THE SOCIAL UNCONSCIOUS
IN PERSONS, GROUPS,
AND SOCIETIES

NEW INTERNATIONAL LIBRARY OF GROUP ANALYSIS

Series Editor: Earl Hopper

Other titles in the Series

Contributions of Self Psychology to Group Psychotherapy
  by Walter N. Stone

Difficult Topics in Group Psychotherapy: My Journey from Shame to Courage
  by Jerome S. Gans

Resistance, Rebellion and Refusal in Groups: The 3 Rs
  by Richard M. Billow

THE SOCIAL UNCONSCIOUS IN PERSONS, GROUPS, AND SOCIETIES

Volume 1: Mainly Theory

Edited by
Earl Hopper and Haim Weinberg

KARNAC

First published in 2011 by
Karnac Books Ltd
118 Finchley Road, London NW3 5HT

British Library Cataloguing in Publication Data

A C.I.P. for this book is available from the British Library

ISBN 978 1 85575 768 4

Edited, designed and produced by The Studio Publishing Services Ltd
www.publishingservicesuk.co.uk
e-mail: studio@publishingservicesuk.co.uk

Printed in Great Britain

www.karnacbooks.com

CONTENTS

ACKNOWLEDGEMENTS   ix

ABOUT THE EDITORS AND CONTRIBUTORS   xi

FOREWORD   xvii
   Earl Hopper, Editor of NILGA

INTRODUCTION   xxiii
   Earl Hopper and Haim Weinberg

PART I
THE ORIGINS OF THE CONCEPT OF THE
SOCIAL UNCONSCIOUS

CHAPTER ONE
The concept of the social unconscious in the work   3
of S. H. Foulkes
   Dieter Nitzgen

CHAPTER TWO
The concept of the co-unconscious in Moreno's psychodrama   23
   Heloisa Junqueira Fleury and Anna Maria Knobel

CHAPTER THREE
Enrique Pichon-Rivière: the social unconscious   45
in the Latin-American tradition of group analysis
   Juan Tubert-Oklander

PART II
THE ORGANISMIC AND NEUROBIOLOGICAL PERSPECTIVE

Introduction   71
   Malcolm Pines

CHAPTER FOUR
Mirror neurons, sociality, and the species homo sapiens   77
   A. P. Tom Ormay

CHAPTER FIVE
The group mind, systems-centred functional   99
sub-grouping, and interpersonal neurobiology
   Susan P. Gantt and Yvonne M. Agazarian

PART III
THE RELATIONAL AND INTERPERSONAL PERSPECTIVE

Introduction   127
   Robi Friedman

CHAPTER SIX
Working intersubjectively: what does it mean for   133
theory and therapy?
   Martin Weegmann

CHAPTER SEVEN
The lost roots of the theory of group analysis: 155
"interrelational individuals" or "persons"
   Joshua Lavie

PART IV
THE MIND OF THE SOCIAL SYSTEM

Introduction   179
   Felix de Mendelssohn

CHAPTER EIGHT
The false we/the false collective self: 187
a dynamic part of the social unconscious
Helena Klímová

CHAPTER NINE
Manifestations of psychic retreats in social systems   209
Marina Mojović

PART V
THE MATRIX OF THE SOCIAL SYSTEM

Introduction   235
Gerhard Wilke

CHAPTER TEN
The social unconscious and ideology: 243
in clinical theory and practice
Farhad Dalal

CHAPTER ELEVEN
The foundation matrix and the social unconscious   265
Regine Scholz

PART VI
THE NUMINOUS AND THE UNKNOWN

Introduction   289
Amélie Noack

CHAPTER TWELVE
The social unconscious and the collective unconscious: 295
the Jungian perspective
Stephanie Fariss

CHAPTER THIRTEEN
Intuiting knowledge from the social unconscious   321
with special reference to social dreaming
Gordon Lawrence

INDEX   337

For group analysis and group analysts

ACKNOWLEDGEMENTS

We are pleased to acknowledge the help, tolerance, and support of our families, who have once again made many sacrifices for our own professional development and the development of the profession. We are especially grateful to Céline Stakol, whose administrative skills and devoted secretarial help and advice with each chapter and with the manuscript as a whole have proved invaluable to us.

Earl Hopper, PhD
Haim Weinberg, PhD

Yvonne Agazarian, EdD, CGP, DFAGPA, FAPA, is a clinical psychologist, group analyst and a systems-centred practitioner in Philadelphia. She is a member of the Faculty of the Postdoctoral Program in Group Psychotherapy, Adelphi University, the Founder of the Systems-Centered Training and Research Institute, a Distinguished Fellow of the American Group Psychotherapy Association, and a former member of the Board of the International Association for Group Psychotherapy and Group Processes.

Farhad Dalal, PhD, is a psychotherapist and group analyst in private practice. A founder member of the South Devon Psychotherapy and Counselling Service, he also works with organizations. He is a training group analyst for The Institute of Group Analysis (London).

Stephanie Fariss, JD, LCSW, CGP, is a Diplomat Jungian analyst in private practice in Chicago, a training analyst and faculty member of the Analyst Training Program in Analytical Psychology, and the former co-director of the Clinical Training Program in Analytical Psychology at The C.G. Jung Institute of Chicago. She is currently a candidate at the Chicago Institute for Psychoanalysis and has a long-standing interest in American Studies.

Heloisa Junqueira Fleury, MA, is a clinical psychologist and psychodramatist in private practice in São Paulo, a faculty member of the Psychodrama Training Program in Sedes Sapientiae Institute, and a teacher and supervisor at the School of Medicine, University of Sao Paulo. The Honorary Treasurer (2009–2012) of the International Association for Group Psychotherapy and Group Processes, and a former President of the Brazilian Federation of Psychodrama.

Robi Friedman, PhD, is a clinical psychologist and group analyst in private practice in Israel, the Chair of the Israeli Institute of Group Analysis, a former President of the Israeli Association of Group Psychotherapy, and a member of the Management Committee of the Group Analytic Society. He teaches psychoanalytic individual and group psychotherapy in Haifa University the understanding of dreams and dreamtelling and Relation Disorders. He is a former member of the Board of the International Association for Group Psychotherapy and Group Processes.

Susan Gantt, PhD, ABPP, CGP, FAGPA, FAPA, is a psychologist in private practice in Atlanta, Assistant Professor in Psychiatry at Emory University School of Medicine, and Director of the Systems-Centered Training and Research Institute. She is also a Diplomate in Group Psychology for the American Board of Professional Psychology, and a consultant to organizations and a supervisor and conference director in systems-centered training in the USA and Europe.

Earl Hopper, PhD, CGP, FAGPA, is a psychoanalyst, group analyst and organizational consultant in private practice in London. He is a supervisor and training analyst for the Institute of Group Analysis, the British Association of Psychotherapists, and the London Centre for Psychotherapy, a Fellow of the British Psycho-analytical Society and a member of the Group Analytic Society. He is an Honorary Tutor at The Tavistock and Portman NHS Trust and a member of the Faculty of the Post-Doctoral Program at Adelphi University, New York. He is also a Fellow of the American Group Psychotherapy Association, a former President of the International

Association for Group Psychotherapy and Group Processes, a former Chairman of the Association of Independent Psychoanalysts of the British Psychoanalytical Society, and a former member of the Executive Committee of the Group Analytic Society (London).

Helena Klímová, Mgr, is a group analyst and psychoanalytic psychotherapist in private practice in Prague, specializing in the treatment and study of Holocaust trauma and of totalitarian systems. Co-founder of the Czech Society for Psychoanalytic Psychotherapy, of IGA Prague and of Rafael Institute, and an Honorary Member of GAS (London). She is a trainer, supervisor, and publicist, has been married for fifty-three years, and has two children, four grandchildren, and two great-grandsons.

Anna Maria Knobel, MA, is a clinical psychologist and psychodramatist in private practice in Sao Paulo. She is also a faculty member and supervisor of the Psychodrama Training Program in Sedes Sapientiae Institute, a teacher of Sociometry and Group Work, and specializes in clinical work by the Federal Council of Psychology (CFP). She is Group Director of Psychodrama in Sao Paulo, Brazil.

Joshua Lavie, MA, is a clinical psychologist and group analyst in Tel-Aviv and a PhD candidate at the Cohn Institute for the History and Philosophy of Science and Ideas at Tel Aviv University. He is also a teacher and supervisor for the Israeli Institute of Group Analysis, a member of its Board of Directors, and is Co-founder of *Mikbatz—The Israeli Journal of Group Psychotherapy*.

Gordon Lawrence, Dr. rer. oec, is a visiting Professor at the New Bulgarian University, Sofia, and formerly of Cranfield University. He is a Distinguished Member of the International Society for Psychoanalytic Study of Organization. He was a former member of the scientific staff of the Tavistock Institute, where he discovered social dreaming. He is now a director of Social Dreaming Solutions, Ltd.

Felix de Mendelssohn is a psychoanalyst and group analyst in private practice in Vienna and Berlin, Head of Department of Psychoanalytic Studies at the Sigmund-Freud University, Vienna, and a former chairman of the Group Analytic Section of the International Association for Group Psychotherapy and Group Processes.

Marina Mojović, MD, MSc, is a psychiatrist, psychoanalytic psychotherapist, group analyst, and organizational consultant in private practice in Belgrade. She is an educator in the Serbian Society for Psychoanalytic Psychotherapy, and in the Group Analytic Society–Belgrade a training group analyst and a founder of the Section for Psychodynamic Studies of Institutions, Organisations and Society of The Group Analytic Society. She is a member of the Group Analytic Society–London and of several international organizations.

Dieter Nitzgen, MA is a group analyst. He is a training analyst and supervisor of the IGA Heidelberg and the German Association of Group Psychotherapy and Group Dynamics (DAGG). He is a member of the Association of Freudian Psychoanalysis (AFP), Head of the Department of Psychotherapy of Rehaklinik Birkenbuck, Chairman of the Scientific Committee of the Group Analytic Society (GAS), and a member of the Executive Committee of the Group Analytic Society.

Amelie Noack, MA, MSc, is a Jungian analyst and training group analyst in private practice in London and Bristol. A member of the British Association of Psychotherapists (Jungian section) and a supervisor and training analyst for The Institute of Group Analysis. She is a Member and Honorary Secretary of The European Group Analytic Training Institutes Network, a teacher and supervisor in the UK and abroad, and a convenor of events in social dreaming.

A. P. Tom Ormay, BA, is a group analyst and psychoanalytical psychotherapist in private practice in Budapest. He is a member of The London Centre for Psychotherapy, a member of The Institute of Group Analysis (London), a teacher in the University of Physical Education, and in the John Wesley University in Budapest and in the University of Szeged, Hungary. He is a supervisor and training analyst for the Hungarian Institute of Group Analysis, a member of the Group Analytic Society (Budapest), and an ex-officio member of the Executive Committee of The Group Analytic Society (London). He is the editor of *Group Analysis*.

Malcolm Pines, MD, is a former consultant psychotherapist at the Tavistock Clinic and the Maudsley Hospital. He is a Founder Member of The Institute of Group Analysis, a former President of the International Association for Group Psychotherapy and Group Processes, and a former President of The Group Analytic Society. He is also a former Editor of *Group Analysis*.

Regine Scholz, PhD, is a clinical psychologist and group analyst in private practice in Duesseldorf. She is a supervisor and training group analyst for the IGA (Muenster), Vice Chair of Section Klinik und Praxis (KuP) of the German Association of Group Psychotherapy and Group Dynamics (DAGG), a Member of the Executive Committee of the Group Analytic Society (London), and Editor of *Arbeitshefte Gruppenanalyse* in co-operation with *psychosozial*.

Juan Tubert-Oklander, MD, PhD, is a psychoanalyst, group analyst, and family therapist in private practice in Mexico City, a training and supervising analyst at the Institute of the Mexican Psychoanalytic Association, a member of the Group-Analytic Society (London), the Mexican Psychoanalytic Association, and the Argentine Psychoanalytic Association.

Martin Weegmann, BA, is a group analyst and consultant clinical psychologist. He works full time in the UK's National Health Service as lead psychologist for substance misuse services, S. West London. He teaches in many psychotherapy organizations, including the Institute of Group Analysis (London & Manchester).

Haim Weinberg, PhD, is a clinical psychologist and group analyst in private practice in California. He is the Director of the International Program at the Professional School of Psychology, Sacramento, California, Adjunct Professor at the Wright Institute, Berkeley, and at the Alliant International University, Sacramento. He is a faculty member of the Group Facilitators Training Program in Tel-Aviv University. He is also current president of the Northern California Group Psychotherapy Society, a former President of the Israeli Association of Group Therapy, and a former member of the

Board of the International Association of Group Psychotherapy and Group Processes.

Gerhard Wilke, MA Cantab. Dip. FHE, is a group analyst and organizational consultant in private practice in London. He is an Associate of the Ashridge Business School, a teacher on the MA Course in Group Analysis at The Institute of Group Analysis and Birkbeck College, London, a former member of the Board of the International Association for Group Psychotherapy and Group Processes, and a former member of the Executive Committee of The Group Analytic Society (London).

The conceptualization of the social unconscious is the essence of group analysis, both as a perspective in the study of personality and social systems, and in the healing of psychopathology within the context of human relationships. Unfortunately, psychoanalysis continues to degrade the importance of the sociality of human nature, as reflected in the constraints and restraints of social facts, such as those of gender, class, race, ethnicity, nationality, language groupings, family structures, and organizational life, not to mention massive social trauma; similarly, the social sciences continue to ignore the importance of the unconscious mind and the many expressions of it in the relational life of persons within their overlapping social contexts. Fortunately, group analysis offers a space for the integration of these multiple frames of reference, based on an appreciation of binocular vision and the *gestalt* of our perceptions, both as scientists and as healers.

Janus-faced, we look inwards and outwards, backward towards our origins and forward towards our co-constructed destinies, as we choose tragically and comically from among a limited number of alternatives. The study of the social unconscious is always both a political and religious or philosophical project. As students of this complex and necessarily abstract phenomenon, we are drawn to the work of Freud, Klein, Bion, and Lacan, as well as that of Foulkes, Moreno, and Pichon-Rivière, although few of us are equally at home in the work of each. We use data and hypotheses from the social sciences, depth psychologies, and the neurosciences, but we recognize that life is located within the cosmos as a whole. Although the universe exists in a grain of sand, the study of human relationships and their vicissitudes cannot be reduced to the study of instincts and the projected phantasies associated with them. Ultimately, the meaning of human affairs always requires that we contextualize them in time and social space in appreciation of open living systems, whether in terms of concentric circles or, preferably, a set of intertwined and interpenetrating spirals.

Although the authors of the chapters in this volume offer many examples of their basic arguments, at the core of their projects is the theorization of the recursive and compulsive perpetuation of traumatic experience. Each of us is preoccupied with reaching a more comprehensive understanding of human nature, primarily in order to help alleviate human suffering. Although insight does not always bring increased personal and social control, it increases the likelihood that we can make more informed and just decisions, enabling us to become wiser—if sadder—human beings.

The history of this series of volumes about the social unconscious in persons, groups, and societies might be of interest. Following the death of the founders of group psychotherapy, colleagues in various countries have continued to refer to the importance of our understanding of the social unconscious. However, very few of them have attempted to meet the theoretical, empirical, and clinical challenges that they have set. In this context, Haim Weinberg suggested to me that it would be a good idea to co-edit a volume of invited chapters on the topic of the social unconscious, attempting to go beyond my own work. I offered The New International Library of Group Analysis as an appropriate context for this. We used the 14th European Symposium in Group Analysis in August 2008 in Dublin, entitled "Despair, Dialogue, Desire" as an opportunity for starting to select these chapters. However, it soon became apparent that a series of volumes was in order. We decided to divide The Social Unconscious in Persons, Groups and Societies into

Volume I: Mainly Theory, Volume II: Mainly Matrices, and *Volume III: Mainly Clinical Work.*

It has taken us about three years to prepare Volume I. English is not the first language of many of our contributors. Authors who readily agreed that the study of the social unconscious was essential in their work later differed in their emphases on the multiple foci of the topic. International communication through modern information technology carries its own problems, not least the consequences of the discrepancy between the idealized expectation that editing a book of this kind will be easy and the reality that it is not.

Another reason for the delay in the publication of Volume I was the difficulty that Haim Weinberg and I had in writing the Introduction together. It is likely that our work has been influenced unconsciously by the topics of the chapters and even the structure of the book. Formerly a sociologist, I am both a psychoanalyst and a group analyst, and have made my own personal integration of these disciplines. Haim, formerly an electrical engineer who became a clinical psychologist, then a group psychotherapist, and eventually a group analyst through block training in Israel, has also made his own personal integration of these disciplines. I am an American who lives in England, and he is an Israeli who lives in America. We are from different generations. It is not irrelevant that I am an eldest son, and he is a middle son. He is better than I at editorial compromise, but this may be a displacement from efforts to resolve the conflicts of the Middle East. None the less, despite our differences, and perhaps as a consequence of them, we have learnt from the dialogue that has been necessary in order to complete our project. The lucidity of the Introduction is in no small measure due to my having to explain myself to my co-Editor, who was able to hold on to his own point of view.

Volume I: Mainly Theory is comprised of six Parts, each of which pertains to a particular aspect of the social unconscious. Following the Introduction, Part I, The Origins of the Concept of the Social Unconscious, consists of three chapters that discuss the work of S. H. Foulkes, Enrique Pichon-Rivière, and Jacob Moreno, who might be called the fathers of group psychotherapy in its broadest sense. Foulkes, originally from Frankfurt, began his work with groups in England, where he collaborated with James Anthony and many other colleagues and students. The various ways in which Foulkes used the term "social unconscious" is summarized in Chapter One, by Dieter Nitzgen, who has also indicated the various contexts in which the meaning of the concept might be specified. Jacob Moreno, first in Vienna and later in New York, from where his work spread quickly to South America, attempted to conceptualize the interpersonal dimension of the unconscious. He coined the term "co-unconscious". Influenced by the work of Jung, Moreno argued that a complete understanding of the mind required its contextualization within the cosmos as a whole. His work is discussed in Chapter Two, by Heloisa Fleury and Anna Maria Knobel. Enrique Pichon-Rivière, in Argentina and Brazil, focused on the ways in which people personified social, cultural, economic, and political forces. It was important to locate people within their societal contexts. He coined the term "operative groups". His contribution is discussed by Juan Tubert-Oklander in Chapter Three.

In his Introduction to Part II, The Organismic and Neurobiological Perspective, Malcolm Pines explains that it is essential to think in terms of the "social brain", which is consistent with the basic orientation of group analysis. As A. P. Tom Ormay makes clear in Chapter Four, the social brain is characterized by the capacity for "we-centric" space. In Chapter Five, Yvonne Agazarian and Susan Gantt postulate the existence of a group mind on the basis of modern neurobiology concerning flows of energy and information.

In his Introduction to Part III, The Relational and Interpersonal Perspective, Robi Friedman explains that persons and their groupings are interrelational. Moreover, as Martin Weegmann argues in Chapter Six, both persons and their groupings are, in essence, interpenetrating and intersubjective. And as Joshua Lavie outlines in Chapter Seven, the early work of Foulkes concerning the sociality of human nature was based on the ideas of Norbert Elias concerning the paradox of simultaneous socialization and individuation, and his view that societal social systems were not in opposition and in contradistinction to the individual members of them, but comprised interrelational persons.

In his Introduction to Part IV, The Mind of the Social System, Felix de Mendelssohn, who, from his vantage point of Vienna, has been both so near and at the same time so far from the scenes of European social turmoil, notes that the most painful aspects of the human condition are deeply entrenched in both persons and their societies. The possible development of the collective false self in Czechoslovakia is explored by Helena Klímová in Chapter Eight, and the co-operation of social psychic retreats in Serbia is explored by Marina Mojović in Chapter Nine. These authors discuss how properties of traumatized people are manifest in properties of totalitarian social systems, and, vice versa, how totalitarian societies are a source of traumatic experience for their "citizens".

In his Introduction to Part V, The Matrix of the Social System, Gerhard Wilke observes how important it is to discuss the properties of matrices in their own terms, and not to reduce them to properties of the people who participate in them, and not to confuse the foundation matrix of the societal social system with the dynamic matrices of the groups within it. Farhad Dalal, in Chapter Ten, directs our attention to the social defence of ideology that protects against the anxieties that are associated with the recognition of social powerlessness. And Regine Scholz, in Chapter Eleven, considers how the foundation matrix of a society constrains and restrains the measurement of time in connection with the partly coterminus life trajectories of both persons and their societies.

As Amelie Noack suggests in her Introduction to Part VI, The Numinous and the Unknown, the theory of social regression in response to trauma has much in common with the new Jungian theory of the cultural complex, which can be seen in patterns of social dreaming. She is sensitive to the possibilities for integration of ideas from psychoanalysis, analytical psychology, and group analysis. In Chapter Twelve, Fariss illustrates the constraints of a cultural complex in connection with conflict laden interactions between different racial groups in the USA, linking these interactions with unresolved social trauma in the USA and in the slave-trading world. As Gordon Lawrence suggests in Chapter Thirteen, the study of social dreaming in the context of a social dreaming matrix shows that the collective and interrelational dreams of the members of any social system contain information about their common predicaments, concerns, and even their anticipation of their future. In other words, dreams contain both secular information in the context of their society, and sacred messages in the context of the cosmos.

These chapters create a fascinating mosaic of the many facets of the theory and concept of the social unconscious. Their authors and their works are important nodal points in a socio-cultural–communicational network of colleagues and ideas.

Earl Hopper
London

Introduction

Earl Hopper and Haim Weinberg

In this Introduction we outline the development of the concept of
the social unconscious, and identify several of the current areas of
interest in it. We believe that the study of the social unconscious is
at the heart of the group analytic project, which continues to change
and to develop.

I

Before Freud, the notion of the unconscious mind was often used
by philosophers such as Spinoza, Leibniz, Schopenhauer, and
Nietzsche. For them, the "unconscious mind" referred to perceptions, thoughts, feelings, and sensations that, at any given time, are
outside the field of consciousness. Working within this tradition,
but at the same time attempting to break free from it, Freud developed a topographical model of the personality in which psychic life
could be represented in terms of three levels of consciousness: the
conscious, the preconscious, and the unconscious, including the
non-conscious. As a noun, "unconscious" referred to mental or psychic processes, phenomena, and structures that occur or exist in the

absence of conscious awareness; as a verb, it referred to the action of making or having made these processes and phenomena, and structures unconscious, in the sense of suppressing, repressing and/or splitting off, as an adjective and/or adverb, unconscious referred to the fact that such psychic processes, phenomena, and structures are outside and/or have been put outside a person's conscious awareness. It was assumed that the unconscious is a matter of degree, and not a permanent condition. It was also assumed that, in one way or another, the unconscious originates within the human body and in the human species.

At first, Freud emphasized that since the unconscious mind was associated with the id, which was located in a particular part of the brain, the unconscious mind functioned differently from the conscious mind, which was associated with the ego, which was also located in a different part of the brain. This model of personality was revised many times. Eventually, it was hypothesized that parts of the ego and superego and their various functions were also unconscious. And the much later and more evolved structural model of the personality recognized the internalization of external objects.

Whereas the conscious mind was said to function according to reality testing, rational thinking, logical codes, and secondary process in general, the unconscious mind functioned according to the laws and principles of primary process.[1] Freud believed that many significant aspects of human thought, feeling, and behaviour were shaped and directed by these unconscious irrational forces, and these forces were inadmissible to direct conscious awareness. However, it was possible to learn about the unconscious through the study of parapraxes, fantasies, free associations, dreams, clinical symptoms, etc.

The contents of the unconscious system were not merely outside the field of consciousness, they were also radically separated from it by the exercise of so-called "defences" against the painful anxieties that would arise if a person became aware of these phenomena. In other words, the contents of the unconscious mind were prevented from entering the conscious mind as a consequence of repression and/or splitting. Unconscious processes and phenomena could not enter or re-enter the conscious–preconscious system without undergoing various kinds and degrees of distortion which made this material more acceptable to the conscious mind of the ego and superego. In other words, the unconscious was a reservoir for fantasies, ideas, wishes, desires, traumatic memories, etc., which were unacceptable because they were associated with painful emotions. Moreover, the defence mechanisms, which prevented the threatening material from emerging into consciousness, were also unconscious.

During the 1920s and 1930s, psychoanalysts learnt that it was much too limiting to focus entirely on the so-called "individual" and his body as the only, or even the main, source of non-conscious, unconscious, and pre-conscious phenomena. It was essential to give more emphasis to the influence of human interrelationships through the life trajectory from conception to death within the context of society and culture. Although the embodied id was a source of energy in mental and emotional life, so, too, were the family, group, and wider society. People internalized their social worlds, and much was projected into them.

It was recognized that the history of these social groupings is very different from the history of the body: whereas the body begins with conception, social groupings begin in time immemorial. Societies and their cultures change and develop, and the manifestations of human creativity in socio-cultural patterns are internalized, shared, and transmitted across the generations. None the less, it was not clear just how processes of transgenerational cultural transmission occurred.

Several psychoanalysts and sociologists began to theorize the effects of the social world on the unconscious life of people, and vice versa: for example, Jung's theory of the collective unconscious is especially important, and we will return to this contribution in due course. However, within the context of Freudian psychoanalysis, the work of Erich Fromm warrants special attention. Moving away from a long line of explanations of the social world in terms of what was projected into it, Fromm sought to elucidate how the unconscious mind was moulded by both the body and the society. None the less, drawing on the traditional study of ur-themes in German philosophy and philology, he also regarded the society as a kind of organism that was characterized not only by social, cultural, economic, and political structures, but also by libidinal and death instincts that were specific to it. In fact, he referred to the unconscious mind of the society, and was the first to use the term "social unconscious".

However, Fromm was not clear whether his focus was on the social sources of the mental processes and phenomena of which the members of a particular society or type of society were unconscious, or on those particular mental processes and phenomena which were also a source of the structure of the society.

The study and clinical application of the social unconscious was of central importance in the work of S. H. Foulkes. Prior to the Second World War, Foulkes was influenced by existentialist philosophy and sociology in Frankfurt, and by German psychoanalysis, as seen in the early work of Bernfeld, Fromm, Fromm-Reichmann, Horney, and others who were preoccupied with such matters as the effects on personality of class structures, gender roles, and the power structures of society. However, he, too, used the concept of the social unconscious in reference both to the internalized social world of which people were unaware and to the properties of the external social world of which people were unaware. His first paper to the British Psychoanalytical Society concerned the process of introjection, which is of interest mainly because at the time the psychoanalysts in London were focusing primarily on projection processes. Foulkes rarely used the notion of a social organism.

Foulkes stressed that people are unconscious of many social and cultural factors and forces in the same way that they are of many biological factors and forces. Denoting the latter as "the unconscious in the Freudian sense" of the term, he wrote that there was

> a totally different area of which the individual is equally unaware ... [and is] ... as much compelled and moulded by these colossal forces as by his own id, and defends himself as strongly against their recognition without being aware of it, but in quite different ways and modes. One might speak of a social or interpersonal unconscious. [Foulkes, 1964, p. 52]

Subsequently, he dropped the notion of an interpersonal unconscious, but continued to refer to the social unconscious of people and their groupings.

Unfortunately, Foulkes did not elaborate on his conceptualization of the social unconscious, and did not define the concept in a systematic way or explain how he used it in clinical work. However, Foulkes believed that the body, mind, and society were completely interdependent and intertwined with one another. Thus,

"Individuals" and their "Groups" are abstractions constructed by the observer of them, and a matter of the figure and ground of an observer's perception of them.

Bion, one of the fathers of the psychoanalytical study of group dynamics, if not of group therapy itself, did not use the concept of the social unconscious. However, he did refer to the mentality of the group. He was, of course, interested in what he called "basic assumptions" as group phenomena, but primarily as products of the projected creations of the members of groups. He was also interested in "leadership", but primarily in terms of valence for particular roles associated with basic assumptions, that is, the leadership of "basic assumption groups"; the leadership of "work groups" remained a residual category, as did work groups themselves. However, Bion did not focus on the reality of group phenomena and/or the internalization of group phenomena. Although Bion used the notion of "group mentality", and referred to the importance of being able to use "binocular vision" with respect to focusing on persons and/or their groups, he was ambiguous about the reality of social facts. Therefore, it is not surprising that Bion did not use the concept of the social unconscious.

In parallel with the work of Foulkes and Bion, Moreno, in the context of psychodrama, and Pichon-Rivière, in the context of "group work" more generally, also focused on the recursive processes of the mind in society and the society in the mind. Moreno used the terms "co-unconscious" and "inter-personal unconscious" in connection with the dyadic co-construction of the mind, and he studied the structure of social systems through sociometry. Pichon-Rivière's work with groups in their natural settings was really one of the first examples of applied group analysis. His studies of the personification of socio-cultural–communicational patterns were perhaps more akin to the perspective of Foulkes than to Bion's study of valence with respect to the roles that comprised basic assumptions.

II

It is generally agreed that during the 1960s in London, New York, Buenos Aires, and other capital cities, group analysts, psychoanalytical group psychotherapists, and students of group dynamics had not yet adopted the concepts of the social unconscious and the interpersonal unconscious, and were somewhat ambivalent about combining the notions of "unconscious" with those of "social" and "cultural". However, mainly in association with Foulkes and his colleagues, several group analysts began to use the concept of the social unconscious, sometimes referring to persons, sometimes to groups and other kinds of social system, and sometimes to both. These group analysts began to distinguish themselves from psychoanalysts in terms of their sensitivity to the unconscious structuring of personality by social factors and forces, and by their study of groups and social systems from both a psychoanalytical and a sociological point of view. Although they were in dialogue with Bion, Ezriel, Turquet, and others, who helped to develop the Group Relations movement associated with the Tavistock, they eschewed the use of the Kleinian model of the mind on which this work was based. Instead, they used a model of the mind that was developed by Winnicott and various members of the Group of Independent Psychoanalysts who developed the British object relations school of thought (Hopper, 2003a).

This perspective concerning the social unconscious and British object relations thinking, or what is usually regarded as Winnicottian object relations thinking, has been articulated and elaborated by Earl Hopper: first as a sociologist in dialogue with Norbert Elias in the Department of Sociology at the University of Leicester, later in consultation with S. H. Foulkes in the context of the Group Analytic Society in London, and still later as a psychoanalyst and group analyst who continued to draw on his knowledge of sociology. When Hopper began to train as a group analyst he discussed his PhD thesis with Foulkes, who understood his attempt to elucidate the social sources of insatiability for stratification goals rather than to focus exclusively on its Oedipal sources. This thesis, which was an attempt to develop the work of Horney, was later published in 1981 as *Social Mobility: A Study of Social Control and Insatiability*. Foulkes agreed that it was essential for group analysis to include many traditions of thinking and scholarship in sociology, anthropology, social psychology and even in contemporary psychoanalysis. For example, in sociology, the work of Robert Merton on anomie, Talcott Parsons on social and personality systems, and Anne Parsons on the inverse Oedipus complex as found in

Southern Italy; in anthropology, the work of Malinowski on alternative forms of the Oedipus complex based on social and cultural structures, of Margaret Mead on gender identity, and of other members of the culture and personality school of thought which was so important in the USA; in social psychology the work of G. H. Mead on symbolic interaction, of Benjamin Worff and other students of socio-linguistics; and in contemporary psychoanalysis, studies of gender identity by Mitchell and others. Hopper introduced this material into the curriculum of the first Qualifying Course at the Institute of Group Analysis (London). This became the core of "Mind, Self and Society" convened for many years by Malcolm Pines.

In the context of his work with Foulkes and his colleagues, Hopper published a series of articles concerning the socio-cultural sources of various patterns of anxiety and of various personality characteristics more generally. At the same time, he also published a series of articles concerning various aspects of groups and other kinds of social system, for example, education systems, stratification systems, patterns of social aggression, massive social trauma, the problem of context and open systems thinking, the dynamics of large groups, equivalence, etc. In other words, Hopper attempted to develop the two foci of the Foulkesian project concerning the social unconscious: the internalization of various properties of groups and other kinds of social system, and the elucidation of the social world in its own terms. Several of these articles were later included in *The Social Unconscious: Selected Papers* (Hopper, 2003a).

Essentially, Hopper accepted the view that the "social unconscious" refers to the fact that people are likely to be unconscious of social factors and forces, but noted that the concept is also used to refer to the social factors and forces of which they are unconscious, which paralleled the way that the more traditional notion of "unconscious" refers both to the fact that people are unconscious of a variety of biological and, subsequently, a variety of psychological factors and forces, and to those biological and psychological factors and forces of which they are unconscious. Although this dual usage was confusing, because it refers both to aspects of the psychic life of a person and to aspects of the group that have been internalized, there seemed to be no alternative to this usage. However, he argued that in the discussion of these processes and objects involved in them, it was necessary to be absolutely clear about whether one is referring to person systems or to their social systems. In other words, he emphasized that the meaning of the concept of the social unconscious depends on the gestalt of an observer's perception and the focus of his binocular vision. He also stressed that making these distinctions would almost always require the specification of what Pines (1998) later called "frames of reference".

More specifically, Hopper defined the social unconscious in terms of the existence of social, cultural, and communicational "arrangements" of which people are "unaware". "Arrangements" is a kind of euphemism for systems and structures and their various manifestations, such as, in the case of societies, their specific institutions and organizations, and, at a more abstract level of analysis, their various subsystems, such as the political, economic, educational, etc. Although Hopper also used the notions of "interaction system", "normative system", and "communication system", and "social structure", "culture structure", and "communication structure", this sociological nomenclature has seldom been adopted by group analysts.

"Unaware" is also a euphemism for unconscious processes in their entirety. However, as in the traditional concept of the biologically based unconscious, the social unconscious involves the "nonconscious", the "dynamic unconscious" of the "repressed" and the "split-off", and the "pre-conscious" with respect to the external world and the internal representations of it. Moreover, being unaware of the social, cultural, and communicational arrangements in the external world is a relational process involving three or more persons, and is never merely a matter of a single individual's knowledge of the external social world. For interrelational persons, the social world is not a matter of what is "outside" the mind and of which one is unconscious (or conscious or pre-conscious or nonconscious), but a matter of transitional objects and transitional phenomena that have been both discovered and/or invented, or, to be more precise, co-invented. The "external world" is often used as a synonym for the "social world". However, whereas all aspects of the social world are aspects of the external world, not all aspects of the external world of any particular person are aspects of the social world that are likely to be shared by a larger number of persons. In fact, some aspects of the external world are not really aspects of the social world, although all perceptions of the external world will be mediated through perceptual processes that involve concepts that are embedded in systems of communication and specifically language. Although this is a matter of the frame of reference of the discussion, care must be taken to identify the social objects in question, and to accept the possibility of personal variation and diversity within any social system.

With respect to processes of internalization, the social unconscious always refers to the unconscious *constraints* of social objects that have been internalized, and to the unconscious *restraints* of those that have not. The concept of constraint is not meant to imply only "inhibition" and "limitation", but also "facilitation" and "development". For example, processes of constraint govern even the transformation of sensations into feelings, and of concepts into thought and thinking. This point about both limitations and facilitations can also be made concerning the influence of the body and the species on the internal world. The concept of "constraint" is taken specifically from the work of Durkheim and other early French sociologists, who used the term with respect to the unconscious constraints of "social facts"; they did not refer to the "social unconscious", but to the *conscience collective*, which was not intended to imply the "unconscious of the society", but was based on an appreciation of the existence of "social facts" that were internalized and shared by the members of a particular society. The notion of restraint is based on the Freudian view of "society against man", and the notion of constraint is intended as a modification of this idea. However, the development of the structural model in psychoanalysis, with its emphasis on internalized objects, has meant that it is incorrect to polarize a theory of constraint from a theory of restraint. In effect, a restraint tends to become an internalized constraint.

Interrelational persons are not merely in interaction with one another from conception to death. In the beginning there is no such thing as an infant, but only an infant in relationship with its mother (Winnicott, 1952); there is no such thing as an "individual", but only an individual within a society (Dalal, 1998); there is no such thing as a "first" human being, but only a person born into a breeding group (Hopper, 2003a). Before birth, the zygote is physically part of the mother and vice versa; during gestation and birth, the foetus and mother influence and respond to each other; in fact, the foetus and the mother constitute a unique interrelational object (Puget, 1986). After birth, introjections and projections occur within the context of processes of mutual engagement and attachment between infant and (m)other within a network of relationships. People start life with the need and the desire for relationships, as much as, if not more than, the need and the desire for instinctual satisfaction. They seek a sense of both "we-ness" and "other-ness", somewhere between merger and individuation. Identities and identifications are both affiliative and oppositional. People are born into relationships, families, and groups of various kinds, which shape the personalities of the people who participate in them, and who, in turn, shape their groupings. This continues throughout life (Scheidlinger, 1990).

It follows from this perspective that the mind is not a function of the monadic brain of a single individual. The mind is a relational mind. In fact, the concepts of the co-conscious, the shared conscious, the co-unconscious, and/or the shared unconscious, not to mention what Foulkes and Moreno, more or less *en passant*, called the interpersonal unconscious, all recognize the existence of the relational mind in general and the relational mind of certain relationships in particular.

Much more recently, and apparently not cognizant of the contribution of Foulkes, Moreno, and Pichon-Rivière, among others, relational psychoanalysts have argued that their project

> is based on the shift from the classical idea that it is the patient's mind that is being studied (where mind is seen as existing independently and autonomously within the boundaries of individuals) to the relational notion that mind is inherently dyadic, social, interactional and interpersonal. [Aron, 1996, p. x]

In this context, Zeisel (2009) and other "Modern Analysts" have even begun to refer to a "relational ego". With very few exceptions, such as Tubert-Oklander and Billow, relational analysts have rarely acknowledged the influence of group analysis on their thinking, for example in connection with the so-called "third position". Ogden seems to be particularly oblivious to group analysis. Something similar occurred in Winnicott's last works, when he began to discuss society and culture as transitional phenomena, using the concepts of matrix and other terminology borrowed from sociology and group analysis.

It also follows that the relational mind is dynamic. Although the brain itself is subject to change through growth and development, as well as through degeneration, the relational mind "knows no time and knows no space" in ways that may not have been fully appreciated by Freud and later by Bion in their discussions of the unconscious mind of individuals and the unconscious basic assumption processes of groups. The relational mind is defined by the boundaries of the minds of those with whom a person is in relationship, and is regulated by changes in a person's social, cultural, and communicational networks.

A third implication of this perspective is that the socially unconscious mind involves the possibility of creativity and creation. Even the ability and willingness to exercise the transcendent imagination is an action of an interrelational person. In other words, hope is a collective virtue.

The internalization of social, cultural, and communicational arrangements is based on many neurobiological processes, ranging from social instincts to patterns of infant–mother communication, including the use of all of the senses and the apparatus. For example, mirroring based on mirror neurons is of special importance, but so, too, are many other barely understood aspects of the social brain.

Verbal communication, or language, is fundamental to the formation of the social unconscious. Language is the primary tool by which and through which social reality is perceived and constructed. Language defines, names, and describes objects. It moulds and shapes the perception of all external phenomena. It structures the formation of concepts and, therefore, of thinking itself. These are reciprocal and recursive processes (Derrida, 1974; Lacan, 1977). Although the development of verbal communication is governed by a variety of innate factors, and the acquisition of language is preceded by communicational gestures, learning a language facilitates taking qualitatively new steps in the development of intelligence and personality. What really sets us apart from other species is our capacity to think and communicate using language and symbolic systems, which is the foundation of our rationality and religiosity, and of our desire to create long-term goals and to formulate abstract concepts like justice and truth; therefore, it is the basis of complex culture (Cassirer, 1946).

It is important to recognize that *even in the beginning* the ego is both a body ego and a society ego. Despite the assumptions of classical psychoanalysis that internalized objects have always been coloured by the unconscious fantasies that have been projected into them before they have been internalized, external objects can be and often are internalized in more or less their pristine forms. Although external social objects may have been co-constructed, internalized social objects are not necessarily contaminated by prior projections. In other words, "bad" objects are not based *only* on the internalization of objects that have been modified by prior projections of anxiety and fantasies associated with the so-called death instinct. Such projections are not the very first psychic actions; and bad internal objects are almost always based on the internalization of bad external objects. It follows that, at least theoretically, it is possible to have and/or to build a good enough society in general and a good enough mother and family in particular, the internalization of whom can modify the development of a primal bad object, if not prevent it in the first place. It is virtually impossible to disentangle clinical theory from socio-political orientations and values. Thus, a clinical intervention that addresses an aetiological chain or series of events is a kind of political act, and, with regard to "first causes", a kind of religious act.

Social objects are internalized through positive processes involving identifications with loving and nurturing objects of various kinds, and through negative processes involving identifications with aggressors of various kinds. It is likely that the internalization of social objects is, to some degree, always associated with a sense of absence, loss, and/or separation from objects on whom subjects are dependent. Thus, the foundations of intrapsychic life are always rooted in traumatic experience, whether in connection with the inevitable trauma of the vicissitudes of birth, or those of early maternal deprivation within the context of family life (Hopper, 1991). These internal objects are retained within positive and negative encapsulations, and the very structure of an intrapsychic representation might be based on an attempt to recreate the lost uterus.

In terms of this perspective, the social unconscious is maintained through a series of protective defences against the experience of painful anxieties that would follow from the recognition of certain social phenomena: social objects are not perceived (not "known"), and if perceived, not acknowledged ("denied"), and if acknowledged, not taken as problematic ("given"), and if taken as problematic, not considered with an optimal degree of detachment and objectivity ("conviction"). This series runs more or less in parallel with the main defences associated with the biologically based unconscious, ranging from disavowal, denial, splitting, and repression in general to the more superficial phenomenon of conscious suppression. However, when the defences against anxieties that follow from the recognition of social reality are weakened or failed, people try to avoid their anxieties through various coping strategies and forms of instrumental adjustment including legitimate and illegitimate innovation, rebellion and revolution, and various forms of alienation, such as ritualism, retreatism, and mechanism, both personally and collectively (Hopper, 1981).

In sum, when Foulkes wrote that the individual is "social through and through", he meant that the unconscious mind of a person is always a socially unconscious mind in its origins, content, development, and maintenance, which is not to deny the importance of the continuing representation of biological needs, drives, and instincts (Knauss, 2006). In terms of this perspective, were it not for the fact that most psychoanalysts continue to ignore the existence and the importance of the constraints of social objects, there would be no need for the concept of the social unconscious.

III

Focusing on the internalization of the social world, several group analysts have contributed to the development of Hopper's definition of the concept of the social unconscious. Some have begun to use the concept of the cultural unconscious, mainly in order to emphasize the importance of the internalization of values, norms, and other essential elements of what is usually known as the "culture" of a particular society (e.g., Spector-Person (1992) in the USA, and Pines (2009) in the UK). This notion of the cultural unconscious is entirely consistent with the perspective that underlies the "personality and culture" school of thought in American anthropology, which takes as its focus the ways in which the culture of a particular society influences the personalities of the members of it, and vice versa. French psychoanalysts and group analysts tend to distinguish the "cultural" from the "social" (e.g., Devereux (1982), Le Roy (1994), Rouchy (1987) and Kaes (1987)). However, and perhaps ironically, this is a practice that Durkheim and other founders of French sociology would have thought to be neither necessary nor desirable. This specification of the cultural unconscious does not recognize that social scientists use "social" to include cultural phenomena in general, sometimes with a hyphen (-): socio-cultural. They use the concept of cultural as distinct from the concept of social only when it is necessary to draw attention to a cultural aspect, property, or dimension of social reality, for example, the values and norms of a social system, rather than to a property of the interaction system, such as the frequency with which certain people are in contact with one another.

Some group analysts focus on the internalization of particular external objects rather than others. For example, Dalal (1998) writes that the social unconscious "... is a representation of the institutionalisation of social power relations in the structure of the psyche itself. In this sense, it is a bridge between the social and the psychological" (p. 209). However, although societal power relations are of vital importance in the formation of the social unconscious, they are hardly either the only or the most important social objects that are introjected. For example, with respect to power relations, it is essential to specify the introjection of the father, not only in terms of the Oedipus complex in the context of his location in the family, but also in terms of his and his family's location in the power structure of the society. Moreover, the projections of all internal objects into the external world function as bridges between the psychological and the social. So, too, do introjections. Dalal's orientation is reminiscent of Erich Fromm's views concerning the importance of psychic representations of economic and political structures. Actually, de Maré (1972), one of the founders of group analysis, also emphasized the importance of the representations in the mind of the nexus of economic and political phenomena in the society, and assumed that economic power structures social relations, which, in turn, structures cultural "content". The echoes of this Marxist idea are still important in the group analytical perspective.

It is also important to take note of the fact that the members of particular social systems are likely to have internalized the same social objects. Thus, the social unconscious pertains to particular social systems and not to social systems in general. (This was the basis of Freud's definition of a "group", although he focused on the common internalization of the leader of the group.) However, whereas some of the social objects that are internalized by a particular person within a particular social system are likely to be the same as those that are internalized by others within the system, some are likely to be different. The variation and diversity of these internalized objects depend on the size and structural complexity of the system, on the positions of persons within it, and even on the degree to which the system is "totalitarian" in its political and civic cultures and modes of social control.

A list of those aspects of socio-cultural–communicational arrangements that are especially important in the formation of the social unconscious of the members of a particular social system would include collective assumptions about social reality, disavowals, social defences, and forms of structural oppression (Brown, 2001). Of course, a "disavowal" is a social defence, because it is directed against social reality and likely to be shared with other people; and a disavowal is the strongest social defence, because it is directed against the fear of annihilation that would be caused by the perception of a particular external reality as a threat to survival. A disavowal of structural oppression may be a matter of "strain" and "cumulative" social trauma, as in the case of totalitarian societies in which one of the main functions of ideology is to maintain the social defence of disavowal. With respect to social defences, it would be useful to study the manifestations of various forms of intrumental adjustment within various kinds of disordered relationships (Friedman, 2004). Of particular interest is Cohen's (2001) consideration of "literal" denial, "interpretative" denial, and "implicatory" denial of social trauma.

Weinberg (2007) agrees that a definition of the social unconscious should specify the contents of it, primarily in order to operationalize the concept and make it more accessible for empirical research. Anxieties, defences, fantasies, myths, and collective memories are of special importance. Moreover, he argues that collective memories of social trauma and social glories, whether or not they are "chosen" (Volkan, 2001), should be regarded as the building blocks of the social unconscious of the members of a particular social system, primarily because they shape the identity of the system, and, therefore, the social identities of its members (Halbwachs, 1992). Collective memories can be defined as the representations of the past that the members of a system collectively adopt (Kansteiner, 2002). These representations contribute to the formation of a coherent narrative of the history of the system. Although they do not provide an accurate historical account of what happened in reality, they come to answer particular needs, crystallize the consciousness of the system, create a sense of continuity, and build a sense of solidarity.

These cultural legacies may be transformed into myths, which are more elaborated stories of important events, usually containing some heroic and wishful elements. Myths are neither true nor false, but contain a mixture of fact and fantasy. Some myths have existed since time immemorial, but some are created quite quickly in an attempt to make sense of important collective events. Myths have many functions, and can be explained in a myriad of ways. The elaboration of collective memories and the making of myths are like secondary revision in dreamwork.

Weinberg emphasizes that whereas the members of a particular societal social system are likely to be conscious or pre-conscious of their myths and collective memories, they are likely to be unconscious of the defensive functions of these myths and collective memories, especially those concerning shared anxieties associated with social powerlessness and social identity. They are also likely to be unaware of the constraints and restraints of these phenomena on their daily life. He would also distinguish between the "weak ingredients" and the "strong ingredients" of the social unconscious, or between the peripheral and the core ingredients of it.

In editing this series of volumes and in preparing this Introduction to Volume I, Hopper and Weinberg have begun a dialogue about the concept of the social unconscious and the theory of it. Hopper has argued that the members of a particular social system are likely to introject an infinite number and variety of aspects of it, and that it is virtually impossible to circumscribe a set of social objects that comprises the elements of the social unconscious of the members of the particular social system. No list of the so-called contents of the social unconscious can be complete. For example: with respect to societal social systems, it is necessary to include language and communication systems in general, regardless of what is being communicated. Especially important are aspects of family structure, class and status group formations, ethnicity and classical classifications, gender and social roles, and age grades, as well as the basic beliefs and mores of a society.

Hopper has also suggested that the distinctions between weak and strong, or peripheral and core depend on the particular interests of an observer, which are likely to vary over time. Although primal internalization processes are always coloured by the traumatic experience of loss, separation, and failed dependency, and are a predisposing factor in the secondary internalization of collective memories of social trauma, the emphasis on traumatic experience might be a function of the interests of group analysts, who tend to believe that helplessness and traumatic experience are at the heart of the human condition, rather than envy and the death instinct. The norms that govern the socio-biological order of the society would seem to be of universal importance, and perhaps especially relevant to the theory of the social unconscious in terms of properties of the environmental mother. The importance of trauma in the social and intellectual identity of group analysis is reviewed by Hopper (2009, 2011). A useful review of some aspects of the internalization of the traumatizing social world is provided by Garwood (2001).

IV

Another line of development in the concept of the social unconscious has been based on a shift in emphasis from the internalization of the co-constructed social world to the co-constructed social world itself, and from the focus on the unconscious representation of the properties of the co-constructed social world to the unconscious co-construction of these properties. The development of psychoanalysis from a one-body to a two-body psychology, and then to a two-person psychology, which means, virtually by definition, a three-person psychology, if not a multi-person, multi-layered, and multi-dimensional psychology, has led to the recognition of the reality of social and social psychological "fields of influence" and "transitional spaces".

It has long been axiomatic in group analysis that although social reality differs from psychic reality, and both social reality and psychic reality differ from organismic reality, social reality and psychic reality are, none the less, *real*. The recognition of the reality and the validity of the social fact is the basis of sociology, and of the social sciences in general, and the recognition of the reality and the validity of the psychic fact is the basis of all depth psychologies. The recognition of the validity of both the social fact and the psychic fact is the basis of group analysis.

Although Moreno, Pichon-Rivière, Bion, and others referred to the "mentality of the group", Foulkes (1964) went further, writing, "we can postulate the existence of a group 'mind' in the same way as we postulate the existence of an individual mind" (p. 118). He argued that the mind is a property of a social system, and that the mind of a social system transcends the minds of the members of it. The mind of a group or the mind of a social system is also more than the simple summation of the minds of the individual members of the group or social system. In fact, Foulkes argued that the free-floating conversations among the members of a group who met for the purpose of psychotherapy in the group were actually akin to the free associations of an individual patient in psychoanalysis. Moreover, the mind of a particular group must be contextualized within the mind of its contextual social system. In other words, the mind of a particular group is a part of the mind of the society and/or of the minds of its intermediate institutions and organizations in which the group exists. In terms of this perspective, the mind of a group or of any other kind of social system is, virtually by definition, a socially unconscious mind, although it may be regarded in terms of its pre-conscious and non-conscious elements.

Within the context of the emergence of group analysis in London, the idea of a group mind can also be traced in part to the work of Hutton (1976) and other scientists and philosophers who participated in the intellectual life of the Group Analytic Society. They stressed the importance of understanding all human phenomena in terms of communication as flows of information.

Bohm's (1980) early work on the implicate order was important, as were various lectures and seminars on the philosophy of science, with special reference to the study of sub-atomic particles, energy, chaos, and complexity theory, etc. Group analysts also discussed the possibility that in order to understand more fully the mind of a society and/or of its component subsystems, they should also study the social formations of the species of Homo sapiens, as well as those social formations of other species, ranging from colonies of primates (Chance & Jolly, 1970) to flocks, schools, herds, and "smart swarms" in general (Miller, 2010). However, the study of social formations is more relevant to those species that are dominated by their neurobiological structures than to species that are dominated by their cultures. Recent studies of "collective intelligence" of groups and other social systems imply that the notion of a "group brain" is on the agenda (Woolley, Chabris, Pentland, Hashmi, & Malone, 2010).

Whereas Hopper and Weinberg agree concerning the recognition of the reality and validity of the social psychological field and the transitional space of the group and of social systems in general, they disagree about the value and utility of thinking in terms of group mentality and the concept of the group mind. We will now outline some aspects of this disagreement.

Hopper argues that if a social system has a mind, it follows that it has a conscious mind and an unconscious mind, and that by definition the unconscious mind of a social system is its socially unconscious mind. However, Hopper doubts the value and utility of using the concept of the mind of a social system, and, therefore, using the concept of the social unconscious with respect to the so-called "mind" of a social system, whether a group or even a society as a whole. Many social scientists, group analysts, and psychoanalytical group therapists, especially in the USA, refuse to speak of "group mentality", "group mind", "group unconscious mind", "group unconscious", "group social unconscious", etc. Although some colleagues eschew the use of these concepts, because they do not accept the reality and validity of social facts (for them, only the individual organism is real, and social facts are regarded as projective creations), many colleagues eschew them for more adequate reasons. For example, they recognize that the greater the size of a social system, the greater are the difficulties associated with the notion that such a system has an overarching "mind". It is virtually impossible to assume the isomorphy of the societal social system with any of its component social systems, and the isomorphy of any of these systems with the members of them. Furthermore, it is important to avoid using terminology for the discussion of properties of persons in order to describe properties of social systems, such as a "phallic society" or a "narcissistic society"; similarly, terminology that has been developed for the discussion of properties of social systems in order to describe properties of persons, such as a "bureaucratic personality" or an "efficient personality". These colleagues understand the connotations of such terms, but regard them as ambiguous. They argue that collapsing the distinctions between social systems and the person systems of their members makes it impossible to study their general and specific connections. It is especially important not to imply that all groups and social systems possess "collective intentionality" (Searle, 1995), because the development of collective intentionality and the specific structures through which it is developed and maintained is problematic and variable.

Hopper also argues that in order to have a so-called "mind", it is necessary for the system to have a brain. Social systems do not have brains. Therefore, social systems do not have minds (Winnicott, 1949). The counterpart to this is that in order for a person to have a mind, it is necessary for him to have a society and culture. It is not enough for him to have a brain. Although Hopper and Dalal insist that persons always exist within the context of their societies, persons are not always integrated into their communities or acculturated into their potential cultures. This is the basis for understanding some psychopathology in terms of the autistic spectrum: a brain without a mind or a mind that is disturbed in terms of a person's ability to communicate with others.

The notion of the "mind" of the social system is really based on the metaphor that social systems are *like* people. This metaphor is a heuristic device that directs our attention and curiosity towards certain parts, aspects, and processes of social systems in an attempt to improve our understanding of them. Unfortunately, organismic and personistic analogies that social systems are *like* organisms and persons tend to become homologies that social systems are, in fact, organisms and persons. Colleagues who use these analogies tend to be unaware of the implications of this way of thinking. For example, they favour attempts to maintain the stability of the system rather than to foster its potential for change, and they approve of the existing power structure rather than alternatives to it.

That what might be regarded metaphorically as the mind and as the unconscious mind of a social system is mistakenly regarded to be the mind and the unconscious mind of it is reminiscent of the fact that in the nineteenth century, in the first edition of *Society*, the great sociologist Herbert Spencer wrote that society is *like* an organism, but in the second edition of it he wrote that society *is* an organism, thus exposing himself to many arguments and difficulties concerning various issues about social change and its desirability. This fallacy is reminiscent of the opening speech by Menenius, the avuncular figure in Shakespeare's *Coriolanus*, who speaks of Rome in terms of the "body politic", using the homology that Rome was a human organism whose various parts could be compared to various classes of the society, and regarding those in power as the brain and the heart of the society, and those without power, as its stomach and genitals. The Menenius Fallacy can also be seen in the use of "personistic" analogies and homologies, which is commonplace among psychologists and psychoanalysts who take social systems as the object of their study, usually seen in references to the id, superego, and ego of the group. This way of thinking extends to the use of mechanistic analogies and homologies: that is, the social system is a machine rather than like a machine, which implies that the system can be changed endlessly in an infinite number and variety of ways, often without concern for the members of the social system involved, hence, the notion of social engineering.

Hopper has hypothesized that the one exception to this general rule that we should avoid using organismic and personistic homologies concerning the mind of a social system involves what might be called a "traumatized" social system, or a "wounded" or "broken" one. In *Traumatic Experience in the Unconscious Life of Groups*, he (Hopper, 2003b) argues that wounded people regress in ways that involve a sense of interpersonal merger, fusion and confusion with others as a defence against the fear of annihilation that follows from traumatic experience. Hence, the social systems of wounded people also regress, for example, from complexity to simplicity: societies become like groups and groups become like their individual members. The structures of systems in which their participants have been traumatized are likely to weaken and collapse, and the participants in these systems are likely to become "lost", not only in translation, but also in their interpersonal relationships, and in their commitment to shared values and norms. Although isomorphy among organisms, persons, groups, and larger and more complex social systems is always a matter of degree, when systems are traumatized the degree of isomorphy among their component systems is high. Traumatized people become fractals of their traumatized social systems, and vice versa. In response to the failed dependency of traumatic experience, and, in turn, under conditions of time-collapse, the members of a group are likely to re-live and even to re-enact their unmourned and unresolved "issues", both from their own pasts and from the pasts of previous generations that have been transmitted to them. In this context, it would seem to be appropriate to refer to the mind of the social system.

In sum, social systems have cultures and patterns of communication of which the members of the systems are, to varying degrees, unconscious, even though they have both co-constructed these cultures and patterns of communication, internalized, shared, inherited, and transmitted them. Hopper prefers to use the concepts of social system, society, culture, and communication systems, etc., that have been developed in sociology and anthropology, rather than the concept of a societal mind, a group mind, or, for that matter, a family mind, an organizational mind, etc. He stresses that whereas the notion of a dyadic mind is entirely acceptable, it is different from the notion of a mind of a dyad. However, Hopper argues that it may be apposite to refer to the mind of a traumatized social system, because the participants in these systems are likely to be engaged self-protectively in processes of mutual merger.

In contradistinction to Hopper's point of view, Weinberg argues that a debate about the validity of referring to the mind of a social system must start with a definition of the "mind". Quoting Siegel (2006, p. 248) that "the mind can be defined as a process that regulates the flow of energy and information . . . (t)he mind emerges in the transaction of . . . neurobiological and interpersonal processes", and that ". . . [e]nergy and information can flow within one brain or *between brains*" (our italics),Weinberg believes that in order to have a mind, a social system does not need to have a brain. It is sufficient for the members of a social system to possess brains and to interact with one another. In other words, the flow of energy and information *between* the members of the social system *is* the mind of the social system. Thus, the mind of the social system exists within the transitional space that is co-created by all the members of the system, and is a function of their interpersonal relations and of their capacity for "we-centric" space. Moreover, Weinberg believes that, in so far as social trauma and its vicissitudes constitute the core elements of the social unconscious of all societies, and, therefore, that the degree of isomorphism between societies and their members is always high, traumatized societies do not constitute a special case. Thus, he is prepared to refer to the mind of a social system, not only as a synonym for the culture and/or social organization of a social system, but as a matter of substance.

V

It is noteworthy that, as of the early 1970s, Foulkes more or less stopped using the concept of the group mind in favour of his concept of the matrix. This concept is not based on a homology between the social system and a person, which makes the concept of the matrix more useful than the concept of the group mind. Foulkes (1973, 1975) defined the matrix as a ". . . hypothetical web of communications *and* [r]elationships". In other words, the matrix refers to what sociologists called the "organization" of a social system or the "social organization". The organization of a social system is multi-dimensional, and it is possible to consider many properties of it, such as patterns of interaction, normation, communication, and so on. However, the word "matrix" was intended to connote womb, mater/mother, material, mould, multi-variate, multi-dimensionality, and, perhaps above all, network or socio-cultural–communicational network (e.g., Roberts, 1982; Lintott, 1983; Ahlin, 1988; Hinshelwood, 1989). This notion was also used by Moreno.

Most group analysts welcomed the introduction of the concept of matrix and the relegation of the concept of group mind. Although we needed a concept and a term in order to denote a social system and its various properties, we believed that the concept of mind should be reserved for reference to persons. Yet, in the English language and in Western philosophical traditions, it was barely possible to denote social facts that were neither objective nor subjective but were co-constructed and intersubjective or, in effect, "transitional". Of course, an important exception to this development is the work of de Maré, whose interest in large groups and in so-called "median groups" of 30–35 people was really more about his continuing study of the group mind than it was about the dynamics of small "large groups" or large "small groups" (Lenn & Stefano, 2011).

Foulkes used the term "dynamic matrix" in reference to the social organization of the group, and the term "foundation matrix" in reference to the social organization of the society. He did not have a concept for denoting the matrix of social systems that were larger and more complex than groups, but smaller and more simple than societies, such as organizations; neither did he have a concept for denoting the matrix of a family, which is not quite a group in the sense that all families are groups, but not all groups are families. However, several group analysts have discussed the matrices of organizations and of families, using the concept of dynamic matrix in reference to them.

The dynamic matrix of a group is based primarily on the structure of its communication system (which is why it can be argued that the cohesion of a group is based on the coherence of its communication system). The foundation matrix of a society is based on its communication system as well as on other dimensions and elements of relations among people within a particular territory over time (which is why its cohesion is based on the integration of its interaction system and on the solidarity of its normative system) (Hopper, 2003b).

The matrix of a social system was conceptualized as a source of constraint and restraint on the members of the particular social system. However, the dynamic matrix of a group always reflects the constraints and restraints of the foundation matrix. In fact, the very existence of a group depends on its relations with its contextual social systems. Groups always exist inside societies, which provide the "common ground" for the members of a group even before they enter it, and which continues to influence them while they are in the group. Foulkes (1975) referred to the foundation matrix of a society as 'the pre-existing community . . . between the members [of it], founded [ultimately] on the basis that they are all human" (p. 212). Thus, some elements of the foundation matrix of a particular society are based on the social, cultural, and communicational arrangements that are typical of that kind of society, some elements are based on the arrangements of the particular society, and some elements of the foundation matrix are based on the species Homo sapiens, and, therefore, are likely to be universal, that is, to be found in all societies. (Many psycho-dramatists and socio-dramatists refer to the foundation matrix as the "socius", meaning the mentality of the society, as expressed in its social-cultural–communicational relations.)

Although matrices both create and are created by the inter-relational persons who participate in them, matrices have their own structure and functional autonomy. Dynamic matrices are in flux, by definition. Foundation matrices are also in flux, but they are transgenerational in their origins and development.

The matrix of a system must always be contextualized in terms of an open-systems perspective. Although the distinction between the boundaries of the social system and the boundaries of its participants must be maintained, the matrix of any social system is located midway between the matrices of its subsystems and the matrices of its larger contextual systems. Thus, global dynamics may be recapitulated within societies, and societal dynamics may be recapitulated within regions and specific locales, organizations, families, dyads, etc., and, of course, vice versa. This kind of recapitalization is termed "equivalence", which is based on projective and introjective communications involving the compulsion to repeat a narrative of pain that cannot be expressed in the situation in which it was originally spawned (Hopper, 2003b).

One of the dimensions of dynamic and foundational matrices that has been almost entirely neglected by group analysts is technology and economic organization. The development of information technology, for example, has challenged our understanding of individuality and sociality in that access to such technology involves actual isolation combined with virtual relation to others. Facebook has forced the rediscovery of the sociometry of human relationships.

Having unconsciously co-constructed the matrices of their social systems, people are always involved in the personification of them. In this sense, the person and his social systems are always two sides of the same coin. Specifically, with respect to the system of communication and levels of it, the members of a social system are always to some degree spokespersons for all the members of the system. This is not merely a matter of vulnerability to the suction of particular roles (Kernberg, 1998; Redl, 1963), or having a valence for fulfilling particular roles associated with basic assumption processes (Bion, 1961). It is often a matter for prolonged reflection and negotiation as to the degree to which a person speaks for himself, for various subgroups and/or for all the members of a social system. In fact, such negotiation always leads to a consideration of the boundaries of persons and their groupings, and, therefore, to the social unconscious. Some of these issues will be explored in depth in Volume II of this series, which is mainly about the dynamic and foundation matrices of various groups, organizations and societies.

VI

Many people confuse the concept of the social unconscious with the concept of the collective unconscious. In fact, these two concepts are similar but different. Although Jung did not refer to the unconscious mind as such, it can be said that Jung (1936) distinguished the collective unconscious mind of each human being as a member of the species Homo sapiens from the personal unconscious mind of each particular human being. It follows that human beings are identical with respect to their collective unconscious minds, but different with respect to their personal unconscious minds.

The collective unconscious contains images of "archetypes", and is not actually a store of archetypes themselves. Archetypes are not really knowable except through traces of them, which is similar to Plato's discussion of epistemology in the context of the Cave. These images of archetypes would seem to be universal and timeless, because they are derived from the biologically innate archetypes. These archetypes and images of them are said to be inherited by the species on the basis of acquired characteristics that originated in situations that occurred eons ago. However, some images of archetypes are universal and timeless because they are associated with "life events" that are themselves universal and timeless, such as birth, stages of maturation, death, etc.

This classical Jungian point of view is similar to Freud's classical point of view in *Totem and Taboo* (1912–1913). Jung and Freud assumed that the trials and tribulations of the first breeding groups of human beings were encoded into their genetic structure, and were transmitted to subsequent generations in terms of archetypes or something like archetypes. This idea was later developed in terms of the instinctual sources of what later Kleinian psychoanalysts asserted were a source of "unconscious phantasies" (Solomon, 2007).

Although Jung was somewhat ambiguous about the phylogenetic basis of the collective unconscious, he accepted that there was a very close parallel between the biological, psychological, and sociological development of societies and cultures, on the one hand, and organisms and persons, on the other. Jung assumed that mental life and biological life are governed by the principle that ontogeny recapitulates phylogeny. Thus, the great phenotypical diversity of cultures is underpinned by a much smaller number of basic, innate, elemental archetypes and images of them. These primal fantasies predispose human beings to produce the same or similar mythical ideas and other collective phenomena over and over again. However, Jung argued that these predispositions are not only restraints but also constraints, which can be generative, and associated with creativity, imagination, and problem solving, as has been said of dreams (Hadfield, 1954).

Many Jungians believe that the religions of contemporary tribal peoples express essential truths that have been more or less extinguished or at least submerged within the belief systems of more "modern" peoples. They also regard ancient and contemporary myths, especially religious myths, as collective memories of important events that occurred in the beginning of human civilization. In this connection, the collective unconscious has a "cosmic" dimension, and is open to determinate influences from the numinous world of spirits. This is a way of saying that the species is rooted in the mind of God, which some Jungians would argue is a more poetic way of connecting the concept of the collective unconscious with theories of synchronicity and spontaneity in the context of contemporary theories of chaos and complexity, or vice versa.

Several modern Jungians have used the concept of the collective unconscious in order to emphasize the interpersonal unconscious and the shared unconscious as the basis for the co-construction of social reality and the co-construction of anxieties and defences (Zinkin, 1979). In this context, they also focus on the importance of socialization processes. The consensus among contemporary Jungians is that the concept of the collective unconscious should be used in order to emphasize the importance of the internalization of culture, and of certain aspects of culture. Henderson (1984) referred to the "cultural unconscious" of native Americans, arguing that what Jung originally called the "collective" is dependent on the culture. In other words, archetypes, which are always rooted in biology, develop their particular content in every culture and era through the process of "cultural ingraining". Thus, every culture is an expression of the universal themes of the collective unconscious and the particular themes of the culture of a particular social system, which, in turn, gives rise to the cultural component of the collective unconscious of its members. Especially important is the new concept of the cultural complex (Singer & Kimbles, 2004) which refers to internalized configurations of values, norms, and beliefs which are transmitted through the generations. Many cultural complexes are associated with social tension and conflict, as well as with values, norms, and beliefs that are, quite simply, taken for granted. As is the case for culture more generally, cultural complexes are like the air that we breathe: we do not become aware of air until we lose our access to it.

These modifications of the classical Jungian concept of the collective unconscious, namely, the shared unconscious, the interpersonal unconscious, socialization, cultural ingraining, and the cultural complex, make the contemporary Jungian concept of the collective unconscious virtually identical to the Foulkesian concept of the social unconscious. However, the concept of the social unconscious does not assume an ultimate cosmic context. The unknown and the new might be a function of the dynamics of group relations. Neither does the concept of the social unconscious assume the inheritance of acquired characteristics (although for some this remains an open question); the social unconscious is based on transgenerational cultural inheritance through a variety of institutions such as education, child-rearing practices, and socialization more generally. In the same way that the collective unconscious unites all human beings as members of the same species, Homo sapiens, the collective unconscious also unites all societies and cultures. However, whereas the social unconscious unites the members of particular social systems, it distinguishes the members of one social system from the members of another. It must be acknowledged that despite these patterns of similarity and difference at the level of species and societal social systems, we will always be challenged to explain patterns of diversity among persons.

VII

It is difficult to analyse the resistances to an appreciation of the social unconscious and interpretation of it, whether in the dyads of classical psychoanalysis, the small groups of group analysis and other forms of group psychotherapy, or even in the large group settings of workshops and conferences in which the participants have contracted to explore the dynamics of the social unconscious. The recognition and understanding of the social unconscious constitutes another painful blow to our narcissistic grandiosity, omnipotence, and omniscience (which is why the insights of Durkheim and Marx are as important as those of Darwin, Freud, Jung, Bion, and Foulkes, not to mention those of Galileo, Einstein, Crick and Watson, etc., all of whom have relegated us from the centre of the universe to the periphery of it). The motivation for remaining unconscious of social objects is the need to regulate the anxiety that would follow from the recognition of them, and from understanding the nature of their constraints and restraints, and especially in connection with a sense of helplessness and powerlessness. Moreover, it is difficult to be committed to ethical living when our insights into the power of the social unconscious make it so difficult to believe in "free will", to accept that we have the freedom to choose our actions and even to choose not to act in good faith. Understanding the social unconscious can lead to an inurnment to core values and moral norms, based on an extreme interpretation of cultural relativity, which can lead, in turn, to a degree of freedom from guilt and shame, on the one hand, and to the consequences of what Fromm called escape from freedom, on the other. As in the understanding of unconscious processes more generally, it is possible to gain intellectual insight into the social unconscious without the experience of the emotions connected with the constraints and restraints of it.

These resistances are rooted in anxieties associated with early life experience, starting with the painful awareness by the foetus that not only is it attached to a womb, but that the womb is also attached to a larger object, the mother, and, in turn, that not only is the mother "attached" to the father, but that the parental couple is also "attached" to a larger family, and, in turn, that the family is attached to larger and more comprehensive social, cultural and political structures. An important aspect of this painful insight is the awareness that these others and, in turn, their others, have minds of their own. How small and vulnerable we are . . . so limited in our freedom to make the world as we would please (Hopper, 2007).

Several other factors are also involved. One is that in modern industrial and post-industrial societies, especially those of the West, ideologies of individualism prevail, and the reality of the interpersonal relationship is difficult to comprehend. Many people are able to perceive material facts, such as their own bodies, but neither psychic facts nor social facts, such as their own minds and their interpersonal relationships, groups, group processes, organizations, societies, etc. To them, the concept of the social brain seems to be a contradiction in terms. Another factor is that not many clinicians have been trained in the social sciences, and, therefore, they are reluctant to discuss the reality of the external social world. Also, the very term "social" is often taken to imply "socialism", which seems to be even more of a "no-no" today than it used to be.

More speculatively, we wonder if another source of resistance to understanding the social unconscious is the difficulties people have in the appreciation of spirituality, and of numinosity in general, and in asking questions about liminal transitions. Of course, this, too, is a product of the constraints of the social unconscious, because in other cultures people do not have these particular difficulties: they find it easier to consider spirituality than the material world, and for them the split between the spiritual world and the material world does not exist.

Clinical work involving the analysis of the repetition of the concentric and spiralling nature of early life experience within transference and countertransference processes is likely to increase the ability and willingness to be interested in what transpires between people and their groups both at any one time and across the generations.

Note

1. The capacity to be "unconscious" is a function of the brain and the body. Cognitive psychology has shown that we can perceive emotionally loaded words unconsciously. The neurosciences have discovered much evidence for the existence of unconscious processes. For example, Cozolino (2006) claims that right brain functions are similar to Freud's notion of unconscious processes, and these functions would seem to develop earlier, to be guided by emotional and bodily reactions, and to be characterized by a non-linear mode of processing, which allows for the perception of multiple overlapping realities. The ventromesial quadrant of the frontal lobe has been identified as the brain subsystem that, when damaged, frees the functions that Freud (1923b) related to the unconscious system, for example, exemption from mutual contradiction, mobility of cathexis, timelessness, and replacing external reality with psychic reality, or, in other words, primary process as opposed to secondary process.

References

Ahlin, G. (1988). Reaching for the group matrix. *Group Analysis, 21*(3): 211–226.

Aron, L. (1996). *A Meeting of Minds*. Hillsdale, NJ: Analytic Press.

Bion, W. R. (1961). *Experiences in Groups and Other Papers*. London: Tavistock.

Bohm, D. (1980). *Wholeness and the Implicate Order*. London: Routledge.

Brown, D. (2001). A contribution to the understanding of the social unconscious. *Group Analysis, 34*(1): 29–38.

Cassirer, E. (1946). *The Myth of the State*. New Haven, CT: Yale University Press.

Chance, M., & Jolly, C. (1970). *Social Groups of Monkeys, Apes and Men.* London: Jonathan Cape.

Cohen, S. (2001). *States of Denial: Knowing about Atrocities and Suffering.* Cambridge: Polity Press.

Cozolino, L. (2006). *The Neuroscience of Human Relationships: Attachment and the Developing Social Brain.* New York: W. W. Norton.

Dalal, F. (1998). *Taking the Group Seriously.* London: Jessica Kingsley.

De Maré, P. (1972). *Perspectives in Group Psychotherapy.* London: Allen and Unwin.

Derrida, J. (1974). *Of Grammatology.* Baltimore,MD: Johns Hopkins University Press.

Devereux, G. (1982). *Femme et Mythe.* Paris: Flammarion.

Foulkes, S. H. (1964). *Therapeutic Group Analysis.* London: Allen and Unwin.

Foulkes, S. H. (1973). The group as matrix of the individuals' mental life. In: E. Foulkes (Ed.), *S. H. Foulkes Selected Papers.* London: Karnac, 1990.

Foulkes, S. H. (1975). A short outline of the therapeutic process in group analytic psychotherapy. *Group Analysis, 8:* 59–63.

Freud, S. (1912–1913). *Totem and Taboo. S.E., 13:* 1–161. London: Hogarth Press.

Freud, S. (1923b). *The Ego and the Id. S.E., 19:* 3–66. London: Hogarth Press.

Friedman, R. (2004). Safe space and relational pathology. *International Journal of Counselling and Psychotherapy, 2:* 108–114.

Garwood, A. (2001). Life, death and the power of powerlessness. *Group Analysis, 34(1):* 153–168.

Hadfield, J. A. (1954). *Dreams and Nightmares.* London: Penguin.

Halbwachs, M. (1992). *On Collective Memory.* Chicago, IL: University of Chicago Press.

Henderson, J. L. (1984). *Cultural Attitudes in Psychological Perspective.* Toronto: Inner City Books.

Hinshelwood, R. (1989). Communication flow in the matrix. *Group Analysis, 22(3):* 261–270.

Hopper, E. (1981). *Social Mobility: A Study of Social Control and Insatiability.* Oxford: Basil Blackwell.

Hopper, E. (1991). Encapsulation as a defence against the fear of annihilation. *International Journal of Psychoanalysis, 72(4):* 607–624.

Hopper, E. (2003a). *The Social Unconscious: Selected Papers.* London: Jessica Kingsley.

Hopper, E. (2003b). *Traumatic Experience in the Unconscious Life of Groups.* London: Jessica Kingsley.

Hopper, E. (2007). Theoretical and conceptual notes concerning transference and countertransference processes in groups and by groups, and the social unconscious, Part II. *Group Analysis, 40*(1): 29–42.

Hopper, E. (2009). Building bridges between psychoanalysis and group analysis in theory and clinical practice. *Group Analysis, 42*(4): 406–425.

Hopper, E. (Ed.) (2011). The theory of the basic assumption of incohesion: aggregation/massification or (ba) I:A/M. Appendix to *Trauma and Organizations*. London: Karnac.

Hutton, E. H. (1976). The scientific status of psychoanalysis and of group analysis. *GAIPAC-Letters*, No. 4. The Group Analytic Society (London).

Jung, C. G. (1936). The concept of the collective unconscious. *Journal of St. Bartholomew's Hospital (London)*, XLIV.

Kaes, R. (1987). La troisième difference. *Revue de Psychothérapie Psychanalytique de Groupe, 9–10*: 5–30.

Kansteiner, W. (2002). Finding meaning in memory: methodological critique of collective memory studies. *History and Theory, 41*: 179–197.

Kernberg, O. (1998). *Ideology, Conflict and Leadership in Groups and Organizations*. New Haven, CT: Yale University Press.

Knauss, W. (2006). The group in the unconscious: a bridge between the individuals and the society. *Group Analysis, 39*(2): 159–170.

Lacan, J. (1977). *Ecrits: A Selection*, A. Sheridan (Trans.). New York: Norton.

Lenn, R., & Stefano, K. (Eds.) (2011). *Patrick de Maré: Small, Large and Median Groups*. London: Karnac.

Le Roy, J. (1994). Group analysis and culture. In: D. Brown & L. Zinkin (Eds.), *The Psyche and the Social World*. London: Routledge.

Lintott, B. (1983). Mind and matrix in the writing of S. H. Foulkes. *Group Analysis, 16*(3): 242–247.

Miller, P. (2010). *Smart Swarms*. London: HarperCollins.

Pines, M. (1998). Psychic development and the group-analytic situation. In: *Circular Reflections: Selected Papers on Group Analysis and Psychoanalysis* (pp. 59–76). London: Jessica Kingsley.

Pines, M. (2009). Personal communication concerning the "cultural unconscious".

Puget, J. (1986). Personal communication concerning what she calls "overlapping worlds".

Redl, F. (1963). Psychoanalysis and group therapy: a developmental point of view. *American Journal of Orthopsychiatry, 33*: 135–147.

Roberts, J. P. (1982). Foulkes's concept of the matrix. *Group Analysis, XV/2*: 111–126.

Rouchy, J. C. (1987). Identité culturelle et groups d'appartenance. *Connexions, 55*: 45–56.

Scheidlinger, S. (1990). On internalization in group psychology: the group within. *Journal of the American Academy of Psychoanalysis, 18*(3): 494–504.

Searle, J. R. (1995). *The Construction of Social Reality*. New York: Free Press.

Siegel, D. J. (2006). An interpersonal neurobiology approach to psycho-therapy: awareness, mirror neurons, and neural plasticity in the development of well-being. *Psychiatric Annals, 36*(4): 247–258.

Singer, T., & Kimbles, S. (Eds.) (2004). *The Cultural Complex: Contemporary Jungian Perspectives on Psyche and Society*. London: Brunner-Routledge.

Solomon, H. (2007). *The Self in Transformation*. London: Karnac.

Spector-Person, E. (1992). Romantic love: at the intersection of the psyche and the cultural unconscious. In: T. Shapiro & R. Emde (Eds.), *Affect Psychoanalytic Perspective*. New York: International Universities Press.

Volkan, V. (2001). Transgenerational transmissions and chosen traumas: an aspect of large group identity. *Group Analysis, 34*(1): 79–97.

Weinberg, H. (2007). So what is this social unconscious anyway? *Group Analysis, 40*(3): 307–322.

Winnicott, D. W. (1949). Mind and its relation to the psyche-soma. In: *Through Paediatrics to Psycho-Analysis*. London: Hogarth Press, 1982.

Winnicott, D. W. (1952). Anxiety associated with insecurity. In: *Through Paediatrics to Psycho-Analysis*. London: Hogarth Press, 1982.

Woolley, A. W., Chabris, C., Pentland, A., Hashmi, N., & Malone, T. (2010). Evidence for a collective intelligence factor in the performance of human groups; *Science, 330*(6004): 686–688.

Zeisel, E. (2009). Affect education and the development of the interpersonal ego in modern group psychoanalysis. *International Journal of Group Psychotherapy, 59*(3): 421–432.

Zinkin, L. (1979). The collective and the personal. *Journal of Analytical Psychology, 24*: 227–250.

PART I

THE ORIGINS OF THE CONCEPT
OF THE SOCIAL UNCONSCIOUS

CHAPTER ONE

The concept of the social unconscious in the work of S. H. Foulkes

Dieter Nitzgen

The "basic nature of social influences" in psychoanalysis and group analysis was one of the main concerns of S. H. Foulkes. Even in his first book, *Introduction to Group Analytic Psychotherapy* (Foulkes, 1948), he welcomed the "growing recognition of the basic importance of society" in psychoanalysis (p. 11). In fact, group analysis can be seen in terms of the recognition of the importance of the concept of the social unconscious, which Foulkes introduced as a supplement to Freud's concept of dynamic unconscious. However, the references Foulkes made to this concept are scarce and scattered, and taken from and relating to very different contexts, such as neurobiology, psychiatry, psychoanalysis, sociology, and social anthropology, as well as epistemology. Moreover, these references are dense and need unpacking. This chapter will review Foulkes' main references to the social unconscious, and provide relevant background information regarding the contexts of them.

Foulkes' references to the social unconscious

In a first paper on group analysis, written together with E. Lewis and published in 1944, Foulkes and Lewis listed four group-specific therapeutic factors brought about by the loosening and stimulating effects of the group situation itself (Foulkes & Lewis, 1944, in Foulkes, 1964, p. 34; cf. Foulkes, 1983[1948], p. 167; Foulkes & Anthony, 1957, p. 151): social integration and relief from isolation, mirror reactions, the activation of the collective unconscious, and interpersonal exchange.

For Foulkes and Lewis, it is "as if the collective unconscious acted as a condenser" (Foulkes & Lewis, 1944, in Foulkes, 1964, p. 34). Clearly, this notion of the "collective unconscious" had Jungian overtones (bearing in mind that Eve Lewis was a Jungian analyst working in a Jungian art therapeutic community (cf. Pines, 1999). In *Introduction to Group Analytic Psychotherapy*, Foulkes (1948) supplemented these four group specific factors with a fifth and sixth factor, describing the functions of the group as "Forum" and "Support" (pp. 167–168), and again evoked the idea of a "collective unconscious" acting as a condenser in the group.

Shortly afterwards, in a paper read to the American Group Psychotherapy Association, Foulkes (1949), discussed the group's relation to its leader in some detail. He differentiated several forms of transference reactions in groups, and made the important distinction between "familial" and "non-familial" types of transference, maintaining that although the family is a group, the group is not necessarily a family:

> In the unconscious phantasy of the group, the therapist is put in the position of the primordial leader; he is omniscient and omnipotent and the group expects magical help from him. He can actually be said to be a father figure and it is all too easy to interpret his position really as that of a father or mother and see the group representing a family. This is not my impression. Whereas family transference reactions between the members of the group and the leader can occasionally be seen the configuration as a whole does not, by any means, shape according to the family pattern. *It is true that the family is a group, but not that the group is a family.* [1984(1964), p. 59; my italics]

Claiming there are non-familial types of transference at work in groups, such as a transference to the community and/or society as a whole, Foulkes went beyond the established psychoanalytic model of group dynamics and group psychotherapy: that is,

Freud's (1921c) understanding of *Group Psychology and the Analysis of the Ego* (p. 65) and Bion's (1961) *Experiences in Groups*.

The first explicit reference to the "social unconscious" as a group analytic concept is found in "Group therapy" (Foulkes, 1950). He wrote,

> . . . the group analytic situation, while dealing intensively with the unconscious in the Freudian sense, brings into operation and perspective a totally different area of which the individual is equally unaware. Moreover, the individual is as much compelled by these colossal forces as by his own *id* and defends himself against their recognition without being aware of it, but in different ways and modes. One might speak of a "social or interpersonal unconscious". [p. 52]

In *Group Psychotherapy: The Psychoanalytic Approach* (Foulkes & Anthony, 1957), Foulkes amplified this first statement. He now explained that the "social unconscious" consists of "such *social relationships* as are not usually revealed, or are not even conscious" (1984[1957], p. 56, my italics). He again emphasized the "advantage of the group situation" and "the opportunity it affords for the exploration of what may be called the "social unconscious" (*ibid.*, p. 42). In groups, "each individual's feelings and reactions will reflect the influences exerted on him by other individuals in the group and by the group as a whole, however little he is aware of this" (*ibid.*). Therefore, it is *in* and *by* the group setting that unconscious social relations become "particularly open to exact investigation", sometimes with results "which can be surprising" (*ibid.*). With regard to clinical practice, he maintained that the "translation" of the "social unconscious" follows the same principles as the translation of Freudian "repressed unconscious" (*ibid.*, pp. 55–56).

The last reference to the social unconscious in his published work is to be found in "Problems of the large group" (Foulkes, 1975). In it, Foulkes discussed this concept in relationship to mental processes that he again suggested should not be considered as intrapsychic, but as *"per se* being multipersonal" (1990[1975], p. 253). He reaffirmed his earlier views on the social unconscious, and emphasized that the group analytic understanding of "translation" applied to the repressed unconscious of Freudian psychoanalysis and to the social unconscious alike (*ibid.*, p. 252).

The various contexts of the concept of the social unconscious in the work of Foulkes

Foulkes's references to the social unconscious suggest a variety of contexts, all of which are relevant to illuminating the full meaning of this concept. In his very first communication on group analysis, presented in April 1946 to the British Psychoanalytical Society, he took pains to explain that in group analysis "the qualifying word 'analysis' does not refer to psychoanalysis alone, but reflects at least *three different influences, all of which operate actively*" (1990[1946], p. 129). As the first of these influences, he mentioned "psychological analysis" as being evolved by Kurt Goldstein and Adhémar Gelb (*ibid.*, p. 129); the second was the influence of Freudian psychoanalysis, and the third was "sociological analysis" or "socioanalysis". Accordingly, we may assume that, for Foulkes, the idea of the social unconscious also reflected these three influences. I will return to the interesting fact that Foulkes did not list the influence of cultural anthropology.

Against localization: the neurobiological context

Although the social unconscious as a concept has a Freudian core, the idea of non-conscious relations between the "individual" and the "social other" precedes Foulkes's psychoanalytic training from 1928 to 1930 in Vienna, and dates back to his formative years as a psychiatrist, when, from 1924 to 1926, he had worked in Kurt Goldstein's neurological clinic in Frankfurt. On the basis of his clinical work with brain injured patients during and after the First World War, Goldstein had argued against the assumption of "localized" lesions in the brain put forward by classical neuron theory (Gelb & Goldstein, 1918). Instead, he advocated that the nervous system normally and pathologically always "reacted as whole". Therefore, he argued, disorders of the brain could not be "localized" in local lesions, but were to be considered as dysfunctions of the nervous system as a whole. In a careful review of Goldstein's (1934) book, *The Organism*, Foulkes (1936) had given a detailed account of Goldstein's neurobiological findings and their epistemological implications. He reaffirmed that the nervous system always reacted as a whole, and that this reaction was determined by what

Goldstein had called the "total situation" (Nitzgen, 2007, 2008, 2010). He emphasized Goldstein's methodological principle that "no finding is to be considered without reference to the *whole organism* and the *total situation*" (Foulkes, 1990[1936], p. 43, my italics). Foulkes went on to widen the scope of these neurobiological findings from the nervous system to the organism to the individual as a whole, and finally to the society as a "network", more or less as described by Elias (1939).

Accordingly, in 1948, his focus of interest shifted from neuro-(bio)logical to social networks. Drawing from his early group analytic experiments in Exeter and his experiences of British wartime psychiatry in Northfield, Foulkes was eventually able to transfer Goldstein's original insights to the social field and to apply them to socio-psychological phenomena. The subject of his (Foulkes, 1948) *Introduction to Group Analytic Psychotherapy* is "The individual as whole in a total situation" (p. 1). Here, he explained that what happens psychologically within the individual is determined by its "total situation", that is, its surrounding social network. This led to a totally new perspective on the nature and origins of psychic disturbances. As Foulkes saw it, such disturbances could no longer be *localized* within in the individual psyche but were to be *located* in a total field of interaction, the group matrix. Taking this view, he repeated Goldstein's earlier criticism of "localized" brain functions beyond neurology. By taking this step, he finally arrived at a "general formulation" regarding psychic disturbances:

> All this leads us to the general formulation that the disturbance we see in front of us, embodied in a particular patient, is in fact the expression of a disturbed balance in a total field of interaction which involves a number of different people as participants. [Foulkes & Anthony, 1984(1957), p. 54]

It is not difficult to see that the understanding of the individual as a whole in a total situation anticipates the later concept of the social unconscious. In both, the individual is considered to be "determined" by the conscious and non-conscious social relations of a given situation. For Foulkes, such a holistic or systemic perspective implies an altered view of the psychoanalytic situation itself. Thus, he insisted that we must perceive and evaluate the analytical situation including all its 'unconscious' components as determined by the patient's total life situation and not, contrariwise, see 'life' and 'reality' merely as a projection, screen and reflector of his 'unconscious phantasies', which they are indeed, at the same time. [Foulkes, 1948, p. 15]

This was in direct opposition to the ascendant view in the UK concerning the Kleinian emphasis on the centrality of innate unconscious phantasy. In contrast, Foulkes maintained that the general principle of a specifically group analytic orientation is that the group analyst "orientates himself in the light of the total situation and its context" (1990[1968a], p. 183).

Foulkes's epistemological orientation

It is necessary to consider Foulkes's clinical perspective in the context of the epistemological orientation that informs group analysis. In "Problems of the large group" (Foulkes, 1975), he maintained that "we cannot isolate biological, social, cultural and economic factors, except by special abstraction". "Mental life", he said, "is the expression of all these forces, both looked at horizontally, as it were in the strictly present reality, and vertically in relation to past inheritance" (1975, p. 252). In this statement, Foulkes recurred to Goldstein's epistemological perspective, which he himself had outlined in *Introduction to Group Analytic Psychotherapy* (Foulkes, 1948), stating that "the old juxtapositions of an inside and outside world, constitution and environment, individual and society, phantasy and reality, body and mind and so on, are untenable" (p. 10). For Foulkes, they are "untenable" because, as juxtapositions, they are not substantial but "artificial, though plausible abstractions", referring to an underlying life process which remains outside all positive knowledge (like Kant's thing-in-itself, which in itself is unknowable). This is the essence of Goldstein's epistemological legacy to Foulkes. As I have shown elsewhere (Nitzgen, 2010), this legacy also reflected the influence of Goldstein's cousin, the philosopher Ernst Cassirer (cf. Cassirer, 1910), and informed Foulkes's entire clinical thinking, pushing it relentlessly towards the uncompleted project of a group analytic theory of mind (Foulkes, 2003).

The social location of neurosis: the psychoanalytical context

It is likely that Foulkes was also influenced by the work of Bernfeld. An influential member of Anna Freud's inner circle, Bernfeld was a partisan of socialist ideals and ideas, and a pioneer of psychoanalytically informed education. In 1925, he went to Berlin, continuing his seminar on psychoanalysis and education. (In his autobiographical notes, Foulkes (1968b, p. 120) mentioned that when he arrived in Vienna, Bernfeld had "already departed to Berlin".) In 1929, Bernfeld published a paper on the relevance of the "social location" for the understanding of "neurosis, deprivation and education". Although Foulkes does not refer to it in his written work, it is more than likely that he had learnt of it during his psychoanalytic training from 1928 to 1930 in Vienna, where Bernfeld had been a member of the teaching staff from 1922 until 1925. Bernfeld's paper was part of the ongoing dialogue between psychoanalysis and Marxism in the 1930s (Bernfeld, Reich, Jurinetz, Sapir, Stoljarov, 1970). Although Bernfeld acknowledged the correctness of Freud's theory of the drives, he maintained that their "vicissitudes" (Freud, 1915c) were moulded by the social situation in which they originated no less than by biological factors. Accordingly, he maintained that "normal and pathological mechanisms" do have a "historical aspect": "We may resume the question of the historical aspect and the social moulding of a mental process in terms of the perspective of the social location" (1929, p. 210; my translation). For Bernfeld, the concept of a social location of neurosis was useful in clinical psychoanalysis (Bernfeld, 1931) as well as in education (Bernfeld, 1935). In terms of language, it is interesting to note that his original German expression: *der soziale Ort* can equally well be translated into English as the social *situation* or the social *location*.

Bernfeld's concept was not the only influence of the Freudian left on Foulkes. Moving from Vienna back to Frankfurt in 1930, Foulkes also became geographically and intellectually drawn to the work of the Institute of Social Research, which at the time also housed the Frankfurt Institute of Psychoanalysis (Schivelbusch, 1982, p. 80). Foulkes was in charge of its outpatient department until he emigrated in 1933. The social foundations of character formation and its empirical research on "Authority and the family"

(Fromm, 1936), had become the focus of psychoanalytic attention, which had shifted from symptom to character formation (cf. Freud, 1908b). The relevant model of character formation of classical psychoanalysis (impulse–conflict–defence–symptom/character) was supplemented by a second, more socially orientated model (society–conflict–adaptation–character) (Hoffmann, 1984, p. 62). This latter model was closely associated with the psychoanalytic works of Fromm (1932) and his description of an "authoritarian" or "authoritarian–masochistic" character (Fromm, 1936). In contrast to the understanding of character formation as *Triebschicksal*, as a "vicissitude of the drives" (Freud, 1915c), Fromm's elaboration was more social psychologically focused: that is, based on unconscious social structures, family relations, and power issues. In fact, Fromm later stopped using libido theory altogether.

Among the classical analysts, it was Fenichel who synthesized Freud's genetic point of view with the findings of ego psychology and the importance of social factors. For Fenichel, "the character of man is socially determined" (Fenichel, 1945, p. 464). Like Bernfeld before him, Fenichel emphasized that "different societies, stressing different values and applying different educational measures *create different anomalies*" (*ibid*, my italics). Unlike Fromm, he maintained that character formation was due to internal demands and external constraints. He wrote,

> Character, as the habitual mode of bringing into harmony the tasks presented by internal demands and by the external world, is necessarily a function of the constant, organizing and integrating part of the personality which is the ego . . . [1945, p. 467]

As a psychoanalyst and as a group analyst, Foulkes (1964) affirmed this view when he stated that "conceiving the social nature of man as basic does not deny or reduce the importance of the sexual instinct in the sense of psycho-analysis, nor the aggressive instinct" (p. 109). Another decisive influence on Foulkes was the work of Homburger-Erikson, who trained in Vienna at the same time as Foulkes himself. In his first book, Foulkes, drawing extensively from Erik Erikson's (1946) paper, "Ego development and historical change", which he saw as a "remarkable contribution" to the appreciation of the "basic nature of social influences" in psychoanalytic

theory and practice (Foulkes, 1948, p. 11). He especially approved
of Erikson's revised notion of the goal of psychoanalytic treatment.
In his paper published in 1946, Erikson had suggested that "the
individual's mastery over his neurosis begins, where he is put in a
position to accept the historical necessity which made him was he
is" (quoted by Foulkes, 1983[1948], p. 13). Accordingly, psychoanalytic treatment could no longer be restricted to the "increase of
the mobility of the id, the tolerance of the superego and the synthe-
sizing power of the ego" but should also encompass the analysis of
"the individual ego-identity in its relation to the historical changes
which dominated his childhood milieu" (Foulkes, 1948). Viewed in
the context of the psychoanalytic contributions of Bernfeld, Erikson,
Fromm, Homburger-Erikson, and Fenichel, the concept of the
"social unconscious" can be seen as a contribution to, as well as an
extension of, the psychoanalytic debate on the social location of
neurosis, character formation, and the development of ego-identity.

The roots of the concept of the social unconscious in sociology and social anthropology

Although the roots of group analysis were firmly planted in the soil
of psychoanalysis, group analysis was decisively shaped by sociological thinking, too. In his reference to "sociological analysis", or
"socio-analysis', as one of the three formative influences operative
in the development of group analysis, Foulkes acknowledged the
influence of Karl Mannheim, who was the first to have used the
term "group analysis" in *Diagnosis of Our Time* (Foulkes, 1990[1946]
p. 131; cf. Mannheim, 1943). However, in *Introduction to Group
Analytic Psychotherapy*, he especially referred to the sociological
work of Norbert Elias. Reminding the reader of his review of Elias's
(1938) book *The Civilizing Process*, Foulkes (1938) summarized
Elias's sociological views by saying that the individual "is part of a
social network, a little nodal point, as it were, in this network and
can only artificially be considered in isolation (1983[1948], p. 14). In
this phrase, Foulkes implicitly referred to Elias's notion of society
as a "network" first put forward in 1939 (cf. Elias, 1939). Although
Elias himself does not use the phrase "the social unconscious", it is
implicit in his sociological theory: first of all, as part of his overall
perspective of civilizing processes and their dis/integration, and

later in his notion of individual "habitus" formed by specific social "figurations" as described, for instance, in his (Elias, 1989) study *The Germans*. In his autobiographical notes dating from 1973, Foulkes acknowledged that he had learnt much "from his sociological friends" (Foulkes, 1990[1973], p. 79), referring mainly to Norbert Elias. However, in the book written with Anthony (Foulkes & Anthony, 1984[1957], p. 23), he mentioned Franz Borkenau as a another major influence from sociology, without being specific about the nature of his contribution. (Borkenau, who Foulkes had known from his Frankfurt days, was born in 1900 in Vienna. He had been a dedicated communist working in the service of the Communist International until his split with the party in 1929. A trained historian and sociologist, he was also an early member of the Institute of Social Research in Frankfurt, and became well known for his book on the transition from the feudal to the bourgeois world view (1934). Like Foulkes, he emigrated from Germany in 1933, first to Vienna, then to Paris, and finally to the UK, where he arrived in early 1934. At that time, he was listed among the students of Malinowski's seminar at the London School of Economics where he studied until 1935. With the help of Malinowski, he then took a short professorship in Panama, and after his return to London went on to Spain, where he worked as a freelance journalist. Until today, his book *The Spanish Cockpit* (1938) is a key account of the Civil War in Spain, disclosing the author's utter disillusionment with the role of the communist party in Spain (comparable with that of Arthur Koestler and George Orwell). Summing up what he had gained from Malinowski's seminar, Borkenau wrote in his curriculum vitae for the London School of Economics: "I am convinced, that a combination of historical and field-work is the ideal approach to the understanding of social developments, wherever it can be applied" (PEC Bos 45). He first applied this anthropological knowledge to evaluate the events in Spain and ended his book with a chapter on Spanish "mentality". With his second wife, Lucie Vargas, who at that time was working in Paris with Lucien Febvre and Marc Bloch, the founders of the famous historical school of the Annales (cf. Schöttler, 1994, 1996), Borkenau discussed questions of mentality, too. Vargas, who had studied with Alfred Dopsch in Vienna, was one of the first historians to apply the principles learnt from Malinowski (whom she knew) to historical research. From this, she came to understand Hitler and his National Socialism not only as a political phenomenon, but also as a cultural one. Like Eric Voegelin, who coined the term (cf. Voegelin, 1938), Vargas thus came to view it as a "political religion". Even after their divorce in 1936, Borkenau continued to follow her intellectual tracks. Traces of these are visible in his (Borkenau, 1981) last book on the cycles of cultures.) Despite these brief remarks, Borkenau's influence on Foulkes remains somewhat obscure. Foulkes did not list social anthropology as particularly relevant to the development of the concept of the social unconscious. None the less, he referred to the anthropological works of Bronislaw Malinowski as a source of inspiration for his work in Northfield (1948, p. 16–17). He quoted at length from Malinowski's (1926) paper on "Myth in primitive psychology", and reasserted his view regarding the essential function of myth for society:

> Myth is not merely a story told, but a reality lived. Myth fulfils in primitive culture an indispensable function. . . . Myth is thus a vital ingredient of human civilisation, it is not an idle tale, but a hard worked active force. [Malinowski, quoted by Foulkes, 1948, p. 16]

Accordingly, Foulkes stated that "the group situation—a collective of human beings in a social setting—is the best place to study the Group, as well as the Individual in its social aspects, alive and direct" (ibid.). Moreover, he acknowledged Malinowski's influence on him not only in terms of theory, but also with regard to his clinical practice. "Malinowski's description of the move from 'Arm Chair Anthropology' to 'Open Air Anthropology'", he said, "fits exactly my own development at Northfield; away from consulting room psychiatry, into living 'open air' psychiatry, into the soldier's life, his Army Mythology, of his 'neurosis' in the reality of his life" (ibid., p. 17). This sheds light on how Foulkes conceived his occupation in Northfield Military Hospital. His role and task were akin to those of an anthropologist in a foreign culture and society, as a ethnographer or a "participant observer" (Foulkes, ibid.; cf. Devereux, 1972). Foulkes's remarks on Malinowski also introduce a non-Jungian element into what Foulkes and Lewis originally had called the "collective unconscious" in the sense that Jung had used the term concerning myth and mythology. Foulkes was aware of the debate between Ernest Jones and Malinowski concerning what Jones called the Oedipus complex and Malinowski called the family complex, following Freud's original notion of it, and it is likely that Foulkes and Elias had discussed Malinowski's *Sex and Repression in a Savage Society* (1927). Hopper (personal communication) reports that Foulkes encouraged him to teach this material in the first Qualifying Course at the Institute of Group Analysis in London.

Regarding method: access to the social unconscious

Foulkes was not content to elaborate the notion of the social unconscious only in theoretical terms. As a practising psychoanalyst and group analyst, he was equally keen to describe a "method of access to unconscious social processes in groups and group-like social systems and to devise its 'technical tools'" (cf. Foulkes, 1971). For Foulkes, the basic tool for this was Freud's psychoanalytic method of free association. He wrote, "With respect to the translation of the repressed unconscious, the basic tool is free association; that is, the communication of everything in the patient's mind without censorship" (Foulkes & Anthony, 1984[1957], p. 40). However, in group analytic groups, he noted, "we want means of communication under reduced censorship" (*ibid.*, p. 56). For Foulkes, the reduction of "censorship" does not only apply to the repressed unconscious in the Freudian sense, but also to the social unconscious. "This reduced censorship", he claimed, "must apply *also* to the patient's relationships to others, including the conductor" (*ibid.*, my italics). According to Foulkes, "this very important feature *enables us* to approach what might be called the social unconscious, i.e. such social relationships as are not usually revealed, or are even not conscious" (*ibid.*, my italics). Conceptually, reduced censorship is, thus, key to translate both repressed unconscious (internal) impulses *and* unconscious (external) social relations. This is a complex statement, one that is not without significant riddles. To grasp its basic logic, we have to reconsider Foulkes's crucial distinction between individual associations, as known from psychoanalysis and group associations. While the "individual associations" are "based on traces in the brain", and associated with Freud's memory traces, group associations are based "on the common ground of unconscious *instinctive understanding*" of the group members (*ibid.*, p. 28, original italics). Consequently, Foulkes now considered all communications in a given group as *"meaningful associations in the context of group"* (Foulkes, 1990[1968a], p. 181; my italics, Foulkes & Anthony, 1984[1957], p. 29). Eventually Foulkes recognized that thereby they acquired "the value of *unconscious interpretations"* (*ibid.*, original italics). Making this *"decisive* step in theory and practice", as he himself claimed (*ibid.*, p. 29, my italics), enabled him to relate Goldstein's systemic view—his concept of the "total situation"—to Freud's method of access to the unconscious mind (cf. Foulkes, 1983[1948], p. 5). Based on clinical observation, Foulkes realized that *"free association is in no way independent of the total situation"* (*ibid.*, p. 71, my italics). Regarding theory and practice, this insight is the conceptual core for the group analytic access to all that has been repressed, including the social unconscious. However, Foulkes did not clarify what he really meant by "unconscious intuitive understanding of group members": for example, was it akin to what Bion had begun to call basic assumptions, or what Freud had called sexual and aggressive drives, based on an analogy between the group and the organism?

Concluding comment

From Foulkes's references, we can gather that for him the concept of the social unconscious was more or less an "intuition" with which he grappled throughout his career without being able to resolve many of the conceptual difficulties involved in using it. From the beginning, Foulkes struggled to disentangle the *social* from the *collective* unconscious. In his first works, especially in the paper with Lewis (1944), he used the two terms more or less anonymously. In later works, Foulkes distinguished more clearly between the social and the collective unconscious. Part of this differentiation is the description of a "primordial level" of group communication governed by "universal symbols" and "archaic images" (Foulkes, 1990[1968a], p. 183), for which Foulkes conceded that *"perhaps Jung's concept of the collective unconscious is relevant here"* (*ibid.*, my italics). It is surprising that he did not draw more from social anthropology and contemporary sociology. These ideas would have provided him with an alternative frame of reference, for example,

Malinowski's (1926, 1936) elaborations of the function of myth in society, or Borkenau's (1967) historical understanding of myth and archetypes, or Voegelin (1938) and Vargas' notion of political religion (cf. Schöttler, 1997). These ideas all differed from Jung's a-political vision of myth and mythology. Perhaps Foulkes, as an emigrant, did not want be associated with their political orientations, which, in Borkenau's case, had been to the extreme "left" before the war, and violently anti-communist after the war. However, this stance deprived Foulkes of the conceptual tools with which he could have elaborated important aspects of what he called the "colossal forces" of unconscious social facts. As a result, his references to "fathers and mothers as archetypes" (Foulkes & Anthony, 1984[1957], p. 27) and the "primordial level of group communication" were ambiguous and devoid of political, sociological, anthropological, and also philosophical, substance. By insisting on not republishing his early paper on Goldstein (1936) in English during his lifetime, Foulkes also obliterated other important traces of his own intellectual legacy: for instance, references to the collaboration of Goldstein with his cousin, the philosopher Ernst Cassirer (Nitzgen, 2010), which are entirely relevant for a deeper understanding of the concept of the social unconscious. It had been Cassirer (1923, 1925, 1929) who, in *The Philosophy of Symbolic Forms*, had defined mythical thinking as the symbolic "matrix" of all other symbolic forms, such as language, art, religion, and science. In his last book, *The Myth of the State*, Cassirer (1946) had extended Goldstein's early studies on individual symbol pathologies (like aphasia) to the social field. Referring to Malinowski's view of the essential function of myth for society, he described collective symbol pathologies at work on modern societies in form of calculated, technologically produced "political myths".

From a more clinical point of view, Foulkes never explained how social facts impinged on the individual psyche. Although he merely hinted at their double nature as inhibiting and facilitating forces, he did not elucidate the process of their psychic representation. Unlike the repressed unconscious of psychoanalysis, which was based on *specific* mechanisms of defence, mainly repression employed against the drives of sexuality and aggression, he did not outline in any detail the defensive process associated with unconscious social facts. Instead, he resorted to Freud's early concept of "censorship" (Foulkes & Anthony, 1984[1957], p. 56), which he claimed was operative towards psychic and social facts alike. Therefore, from a psychodynamic point of view, the concept of the social unconscious is more descriptive than explanatory. However, like Bernfeld's notion of the social location of neuroses, it lends itself to a comprehension beyond the domain of the strictly social. According to Foulkes, the social unconscious also spans cultural development as such:

> The cultures and values of a community are inescapably trans-
> ferred to the growing infant by its individual father and mother as
> determined by their particular nation, class, religion, and region.
> They are transmitted verbally and non-verbally, instinctively, and
> emotionally, twenty-four hours a day and night. Even objects,
> movements, gestures and accents are determined in this way by the
> representation of the cultural group. [*ibid.*, p. 27]

In this extended sense, the notion of the social unconscious is linked to the concept socialization and theory of socialization. This is what the authors of the Institute of Social Research, Adorno, Horkheimer, and Fromm were looking for when they started their research into the social-psychological foundations of the "authoritarian character" in the 1930s. In Germany, such a psychoanalytically informed theory of socialization was eventually outlined by Lorenzer (1972), a psychoanalyst and social scientist working at the Sigmund Freud Institut in Frankfurt. In France, a similar project was undertaken by Castoriadis (1975), a Greek-born philosopher and psychoanalyst. Over the years, Foulkes (1972) emphasized more and more the importance of cultural transmission over what Freud had considered to be a predominantly "organic heritage", specifically in his notes on the "Oedipus-Complex and regression" (p. 238). In his paper on the large group, Foulkes (1975) asserted that "In the group analytic view, this inheritance is not seen entirely, or even predominantly, as a genetic and biological one, but more as a cultural inheritance, a transmission from generation to generation, from the earliest days onwards" (p. 252). (Recently, the particular mechanisms and dynamics of such a cultural inheritance have been elucidated in more psychoanalytical, biological, historical, and philosophical terms by Stanley Greenspan and Stuart Shanker (2004) in their book *The First Idea*.)

Viewed from the perspective of Foulkes'epistemological orientation, the social unconscious is also an abstraction, pertaining to a distinct area of knowledge and meaning won from what Castoriadis (1981) has called the "magma" of the social-historical process.

References

Bernfeld, S. (1929). Der Soziale Ort und seine Bedeutung für Neurose, Verwahrlosung und Pädagogik. In: L. von Werder & R. Wolff (Eds.), *Antiautoritäre Erziehung und Psychoanalyse. Ausgewählte Schriften Bd.* (pp. 209–225). Frankfurt: Ullstein, 1971.

Bernfeld, S. (1931). Die Tantalussituation. In: L. von Werder & R. Wolff (Eds.), *Antiautoritäre Erziehung und Psychoanalyse. Ausgewählte Schriften Bd. 2* (pp. 329–346). Frankfurt: Ullstein.

Bernfeld, S. (1935). Über die einfache männliche Pubertät. In: L. von Werder & R. Wolff (Eds.), *Antiautoritäre Erziehung und Psychoanalyse. Ausgewählte Schriften Bd. 2* (pp. 308–329). Frankfurt: Ullstein, 1970.

Bernfeld, S., Reich, W., Jurinetz, W., Sapir, I., Stoljarov, A. (1970). *Psychoanalyse und Marxismus. Dokumentation einer Kontroverse.* Frankfurt: a.M. Suhrkamp.

Bion, W. R. (1961). *Experiences in Groups and Other Papers.* London: Tavistock.

Borkenau, F. (1934). *Der Übergang von feudalen zum bürgerlichen Weltbild.* Paris: Felix Alcan [reprinted Darmstadt: Wissenschaftliche Buchgesellschaft, 1971].

Borkenau, F. (1938). *The Spanish Cockpit. London: An Eye Witness Account of the Political and Social Conflicts of the Spanish Civil War.* London: Faber & Faber.

Borkenau, F. (1967). *End and Beginning: On the Generations of Cultures and the Origins of the West.* New York: Columbia University Press.

Borkenau, F. (1981). *End and Beginning: On The Generations of Culture and The Origins of The West.* New York: Columbia University Press.

Cassirer, E. (1910). *Substance and Function and Einstein's Theory of Relativity,* W. Curtis Swabey, & M. Collins Swabey (Trans.). New York: Dover, 1953.

Cassirer, E. (1923). *The Philosophy of Symbolic Forms. Volume 1: Language,* R. Mannheim (Trans.). New Haven, CT: Yale University Press, 1953.

Cassirer, E. (1925). *The Philosophy of Symbolic Forms. Volume 2: Mythical Thought*, R. Mannheim (Trans.). New Haven, CT: Yale University Press, 1955.

Cassirer, E. (1929). *The Philosophy of Symbolic Forms. Volume 3: Phenomenology of Knowledge*, R. Mannheim (Trans.). New Haven, CT: Yale University Press, 1957.

Cassirer, E. (1946). *The Myth of the State*. New Haven, CT: Yale University Press.

Castoriadis, C. (1975). *The Imaginary Institution of Society. Creativity and Autonomy in the Social-Historical World*. New York: Polity Press, 1997.

Castoriadis, C. (1981). Le logique des magmas et la question de l'autonomie. Domaines de l'homme. In: *Les Carrefours du Labyrinthe II* (pp. 385–418). Paris: Le Seuil, 1986.

Devereux, G. (1972). *Ethnopsychanalyse, Complémentaristes*. Paris: Flammarion.

Elias, N. (1939). *The Society of the Individuals*. Oxford: Blackwell, 1991.

Elias, N. (1989). *The Germans. Power Struggles and the Development of Habitus in the 19th and 20th Centuries*. Cambridge: Policy Press, 1996.

Erikson, E. (1946). Ego development and historical change. In: *Identity and the Life Cycle (Psychological Issues Monograph)* (pp. 18–49). New York: International Universities Press, 1959.

Fenichel, O. (1945). *The Psychoanalytic Theory of Neurosis*. New York: Norton.

Foulkes, S. H. (1936). Zum Stand der heutigen Biologie. Dargestellt an Kurt Goldstein: der Aufbau des Organismus. *Imago 22*, pp. 210–241 [English version: Biology in the light of the work of Kurt Goldstein. In: S. H. Foulkes, *Selected Papers* (pp. 39–56). London: Karnac, 1990].

Foulkes, S. H. (1938). Book review of Norbert Elias' *The Civilizing Process*. In: *Selected Papers* (pp. 79–82). London: Karnac, 1990.

Foulkes, S. H. (1946). On group analysis. *International Journal of Psychoanalysis, 27*: 46–51 [also in S. H. Foulkes, *Selected Papers* (pp. 127–136). London: Karnac, 1990].

Foulkes, S. H. (1948). *Introduction to Group Analytic Psychotherapy*. London: Karnac, 1983.

Foulkes, S. H. (1949). Concerning leadership in group analytic psychotherapy. In: *Therapeutic Group Analysis* (pp. 54–65). London: Karnac, 1984.

Foulkes, S. H. (1950). Group therapy. Survey, orientation, classification. In: *Therapeutic Group Analysis* (pp. 47–54). London: Karnac, 1984.

Foulkes, S. H. (1964). *Therapeutic Group Analysis*. London: Karnac, 1984.

Foulkes, S. H. (1968a). Group dynamic processes and group analysis. In: *Selected Papers* (pp. 175–186). London: Karnac, 1990.

Foulkes, S. H. (1968b). Some autobiographical notes. *Group Analysis, 1*: 117–122.

Foulkes, S. H. (1971). Access to unconscious processes in the group analytic group. In: *Selected Papers* (pp. 209–222). London: Karnac, 1990.

Foulkes, S. H. (1972). Oedipus conflict and regression. In: *Selected Papers* (pp. 235–248). London: Karnac, 1990.

Foulkes, S. H. (1975). Problems of the large group. In: *Selected Papers* (pp. 249–270). London: Karnac, 1990.

Foulkes, S. H. (2003). Mind. *Group Analysis, 36*(3): 315–321.

Foulkes, S. H., & Anthony, E. J. (1957). *Group Psychotherapy. The Psychoanalytical Approach*. London: Karnac, 1984.

Foulkes, S. H., & Lewis, E. (1944). Group analysis: studies in the treatment of groups on psychoanalytical lines. *British Journal of Medical Psychology, 20*: 175–184 [reprinted in: Foulkes, S. H. (1964). *Therapeutic Group Analysis* (pp. 20–38). London: Karnac, 1984].

Freud, S. (1908b). Character and anal erotism. *S.E., 9*: 167–175. London: Hogarth.

Freud, S. (1915c). Instincts and their vicissitudes. *S.E., 14*: 109–140. London: Hogarth.

Freud, S. (1921c). *Group Psychology and the Analysis of the Ego. S.E., 18*: 65–143. London: Hogarth.

Fromm, E. (1932). Die psychoanalytische Charakterologie nd ihre Bedetung für die Sozialpsychologie. *Zschrf. f. Sozialforschung, 1*: 253–277.

Fromm, E. (1936). Autorität und Familie. Sozialpsychologischer Teil. In: M. Horkheimer (Ed.), *Autorität und Familie* (pp. 77–135). Paris: Felix Alcan.

Gelb, A., & Goldstein, K. (1918). Zur Psychologie des optischen Wahrnehmungs- und Erkennungsvorgangs (Psychologische Analysise hirnpathologischer Fälle aufgrund von Untersuchungen Hirnverletzter). *Ztschr.f.d. Ges. Neurologie u. Physiologie, 41*: 1–143 [reprinted in: W. D. Ellis (Trans.), *Sourcebook of Gestalt Psychology* (pp. 315–325). London: Kegan Paul, Trench, Trubner & Co. Ltd, 1938].

Goldstein, K. (1934). *The Organism. A Holistic Approach to Biology Derived from Pathological Data in Man*. New York: American Book Company, 1939.

Greenspan, S., & Shanker, S. (2004). *The Frist Idea How Symbols, Language and Intelligence Evolved From our Primate Ancestors to Modern Humans*. Cambridge, MA: Da Capo Press.

Hoffmann, S. O. (1984). *Charakter und Neurose. Ansätze zu einer psychoanalytischen Charakterologie*. Frankfurt: Suhrkamp.

Lorenzer, A. (1972). *Zur Begründung einer materialistischen Sozialisationstheorie*. Frankfurt: Suhrkamp.

Malinowski, B. (1926). *Myth in Primitive Psychology*. London: Kegan Paul.

Malinowski, B. (1927). *Sex and Repression in a Savage Society*. London: Routledge Classics (Psychology Press), 2001.

Malinowski, B. (1936). *The Foundation of Faith and Morals*. London: Riddell Memorial Lectures 7th Series.

Mannheim, K. (1943). *Diagnosis of Our Time*. London: Kegan Paul.

Nitzgen, D. (2007). Development by adaptation. Notes on "applied" group analysis. *Group Analysis, 41*(3): 240–252.

Nitzgen, D. (2008). The group analytic moment sixty years on: revisiting introduction to group analytic psychotherapy by S. H. Foulkes. 32nd Foulkes Annual Lecture. *Group Analysis, 41*(4): 319–340.

Nitzgen, D. (2010). Hidden legacies. S. H. Foulkes, Kurt Goldstein, Ernst Cassirer. *Group Analysis, 43*(3): 354–371.

Pines, M. (1999). Forgotten pioneers: the unwritten history of the therapeutic community movement. *Therapeutic Communities. The International Journal for Therapeutic and Supportive Organization, 20*(1): 23–42.

Schivelbusch, W. (1982). *Intellektuellendämmerung. Zur Lage der Frankfurter Intelligenz in den zwanziger Jahren*. Frankfurt: Die Hessen Bibliothek im Insel Verlag.

Schöttler, P. (1994). Lucie Vargas Bücher. Erfahrungen mit einer unabgeschlosenen Biographie. *Werkstatt Geschichte, 7*: 63–67.

Schöttler, P. (1996). Rationalisierter Fanatismus, archaische Mentalitäten. Marc Bloch und Lucien Febvre als Kritiker des nationalsozialistischen Deutschland. *Werkstatt Geschichte, 14*: 5–21.

Schöttler, P. (1997). Das Konzept der politischen Religionen bei Lucie Varga und Franz Borkenau. In: M. Ley & J. Schoeps (Eds.), *Der Nationalsozialismus als politische Religion* (pp. 186–205). Bodenheim: Syndikat.

Voegelin, E. (1938). *Die politischen Religionen*. München.

CHAPTER TWO

The concept of the co-unconscious in Moreno's psychodrama*

Heloisa Junqueira Fleury and Anna Maria Knobel

Introduction

Around 1937, J. L. Moreno defined his hypothesis regarding the shared unconscious within the theory of psychodrama, which, in his opinion, represents one of the dimensions of the interpersonal process itself. In his view, individuals with a stable, meaningful relationship, such as married couples, families, and professional partners, develop both specific and shared forms of subjectivity that constitute co-conscious and co-unconscious states. The former is remembered as part of their life history, as a component of their identity. The latter consists of what each individual has experienced, heard of, or known at some time, but is no longer able to remember. The co-unconscious state may also be related to something the individuals never really "knew" but which they experienced within their field of meaningful relationships, irrespective of whether these individuals were dead or alive. These

*Part of this chapter was presented at the 17th International Congress of Group Psychotherapy, Rome 2009.

elements constitute a continuum of relational transmitted meanings that give experiences a colorful and unique quality.

Even before making a connection to the co-unconscious, Moreno, in 1923, wrote his first observations of an interpersonal communication out of participant awareness:

> There are players [in the Theatre of Spontaneity] who are connected with one another by an invisible correspondence of feelings, who have a sort of heightened sensitivity for their mutual inner process. One gesture is sufficient and often they do not have to look at one another, they are telepathic for one another. They communicate through a new sense, as if by a "medial" understanding. [1973 (1923), p. 68]

In a footnote referring to an article dated 1937, Moreno connected this former text to his writings on shared unconscious, "that could be called co-unconscious" (Moreno, 1983[1959b], p. 65).

However, Moreno contributed very little towards clarifying this concept. According to Ancelin-Shützenberger (2007), who worked closely with him for over twenty-five years, his work on this concept of the co-unconscious remained confined to his seminars and lectures and general discussions with colleagues.

His few texts on the subject are vague and lack unity, perhaps because the subject deals mainly with the psychological dimension of existence with which he concerned himself least, since his major interests were the study of creativity and the spontaneity of relationships, in investigating how groups were formed and how they functioned, and in developing the theory of roles, techniques, and strategies within dramatic action. Furthermore, in the 1940s, science placed great emphasis on correlations of cause and effect (the medical model) supported by statistics (the quantitative model), which hampered the comprehension of this phenomenon.

To this day, few contemporary psychodramatists have interested themselves in developing this theme conceptually. The objective of this chapter is to discuss what characterizes the co-conscious and co-unconscious states of mind, as defined by Moreno, presenting Moreno's few texts about the concept, and to discuss the way in which this concept is used in psychodrama, based on contributions from selected contemporary psychodramatists.

Morin's *Introduction à la Pensée Complexe* (1991) stimulates us to consider the significance of some paradoxical phenomena that occur in all living beings, such as, for example, their capacity for self-organization, which allows them to remain always the same despite the fact that their parts (cells and molecules) are in a constant state of renewal. This perspective distances us from reductionism as a result of two apparently conflicting movements: complex organization and disorganization function in living beings in a strictly co-dependent manner. As a result of this new epistemological paradigm, more specific tools of thinking are available nowadays that permit us to understand co-unconscious processes.

Another important consideration is that subject and object are inseparable, one being essential to the other. The observer, by analysing a given phenomenon, interferes with and modifies what he/she is observing, thus extinguishing the notion of an object that exists autonomously and separately from a subject. The world is contained within our minds, which are contained within the world, and this does not result in unification but, rather, in a path along which both subject and object mutually interrupt one another. Therefore, the subject emerges while simultaneously creating the world. This provides human beings with the possibility for self-thought which permits the possibility of self-awareness.

Wechsler (2007, p. 73) summarizes these ideas well in the following statement:

> There is no *a priori* reality. Irrespective of the subject, it is co-constructed by agents that inhabit the phenomenon within each agent's structural and functional possibilities. . . . Therefore, the *relational experience* that supports the constitution of intra and inter-psychic realities is supported by the *complementariness* of the roles, in the *interdependence* and in the impossibility of *dissociating* subject from phenomenon, although each one remains irreducible in relation to the other.

This more complex way of thinking establishes new zones of meaning by understanding both the formation of the self and the co-unconscious. Rey (1996) shows that the development of theoretical thought was a necessary step in enabling human beings to understand some spaces of reality. Therefore, in Moreno's time, and perhaps until the advent of the latest discoveries in neurobiology, phenomena such as the co-unconscious were unable to form part of the field of scientific knowledge and were described by Moreno using metaphorical approximations.

The constitution of self and the theory of roles

According to the theory of psychodrama, human development is organized on the basis of an infant's relationship with others via role-playing, which takes place in the physiological, psychological, and social dimensions. From this starting point, relatively stable forms of being are organized: the partial body, family and social selves. These partial selves often work in harmony but may also contradict each other. Therefore, since the complete self emerges from the roles played and not the other way around, this dynamic process between roles and counter-roles in their multiplicity of functions promotes gradual clustering and unification of multiple partial selves to what would be considered a global self that guarantees the continuity of the self and the ability to recognize oneself as single and unique. The multiple combinations of these factors confer great complexity to the global self. For example, as a consequence of this process, the same person may be assertive and pragmatic in his/her professional capacities, but reserved and tense in affective relationships in which he/she always fears rejection. This is the same self in its multiple roles/facets. Therefore, according to Moreno, memory and the co-unconscious are constituted and activated in accordance with relationships and active roles, which means that co-unconscious evocations are based on these roles.

The notion of the role also helps us to understand the convergence of collective and private elements in forming the overall self; therefore, it is highly operational. In its collective aspects, such as cultural units of behaviour, the roles convey the codes, values, beliefs, and specific cultural habits of a certain group, such as, for example, the appropriate level of physical proximity, the boundaries of privacy, the appropriate degree of social extroversion, etc. In its private domain, the roles express the specific myths of a family, which are transmitted either openly or implicitly or co-unconsciously from one generation to the next. For example: the firstborn male child will grow up to become a physician; marriages should be made within the group of origin of the immigrant grand-parents; only the elders know how to deal with problems; the significance of gender, etc.

Co-conscious and co-unconscious states and the inter-psyche

Two of Moreno's written statements about this subject merit partic-ular attention. In the first, he says:

> Co-conscious and co-unconscious states are by definition states that partners have experienced and produced together and that can therefore be reproduced or reenacted together. A co-conscious or co-unconscious state cannot be the property of one individual alone. It is always a *common* property that can only be reproduced by a joint effort. [Moreno, 1994(1946), p. vii]

It is clear from this text that, according to Moreno, co-conscious/co-unconscious goes beyond the limits of individual psychic space, belonging simultaneously to various individuals who, because of the solid intimacy existing in their relationship, are able to co-create them. It may be relived and re-enacted by them, but this may also apply to other individuals who may relate naturally to these sets of feelings, sensations, and beliefs. They constitute a relational dimen-sion that results in what Moreno (1994[1946], p. vi) refers to as the *inter-psyche*, that is, a network of interconnected meanings, specific ways of being and of relating, that originate from two or more indi-viduals and might or might not be accessible to the conscience.

These ideas are in accordance with the most recent studies conducted in the field of neuroscience, which point to the mirror neurons as being responsible for the complex condition that is now referred to as intersubjectivity. In fact, within the perspective of neurobiology, intersubjectivity is based on the process of transfer-ring mental activity between individuals through unconscious motor resonance mechanisms (Hug, 2008). When an individual performs an action, expresses emotions or experiences sensations, he/she activates the same neural circuits in an observer through an automatic process that is mediated by a system of mirror neurons. This shared activation suggests a functional mechanism of auto-matic imitation of sensations, emotions, and actions in the body of an observer, constituting a possible biological basis for understanding the mind of the other person and unconscious communication (Gallese, Eagle, & Migone, 2007).

The phenomenon of resonance is provoked by the dynamic interaction between an individual and his/her environment. Shared representations are formed (sometimes out of awareness) as a nucleus of cultural cohesion that serves as a basis for sharing human emotions (Fleury & Hug, 2008). This automatic sharing of emotions between individuals is the basic mechanism involved in social cognition and in the development of empathy. The emotional expression of one of the individuals guides the subjective and physiological experience of the other, serving as an interdependent social guide to maintain emotional reciprocity between pairs and groups (Decety & Meyer, 2008).

In child development, there is a mechanism mediated by the child's mirror neuron system that combines the perception and execution of actions in the newborn infant so that the child and its care-giver mutually regulate the effect of one on the other through implicit emotional communication (Fleury & Hug, 2008). Based on detailed studies performed with non-verbal babies (of 4–12 months), Stern and his collaborators (1984, cited in Stern, 2007, p. 106) concluded that there exists what these authors referred to as *affective harmonization* between mother and infant. Jaffe and co-authors (2001, cited in Stern, 2007, p. 106) described a certain rhythmic binding between the two within a time, which implies not only the possibility of capturing what is occurring with the other person, but of a synchronicity between the associated experiences. This synchronicity, which occurs automatically and without the participants being aware of it, creates a shared experience of togetherness (an interpsychic phenomenon), thus establishing a secure attachment (an intrapsychic structure).

Furthermore, there appears to be agreement among investigators studying the neurophysiological bases of communication between individuals that, since birth, human babies have what is referred to as a psychology of *mutually sensitive minds* (our italics). Fleury and Hug (2008) reviewed several studies and found that the initial development of the baby's brain occurs principally in the right cerebral hemisphere, where the early processes related to emotions, relationships, and attachments (unconscious processes) are stored in the implicit domain of learning and memory. Later, development increases in the left cerebral hemisphere, which is associated with verbal and linguistic development and information that is important for the infant's adaptation to culture, in the explicit domain of learning and memory. The full development of the child is reflected in the integration between the two brain hemispheres, which occurs through the corpus callosum.

Therefore, since the co-unconscious, according to Moreno, constellates among individuals, it generates states: that is, mobile clusters of joint qualities and characteristics that are organized, in part intentionally and in part by chance, within stable and significant relationships. They form a foundation of relational fabric, a matrix shared by individuals (inter) that leaves traces and fragments of these shared experiences in people (intra) and remains as stories, myths, and cultural traditions that go beyond the actual individuals themselves. It encompasses not only models of relationships within families, but also their meanings derived from social and cultural experiences.

In psychodrama, the notion of matrix is always associated with the idea of *locus* (where) and of *status nascendi* (when), that is, the psychic phenomena occur in a space–time and following a certain relational movement through which an emotional *modus operandi* (how) is organized by individuals belonging to the same family, to the same social group or to the same culture. This is a two-way process, "a still deeper reality in which the unconscious states of two or more individuals are interconnected to a system of co-unconscious states" (Moreno, 1994[1946], p. vii).

When this process is used to describe what sustains the development of the human infant, its emotional learning process within relationships, and through the roles that are fundamental to sustaining life, the matrix is then referred to as the identity matrix:

> In the feeding situation, the active role of the person giving the food (the donor) is performed by an auxiliary ego (the mother) and the role of the individual receiving the food is acted out by the infant receiving nourishment. By giving the food, the mother preliminarily warms herself up to actions concerning the child that have a certain consistency. The child, in turn, by receiving the food warms up to a series of acts that also develop some degree of internal consistency. The result of this interaction is that a certain reciprocal

style of mutual role expectancy acts as a basis for all future role-playing between the infant and his/her *auxiliary egos*. [Moreno, 1994(1946), p. 62]

Zuretti (1998) identified the first action involving two human beings linked in the same space and time, which is childbirth, the beginning of the active co-unconscious process, thus confirming that it is these reciprocal expectations in roles that indicate co-unconscious states in which the participants are unaware and that are complementary and attuned. Indeed, one cannot exist without the other.

In his second statement, Moreno (1983[1959b], pp. 61–63) goes beyond this to define the subject more specifically. He writes,

We need to change the meaning of unconscious, looking for a counterpoint, a kind of musical key that would be able to relate every event in the unconscious of A to every event in the unconscious of B, or we need to seek concepts constructed in such a way that their existence is not derived from the resistances of an individual psyche, but rather from an even deeper reality in which the unconscious of various individuals is entwined in a co-unconscious. [p. 61]

If, metaphorically speaking, the co-unconscious is the musical counterpoint, a technique of composition made up of two or more melodic voices that perceive each other simultaneously within a harmonious relational dialogue, in real relationships there needs to be a functional complementariness between the co-unconscious states of the different individuals in this relationship. To enable everyone to contribute in such a combined and organized way, there needs to be a bonding factor. Ferreira (1963, cited in Penso, Costa, & Ribeiro, 2008, p. 11) referred to the defence mechanism that protects the family group against the threat of destruction and chaos as a family myth perpetuated through rules, beliefs, roles, and rituals. Therefore, as a result of this collective family creation, all the participants contribute towards assuring that the dangers, fears, secrets, and shames from the past remain invisible in the here and now of the relationship. A second element then emerges: the impossibility of the participants in this relationship to deal with these contents and processes, leading them to comply organically with specific ways of avoiding family or social or cultural realities, depending on how unbearable and threatening they are to the self. This avoidance creates family defences or, in the broader system, cultural defences.

A result of this relatively stable complexity of meanings conferred by the experiences of the past is the impoverishment of existence. As a predefined game of repetition, it keeps alive issues of the *there and then* of another time and another place in detriment to what could be experienced spontaneously in the *here* and *now* of the relationship. These "living" issues, shared as co-unconscious states, push the individual to unconsciously repeat issues from the past, not only personal ones, but also family and cultural ones. According to Ancelin-Schützenberger (2007, p. 155): "it is not just sin, faults, mistakes and errors that may be passed down unaddressed from generation to generation, but also unresolved traumas, unmourned losses, family or personal secrets and any other unfinished business".

How psychodrama operates with the co-unconscious

Since psychodrama is a method of action in which concrete situations may be embodied in scenes and plots that allow the members of the group to experience, understand and resolve their conflicts on stage, psychodrama functions in a relaxed atmosphere, offering protection and a safe environment for the members of the group. It allows a type of communication between the therapist and the client that includes words but also incorporates action in roles, scripts and expressive manifestations of the body.

This non-verbal communication between the therapist and the patient creates a context in which the explicit verbal domain is able to interact with the implicit domain of memory (images, feelings, intuitions) within the patient–therapist relationship (Stern, 2007).

According to Moreno, this state of harmony between the therapist and his/her client depends on the "tele factor", a type of bilateral empathy that develops between individuals who maintain continuous links. The tele factor is "the basis of all healthy interpersonal relationships and an essential component of every method used in psychotherapy" (Moreno, 1969[1958a], p. 45). Thanks to the progress made in neuroscience, it is possible to understand how this type of empathetic communication works neurologically between individuals.

Furthermore, there are always two standpoints in the therapeutic interaction: the interaction itself and the creation of images, feelings, fantasies, and intuitions influenced by the relational patterns situated in the implicit domain of the memory. This also occurs in groups as well as in dyads. Co-conscious and co-unconscious conflicts and mandates manifest themselves in two ways: first, as the topic of one participant who introduces a situation from his/her life history. While being incorporated into a character, through its very action it recovers new meanings that are then shared by all. This type of work performed with a protagonic scene is generally well accepted by the other members of the group. A second way for the co-unconscious to be revealed is as a symptom of the group, reflected in forms of attachment or in tacit agreements (group defence) that prevent communication from flowing. This second form of tension provides a better description of how the co-unconscious operates in a group.

In looking for these connections between different meanings in the past, present, and future of a participant or of various participants, psychodrama follows a phenomenological–existential psychotherapeutic model that values the original experience of each individual and his/her relationship with others, with the world and with him/herself. It deals with the phenomenological reality of the present moment without searching for connections of cause and effects.

The interrelational processes in this phenomenological paradigm take three fundamental characteristics into consideration: intentionality, intuition, and intersubjectivity (Almeida, 2006):

> *Intentionality* is close to knowledge, not as an agglomeration of cognitive images but as an insertion of the theme into an open reality that illuminates the present moment. This opening to the world seeks to identify the meanings of the phenomena in its relationship with the conscience. [p. 35]

Almeida defines intuition as the capacity to perceive the truth clearly and correctly before thinking or reflecting. Intuition is predominantly the result of pre-reflexive perception.

Intersubjectivity implies an encounter in such a way that two subjectivities meet each other. Moreno's concept of encounter expresses the basic characteristics of intersubjectivity, meaning that not only do two individuals meet, but they also share mutual experiences and understand each other. This encounter of two individuals (Moreno, 1994[1946], p. 251) may also be hostile: with one participant in opposition to the other (*ibid.*, p. 72).

Within the perspective of neuroscience, these three interrelational processes are equivalent to the processes of unconscious resonance mediated at least partially by the mirror neurons. According to Schore (2003, p. 264), in the affective transactions between therapist and patient, a co-creation of an intersubjective context occurs, leading both of them to structural growth and to new brain connections.

Schore also suggests that, due to this resonance, the subjectivity of the therapist may become empathically attuned to the internal states of the patient, favouring the regulation of affections and the processing of cognitive–emotional interactions.

In groups, this phenomenon of multi-personal resonance plays an important role both in constituting the group and in developing its culture. When a psychodrama group gets together for the first time, it is the co-ordinator who creates the necessary conditions for the tenuous connection that starts developing among participants, beginning in small subgroups. These links may become stronger, depending on the need to include one another. Thus, this relational network is affected by the environment, by the group's history, by the similarities and differences between the participants, by leaderships, and by political and/or social determinants, etc. (Rodrigues, 2005). However, sometimes this fails to occur because, according to Moreno, some individuals are continuously excluded or marginalized from the process of communication and social contact, while others are greatly favoured. He refers to this effect as "sociodynamic law" (Moreno, 1934).

Groups also create connections that follow specific regulations, part of which are conscious (e.g., the objective of the meeting, etc.), while others are co-unconscious (myths, codes, etc.). Thus, the co-unconscious states may facilitate or restrict the constitution and maintenance of the group (Rodrigues, 2005).

Moreno (1961, p. 237) also points out that the co-unconscious states might be

> the result of direct interpersonal experience between intimate ensembles of individuals. But they may also be the result of experiences shared on a social and cultural level. The personal contact of the intimate ensembles is then replaced by indirect, transpersonal or symbolic contact. The familial interpsyche is replaced then by a "cultural interpsyche." The sociodrama of a global group of participants becomes feasible . . . in which common experiences shared by people from all walks of life were brought to enactment.

These unconscious relational patterns are located in the right hemisphere of the brain; therefore, they are non-verbal and unconscious. They are manifested as actions or as metaphors or symbolisms that express internal resonance at that precise moment. As the co-conscious and co-unconscious states are experienced and produced in conjunction, they become dependent on relational experience to be transformed into one of these possibilities. Contents recognized by the explicit domain of individual or group memory become part of the co-conscious state (Fleury & Hug, 2008).

In the initial moments of a group session in psychodrama, it is the co-ordinator who centralizes communication, helps the group warm up, and offers support, guaranteeing an atmosphere of tranquility and confidence until some significant proposal (individual or collective) is represented on the "stage", the empty scenic space given over to the imagination. When these strategies fail to produce effects, in general there is a hidden theme that leads to this loss of spontaneity, this fear of being exposed and this paralysis in the group, and it must be identified. This discomfort very often generates attacks aimed either at the co-ordinator or at some scapegoat chosen *ad hoc*, who receives negative feelings that are not actually theirs. At this moment, the focus has to be on group themes, which, in psychodrama, may be conducted from three different perspectives: through protagonists, by spontaneous action, or with the group itself.

In the first model, several short sequential dramatizations are usually created by different individuals or subgroups called "group emergents", who direct the plots until one of the characters is able to scenically explain and resolve the central conflict of the group. The action of this individual, who is denominated the protagonist, produces catharsis and integration, leading to a new existential synthesis towards the issue.

The second model of psychodrama focuses on spontaneous practices such as the "theatre of spontaneity" and the "living newspaper", in which the director works with a team of trained auxiliary egos, allowing the proposed themes to be played out artistically. According to Burmeister (2008):

This connection with the mythic function of drama . . . addresses the universal dimension and inherent universal conflicts instead of focusing directly on real social contexts in the here and now. In the shadow of the myth and protected by its "symbolic" qualities, real social conflicts may arise and may be dealt with "indirectly" in an "un-conscious agenda" resulting in an improvement in the management of these conflicts. . . . . The same may be true for theatre improvisations which will be effective even without being translated into the real social processes to which they refer (e.g. catharsis effects). [p. 2]

In the "playback theatre", developed by Jonathan Fox (1986) and Jo Salas (1993), the scenes are described by people in the audience and experienced spontaneously by the artists on stage. Because they operate within the domain of fantasy, sensitivity, and artistic singularity, the spontaneous methods map the co-conscious/co-unconscious elements present in the group.

The third type of direction is sociodramatic (a method focused on the group), which acts in accordance with the steps or phases of relational organization of the group: isolation, horizontal differentiation, and vertical differentiation (Moreno, 1934). In this model, moments of introspection are offered to permit self-recognition within the referred context, followed by multiple forms of identity expressions, emphasizing the plurality of ways of being that exist within the group. Finally, leaders from the group are encouraged to help the group in its search for solutions for these specific problems (Knobel, 1996, 2006). As a result of this collective co-unconscious creation, the group succeeds in identifying, dealing with, and overcoming what had existed before as a symptom.

Some specific techniques of psychodrama are also particularly useful. Since the most valuable and most reliable signs of these psychological obstacles are reflected in the bodies of the participants (preverbal field), the techniques of maximization and materialization tend to be useful. In the former, the client "takes it to the limits by exaggerating certain body or verbal expressions" (Menegazzo,

Tomasini, & Zuretti, 1995, p. 130). In materialization, body tension is connected to images, characters, or movements that clearly show what that discomfort causes to their bodies, helping to clarify what had appeared earlier as a clue.

These strategies give voice and shape to hidden feelings that may be played as characters in the "as if" of the psychodrama stage. By being enacted in this way, the product of some participants' imagination then comes to belong to all the members and the imagination of all the others is then able to retouch its complexity. Within this rich inter-game of creation, many singular meanings associated with shared beliefs and customs emerge, turning something that was opaque into something more transparent.

It is important to emphasize that whatever is produced in the drama is there specifically to serve the protagonist and/or the group, not only because the stage is empty and available for any and every fantasy or anxiety, but also because the auxiliary egos are polymorphic: that is, they are there to enact any possible complementary role required by the participants. To conduct the movements contained in the scenes, the co-ordinator also has to define him/herself as a presence/absence, as someone who provides support but who does not interfere in the production itself.

The intervention model proposed by Feo (2008, 2010) is very interesting because it functions in two distinct phases: first, it introduces "tacit suspension of otherness", which, according to this author,

> is related to an ensemble of strategies that a director [of psychodrama] applies to encourage the use of the psychodrama stage as a space for the maximum expression of singular feeling, actions and thinking that inhabit a certain individual or sub-group. . . . During tacit suspension of otherness the director has to oppose resistance to any sovereign expression of otherness (any form of expression that attempts to impose itself as hegemonic and based on the desire of others) against the messenger of the group, since he/she is the one with the final word regarding the scenes. [2008, p. 15]

At a second moment, Feo proposes the "scenic introduction of otherness" in which

> the sovereign perspective (anyone expressing him/herself as a creator of new versions to be enacted) now belongs to those who

did not have it beforehand, and the stage is now inhabited by their wishes and desires. Therefore, to suspend and to introduce otherness are simultaneous movements related to whoever is in charge of how the scenes are developing at that moment. With all [the participants] together, the objective is to achieve the maximum expression of how each one represents the scene and how they wish to transform it. [*ibid.*, p. 16]

Therefore, since this occurs in a relational, protected locus, maintained democratic and free by the director, the psychodramatic action that alternates the suspension and the introduction of otherness allows the participants to develop not only the ability to tolerate differences, but also confidence in the power of egalitarian relations. The commitment and the expansion of the scenes produced sequentially by several members of the group tend to reveal the complexity of meanings enacted from the imagination of the group.

It is important to emphasize that although this model is only one of the many possibilities in psychodrama, it appears to constitute a highly successful way of mapping and reaching the co-conscious/co-unconscious states because of its low level of interference at the specific moment of creation. In addition, it sustains the imaginary production of all participants and produces scenic co-narratives that facilitate the experience of the co-unconscious matrix of the group.

Ferro (2005, cited in Neri, 2007, p. 26) refers to the psychoanalytical co-narrative by saying,

It is as if analyst and patient constructed a play together in which the plots come together, are articulated and developed, often randomly and unintentionally by the two co-narrators, in such a way that neither of them is the keeper of a pre-established truth: [proceeding] in this way, the co-narrative transformation replaces interpretation.

According to Zerka Moreno (Moreno, Blomkvist, & Rutzel, 2000, pp. 45–46), her husband, J. L. Moreno, noticed that

their protagonists moved within areas that were not real to anyone except to themselves, being entirely subjective ... these ideas went beyond fantasy and intuition, they were almost a reverie experience. Therefore, Moreno knew that he would be unable to really reach the protagonist's psyche unless he was able to inhabit this surplus reality together with the protagonist.

Hence, dramatization may lead, via warming up and spontaneity, to altered states of consciousness in which the protagonist (an individual or a group) becomes detached from the realistic parameters of time and space to live in a singular, artistic reality that offers new perspectives of knowledge (Knobel, 2007).

For Zerka Moreno, surplus reality is a dimension that goes beyond subjective and objective reality. It is a form of cosmic reality (Moreno, Blomkvist, & Rützel, 2000, pp. 45–46) that allows the person experiencing it to inhabit the imaginary perspective of infinity. Surplus reality points, therefore, to a knowledge that goes beyond the limits of formal logic, following a standard equivalent to that of dreams, but one that is experienced by a protagonist who is awake and active.

One of the privileged places for the appearance of co-conscious/co-unconscious states is in a large group (Weinberg & Schneider, 2003), particularly an ongoing psychodrama group that meets for several days during specialist group congresses. In this process, the psychodramatist proposes initially small expressive structured situations, which aim to encourage a first contact between the participants and decrease alienation and suspicion among them. He/she also invites them to express feelings, thoughts, fantasies, and emotions increasingly directed to the shared collective event. Following the group phases, he/she allows each participant to experience a first moment of introspection in which an extensive mapping of multiple private experiences is possible. They then organize themselves on partial themes, which can be dramatized collectively by different subgroups, enhancing diversity. This succession of sensitive expressions ends by highlighting a protagonistic collective theme that, by being enacted by representatives of the group as a whole, allows catharsis and understanding. Finally, there is a phase of sharing, reflection and elaboration of the experience as a whole.

During these procedures, when ideals and limits fail to be shared and ways of understanding them are not found within the group, two types of undesirable phenomena appear: the first occurs when the tolerable level of frustration is exceeded and anger and impulsiveness take over, preventing the experience from being worked out conjointly. At the other end of the spectrum, the participants of large groups feel illuminated and immediately capable of transforming social reality in an omnipotent way.

To be able to continue existing, resisting, and creating within the difficult and conflicting reality of our everyday lives is indeed what this possible life requests of us.

New perspectives

This chapter presents the co-conscious and co-unconscious states conceived by Moreno in 1937 as an original creation within sociopsychology, since the idea of a relational and shared unconscious, currently referred to as social unconscious, emerged only in the 1960s.

For Hopper (2003, p. 129),

> The concept of the social unconscious refers to the existence and constraints of social, cultural and communicational arrangements of which people are unaware: unaware, insofar as these arrangements are not perceived (not "known") and if perceived unacknowledged ("denied") and if acknowledged not taken as problematic, not considered with an optimal degree of detachment and objectivity.

Co-unconscious states, defined by Moreno as the social unconscious, also encompass limitations and ways of remaining unknown to oneself, which are relationally constituted as an implicit *modus operandi* arising from an infant's contact with its caregiver.

The psychodramatic proposal of a plural self compounded and brokered by roles allows understanding of how certain unperceived relational patterns operate in specific areas of identity, either to interdict or highlight certain themes, scenes, plots, ancestral mandates, family, group, or ethnic myths.

Therefore, a matrix of modes of being, stories, inventions, and fantasies that are expressed or hidden for generations are transgenerationally transmitted as dissociated elements of the participants' identities.

Based on contributions from the neurosciences, Fleury and Hug (2008) propose a preliminary definition of the co-unconscious

> as a manifestation of the unconscious content of the implicit domain of memory and learning (the right hemisphere of the brain), which is stimulated by the phenomenological experience of the present moment through the interactive process that occurs between individuals or in a group. [p. 18]

As a method, psychodrama provides a set of strategies and techniques of action that operate in the imaginary dimension of the "as if", allowing access to contents from the implicit memory domain. This occurs through warming up, which produces characters and plots (in the plane) of surplus reality that are not subject to conscious control. Their actions establish unexpected connections between elements in the present/past/future. In this way, threatening stories and implicit modes can gain new meanings in the more protected and less disruptive environment of the psychodrama stage.

When dealing with collective issues, psychodrama becomes sociodrama, which is a specific method, defined by Moreno (1934) as "an action method that deals with relationships between and within groups and with collective ideologies", enabling greater confidence in the relationships and in the strength of the groups. As many people take responsibility and enact their conflicts and social aspirations collectively, so original solutions are found for the situations, ways of coexistence are traded, and conflicts are expressed. As "a group learning process focused on providing practice in solving problems of human relations" (Sternberg & Garcia, 2000, p. xvii), sociodrama is a means of expressing and working out co-unconscious group themes.

In Brazil, sociodrama has been used as a privileged method of socio-educational intervention for use in marginalized populations (Marra, 2004), increasing the awareness, understanding, and appreciation of identity elements of the group that, in general, are dispersed and unpowered. Another interesting example of work involving sociodrama with the co-unconscious was conducted by Nery (2010) and enabled mapping of ethnic prejudice in a university in Brasilia, Brazil, resulting in a consequent slowdown of the problem. According to the author (2010, pp. 183–184), flexibility in identity is critical for the success of any inclusion process, as it contributes to the empathic dialogue, [and this can only occur] after the identities present are highlighted, visibility is given to the pain experienced by the individuals, confrontations are allowed and conflicts experienced.

For Nery, sociodrama is the method of choice for projects of social and ethnic inclusion, both as a research tool and for its applicability in sociotherapeutic interventions.

Working with co-unconscious social mandates, sociodrama operates as a social therapy, allowing understanding and changing of anachronistic attitudes displaced in time (from other times and social contexts). As a method of research–action, it allows participants to understand and fix distortions that prevent their lives from flowing within a group, as well as forwarding their collective claims to different spheres of local power in a movement that seeks socially engaged solutions.

In our opinion, the psycho-sociodrama model of intervention with the co-unconscious opens a wide range of possibilities for research and action within communities, revealing implicit issues, unperceived beliefs, and deviations in communication and in joint action, transforming the shared social space.

References

Almeida, W. C. (2006). *Psicoterapia aberta: o método do psicodrama, a fenomenologia e a psicanálise* [Open Psychotherapy: the Method of Psychodrama, Phenomenology and Psychoanalysis]. São Paulo: Agora.

Ancelin-Schützenberger, A. (2007). Transgerational analyses and psychodrama. In: C. Baim, J. Burmeister, & M. Maciel (Eds.), *Psychodrama—Advances in Theory and Practice* (pp. 155–174). London: Routledge.

Burmeister, J. (2008). Moreno's co-unconsciousness and the psychodramatic view of the social unconscious. Unpublished.

Decety, J., & Meyer, M. (2008). From emotion resonance to empathic understanding: a social developmental neuroscience account. *Development and Psychopathology, 20*: 1053–1080.

Feo, M. (2008). Direção socionômica multidimensional AGRUUPPA e a fé tácita no eterno retorno [AGRUUPPA Multi-dimensional socionomic direction and the faith in the eternal return]. São Paulo (personal communication).

Feo, M. (2010). A arte de não interpretar interpretando (The art of not interpreting while interpreting). In: M. M. Marra & H. J. Fleury (Eds.), *Sociodrama: um método, diferentes procedimentos* [Sociodrama: One Method, Different Procedures] (pp. 150–177). São Paulo: Ágora.

Fleury, H. J., & Hug, E. (2008). Il co-inconscio di Moreno [Moreno's co-unconscious]. *Psicodramma Classico, 10*: 7–20.

Fox, J. (1986). *Acts of Service: Spontaneity, Commitment, Tradition in the Nonscripted Theatre*. New Paltz, NY: Tusitala.

Gallese, V., Eagle, M. N., & Migone, P. (2007). Intentional attunement: mirror neurons and the neural underpinnings of interpersonal relations. *Journal of the American Psychoanalytical Association, 55*: 131–176.

Hopper, E. (2003). *The Social Unconscious*. London: Jessica Kingsley.

Hug, E. (2008). Neurônios-espelho e o espaço intersubjetivo. In: H. J. Fleury, G. S. Khouri, & E. Hug (Eds.), *Psicodrama e Neurociência* [Psychodrama and Neuroscience] (pp. 31–48). São Paulo: Agora.

Knobel, A. M. (1996). Estratégias de Direção Grupal [Strategies of group direction]. *Revista Brasileira de Psicodrama* [Brazilian Journal of Psychodrama], 4: 49–62.

Knobel, A. M. (2006). Grandes Grupos: história, teoria e práticas psicodramáticas [Large groups: history, theory and psicodramatic practices]. In: H. J. Fleury & M. M. Marra (Eds.), *Práticas Grupais Contemporâneas* [Contemporary Group Practices] (pp. 213–231). São Paulo: Agora.

Knobel, A. M. (2007). Sociometric scenarios and psychotherapy. In: C. Baim, J. Burmeister, & M. Maciel (Eds.), *Psychodrama—Advances in Theory and Practice* (pp. 215–225). London: Routledge.

Marra, M. M. (2004). *O agente social que transforma: o sociodrama na organização dos grupos* [The Social Agent Who Transforms: The Sociodrama in the Organization of the Groups]. São Paulo: Agora.

Menegazzo, C., Tomasini, M., & Zuretti, M. (1995). *Dicionário de Psicodrama e Sociodrama* [Dictionary of Psychodrama and Sociodrama]. São Paulo: Agora.

Moreno, J. L. (1923). *The Theatre of Spontaneity*. New York: Beacon House, 1973.

Moreno, J. L. (1934). *Who Shall Survive? Foundations of Sociometry, Group Psychotherapy and Sociodrama*. Beacon, NY: Beacon House, 1978.

Moreno, J. L. (1937). Interpersonal therapy and the psychopathology of interpersonal relations. *Sociometry, 1*(1/2): 9–76.

Moreno, J. L. (1961). Interpersonal therapy and co-unconscious states: a progress report in psychodramatic theory. *Group Psychotherapy, 14:* 234–241.

Moreno, J. L. (1969)[1959a]. *Psicoterapia de Grupo e Psicodrama* [Group Psychotherapy and Psychodrama] (2nd edn revised). Campinas, SP: Editorial Psy.

Moreno, J. L. (1983)[1959b]. *Fundamentos do Psicodrama* [Psychodrama, Volume 2]. São Paulo: Summus.

Moreno, J. L. (1994)[1946]. *Psychodrama & Group Psychotherapy,* Volume 1. Virginia: American Society for Group Psychotherapy & Psychodrama.

Moreno, Z. T., Blomkvist, L. D., & Rützel, T. (2000). *A realidade suplementar e a arte de curar* [Psychodrama, Surplus Reality and the Art of Healing]. São Paulo: Agora.

Morin, E. (1991). *Introdução ao pensamento complexo* [Introduction to Complex Thought]. Lisboa: Instituto Piaget.

Neri, C. (2007). La notion élargie de Champ [The expanded concept scope]. *Psychotérapies* [Psychotherapies], *27:* 19–30.

Nery, M. P. (2010). *Grupos e intervenção em conflitos* [Groups and Intervention in Conflicts]. São Paulo: Agora.

Penso, M. A., Costa, L. F., & Ribeiro, M. A. (2008). Aspectos teóricos da transmissão transgeracional e do genograma [Theoretical aspects of transgenerational transmission and genogram]. In: M. A. Penso & L. F. Costa (Eds.), *A transmissão geracional em diferentes contextos* [The Generational Transmission in Different Contexts] (pp. 9–23). São Paulo: Summus.

Rey, F. G. (1996). *Epistemologia Cualitativa y Subjetividad* [Qualitative Epistemology and Subjectivity]. São Paulo: Educ—Editora da PUC-SP, 2003.

Rodrigues, R. A. (2005). A escolha profissional na cena do Teatro de Reprise [The professional choice in scene of the Playback Theatre] In: H. F. Fleury & M. M. Marra (Eds.), *Intervenções grupais nos direitos humanos* [Group Interventions in Human Rights] (pp. 69–91). São Paulo: Agora.

Salas, J. (1993). *Improvising Real Life: Personal Story in Playback Theatre.* Dubuque, Iowa: Kendal/Hunt.

Schore, A. N. (2003). *Affect Regulation and the Repair of the Self.* Nova York: W. W. Norton.

Stern, D. N. (2007). *O momento presente na psicoterapia e na vida cotidiana* [The Present Moment in Psychotherapy and Everyday Life]. Rio de Janeiro: Record.

Sternberg, P., & Garcia, A. (2000). *Sociodrama: Who's in Your Shoes?* Westport, CT: Praeger.

Wechsler, M. F. (2007). Pesquisa e Psicodrama [Research and psychodrama]. *Revista Brasileira de Psicodrama* [Brazilian Journal of Psychodrama], *15*: 71–78.

Weinberg, H., & Schneider, S. (2003). Introduction: background, structure and dynamics of the large group. In: S. Schneider & H. Weinberg (Eds.), *The Large Group Revisited: The Herd, Primal Horde, Crowds and Masses* (pp. 13–26). London: Jessica Kingsley.

Zuretti, M. (1998). A tarefa global: compartilhando o tempo e o espaço—o co-inconsciente [Global task: sharing time and space—the co-unconscious]. In: P. Holmes, M. Karp, & M. Watson (Eds.), *O Psicodrama após Moreno* [Psychodrama since Moreno] (pp. 263–365). São Paulo: Ágora.

CHAPTER THREE

Enrique Pichon-Rivière: the social unconscious in the Latin-American tradition of group analysis

Juan Tubert-Oklander

The birth of a tradition

There has been an independent school of group-analytic thinking and practice originating in the work of Enrique Pichon-Rivière, since the late nineteen-thirties, in Buenos Aires. This was further developed in various Latin-American countries by several generations of psychoanalysts and group analysts who identified with the tradition he initiated, including myself.

Although this Latin-American tradition began to be orally conveyed when some South American colleagues settled in London, there has not yet been an English translation of Pichon-Rivière's writings. (There are, however, French translations of his work, which has been introduced in France by René Kaës (Pichon-Rivière, 2004a,b).) In 2004, Hernández de Tubert and I published a book called *Operative Groups: The Latin-American Approach to Group Analysis*, in which we provided historical and biographical information on Pichon-Rivière, and a summary of his concepts on groups, as well as our own theoretical, technical, and clinical approach to group analysis. We deem this work to be a present-day continuation and evolution of his original proposals, in confluence with the Foulkesian tradition.

Enrique Pichon-Rivière (1907–1977)

The Argentine psychoanalyst and group analyst Enrique Pichon-Rivière was born in Geneva, in 1907. His parents were French, but they soon migrated to Chaco, a tropical jungle area in North-Eastern Argentina, where his father tried to raise cotton, with meagre results. The result was that young Enrique lived and grew in a mixed-race area from his fourth year onwards and was, in his own words, "a witness and a participant in the insertion of a European minority group in a primitive life style" (Pichon-Rivière, 1971a, p. 7, my translation). (All quotations from Pichon-Rivière's writings are my own English translation.) Thus, his personality and his thinking were forged in a tricultural crucible: his first language was French, the second was that of the Guaraní Indians, which he learnt from his father's foreman, and only the third was Spanish, acquired by the time he entered elementary school.

He was, therefore, forever split between two conceptions of the world. The first one, which stemmed from his European roots, was strictly rationalistic and found its way in scientific research. The other one came from his contact with the Guaraní culture, which was magical and mythical, and was expressed in his love for poetry and his passion for surrealism and the uncanny poems of Lautréamont. It was like living in two worlds, and only when he found psychoanalysis was he able to reconcile them.

This is characteristic of Latin-American thinking, which is essentially hybrid, unlike the Western European tradition. Latin America was the outcome of the Spanish and Portuguese conquest and interbreeding with natives. This process of mestization brought about a new race and a different way of dealing with existence and thought. For the local cultures are the result of the encounter, violent conflict, and interbreeding of indigenous cultures and those of the European foreign invaders. So, Latin-American culture is unavoidably hybrid; we are all half-breeds, as a result of racial and cultural interbreeding. This is what we call in Spanish *mestizaje*—a term that may be roughly, albeit quite inadequately, translated as "miscegenation" or "interbreeding", since, pretty much like the concept of *negritude*, it implies a cultural and political intention, related to identity and pride. Perhaps a better translation would be "mestization".

One particular expression of this Janus-like duality is to be found in modern Latin-American literature, in the school known as "magical realism", which blends socio-political events and the detailed mechanics of everyday living with magical and wondrous occurrences, in a narrative that flows naturally, without contradictions or explanations, as if it were all commonplace. The best-known example of this trend is Gabriel García Márquez's novel *One Hundred Years of Solitude*, published in 1967, but the movement actually started in the 1950s, with novelists such as Cuba's Alejo Carpentier and Mexico's Juan Rulfo. An equivalent in theoretical thought implies disregarding ordinary categorical dualities, such as inner–outer, individual–group, instinctual–environmental, science–art, reflection–action, analytical–political, and so on, and letting them coexist in a state of generative tension, without cancelling contradictions in an either-or fashion, as in formal logic, or transcending them by generating a synthesis, as in Hegelian or Marxian dialectics.

This peculiar alliance, which gave origin to the Latin-American Baroque (Rojas Mix, 1987), is also to be found in present-day Latin-American philosophy, particularly in *Analogical Hermeneutics*, which is the theoretical proposal of Mexican philosopher Mauricio Beuchot (Beuchot, 1997, 2003; Tubert-Oklander, 2009; Tubert-Oklander & Beuchot Puente, 2008). In the work of Pichon-Rivière, it allowed him to move effortlessly, back and forth, from psychiatry to psychoanalysis, from psychoanalysis to group analysis, from science to art, from critical thinking to political action. His collected papers, published in 1971 under the title *From Psychoanalysis to Social Psychology*, include three volumes: the first one devoted to his contributions to group analysis and social psychology (Pichon-Rivière, 1971a); the second, to his contributions to dynamic psychiatry and psychopathology (1971b), and the third (1971c) gathers his various papers on creativity and the arts, some of them being the result of his collaboration with artists. But this classification is purely formal, since there is a continuity of thought among the various subjects, and the creative process conflates with the therapeutic process and the group process.

And what about the social unconscious?

The social unconscious was very much present in Pichon-Rivière's writings, even though he never used the term. He had no need for it, since it was only natural for him to assume that the inquiry and interpretation of the unconscious dimension of human existence would inevitably lead to the discovery of the individual and collective determinants of experience. In his work with groups, both therapeutic and non-therapeutic, he believed that any member's expressions were necessarily a result of his or her personal motivations, experience, and history—what he called the *vertical interpretation*—as well as of the structure, dynamics, and culture of the group and the wider social systems, a *horizontal interpretation*. The individual member would always act as a *spokesman*, both for himself and for the group, and interpretation should always be twofold: horizontal and vertical, showing what aspect of the group's unconscious experience he was speaking for, but also what part of his personal experience and history had led him to assume this task.

Pichon-Riviere focused on this spokesman function, both in clinical settings—individual psychoanalysis and group analysis—and in his critical analyses of art products and activities, features and routines of everyday life, and current social events (Pichon-Rivière & Pampliega de Quiroga, 1970). Coming from a Marxist background, it was only natural for him to assume that human groups and their members conceived, thought, felt, communicated, and acted in terms of the unrecognized, hidden, and denied economic and power structure of their society. This was expressed through the behaviour of individuals, groups, institutions, and communities, as well as in the collective voice of culture.

In this social analysis, as well as in traditional individual psychoanalysis, the point of departure is always a symptom. This may be a current social habit, an idiomatic expression, collective reactions to common events, rumours, popular songs, or other forms of art, political developments, or crises. This amounts to calling into question the regular certainties and routines of everyday life, an operation that raises severe resistances, since any attempt to turn the ordinary and the well known into a problem with hidden undertones is inevitably unsettling.

A paradigmatic example

Some individuals have, on account of their inborn abilities and their personal histories, the capacity to synthesize and express the feelings of a whole society. Pichon-Rivière did an exercise in this sort of interpretation in the case of Enrique Santos Discépolo, the famous Argentine poet and writer of words and music for tangos. His analysis shows the articulation of Discépolo's personal history, as well as his family's, with Argentina's socio-political evolution, before and during his lifetime. Such complex psycho-social enquiry, which exhibits the dreams, aspirations, frustrations, and tragedies of a whole people, is reminiscent of Erik Erikson's psycho-socio-biographical studies of Gorki and Hitler (1950), Martin Luther (1958) and Ghandi (1969), as well as Reinhard Bendix's (1966) compelling and deeply moving "A memoir of my father", written from a sociological perspective.

It is difficult for a foreigner to understand the meaning and emotional resonance of Discépolo—fondly known as "Discepolín" ("little Discépolo")—for someone born and raised in Argentina. The deeply painful and utterly disenchanted words of his tangos are well-known, not only in Argentina, but also throughout Latin-America. None the less, the full import of their message and its highly ramified connotations may only resonate with a personality built upon the early introjections of primary object relations and the social matrix that convey what we sometimes call the "national character" of Argentina.

This certainly applied to Discépolo, who was nothing if not an Argentine, and allowed him to put into words and music the sorry feelings of his national community in the years that preceded and surrounded the Great Crisis of 1929. Hence, Pichon-Rivière (1965a) took him as a paradigmatic example of what he once called the "implacable interplay of man and the world" (1965b). But his analysis of the mutual relationship between Discépolo and his socio-political context tacitly assumes knowledge in the reader of Argentine history and the social and political climate of the first half of the twentieth century.

I shall, therefore, elaborate on the context of Pichon-Rivière's interpretation of Discépolo and his work. This implies, of course, making explicit what was implicit in his text, and this is a work of interpretation—indeed, for our author, the very definition of the work of analysis is "to make explicit the implicit"—in which the explanation of Pichon-Rivière's references goes hand in hand with the meaning that I am able to construct from my own vantage point.

The context

When the Spaniards arrived to what is now Argentina, they did not find a complex civilization with an established and highly developed culture, as the Incas in Peru and the Aztecs in Mexico, but only a number of miserable and rather primitive tribes, which were either subdued or massacred by the invaders. So, the main source of the country's population was to come from immigration. After Argentina became an independent country, in 1816, and having put an end to a bloody civil war, it was ready to become an integrated state by drawing and passing the Constitution of 1853. Its main artificer, Juan Bautista Alberdi, was particularly worried about the need to increase the population. For this, he favoured fostering European immigration, under the slogan "In America, to govern is to populate". This endeavour had a clear racist inspiration, since he considered the native population unworthy and incapable of becoming the citizens this new State so sorely needed, so that it should have to be overcome and replaced by "civilized Europeans". But even the latter had to be winnowed, since "there are Europeans and Europeans", and the civilizing effort should only bring Europe's best, and not its worst:

> To populate is to civilize when you populate with civilized people, that is, with settlers from civilized Europe. . . . But to populate is not to civilize, but to bestialize, when you populate with the *Chinese*, and Asian *Indians*, and Negroes from Africa. [Alberdi, 1914, p. 18, my translation]

It was within this socio-political and ideological context that the great European immigration wave to Argentina took place. Although this migratory process occurred from 1850 to 1950, the main thrust happened between 1870 and 1930, with a striking predominance of those who came from Italy and Spain. In the first census of 1869, Argentina had less than two million people. By 1914, thirty per cent of the population was foreign-born and, by 1920, half of the inhabitants of Buenos Aires had come from other countries. It has been evaluated that the 1960s' population of twenty million would have been only eight million had there been no immigration (Rechinni de Lattes & Lattes, 1975).

Pichon-Rivière's analysis

For those who came to Argentina, especially from Italy, America was truly a new world, *vis-à-vis* an impoverished Europe, which had nothing to offer them. Their common fantasy was "doing America", that is, to get rich soon from it, with an undertone of exploitation, but for most of them this never happened. Their obvious alien identity and ethnicity blocked their access to the wealthier and refined strata. Hence, the very few who succeeded economically did so because they did their best to leave behind any sign of their humble origins and to incorporate new ways of relating:

> This inclusion in a progressively competitive society splits the migratory communities in two—the poor and the rich—and the bonds between them are severely disturbed, having lost the characteristics they had in their places of origin. Those who have succeeded, the climbers—surely those who have managed to get rid of their origin, not to suffer a paralysing nostalgia, and adapt the instrumentality of their egos to the circumstances—attain communication with the native groups, although in the end their difficulties and the language they use may turn out to be a nucleus of resistance to change. [Pichon-Rivière, 1965a, pp. 162–163]

This is the story of the Discépolos. Santo, the father, was a Neapolitan musician who came to Buenos Aires before the age of twenty, married, had five children, and died early. The eldest son, Armando (1887–1971) became a successful playwright and regisseur. He was eighteen when his father died, and had to take care of his brothers, including Enrique Santos, the youngest, who was five. It was then that he wrote his first play and started a brilliant career. His plays are depressive and pessimistic, with poor and miserable characters, frequently immigrants, who are overwhelmed by an unfair and destructive social reality. His characters are ethnical, and the setting of the story folkloric and sombrely comical. He is considered to be the creator of the style called *Creole grotesque*. But in 1934 he suddenly stopped writing and devoted himself to the "legitimate theatre", directing plays by Tolstoi, Somerset Maugham, Chéjov, Bernard Shaw, and Shakespeare, with all the main actors of his time, until his death at the age eighty-three, when he was still working.

So, Armando fits quite nicely Pichon-Rivière's description of the successful son of immigrants who strives to suppress and leave behind the marks of his alien and humble origin, and become part of the "right people". Enrique Santos (1901–1951), on the other hand, was always true to his proletarian roots in the *barrio*. He was always openly melancholic and withdrawn:

> I had a sad childhood. I was never attracted to playing marbles, or any of the other games children play. I was isolated and taciturn. Unfortunately, this was not unmotivated. I was five when my father died, and lost my mother before I was nine. Then my timidity became fear, and my sadness, affliction. [Discépolo, quoted by Tino Diez, 2010, my translation]

Growing under the supervision of Armando, he started to work with him as an actor in his plays. But soon he turned to writing tangos, as an expression of his pessimism, disenchantment, and melancholy, sometimes manically neutralized by sarcasm and self-mockery. All this echoed the typical Argentine character and the prevailing mood in the population *vis-à-vis* the economic and political situation of the country at the time, as we shall soon see.

Enrique was quite aware of this confluence and resonance of his own feelings and creativity, on the one hand, and the vital and emotional plight of his public, when he said,

> A song is a piece of my life, a suit that is looking for a body that fits it well. The more bodies there are for that suit, the greater will be the success of the song, since if everybody sings it, it is a signal that all of them are living it, feeling it, that it suits them well. [Discépolo, quoted by Diez, 2010, my translation]

This idea is pretty much the same as the other Enrique's (Pichon-Rivière, 1965c) theory of the spokesman function. His interpretation of the evolution and destiny of the two Discépolo brothers articulates their personal history and personality (vertical interpretation) with the anxieties and mood that prevailed in Argentina at the time (horizontal interpretation):

> We cannot determine how much the figure of Don Santo Discépolo, father of "the Discépolos", a musician who attained a certain

renown and who even composed a few tangos, fuses in Armando's imagination with Stéfano, the artist character [of one of his plays], who migrates with the illusion of creating *l'opera fenomenale* [a phenomenal work, in Italian], imposing on his whole family the burden of his ambition and his failure.

We can only assert that Armando becomes, through this identification with his father figure, the spokesman for the family group and the experience of immigration in its general context, of which Stéfano is an archetype, with his load of rootlessness, nostalgia, and insecurity, in a progressively precarious economic situation.

Within this family dynamics, each of the two sons, Armando and Enrique Santos, assumes and realizes two aspects of their father. This real splitting situation [expresses] the fantasy of "doing America", that is, the almost magical attainment of fortune and prestige, [which] activated the immigratory current that flowed on our country. . . . The destiny of each immigrant individual or family group depends on the characteristics of this fantasy and the way in which they implement it. [Pichon-Rivière, 1965a, p. 162]

While Armando assumes the role of the *spokesman* of the family group, Enrique Santos becomes the *spokesman* for the community, with which he has assimilated, being considered a true representative of the country, on account of his intense identification with the features of the Argentine character. Thus, his work becomes transcendent and turns him into a chronicler of his time. Discépolo draws a system for codifying the national character: the tango, and thus reaches an identification with a messianic leader (Perón). Armando, for his part, identifies with the real father, and this will enable him to narrate the vicissitudes of those who, in the articulation of an inner motivation for social ascent, with the fantasy of "doing America" (fostered by the propaganda that came from countries such as ours, interested in an input of qualified workers), decided to migrate. [*ibid.*, p. 161]

Of course, this difference between the brothers may also be understood in terms of their respective ages by the time their father died. At eighteen, Armando was already a man, who was ready to begin his career as playwright, while Enrique Santos was a small child, who would forever feel orphaned, lonely, and hopeless, thus identifying with, and speaking for, a major part of the Argentine population who were deprived and destitute, disbelieved in the political system and its administrators, and despaired of the future. But this requires further contextual information about the Argentinean politics of the 1920s through the 1950s.

The Argentinean politics of the time

Hipólito Yrigoyen (1852–1933) was the leader of the Radical opposition to the conservative government of the National Autonomist Party, through which General Julio Argentino Roca, who was twice elected President, held and pulled the strings of Argentine politics during more than thirty years. Yrigoyen's Radical Civic Union had attempted the revolutionary path on several occasions, from 1890 onwards, but in 1910, when his friend Roque Sáenz Peña was elected President, they made the pact that Yrigoyen would give up armed fighting in return for the passing of a new law imposing a universal, secret, and obligatory vote for all men, in order to put an end to the fraudulent elections of the past. The law was passed in 1912, and this led to Yrigoyen becoming the first President elected by a universal and secret male vote, in 1916.

Yrigoyen was widely popular and attempted liberal reforms, but he had no control of either the Senate or several of the Governorships. He was, therefore, forced to intervene in some of the Provinces (states) and repress, or allow the army to repress, movements by striking workers, which led to massacres for which no one in the government was willing to assume responsibility.

In 1922, he left the Presidency, since the Argentine Constitution did not allow an immediate re-election after the six-year period, in the hands of Marcelo T. de Alvear, who soon became the leader of the "antipersonalist" faction of the Radical Party, which opposed him. In 1928, he was again elected, defeating an alliance between the conservatives and the antipersonalist Radicals. His second presidency, however, was an utter failure, on account of the blatant ineptitude and disorganization of the government. He also had to deal, most ineffectively, with the Great Crisis of 1929. In 1930, his party lost an intermediate election, overcome by the Socialists, who were now carrying the torch of reform. He also made the state oil company YPF intervene in the local oil market, in order to fix its price and put a restriction on foreign oil trusts. All this brought about a military *coup d'état*, led by General José Félix Uriburu, which overthrew the government. The new military government was endorsed by the Supreme Court, thus inaugurating the doctrine of the de facto governments, and Britain and the USA recognized it within a week. Yrigoyen was imprisoned in an island on the River Plate, and died in 1933. His funeral was accompanied by one of the most massive and surprising spontaneous popular demonstrations in Argentine history.

Uriburu's government installed a fascist military control and a violent repression of the opposition, including the institutionalization of torture. One year later, another general, Agustín P. Justo, was elected in a fraudulent election, under the aegis of the conservatives. This started the period known as the Infamous Decade, on account of the prevalence of repression and corruption, and established a system of political control aimed at avoiding any possibility that the radicals might recoup the government, which lasted until 1943.

Analysing the words of his tangos

Such was the climate that surrounded Discepolín's coming of age and his young adulthood. It was a time of disenchantment and despair, and the young writer and composer conveyed this collective feeling loud and clear, with a powerful voice. In 1926, he wrote the words and music of his first tango, humorously called "Qué vachaché"—a slang expression that means something like "What are you to do?", meaning, of course, that there is nothing to be done. This was the epitome of hopelessness, a theme he was to further develop in other famous songs. Here, he said,

> Don't you realize how vain you are?
> Do you believe you'll fix the world?
> Here not even God recoups what's been lost!
> And you want to? Don't make me laugh!

(All the words from songs are quoted from Discépolo (2010), in my own translation. There has been no attempt to recreate the musicality of the original text, or of his regular use of Argentine slang.)

Idealism is then nothing but conceit and foolishness, and the only thing that counts is a ruthless pragmatism:

> What needs be done is to pack a lot of dough,
> vend your soul, raffle your heart,
> squander the little decency you've left . . .
> Money, money, money, and money again . . .
> Then you might get a grub every day,
> Have friends, house, a name . . .
> and whatever you want.
> *Real love was drowned in soup:*
> *the belly reigns, and money's God.*

The last two lines, which I have italicized, are a summary of Discépolo's despondent view of his contemporary society. This did not initially impress or appeal to the public, which noisily whistled it (Pujol, 2010). But, in 1928, the famous singer Azucena Maizani sang his second tango, "Esta noche me emborracho" (Tonight I'm getting drunk), which was an instant success throughout the country and in Europe. The subject was again gloomy despair, but now in a more personal context: the singer circumstantially meeting the cabaret woman with whom he had once been madly in love, now old, battered, and gone to seed. Again, there is nothing to be done, but to get loaded.

After this striking success, that very same year, singer Tita Merello revived "Qué vachaché", which was now cheered. This was the beginning of the author's widely successful career.

These two tangos set the tone for the two main themes in his writing. The first one, stemming from "Qué vachaché", is the criticism of a greedy, corrupt, and ruthless society, seen from the vantage point of the disappointed son of an immigrant, who feels the world to be truly horrible. The same idea is expressed in "Yira, yira" (Round and round), in which he says:

> You'll see that all's a lie,
> you'll see that there's no love . . .
> the world just doesn't care,
> it goes round . . . and round . . .
> Even when your life is wrecked,
> or you're down in biting pain,

> never expect some help,
> never a friendly hand,
> nor a favour from a friend.

The very title of the song is based on a play upon words. "Gira, gira" can be translated as "round and round" or "doing the rounds", but when he playfully turns "gira" into "yira", it acquires an additional connotation. "Yirar" is to wander aimlessly, but also to do the streets, as a prostitute, and "un yiro" is a whore, in the Buenos Aires slang. So, it is not only the case that the world continues revolving, indifferent to the plight of the people, but it is also venal and corrupt.

This was written in 1930, the very year of Yrigoyen's demise. His next version of this argument, "Cambalache" (Flea market), came in 1934, well into the Infamous Decade:

> That the world has always been
> and will ever be
> a pile of crap,
> I know it well . . .
> . . .
> But that this twentieth century
> is a shameless show of evil,
> there's no denying.
> . . .
> Everything's the same!
> Nothing is ever better!
> . . .
> Life has been messed up,
> as in the irreverent display
> of the flea market, and,
> wounded by a seamless steel sabre,
> you can see the Bible weeping,
> side by side with a battered old boiler . . .

The second theme that is found, over and over again, in his songs, is that of the woman, the lost love, sometimes the betrayer or the despoiler. The lover suffers, but he takes it "as a man", swallowing his tears, so that they never show, and sometimes denying manically his own pain, abandoning before being abandoned, or rationalizing the break-up as an altruistic gesture, because "she'll be better off with someone else". In his agonizingly painful song "Uno" (One), which he took a whole year to write, in spite of the desperate demands of band director Mariano Mores, who had already written the music, the man sings of his desperate need to hope, trust, and love, but his faith has been shattered by betrayal, and he suddenly finds that "he has lost his heart". He still craves love and belief, but they are no longer an option for him:

> If I still had a heart . . .
> (The heart I gave away!)
> If I still could, as I used to,
> love without forebodings . . .
> It's just possible that your eyes,
> those eyes that lovingly behold me,
> I might cover with my kisses,
> and not think that they're like
> those other, perverse, eyes
> that wrecked my life away.

But Pichon-Rivière believed that these two themes had a mutual resonance. Armando Santos' experience as an early orphan made it very difficult for him to love and trust another human being, but he was also portraying his disappointment (and that of the Argentine people) with the benign, but weak and ineffective father figure that was Yrigoyen, the expectation that Uriburu would be the strong father that puts the house in order, and the brutal disillusionment when the latter turned out to be a sadistic tyrant and the alleged new order proved to be even more corrupt than the disorganized Yrigoyen government. The internalized imagos of the benign father who takes care of his children, and that of the powerful and effective soldier who would restore order, remained dormant inside Discépolo for a few years, until the emergence, in 1943—the same year in which he finished writing "Uno"—of Coronel Juan Domingo Perón, whom he had met in Chile, as a charismatic populist leader, in whom he would deposit these deep yearnings, as did a large majority of the people.

During his last years, Discépolo was a staunch supporter and personal friend of General Perón, who had been elected President in 1946, and even had a radio programme in which he criticized the conservative opposition. This gained him many enemies among the country's elite. None the less, even though he approved of the social reforms of Peronism, he was also weary of the authoritarianism of the regime and disapproved of the censorship it imposed. Yet, he had managed to "love again".

Pichon-Rivière actually met Discépolo once, acting as a doctor, in a night club the latter had in the exclusive seaside resort of Punta del Este, Uruguay, one year before his untimely death of a heart attack, at the age of fifty. They then had a long conversation, in which they talked about politics, and the writer told him about his ambivalence towards Peronism. He died on 23 December 1951. Apparently, he had finally lost his heart.

The theory

While reading this rendition of Pichon-Rivière's study of Discépolo, the reader may have had the feeling that this was a case history. It is certainly a case study, but, unlike most psychoanalytic studies, the historical and contextual information is not so much about the subject's family and childhood, but about the history of a nation over a 100-year period. Much of this information was kept tacit in the author's explicit text, since he was writing for a professional community of Argentineans, who would be expected to share this experience, even unconsciously, in the case of the younger generations of therapists, who received it from their parents and grandparents.

The same thing happens when this sort of analysis is done in the clinical situation: a great number of social and political references are tacitly shared between therapists and patients. The result is that, when trying to convey what actually happened in a session, there is a need for much more extended historical and contextual information than in the actual telling of the session, especially when the audience is made up of people from another national, cultural, or linguistic area. For instance, Reyna Hernández-Tubert and I presented—in the Dublin 2008 European Symposium of Group Analysis—a co-therapy group-analytic session, in which the analysis oscillated between individual psychodynamics and the social and political context to which all of us belonged, which had to be explained to the audience (Tubert-Oklander, 2010).

But, of course, this sort of analysis—both clinical and applied—is based upon a theory, which needs be made explicit. I shall start with the concepts developed by Pichon-Rivière, and follow with those posed by his disciples and continuators—including myself—which represent the Latin-American tradition he initiated.

In Pichon-Rivière's theory, there is no opposition between individual and collective psychology, since they are two sides of one and the same mental phenomenon. Thus, he quotes John Donne's (1624) famous *Meditation*, when he says: "No man is an island, entire of itself; every man is a piece of the continent, a part of the main".

The metaphor is poignant and clear: neither the island nor the continent are real entities, but only that part of a single irregular ground that can be seen over the level of the waters. Hence, the individual and the group are illusions, derived from our mind's tendency to split and splinter complex wholes, in order to be able to talk and think them through. This clearly reminds us of Foulkes's assertion that "each individual [is] itself an artificial, though plausible, abstraction" (1948, p. 10).

How does Pichon-Rivière carry out his magic trick of leaving utterly aside the dichotomy of "individual" and "group"? This requires a complete revamping of psychoanalytic theory, particularly, discarding the notion of the instinctual drives, to be replaced by that of the *bond* (Pichon-Rivière, 1979). The bond includes, but is not restricted to, what we know as "object relations": "In psychoanalytic theory, we are used to utilize the notion of object relations, but the notion of the bond is much more concrete. The object relation is the inner structure of the bond" (*ibid.*, p. 35). There are two psychological fields in the bond: there is an inner field and an outer field—and here "field" does not only have physical or dynamic connotations, but also those of a football field: a space for groups to play. So, there are internal and external objects, and an internal and an external group, as well as an internal and an external aspect of the bond.

Psychoanalysis has shown greater interest in the inner field, because that is what it can better enquire into with its methodology, but this should not mean ignoring the outer dimension. Besides, "inner" means for the author—as it meant for Foulkes—"intrapsychic", not "intrapersonal", since he considers group phenomena to be truly mental. Foulkes and Anthony (1965) wrote about this: "to us intrapsychic does not convey . . . 'intradermic', and we look upon the dynamic processes in the group not only from the outside, but from inside, as intra-psychic dynamics in their interaction" (p. 21).

There is, then, a perpetual dialectic of the inner and the outer, which is the very stuff of human existence. The internal bonds and the external bonds are integrated in a dialectic spiral process, by means of which that which was originally external becomes internal, and then external again, and so on. There is a fluid interchange between the two fields, which helps to establish the differentiation between the inside and the outside, while at the same time keeping a deep continuity between them. Hence, individual and society form an indissoluble unit, a single dynamic field, because we all carry society within us: "One cannot think in terms of a distinction between the individual and society. It is an abstraction, a reductionism that we cannot accept" (Pichon-Rivière, 1979, p. 57).

So, we are not really studying the inner dynamics of individual personalities, but that of an interaction field; this is the specific object of psychological research. From this point of view, psychoanalytic enquiry is unavoidably group-analytic, even if there are only two people present. The bonding structure then includes not only the subject's relations with his or her internal objects, which have been internalized from the actual experience with external objects, but also his or her interactions—past, present, and wished-for—with the external objects, those same external objects, with their peculiarities, feelings, intentions, and subjectivity, and the groups, communities, and culture to which they all belong: that is, the social, historic, and political context.

The continuators

This emphasis on the unitary and essentially social nature of the human being was further developed by Pichon-Rivière's disciple, José Bleger, whose ideas have been later elaborated by some Latin-American authors, such as Blanca Montevechio and myself, who followed his lead. Bleger (1967, 1971) posed the existence of a deep, primitive, syncretic level of experience, characterized by *ambiguity*, understood as a particular form of object relation in which there is no differentiation between subject and object, but a coexistence of all opposites. This hypothesis, which stems from Freud's (1930a) analysis of the "oceanic feeling" and which is strikingly similar to Hans Loewald's (1980) ideas on the existence of an original fusional level of experience, was, however, phrased in terms of Bleger's Kleinian origins. The result is rather similar to Ogden's (1989) autistic–contiguous position. It also overlaps with Earl Hopper's work on the basic assumption of Incohesion: Aggregation/ Massification or (ba) I:A/M (2003), but a comparative study of the similarities and differences between these various theories goes far beyond the scope of this chapter.

The fact that, in the deepest mental level, there is actually no boundary or membrane separating the individuals, determines the existence of a basic syncytial structure, which underlies individual existence and sets the foundation for groups, institutions, and society (Bleger, 1971, 1974). A syncytium, in biology, is "a multinucleate mass of protoplasm that is not differentiated in cells". Just as in the case of the syncytium there is a common protoplasm containing multiple nuclei, but keeping a continuity in the cytoplasm, the human group would be a single and continuous mass, in which are contained the nuclei of individual identifications and experiences that correspond to the various subjects. This is not conceived as a circumstantial occurrence, but as a continuous state of affairs, a deep level of the individual and the group's mental processes, which underlies everything else.

These ideas were further developed by Montevechio (1999, 2002) in her own conception of syncretism and ambiguity, in terms of a primitive, undifferentiated, and ambiguous organization, in which there is a confluence of opposing passions. This is the most primitive and vital stratum of the mind, from which all social life derives, since in it there is a primal continuity and fusion between individuals and everything that surrounds them. This she represented, after Nietzsche, by the Dionysus myth, which, in conjunction with those of Narcissus and Oedipus, would summarize the human condition. These three organizations of experience coexist and complement each other. She also emphasized the normal and healthy aspects of these primitive forms of experience, in contrast with Bleger's essentially psychopathological perspective.

In my own work (Tubert-Oklander, 2004a,b, 2008) I have elaborated Bleger's and Montevechio's ideas, by adding a fourth, post-
Oedipal organization, consisting in the dialectic interaction of the
three previous organizations, which gives birth to the mature
human subject. Such higher organization emerges from dialogue,
both in the outer group of interpersonal relations and in what
Pichon-Rivière (1965c) called the *inner group*, which underlies all
mental life.

So, from my point of view, derived from the Pichonian and the
Foulkesian traditions, human experience and mental processes are
not coextensive with the boundaries of the human organism. They
are also threefold, since they are simultaneously experienced,
perceived, represented, thought, felt, and acted upon in three
complementary ways. There is a fusional experience of continuity
of everything that is (the Dionysian), which allows a continuous
flow of feeling, thinking, and acting, among human beings. Then,
there is an imaginary, specular, phantasmatic, or iconic experience
of ever reversible relations, in a constant dreaming state (the
Narcissistic). Finally, there is a differentiated experience, in terms of
discrete subjects and objects that interact in a common space, without losing their individuality and their intimate subjectivity, which
contains their feelings, thoughts, fantasies, memories, and conflicts
(the Oedipal). These three alternative experiential worlds coexist
and alternately prevail over the others, but each of them has an
idiosyncratic experience and a symbolic representation of everything that happens, both in the inner and the outer fields.

But what is sauce for the goose is also sauce for the gander, so
the very same dynamics found in the individual apply to collective
mental processes—group, institutional, or social. Foulkes (1964)
acknowledged this when he described four levels of functioning in
the group: (1) the current level, (2) the transference level, (3) the
level of bodily and mental images (projective level), and (4) the primordial level. The first two, which refer to the structural and
dynamic functioning of social systems, and to mature object relations, in interpersonal terms, between group members, corresponds
to the Oedipal level. The third, which is that of the group unconscious fantasy, corresponds to the Narcissistic level. Finally, the
fourth, which Jungians would call "archetypal", represents the
Dionysian level.

If none of these three domains of experience has been repressed, or if, having been repressed, the fluid interchange and dialogue between them has been restored by the analysis, then a new depth is added to the human experience—in both the individual and the group—with the emergence of the post-Oedipal dynamics that bring about wisdom, understood as an increasing awareness of and respect for complex interrelations. This is the final goal of both psychoanalysis and group analysis, although there is a difference of emphasis and aim between them: whereas psychoanalysis carves vertically into the successive strata of individual experience, and only resonates with the echoes of the social unconscious, group analysis expands horizontally in ever widening waves, which tend to reflect the whole gamut of human experience. Therefore, both devices have their assets and their liabilities, and their respective sights bear both highly clear areas and blind spots. Hence, a psychoanalyst has to actively search for the manifestations of the social unconscious, which are not apparent from his or her vantage point, while the group analyst has sometimes to stretch and strain his or her instrument in order to approach and understand the individual's perspective. This is where Pichon-Rivière's dual approach to interpretation and Foulkes's binocular view of the individual and the group go hand in hand, in their effort to provide a wider and deeper understanding of the human experience, as manifested in the group-analytic situation.

References

Alberdi, J. B. (1914). *Bases y puntos de partida para la organización política de la República de Argentina* [Bases and Starting Points for the Political Organisation of the Argentine Republic], F. Cruz (Ed.). In *Scribd.com* (10 May 2010), available at: www.scribd.com/doc/8975894/Juan-Bautista-Alberdi-Bases-y-puntos-de-partida-para-la-organizacion-politica-de-Argentina.

Bendix, R. (1966). A memoir of my father. *Canadian Review of Sociology and Anthropology, 2*(1): 1–18.

Beuchot, M. (1997). *Tratado de hermenéutica analógica* (4th edn) [Treatise of Analogical Hermeneutics]. Mexico City: UNAM/Itaca, 2005.

Beuchot, M. (2003). *Hermenéutica analógica y del umbral* [Analogical and Threshold Hermeneutics]. Salamanca: Editorial San Esteban.

Bleger, J. (1967). *Simbiosis y ambigüedad* [Symbiosis and Ambiguity]. Buenos Aires: Paidós.

Bleger, J. (1971). El grupo como institución y el grupo en las instituciones [The group as an institution and the group in institutions]. In: *Temas de psicología (Entrevista y grupos)* [Themes in Psychology (Interview and Groups)] (pp. 87–104). Buenos Aires, Argentina: Nueva Visión.

Bleger, J. (1974). Schizophrenia, autism, and symbiosis. *Contemporary Psychoanalysis*, *10*:19–25.

Diez, T. (1910). Enrique Santos Discépolo. In: *Terapiatanguera.com.ar* (15 May 2010), available at: www.terapiatanguera.com.ar/Notas% 20y%20articulos/tino_discepolo.htm.

Discépolo, E. S. (2010). Letras de Enrique Santos Discépolo [Words of Enrique Santos Discépolo]. In: *Todotango.com* (15 May 2010), available at: www.todotango.com/spanish/biblioteca/letras/letras_ autor.asp?idc=41

Donne, J. (1624). Meditation XVII. In: *The Literature Network* (30 May 2010), available at: www.online-literature.com/donne/409.

Erikson, E. H. (1950). *Childood and Society*. London: Paladin, 1987.

Erikson, E. H. (1958). *Young Man Luther*. New York: Norton, 1993.

Erikson, E. H. (1969). *Gandhi's Truth*. New York: Norton, 1993.

Foulkes, S. H. (1948). *Introduction to Group-Analytic Psychotherapy*. London: Maresfield, 1984.

Foulkes, S. H. (1964). *Therapeutic Group Analysis*. London: Maresfield, 1984.

Foulkes, S. H., & Anthony, E. J. (1965). *Group Psychotherapy: The Psychoanalytic Approach* (2nd edn). London: Maresfield, 1984.

Freud, S. (1930a). *Civilization and Its Discontents*. S.E., *21*: 64–145. London: Hogarth.

Hopper, E. (2003). *Traumatic Experience in the Unconscious Life of Groups*. London: Jessica Kingsley.

Loewald, H. (1980). *Papers on Psychoanalysis*. New Haven, CT: Yale University Press.

Montevechio, B. (1999). *Las nuevas fronteras del psicoanálisis. Dionisio, Narciso, Edipo* [The New Frontiers of Psychoanalysis: Dionysus, Narcissus, Oedipus]. Buenos Aires: Lumen.

Montevechio, B. (2002). *Más allá de Narciso. La problemática de las identidades* [Beyond Narcissus: The Problematic of Identities]. Buenos Aires: Lumen.

Ogden, T. H. (1989). On the concept of an autistic–contiguous position. *International Journal of Psychoanalysis*, *70*: 127–140.

Pichon-Rivière, E. (1965a). Discépolo: un cronista de su tiempo [Discépolo: a chronicler of his time]. In: *El proceso grupal. Del psicoanálisis a la psicología social (1)* (1971a) [The Group Process: From Psychoanalysis to Social Psychology (I)] (pp. 161–168). Buenos Aires: Nueva Visión.

Pichon-Rivière, E. (1965b). Implacable interjuego del hombre y del mundo [Implacable interplay of man and world]. In: *El proceso grupal. Del psicoanálisis a la psicología social (1)* (1971a) [The Group Process: From Psychoanalysis to Social Psychology (I)] (pp. 169–172). Buenos Aires: Nueva Visión.

Pichon-Rivière, E. (1965c). Grupos operativos y enfermedad única [Operative groups and the single disease]. In: *El proceso grupal. Del psicoanálisis a la psicología social (1)* (1971a) [The Group Process: From Psychoanalysis to Social Psychology (I)] (pp. 121–139). Buenos Aires: Nueva Visión.

Pichon-Rivière, E. (1971a). *El proceso grupal. Del psicoanálisis a la psicología social (1)* [The Group Process: From Psychoanalysis to Social Psychology (I)]. Buenos Aires: Nueva Visión.

Pichon-Rivière, E. (1971b). *La psiquiatría, una nueva problemática. Del psicoanálisis a la psicología social (II)* [A New Problematic for Psychiatry: From Psychoanalysis to Social Psychology (II)]. Buenos Aires: Nueva Visión.

Pichon-Rivière, E. (1971c). *El proceso creador. Del psicoanálisis a la psicología social (III)* [The Creative Process: From Psychoanalysis to Social Psychology (III)]. Buenos Aires: Nueva Visión.

Pichon-Rivière, E. (1979). *Teoría del vínculo* [Theory of the Bond]. Buenos Aires: Nueva Visión.

Pichon-Rivière, E. (2004a). *Le processus groupal.* Paris: Érès [French translation of Pichon-Rivière (1971a)].

Pichon-Rivière, E. (2004b). *Théorie du lien* suivi de *Le processus de création.* Paris: Érès [French translation of Pichon-Rivière (1979) and (1971c)].

Pichon-Rivière, E., & Pampliega de Quiroga, A. (1970). *Psicología de la vida cotidiana* [*Psychology of Everyday Life*] (2nd edn). Buenos Aires: Nueva Visión, 1985.

Pujol, S. (2010). Enrique Santos Discépolo. In: *Todotango.com* (15 May 2010), available at: www.todotango.com/english/creadores/sdiscepolo.html

Rechinni de Lattes, Z., & Lattes, A. E. (Eds.) (1975). *La población de Argentina* [The Argentine Population]. Buenos Aires: CICRED.

Rojas Mix, M. (1987). The angel with the arquebus—Baroque art in Latin America. *UNESCO Courier*, Sept. 1987. Accessed at: *FindArticles.com* (11 May 2010), http://findarticles.com/p/articles/mi_m1310/is_n1_v21/ai_6134023/

Tubert-Oklander, J. (2004a). Dionisio y Narciso. La contribución de Blanca Montevechio al estudio del sincretismo. [Dionysus and narcissus: the contribution of Blanca Montevechio to the study of syncretism]. Paper presented to the 43rd International Congress of Psychoanalysis, New Orleans, March.

Tubert-Oklander, J. (2004b). Mitología, desarrollo y proceso psicoanalítico [Mythology, development, and the psychoanalytic process]. Lecture delivered to the 44th National Congress of Psychoanalysis, Mexican Psychoanalytic Association, Oaxaca, Oax, November.

Tubert-Oklander, J. (2008). An inquiry into the alpha function. *Canadian Journal of Psychoanalysis—Revue canadienne de psychanalyse*, 16(2) : 224–245.

Tubert-Oklander, J. (2009). *Hermenéutica analógica y condición humana* [Analogical Hermeneutics and the Human Condition]. Special Number 24 of *Analogía filosófica*. Mexico City, 2009.

Tubert-Oklander, J. (2010). The matrix of despair: from despair to desire through dialogue. *Group Analysis*, 43(2): 127–140.

Tubert-Oklander, J., & Beuchot Puente, M. (2008). *Ciencia mestiza. Psicoanálisis y hermenéutica analógica* [Hybrid science: Psychoanalysis and Analogical Hermeneutics]. Mexico City: Torres.

Tubert-Oklander, J., & Hernández de Tubert, R. (2004). *Operative Groups: The Latin-American Approach to Group Analysis*. London: Jessica Kingsley.

PART II

THE ORGANISMIC AND NEUROBIOLOGICAL PERSPECTIVE

Introduction

Malcolm Pines

I n the 1970s, the revisionist psychoanalyst George Klein emphasized that psychoanalytic theory had not yet found the rightful
place for what Hopper (2003) has termed the essential "sociality" of human beings. Klein pointed out that in the structural theory
of id, ego, and superego, there was no place and no word for "us-
ness", or "we-ness" as a complement for "ego" and perhaps for
"id" or "it". We needed a concept such as the "we-go", but somehow this was not quite the right word for this. Now, on the basis of
his European classical education, Tom Ormay, who is not only a
group analyst but also a philosopher of science, in "Mirror neurons,
sociality, and the species homo sapiens" has given us the missing
word: "nos".

Ormay does not want to discard Freud's great achievement in
presenting us with his structural theory, with which he replaced his
original drive theory, taking into account the great social forces of
human society. In *Group Psychology and the Analysis of the Ego* (1921c),
Freud wrote that, from the very first, individual psychology is at
the same time social psychology as well: all intrapsychic object relationships can be considered as social phenomena. However, Freud
could not accept the proposal of the American psychoanalyst

Trigant Burrow that psychoanalytic theory itself should be open to what Burrow called "group analysis", the result of his exploration of the dynamics of small groups. Later, Foulkes remembered that he had read these papers, as well as the related work of Fromm, Horney, Adler, and others who shared similar interests.

Ormay's persuasive argument is that we can complete the psychoanalytical structure of a theory of mind by adding a genuine social function that develops from an inherited biological base. That biological base has been the subject of intense investigation into the social life of primates, which quite firmly asserts and proves the biological basis for co-operation. It is clear that complex societies can only develop through the co-operation of their members and the acceptance of complex social structures. It is asserted that to live in a big group requires a big brain, and developing a big brain arises from membership of a big group. In fact, consciousness is the product of nos, which we both create and develop together. As Patrick de Maré has reminded us: the word "consciousness" arises from "con-scio", knowing together.

Ormay tells us that when we look at a person, depending on our viewpoint, we see the personal self, who is private, and the social self, who is a member of his/her community, based on the nos. Social images of the self come about when the person recognizes himself or herself in the various social formations, as in so many mirrors. Self and other: *ego et alter*. There is no self without alter, no alter without self. This brings us close to Foulkes's assertion that we human beings are primarily social, and that the phenomena of mirroring and reso-nance are essential components of our social life. *Ab inicio*, the human infant is immersed in the network of relationships, predominantly with mother as the chief care-giver. I am certain that Foulkes would have had a positive response to Ormay's concept of nos.

These relationships, which lead into a social world and a human society, rest on the basis of reciprocity. Reciprocity is a mutual "reckoning with", the first act of the social. The basis of reciprocity is that the other who responds to me should, in principle, be capa-ble of responding to me as much as I respond to him/her or he/she. The basis of the social is the interaction—mutual, reciprocal and complementary. We foresee the response of the other, that is, the action the other will perform in answer to ours. Meanwhile, the other is going through the same process. The action and interaction therefore emanates not from one but from two, which is the very basis of nos, the word that Ormay has called into being and through which our perspective on human life is illuminated. A very group analytic concept.

Influenced by the theory of group analysis, but drawing more from field theory and the study of group dynamics, Yvonne Agazarian and Susan Gantt, in their beautifully crafted chapter, "Developing the group mind through functional subgrouping: linking systems-centred training and interpersonal neurobiology", demonstrate how systems-centred training and neurobiology can further the development of the group mind, defined as ". . . an embodied and relational process that regulates the flow of energy and information . . .", and which ". . . is a characteristic of every living human system" (Siegel, 1999). Their concept of the group mind is based on Agazarian's theory of living human systems (LHS) and system-centred therapy (SCT). How the development of the group mind is reached through system-centred therapy follows logically from the practice of functional subgrouping.

Gant and Agazarian present us with a clear statement of the conceptual tools provided by systems-centred training and interpersonal neurobiology. Systems-centred training has been fashioned by Agazarian since 1977, later with various co-workers. In this model, the group leaders are indeed "conductors". The task of the conductors is threefold: (1) to develop secure relationship context where moderate levels in emotions are experiences and expressed; (2) to teach conflict resolution through functional subgrouping where differences are discriminated and integrated; (3) to work explicitly to develop a group mind by enabling previously closed minds to become more open by activating the exploratory drive via a "climate of enquiry". The task of the group member is fourfold: (1) to accept the conductor's model and form functional subgroups; (2) to train to join, explore, and validate differences through subgroup learning; (3) to recognize resonances, develop the capacity for attention, communication, nuanced social learning; (4) to focus on attention through intention. The intention of this directed process is to foster the growth of the group mind: as differences are recognized, held, and worked through by the process of directed functional subgrouping, growth can be reached through the enhancement of the group as a whole.

The authors sketch the characteristics of the right and left hemispheres: the left hemisphere linguistic, creating meaningful narratives, the right hemisphere "holistic". Indeed, this chapter is a meaningful narrative of this model in which left hemisphere action by the group leaders predominates, explaining the ways in which the group members are encouraged to explore their similarities and differences. I particularly appreciate the instruction to find out if the anxiety stems from being at the edge of the unknown. Whereas Bion brought to our attention Keats' concept of "negative capability", Agazarian and Gantt suggest the power of "positive capability", using predominantly left hemisphere capacities.

The group analytic model involves more of an "active passivity" on the part of the group conductor, in which she/he opens the mind to right hemisphere reflective and meditative experiences conveyed to the group members as a narrative: what are we doing, where are we going, weighing and balancing the forces experienced within the group analyst's awareness. Being on the edge of the unknown and being sensitive to the emerging truths of experience is to take the position of a "privileged listener". Foulkes described group analysis as "analysis by the group, for the group, including the conductor". Of course, coming from a psychoanalytic background, the aim of group analysis was therapy for its members, but Foulkes allowed for "ego training in action" as part of the consequences of work in and by the group. The concepts of mirroring, resonance, and the group as a whole were basic to the Foulkesian perspectives. Based on his experiences as a psychiatrist with Kurt Goldstein, the great investigator of brain-damaged patients after the First World War, Foulkes established a quasi-neurodynamic model: each person is a nodal point in the relational context. Later, with James Anthony, Foulkes fashioned the concept of Matrix, recognizing patterns of communication and aiding the group in their task of understanding when and where needed, informed by sensitive listening and attention giving. In this model, a group conductor's task is slowly to wean the group from its desire to put the conductor in the role of leader. As a refugee from Germany in 1933, Foulkes would not use the term "leader", because it implied a distinction between leaders and followers and was associated with the psychological enslavement of followers to their leaders.

As group analysts we have always known of and emphasized the value of mirroring and resonance in the face to face situation of our groups, but Gantt and Agazarian have emphasized the importance of knowledge of the neurophysiological process of early infancy, and that these processes contribute to the development of affect regulation by the infant's brain. The external regulation by care-givers, largely with the use of their frontal lobes, is gradually replaced by the organism's own capacity for self-regulation as brain growth proceeds. Interestingly, these exchanges were emphasized by Foulkes when he wrote of the decrescendo of a conductor's authority in the early stages of the group, which is necessary to hold the group boundaries and to lower the levels of initial anxiety. However, as the group acquires its own authority and capacity for self-regulation, so the crescendo in the organization of their collective self contains the decrescendo of the conductor's authority.

Our ways of understanding the social unconscious may themselves be a product of it. I would suggest that in our society today the action of the left brain, with its capacity for close observation, seeing parts but not the whole, gathering knowledge by experience, is highly valued, but "wisdom" is placed outside this limited focus (McGilchrist, 2009). SCT and group analysis occupy different places in those treatments which utilize the power of group dynamics. SCT originates in Lewin's Field theory and in organizational and systems theory; group analysis originates in psychoanalysis, gestalt psychology, sociology, and neurodynamics. We may be able to see these therapies along the dimension of right and left brain activities, both aiming to restore lost balance, to explore and to integrate wisdoms slowly accrued.

References

Freud, S. (1921c). *Group Psychology and the Analysis of the Ego. S.E., 18*: 67–143. London: Hogarth.

Hopper, E. (2003). *The Social Unconscious: Selected Papers*. London: Jessica Kingsley.

McGilchrist, I. (2009). *The Master and His Emissary: The Divided Brain and the Making of the Modern World*. New Haven, CT: Yale University Press.

CHAPTER FOUR

Mirror neurons, sociality, and the species homo sapiens

A. P. Tom Ormay

Need for an instinct theory

In recent years the human genome has been "deciphered". Geneticists managed to identify the three billion chemical formulations that make up our genetic code. It is not yet known what is what, we do not yet know what most of the components do, and a lot more work has to be done. It is also important to consider that the route from genetic code to human relationship must be long and complicated; at one end we have the chemicals we are born with, at the other end we have relating and feelings, and there are many steps between, but suddenly we are in a position to track the way. Common sense always dictated that the human personality is made up of genetics and environment. In the past century we learnt much about the environment, but when it came to the genetic side, we had to resort to speculation. We can say that the twentieth century was for environmental psychology while in the twenty-first we might be able to redress the balance. I expect some people will go overboard, and suddenly think that it is all biology; we shall have to wait and see. Neither has it been a mistake to speculate about what we inherit. We can ask meaningful questions only if we think ahead of our evidence. An open mind is a good thing; an empty mind is not.

In the past, people variously talked about instinct, drive, or motivation. Freud thought it important to include an instinct theory in psychoanalysis because he wanted a psychology that systematically contains a relationship to the body. By systematic, I mean that for him the body was not an afterthought, but an essential part of the human picture with its reflexes and evolutionary aspect. In psychoanalysis, instinct has been the "interface", to use a modern expression, between body and mind. They were, of course, aware of the difficulties. Philosophers have been asking, and essentially leaving unanswered, the body–mind question for centuries. The psychoanalysts did not intend to give final answers. They looked for a tool. A practitioner cannot wait until all questions are resolved. The patients keep coming every day, and the work has to be done as best we can. Psychoanalysis is not alone with the problem of undefined basic concepts. It is known that when Einstein asked Freud if he thought that instinct was a mythological concept, Freud replied that perhaps there were such concepts in physics as well.

If we approach the problem from its practical side, we can ask: how could we understand any problem relating to the body or being in the world, without an instinct theory? We might attempt an answer by referring to symbols, but then we need to understand how symbols work. Any answer to that question would need to include something about energy that makes sense in terms of the psyche as well as the body. We need to understand what happens when we have a thought or a feeling and a part of the body is moved by it. Those who try to do psychoanalysis without instincts might still want to use words like "libido" or "feeling" or "affect" in such a way that implies some kind of driving force.

Recent developments in genetics also restate the importance of inherited factors in the personality. That which Freud called the "phylogenetic" does not go away; on the contrary, it increasingly demands its place and focuses on the lingering question that Winnicott (1964) called the "human potential" and the environment.

Some people try to overcome what has been called the dualistic view of human beings, as I referred to it above, when we talk about a mind and a body. Some argue that machines, like computers, think; the brain is a computer, and the brain thinks. But this kind of reductionism I consider merely a linguistic trick, where a word to describe mental processes is simply applied to a physical object. Then, we might just as well say that computers feel. We may or may not subscribe to dualism, but, at any rate, this kind of reductionism has been far away from psychoanalysis.

Freud's structural theory

Freud said that the id would do anything for pleasure. It is not concerned with morals, or with survival in the real external world. Any pleasurable phantasy could make it act, and so drive it to destruction. In contrast to the id, the ego considers the outcome of an act in realistic and self-centred terms: "how do I benefit if I do such and such?" It means that the ego is an amoral agent. Not immoral, it is not against morality, but thinks in different terms. It sees reality in space–time, and its function is to make sure that I find a place in the world at any given time. The ego follows not moral-ity, but *the principle of survival of the individual*. It also relates to the id by finding ways to satisfy its pleasure by acts which derive the most benefit, or, at any rate, cause the least damage to the person. In other words, the ego tries everything to get away with whatever it can.

On the moral side we have the superego: when the baby "steps out of the cradle" he finds himself in a complex social world and needs guidance to get along in it. He does not know what a cup is for, or how to speak, and the famous potty is a com-pletely alien object. The child has to be told, and taught with skill and patience. He will take into himself, internalize, his parents and guardians, and keep their representations in a special place. The group of these introjects is called the superego, which endures, giving instructions all the time. It will give love when the child has been "good", and it will punish when "bad acts" are per-formed. In Freudian terms, conscience is the ego's relationship to the superego, and a feeling of guilt means fear of punishment. The ego tries to get away with what it can, and the superego dictates the limits.

Nos, the genuinely social function

Adding a genuine social function to the structure of personality makes a fundamental difference. The idea of two basic instincts emerged in the 1960s: the old one initiates self-centred acts and the new one makes us belong. The former has been attributed to Darwin, and makes us experience reality from a personal point of view, and, as we grow up, the personal ego develops from it. With the help of the recently discovered social instinct, we can complete the psychoanalytic structural theory of the mind by adding a genuine social function that develops from an inherited biological base. It enables us to experience reality from a social viewpoint, as we share, do things together, and belong to various groups. We might call such a genuine social function "nos", Latin for "we". Both the ego and nos begin to develop after we are born. The baby observers (Stern, 1973) discovered that we display social responses from the beginning of life. The new personality structure comprises the id, ego, and nos. The superego remains as a part of the ego, and a bridge towards nos, because parents teach us civilization, the content of society, but its basically dictatorial role is reduced by the genuine social function. Now we can clearly state what Freud (1923b) could not, that development of the ego is possible only if, at the same time, a social function, nos, is developing that provides the human context necessary for ego development.

When psychoanalysis was enriched by object relations theories, it began to move in the direction of discovering nos. Many contributors retained an instinct theory, and at the same time emphasis shifted on to the area of relating to others. Nowadays, we understand the baby in its relationship to mother. Winnicott's dictum is well known: "there is no baby, only a baby–mother unit". But with the object relations theories, a conflict appeared: on the one hand it seems that the baby relates to satisfy a selfish instinct, on the other hand relationship becomes an aim in itself. How can we resolve this conflict, if only a self-centred instinct is known, and the ego that develops from it? We come across the difficulty in a direct way when we try to understand what Racker (1968) called "concordant transference". He attempted to explain empathy as an ego function. It is essential that, in empathy, we share somebody's mental state, but the ego does not share, mutuality cannot be an ego function.

The ego makes it clear what is mine and what is yours. It distinguishes between individuals. Stern's (1973) "affective resonance" became stuck in the same way. Money-Kyrle (1956) talked about "normalizing transference" and suggested that quick introjective and projective processes would oscillate, and somehow result in the ego experiencing sharing. This sounds a clever trick to me. Undoubtedly, a large part of our mind is shared by others, but how is that possible? Clearly, it cannot be explained with a self-centred instinct and the ego that grows from it. Some object relations people tried to avoid the problem by abandoning the instinct theory, but then their thinking became inconsistent, because it lacked the foundations Freud considered necessary: an instinct theory to ensure that our picture of a human being includes the body and its evolutionary roots. For example, Fairbairn (1952) risked such inconsistency.

Foulkes (1975) writes,

> In a planned book on theory, I hope to deal with what I believe to be the limitation of the so called *inner-object theory* as against the *theory of interacting processes, and interacting unconscious communications* which I propose. [p. 16]

Foulkes never managed to write his book on theory, but by 1975 the social instinct was scientifically demonstrated by biology. Much earlier, Foulkes (Foulkes & Anthony, 1957) had already speculated about a social instinct:

> Man is primarily a social being, a particle of the group. The apparent possibility for him to live as an isolated "individual" is the result of later, more complex developments. The assumption of a "social instinct" inside this individual could be looked upon as an example of Freud's concept of the "conservative" nature of instincts, in the sense that their "aim" is to restore a previous state of affairs. [p. 234]

At the present time we are beginning to have more knowledge of biological processes, based on what we are born with, mainly in the brain, that obviously play an important role in mental activity. The problems are enormous. The human brain is made up of over 100 billon neurons, and each neuron has synaptic connections with other neurons ranging in number from a few hundred to tens of thousands. All this complexity is compressed into an area smaller than a football. It is difficult to intrude with electrons without causing damage or even death to the person.

Neuro-biology and nos

The brain is not a computer, but there are some similarities between them. A mass of electronic impulses circulate in a computer, and a mass of neuron impulses circulate in the brain. We can use a computer for making calculations, and the brain also calculates. We use our brain to tell that two plus two makes four.

When we produce a picture on the monitor, the computer selects a few of the many thousands of impulses it needs for output. The human brain is able to do something similar in order to sift through a vast mass of sensory data and present us with, on a second to second basis, what may appear on the "monitor" of our consciousness. We enjoy the thought that our consciousness is boundless and has endless capacity. In fact, consciousness is more like a searchlight in a dark room. It is now clearly demonstrated that the bandwidth of consciousness is less than forty bits per second, contrasted with some eleven million bits per second of sensory data delivered to the brain. Consciousness might be in endless motion, darting hither and thither, turning attention to different aspects of our awareness, but cannot, however, cover very much at any given time. Most of our mental content remains unconscious at all times.

In *The Interpretation of Dreams* Freud (1900a) describes the unconscious as

> the true psychic reality; in its innermost nature it is as much unknown to us as the reality of the external world, and it is as incompletely presented to us by the data of consciousness as is the external world by the communication of our sense organs. [p. 681]

Some people try to simplify Freud and say that what Freud calls unconscious is the repressed part of our mind. In the above quotation he writes about reality that is unknowable because we do not have the means to be conscious of it, and not simply because it would be repressed.

To my knowledge, Spinoza was the first philosopher who presented us with a model of the world where most of it is unconscious to us. He said that the real world has an infinite number of attributes, but we human beings are able to sense only two of them. (He thought they were mind and extention.) If this is true, then, as a matter of principle, most of what goes on remains unconscious for us forever. Kant said something similar later on.

Most cognitive scientists maintain today that consciousness plays a small part in our mental life: most of it is unconscious (Bargh & Chartrand, 1999). This is an important change in the direction of psychoanalysis. Brain-damaged patients helped us to reach such conclusions, because we cannot experiment with human beings, but when a damaged part of the brain stops functioning, we observe the change in mental output that results.

Bargh and Chartrand also observed that 95% of our behaviour is determined by unconscious mental activity, and we are responsible only for 5% of it. Thereafter, it became important to discover parts of the brain that are needed for consciousness. Consciousness is the product of nos; we create it together, and continue working on it, developing it together. Society provides the means for that work: for example, language, literature, science, the media. On the part of the body, inborn biological potentials determine the shape of our consciousness.

Modern biology distinguishes between "state" and "content" of consciousness. Mental state is studied, for example, in connection with amnesia: it is found that we may be conscious or awake to various degrees. We find the same in the various dream states. Consciousness is lost by those who suffer injury to the brainstem, a small part of the brain, in the back of the skull, that connects to the spinal cord. It has been discovered that stimuli coming from the brainstem, and not specific stimuli, influence our state of consciousness from the inside. When interpreting a dream, we find meaning by making it public, by bringing it out into the common nos. The same part of the brain is connected to the abdomen. Mental state is the result of the activating system of the brainstem that also checks the internal state of the body. With its help, we are continuously informed about how we feel, the affective state of the "I". Damasio (1999a) maintains that the "content" of consciousness, on the other hand, is determined by the posterior cortical channels that are governed by the external world. So, the content of consciousness is determined by the social world we all live in and arrange our social relationships in—the world of nos.

Damasio (1999b) came to the conclusion that the two components of consciousness that control the external and internal worlds also connect the two, the external object with the self, the external moment with the internal moment. The conscious momentary time units are most probably excited by the forty hertz per minute rhythmic oscillations of the brain. The feeling of what is happening is generated this way, because our impulses are ordered according to time. In our consciousness, the feelings, the evaluation of what is happening around us, are projected out. The internal world is projected on to the external world. The importance of projection is well known in the psychoanalytic picture of human beings. We may note the biological proof of the distinction between the external and the internal world. We have talked about these two worlds as external and internal, and although there have been critics of the above distinction, biology has demonstrated its reality.

The kind of consciousness discussed here is called core consciousness by Damasio (1999a). He writes, " I think we can say that Freud's observations about the nature of consciousness coincide with the most advanced neurological views of our age" (p. 38).

Core consciousness is also called simple, or primary, consciousness and constitutes the first level of consciousness, where we are conscious, but we do not reflect. There is also reflective, or secondary, consciousness that is consciousness of consciousness, when I do not only know what I feel or know, but also reflectively know that I feel it or know it. Thinking about understanding belongs here, and so does the application of images in the process of thinking. Secondary consciousness is determined by the cortex, the new brain, and mainly by the associative cortex, the language zones of the left hemisphere, and the prefrontal lobe, which is most developed in humans. Language, the product of social life, belongs here, so reflective consciousness is nos, and a large part of these biological processes is unconscious. This is the area where we give meaning to the internal representations of the external world according to social norms, where we may observe the past, judge the possible future, where we live not only in the present moment. Reflective consciousness is called narcissistic consciousness by Freud, because we relate to ourselves in it. As long as reflective consciousness helps our object relations, it is healthy, but when too much energy is bound up in it, at the expense of object relating, we call it pathological narcissism. It might be of some use if neurologists examined the quantitative relationship between the associative cortex and primary consciousness.

Mirror neurons

The recently discovered mirror neurons (Iacoboni, 2008) are of particular importance to the social side of our personality. They provide a biological foundation to the group analytic function of mirroring. Nava (2007) refers to Decety and Jackson (2004), who state that empathy is an innate ability, in other words, determined by a social instinct, and it is also a communicational skill, as it has to develop in the group. Their starting point agrees with my concept of nos. They consider three components of empathy in human beings:

1. Perception–action liason. In group analysis we talk about affective sharing between self and others, based on shared perception
2. Conscience. In group analysis we call it sense of belonging between self and other
3. Mental flexibility. In group analysis we call it matrix, which enables self to perceive itself in the place of the other

Knoblich and Flash (2003) observed that perception of the other's way of relating automatically activates the representation of that way of relating in the self.

Studies of monkeys have demonstrated the presence of mirror neurons that discharge in the same mode when relating to another individual, or when other individuals relating are observed (Rizzolatti, Fadiga, Fogassi, & Gallese, 1999). Studies of functional neuro-imaging in human beings demonstrate that the neural circuits involved in relating to another overlap those that are activated in the perception of the same kind of relating (Blackmore & Decety, 2001). This neuronal network is complex; it involves the pre-motor cortex, the parietal lobe, the supplementary motor area, and the cerebellum. With the help of mirroring neurons, we experience ourselves reflected by our environment. The baby will see itself reflected in mother's eyes, in the Winnicottian baby–mother unit. Up to the nineteenth century, we were surrounded by animals. We travelled on horseback, the cart was drawn by ox, etc. In such an environment we experienced our animal nature reflected. We find evidence for it in the arts of the age, where passion and strong feelings provided the dynamics. In the present times, we are surrounded by machines, and as a result we increasingly see ourselves as machines. The scientific picture of human beings and modern arts are clear evidence. And, interestingly enough, long before the discovery of mirror neurons, Plato (1997) wrote in the Alcibiades that the best mirror for a human being is another human being. Mirror neurons perform their reflective function by firing when we act, and firing also when we observe or experience action similar to our own. A similar act is not an identical act: similarity means the same type. When I perform a helpful act, the mirroring neuron fires; when I observe or experience a helpful act, the mirroring neuron fires again, as a kind of recognition of the same kind of act, the same type of act. It means that mirror neurons operate on the social level, where we classify acts according to social types, such as good acts, fearful acts, funny acts, etc.

New structural theory

For reasons mentioned above, many people insist that we do need an instinct theory; however, as long as we stick to the old one and to a structure of id–ego–superego, we cannot understand the social nature of man. Relationship, as an aim in itself, cannot be explained with those ideas. We can only repeat what Freud already said about the connection between the id and the ego, and that we relate for self-centred reasons only. The contradiction is resolved if we recognize the social instinct, and what follows from it: development of a social function of the personality. Then we do not overload the ego with what is not its job, such as the Kleinian sense of guilt, which is not a fear of punishment, but is about the pain the baby feels when it discovers that it has been hurting the same breast that gave him love. Such guilt can only be explained with a feeling of togetherness. Only nos can provide an understanding here, because participation and togetherness are social feelings. I find it interesting that the Kleinians emphasize the baby's responsibility in this mutual reality. They say that the baby creates the good or bad breast, while Winnicott (1964) points to the mother, saying that she creates the good or bad situations. With the help of nos, we can see that mother and baby together create the reality they both participate in, because in nos we experience our relationship as a complete whole. When we look at the baby as a genuine social being, it becomes clear that with my envy I am damaging not just my reality, but I harm *our* reality, which includes everybody who participates in it. Similarly, with my gratitude, I enrich not just my inner world, but the world we all share.

Illusion is a combination of phantasy and reality, and nos develops in such a world, as the child understands, by and by, that he exists as a part of social reality, as a part of some bigger whole.

During the years of learning to become social, the child needs the guidance of the superego; while he does not understand, he needs to be told. But as he grows up and the social side of his personality develops, the superego takes a back seat. The socializing process is accompanied by a feeling of renunciation that comes with anxiety, because we lose the security of the superego, the dictator who told us how things were, and what to do in various situations. Classical psychoanalysis got as far as replacing the cruel dictator with a benign one in the transference, but it is not enough for growing up. As Ferenczi (1933) wrote:

> Parents and adults, in the same way as we analysts, ought to learn to be constantly aware that behind the submissiveness or even the adoration, just as behind the transference of love, of our children, patients and pupils, there lies hidden an ardent desire to get rid of this oppressive love. [p. 164]

A grown-up person is master of himself, and says, "I am going to decide what I want to do." We need nos for that sort of development, because it enables us to understand our various social relationships: for example, at our work place, or in the family, or in any group. Once we get over the anxiety caused by the vanishing role of the superego, we experience great relief, because the superego carries many problems. When we internalize our parents and guardians, we also take in their personalities, mental problems, and social misunderstandings, which are the source of many neuroses. If we care to develop our nos, we shall manage our social life much better than our parents ever did. With consciousness of nos, we understand that co-operation and our existence in the community is to the advantage of all of us. Such recognition fills us with the joy of liberation, while a lack of co-operation makes us feel empty and alienated—in other words, *social guilt*. The fulfilled joy, or the guilt of nos, is different from the personal satisfaction or fear of punishment of the ego. Belonging to the family and the various social groups gives us a positive experience in nos. It tells us that *we are all in one*: of course, not in the space–time meaning of the word, but in a social sense. The "oppressive love" of the superego is replaced by the liberating love of nos.

It is important to point out that the superego will never disappear, because nobody ever grows up completely, and, in as much as we remain children, we retain the personality structure of the child. But the direction of psychic development is dictated by the social function of nos.

Our parents are our source of love in childhood. As we grow up, we necessarily distance ourselves from them. Object relations theories tell us that we have to internalize our parents and thus carry that source of love inside. Indeed, the ego is capable of much internalization, but it can only do some of the job of holding on to love. If we try to find all our love in internalized love objects, we overload the ego and create a narcissistic culture. Much of the love we have is provided by us, as we love each other, not in an internalized world, but in the real social world. The Buddha said, "Love each other, because you do not have your mother and your father any more to love you."

Trying to understand human relationships, Freud had to explain them with the ego. He had to say that when I relate to any object, I relate to its internal representation. I cathect internal representations, I displace one internal representation with another, and so on. If we try to understand how we relate by using a theory based on the ego, we cannot understand how we get from internal representation into the social world. If we only have the ego, we can never get out. The problem deepened later on with object relations theories, because this put the emphasis on relating, but as they only have the ego, they are stuck with inner objects. On the other hand, if we are concerned only with the external social world, we never get in, and that is the problem with socio-therapy. Both the ego and nos are needed if we want a more complete structural theory to explain human relationships.

Social unconscious and nos

We need to clarify the various uses of language when we try to understand our relationships: for example, how we talk about the physical world, the psychic world, and the social world.

As in Freudian psychology we say that the superego is partly conscious, and partly unconscious; with the use of nos we can find a place for the social conscious and the social unconscious. Nos is identical with what we call the social side of life, and with the new theory the social becomes a component of the structural theory of psychoanalysis and it is based on an instinct theory. Sociology is concerned with the social conscious, but the social unconscious also has an extended literature by now. Foulkes and Anthony (1957) used the term, Pines (1983), Hopper (1997, 2001) and Dalal (1998), among others, have written on the subject. It is interesting to note that much earlier Ferenczi (1913) thought about a group mind by considering some of its unconscious components:

> So important an increase in our knowledge of the individual mind could not leave the conception of the manifestations of the group-mind untouched. Freud and his students very soon took the products of the popular mind, above all the myths and fairy tales, as objects for research, and made it clear that in their very allegorical and symbolical manifestations repressed human instincts are demonstrable as they are in the symptoms of hysterics, and in the dreams of healthy people. [p. 428]

Ferenczi refers to certain components in the above, and Hopper (2001) emphasized that the social unconscious includes not only repressions, but everything else that makes up our social relationships. Group analytic psychotherapies are particularly useful for the development of nos because, as Foulkes (1964) pointed out, the full matrix of social relationships becomes accessible in them.

Let us refer back yet again to Freud's instinct theory. He said that an instinct had three components: source, object, and aim. The source is always some biological need, for example, hunger, that releases some energy. The object is what the person relates to in order to satisfy the need, for example, food or mother. The aim is the forward-looking part of the instinct: it is pointing towards the object, and comprises what I have to do to satisfy the need. The aim appears on two levels: on a general level, the aim of an instinct is satisfaction, but there is always a special aim, that which has to be done by the person in the circumstances, to eat if hungry, etc. The instinct is capable of all that, which made Hartman (1964) say that instincts were not irrational, but I would add that they have their own logic. I echo Pascal, who said that the heart had its own reasons. I find it remarkable that the sociologists studied society also from the point of view of source, object, and aim, but they did not make it explicit, and there has been no reference to Freud's instinct theory.

If we examine the various institutions of the social structure, whether it be the family, the police, industry, or education, we find that each has a social function, they satisfy some social need. Such a need is the source. The objects are specific, created, or in some other ways related to, by the institutions. They may be physical objects, for example, industry has many of them, or they may be abstractions, such as the various objects of education. The aims are also specific according to each function, but behind those there is a more general aim, which is more difficult to define, pointing towards forces even bigger than society. Such general forces often contain mystical elements. Some sociologists, like Durkheim (1912), or Max Weber (1920), regarded religion as the general aim of society. Marx thought that beyond the human forces there were natural ones that can be known by human beings. But even he had the idea that behind it all there is historical necessity with its "mystical" depth; of course, he would not have used that adjective. It seems that even social strivings towards the most abstract spiritual aims originate from biological instincts. The connection between sociology and biology appeared in various forms. Spencer (1876) found many similarities, and applied evolutionary logic in his social outlook. Later on, such similarities became more complex: for Lévi-Strauss they became formally structural, which means that society might resemble the human body in its structure, but such resemblance is only formal, because the two are not identical. They all agree that the various social forces and processes are only partially conscious to the human being, so there is a social field where we interact, whether we know it or not, whether we want it or not, because we are all parts of human society. This reality is constituted by nos, where people live their lives. Nos connects individuals, in so far as it develops out of instincts individuals are born with. So far, we can talk about my nos, your nos, etc. But those individual manifestations form one nos, and we all relate in it. This is *participation*. The ego cannot do it, it cannot even understand it, as it is not the ego's job to do so; on the contrary, the ego separates us and ensures that each of us is one person in the community.

We may look at a person from both sides, and, depending on our viewpoint, we get a different picture. On the side of the ego we find the person as the personal self, which is private. Classical psychoanalysis has furnished us with such a viewpoint. If we look at a person from the side of nos, as it is discussed here, we find the social self, as a member of its community. Social images of the self come about when the person recognizes himself or herself in the various social formations, as in so many mirrors. As history went by, the individual dimly recognized that he belonged to various groups: the family, a tribe, humanity, living beings, the universe. It gradually became clear that he was a social being who needs a communal life and knowledge of how to relate. Earlier forms of conscious nos might not appear conscious to a person of our times. Let us remember that we are conscious with the ideas of the age we live in, and mythology is also a form of consciousness, in as much as people of the classical age used it to talk about social facts and forces with an experience of recognition.

The conscious side of our social life is gradually unfolding in our every day life, but most of our social life has been unconscious. I do not think of the social unconscious as a giant ghost floating over us. We are all one in the life of society and the various groups. That unity does not have a body, but it is real, and, in as much as we do not know, it happens unconsciously. Erös (1993), a Hungarian sociologist, uses the idea of social representation, based on the work of Muscovici, a social psychologist, to explain something similar:

> It is based on thoughts, expressions and explanations that come about in personal communications of our everyday life and people learn them from each other. I may not remember anything of Hungarian history as a matter of fact, but if I am in possession of the social representation that says: "the Hungarian people always heroically fought for freedom" or: "the foreign invaders are responsible for everything bad", then I can participate in various discussions even if I did not live in those times referred to by the social representations. Precisely those social representations enable me to join various social formations and processes. [p. 226]

Freud talked about different kinds of unconscious. As most of what we know is unconscious at any given time, there is an unconscious that is readily called into consciousness if we wish. Sometimes, when Freud writes about the preconscious, he seems to mean something like that, yet, he says that the repressing force itself, which keeps the repressed part of the mind unconscious, is also in the preconscious, although it is not easy to make that force conscious. The repressed is often called unconscious proper, or just unconscious in psychoanalysis. But we have already seen that sometimes Freud used the word unconscious to refer to the real world we cannot know. The social unconscious belongs to a special category. Nos is the social reality we live in. We create it together by contributing our own bit to it in our social life. This reality is not the material kind, but equally real and effective. I am a member of my family, the same family my brother is a member of, and so are my parents. We made that family together; it would not exist without us. I say this family is *my family*, my brother says it is *his family*. At the same time, it is *our family*. This is nos and participation. We find such relationships if we look at how the parts form a whole. Wittgenstein (1967) generally called it "family relationship". From the ego's point of view it seems contradictory that I say it is mine, my brother says it is his, at the same time it is ours, and our parents' as well. The ego would find it difficult to understand. But we grew up in families, so we know that there is no contradiction here: it is belonging. My nos is, at the same time, my brother's nos, and also our nos. The ego protests, because its job is to distinguish between us, it makes the point that what is mine is not yours, and vice versa. I think we need both to understand human reality. My ego is only mine, but my nos is also our nos. The various institutions of the social structure are all so many forms of nos, and provide so many social mirrors for people who participate in them. The various kinds of social consciousness intertwine, because the same individual belongs to many social institutions. Thus, the same person appears many times in the various social mirrors. Mead (1956), the American pragmatist and social scientist, would say that a person has many social selves. I would put it slightly differently by saying that a person has many social self-images.

Foulkes (1964) said that we cannot look at a person's associations or dreams in the group as purely individual manifestations. Everything that happens in a group is done by individuals, but the same act is also a group expression. Following his thought, we can say that when we study people's individual behaviour and their social behaviour we do not observe two separate events. Relating has two sides. The very same relationship is individual on one side, and social on the other. When I buy a piece of meat, I buy it, because I am hungry. That happens on the ego side. But, at the same time, I buy meat, and a vegetarian would not; I buy it for lunch, because in our society we have lunch; I buy it for money instead of hunting it, because in our society we have distribution of labour that determines my behaviour that way. All that happens on the side of nos. I like to have lunch that way, because others do it also, and I feel I participate in a social activity. I need that feeling. On the side of the ego, I make a choice with pride, but it usually happens within a typical social situation that is given and determines my individual freedom. If I always had to behave differently from everybody else, I would go mad. There are some who try, and they do go mad, like the schizophrenics. They cannot belong to a community. Their ego is weak and fragmented, therefore it cannot protect their identity; as a result, their nos pulls them into the group with such a force that they fear annihilation. Then they desperately try to declare their identity by performing bizarre acts.

Why did sociologists not make use of instinct theories? Probably because until the 1960s biology provided us only with "selfish" instincts, and from such a viewpoint society is, at best, a necessary evil. Such instinct theories did not help the sociologist. Those who talked, nevertheless, about instinctive action did it on speculative grounds, because they had no scientific backing. It is the business of biology to justify the use of an instinct or drive. In the 1960s, the social instinct was scientifically justified by biology. From then on it became obvious that it is a biological need of human beings to live together in society. In other words, our biological structure predetermines us to create civilizations, social structures, and culture, and that every individual finds its place in that common structure. With the unity of the ego and nos, human beings do not shrink into isolated egos in psychoanalysis, and they become creatures of flesh and blood in sociology.

The ego ideal

Freud, in *Group Psychology and the Analysis of the Ego* (1921c) contributed significantly to the understanding of the group at the time, and also found a place for the group in the system of psychoanalysis, demonstrating that development of the ego demanded a web of human relationships. He wrote that the individual, entering the group, loses identity and dissolves in the mass, but, with the help of the ego-ideal, identity is regained as a more social being.

This idea of Freud's provided a new picture of the group at the time. According to him, the individual discovers or rediscovers identity in the group. I would like to point out that the expression "das Ich" has a double meaning for Freud, as is discussed by Bettelheim (1980). Sometimes it means what later on was defined as the ego, at other times it seems to mean the self. In the *Standard Edition*, Strachey and his collaborators achieved a consistent usage of words, but, at the same time, by uniformly translating "das Ich" into "ego", they managed to produce a text clearer than the original. As it happens, Freud defined the ego as the function creating the experience of reality, carrying its images, and providing the defences in it, only around 1921. Therefore, in his writings after that time, "das Ich" can be consistently translated into "ego", but in his earlier texts it is not clear what Freud means by it. When he writes about somebody discovering or rediscovering himself, the meaning is obviously "self". Such ambiguity, present in the original, gets lost if "das Ich" is uniformly translated into "ego".

The ego ideal provides us with something to share and aim for together; we can unite around it, and have a purpose in life. But Freud was unable to place the ego ideal into some structure. The ego ideal is a type, "it is larger than life", as we say, meaning that it is not an individual. It is also a type that can be shared by many individuals. Therefore, it cannot be in somebody's ego. It has to be somewhere not in the ego, but where many egos have access to it. Now, with the discovery of nos, we have the agent needed for social types. Such shared images require a shared function where they can be "found". I am talking metaphorically here, because social types are not objects, neither are they inner objects of some ego. They are objects in nos, and we can call them social objects of nos to distinguish them from inner objects of the ego. They are often forward looking, and show us something desirable that we might achieve if we get together.

With the help of nos, our understanding of history changes as well. We have already indicated that individual psychoanalytic work tends to move towards group analysis by the introduction of social factors, as is discussed by Hopper (1995, 2001). At the same time, we can apply psychoanalytic concepts to the understanding of historical processes, provided we do not do it mechanically, but we reconsider their use every time. Harmatta and Ormay (2000) write about historical regression:

> Sudden historical changes cause anxiety on social level. Nos defends against it by a characteristic regression that works similarly to the mechanism of the ego, and takes us back to social fixation points that contained similar problems in the past. [p. 85]

Such defence of nos is called social regression. At first, attempts are made to go forward, but, if society is not ready, regression results. Retro movement is made along two different time axes. On the one hand there is a return to historical past, on the other hand, withdrawal occurs into more primitive psychic layers. History provides us with examples of the first kind, and the other is organized as Bion (1970) described it with his basic assumptions: dependence, fight/flight, pairing. To these Hopper (1997) provided a fourth basic assumption: massification–aggregation.

The applied method of thinking is not a deficiency theory, or a conflict theory, but, rather, a growth theory. It presupposes some teleology in history, some development from the simple towards the complex. Thus, we provide the important thought that there is not only survival in history, but a systematic movement, partly conscious, partly unconscious, towards some well- or ill-selected social ideal. Naturally, in such a process, we find deficiency as well as conflict. In traumatic times we are unable to go forward, we look for ego ideals in the past, when we did achieve something, when we had something to be proud of.

The history of the twentieth century provides us with many examples of sudden change. For example, we have the collapse of the Austro-Hungarian Empire, then the decline of the British and the French Empires, and the growing German Empire under the Kaiser, without any permanent solution. In each case, we can observe the denial of the historical change that caused the trauma. It takes national thinking back to the times of a golden age of the Empire. In Nazi Germany, a return to pagan values, an enormous historical regression, goes back to a Teutonic past, and, psychologically, they reached the basic assumption of dependence, where idealized and omnipotent leaders are sought. Nazi Germany shows that ego ideals can be dangerous as well as useful. The Teutonic warlord became their ego ideal, splitting, discriminating, and ready to kill everyone who did not fit into its plan.

The question arises, what determines whether we have positive or negative ego ideals? A simple answer would be that more or less healthy societies have positive ego ideals, and sick societies have negative ego ideals. Now we have to decide what is a healthy society, and what is a sick one independently from looking at their ego ideals, otherwise we go around in a circle. I think nos as developing common agent may lead us towards an answer.

References

Bargh, J. A., & Chartrand, T. L. (1999). The unbearable automaticity of being. *American Psychologist*, 54: 462–479.

Bettelheim, B. (1980). *Some Comments on Privacy in: Surviving and Other Essays*. New York: Vintage Books.

Bion, W. R. (1970). *Experiences in Groups*. London: Tavistock.

Blackmore, S. J., & Decety, J. (2001). From the perception of action to the understanding of intention. *Nature Reviews Neuroscience, 2*: 561–567.

Dalal, F. (1998). *Taking the Group Seriously*. London: Jessica Kingsley.

Damasio, A. (1999a). Commentary on Panksepp. *Neuro-Psychoanalysis, 1*: 38–39.

Damasio, A. (1999b). *The Feeling of What Happens*. London: Heinemann.

Decety, J., & Jackson, P. (2004). The functional architechture of human empathy. *Behavioural and Functional Neurosciences Reviews, 3*(2): 71–100.

Durkheim, E. (1912). *Les Formes Élementaires de la Vie Religieuse*. Paris: Alcan.

Erös, F. (1993). *A válság szociálpszichológiája*. Budapest: T-Twins Kiadó.

Fairbairn, W. R. (1952). *Psychoanalytic Studies of the Personality*. London: Routledge and Kegan Paul.

Ferenczi, S. (1913). Stages in the development of the sense of reality. In: *First Contributions to Psycho-Analysis*. London: Maresfield Reprints, 1980.

Ferenczi, S. (1933). Confusion of tongues between adults and children. In: *Final Contributions*. London: Maresfield Reprints, 1980.

Foulkes, S. H. (1964). *Theraputic Group-Analysis*. London: G. Allen and Unwin.

Foulkes, S. H. (1975). *Group Analytic Psychotherapy*. London: Gordon and Breach.

Foulkes, S. H., & Anthony, E. J. (1957). *Group Psychotherapy, The Psychoanalytic Approach*. Harmondsworth: Penguin.

Freud, S. (1900a). *The Interpretation of Dreams*. S.E., 4–5. London: Hogarth.

Freud, S. (1921c). *Group Psychology and the Analysis of the Ego*. S.E., 18: 67–143. London: Hogarth.

Freud, S. (1923b). *The Ego and the Id*. S.E., 19: 3–66. London: Hogarth.

Harmatta, J., & Ormay, T. (2000). A történelmi regresszió. *Pszichoterápia, IX*: 85–92.

Hartman, H. (1964). *Essays on Ego Psychology*. New York: International Universities Press.

Hopper, E. (1995). The social unconscious in clinical work. *Group, 1955*: 216–241.

Hopper, E. (1997). Traumatic experience in the unconscious life of the group. The fourth basic assumption. *Group Analysis, 30*: 439–470.

Hopper, E. (2001). The social unconscious: theoretical considerations. *Group Analysis, 34*: 9–28.

Iacoboni, M. (2008). *Mirroring People*. New York: Farrar Strauss and Giroux.

Knoblich, G., & Flash, R. (2003). Action identity. evidence from self recognition, perception and coordination. *Consciousness and Cognition, 12*: 620–632.

Mead, G. H. (1956). *The Social Psychology of George Herbert Mead*. Chicago, IL: Anselm Strauss.

Money-Kyrle, R. E. (1956). Normal countertransference and some of its derivations. *International Journal of Psychoanalysis, 37*: 360–366.

Nava, A. S. (2007). Empathy in group analysis: an integrative approach. *Group Analysis, March*: 13–28.

Pines, M. (1983). The group analytic view of culture and civilization. *Group Analysis, XVI*(2): 145–151.

Plato (1997). *Collected Works*. Indianapolis, IN: Hackett.

Rizzolatti, G., Fadiga, L., Fogassi, L., & Gallese, V. (1999). Resonance, behaviours and mirror neurons. *Archives Italiennes de Biologie, 137*: 88–99.

Racker, H. (1968). *Transference and Countertransference*. London: Karnac.

Spencer, H. (1876). *Principles of Sociology*. London: Allen and Unwin.

Stern, D. N. (1973). *The Interpersonal World of the Infant*. New York: Basic Books.

Weber, M. (1920). *A protestáns etika és a kapitalizmus szelleme*. Budapest: Gondolat, 1982.

Winnicott, D. W. (1964). *The Child, the Family, and the Outside World*. Harmondsworth: Penguin.

Wittgenstein, L. (1967). *Philosophical Investigations*. Oxford: Basil Blackwell.

CHAPTER FIVE

The group mind, systems-centred functional subgrouping, and interpersonal neurobiology*

Susan P. Gantt and Yvonne M. Agazarian

I n this chapter, we build a link between the emerging insights of interpersonal neurobiology and the systems-centred group method of functional subgrouping as a tool for developing the "group mind". We propose a definition of group mind that differs from the one formulated by Le Bon (1896), who emphasized crowd psychology, McDougall (1920), who focused on individuals thinking together, and Durkheim (1966), who emphasized the *collective* of the society as an organism. Instead, we propose a definition of "group mind" that builds on interpersonal neurobiology (IPNB) and systems-centred theory (SCT) and practice. Although this new definition is compatible with the group analytic emphasis on the mind as dependent on social and cultural life (Hopper, 2009), it introduces an important difference through linking the neurobiological findings with systems-centred functional subgrouping.

---

*This chapter is adapted from its original publication in the *International Journal of Group Psychotherapy*, 2010, 60(4), and is reprinted here with permission.

Interpersonal neurobiology

The past fifteen years have brought a new understanding of the brain and especially of experience-dependent neuroplasticity (Badenoch, 2008). Certain genetic potentials in the brain are now recognized as experience-dependent for activation (Kandel, 2006). A growing body of research has demonstrated that repeated neuron firings at synapses can increase the density of neural circuits and form new ones, validating Hebb's (1949) idea that repeated firings of one neuron followed by the firing of another strengthen this neuronal connection. For example: individuals who meditate have increased neural thickening in the middle prefrontal cortex and right insula areas of the brain, areas associated with attention, interoception, and sensory processing (Lazar et al., 2005); London cab drivers have larger hippocampal volume, an area of the brain related to spatial mapping (Terrazas & McNaughton, 2000); musicians have thickening in auditory areas of the cortex (Menning, Roberts, & Pantev, 2000); and both novel experience and exercise stimulate the formation of new stem cells (neurogenesis) in the hippocampus (Song, Stevens, & Gage, 2002).

The extraordinary proliferation in research on neuroplasticity has accelerated the focus on the relationship between the brain, the mind, and interpersonal relationships. Notably, Siegel (1999, 2006, 2007), Cozolino (2002, 2006), Schore (2003a,b), and Badenoch (2008) have linked brain functioning and interpersonal experience, an area of focus now called interpersonal neurobiology (IPNB).

Siegel (1999) proposed a definition of mind as an embodied and relational process that regulates the flow of energy and information which "develops at the interface of neurophysiological processes and interpersonal relationships" (Siegel, 1999, p. 21), and which "develops across the lifespan, as the genetically programmed maturation of the nervous system is shaped by ongoing experience" (Siegel, 2006, p. 249). These ideas emphasize the role of interpersonal relationships in brain development and their involvement in the ongoing plasticity of the brain. Siegel (1999, 2007) has highlighted the role of the middle prefrontal region (consisting of the anterior cingulate, orbitofrontal, medial, and ventral regions of the prefrontal cortex) in integrating information from the body, limbic region, and cortex. He has emphasized how crucial this integrative processing is in interpersonal relationships and attachment patterns. Focusing attention activates neuronal firing, which, with repetition, can lead to the development of new and sustained patterns of neuronal activation. Applying this research to psychotherapy, Siegel introduced the acronym, SNAG (stimulating neural activation and growth), or "snagging the brain", as an important conceptual and technical tool for psychotherapists. For example, activating the right-brain with sensory awareness exercises can be useful with avoidantly attached patients to stimulate neural connection between the right and left hemispheres (Siegel & Hartzell, 2003). Last, Siegel (2007) organized the research in terms of domains of neural integration, for example, cortical to subcortical (vertical integration), right to left (horizontal integration), and others that are important in mental health, proposing that effective psychotherapy can enhance these processes of neural integration.

Cozolino (2002, 2006) has also reviewed the brain research literature extensively and identified aspects of psychotherapy that maximize neural integration: (1) the therapeutic relationship makes the attachment circuits in the brain more modifiable; (2) moderate emotional arousal creates the kind of new experience that promotes neural plasticity; (3) neural activation enables a re-regulation between cognitive and emotional processing, including developing narratives that guide new behaviour.

Schore (2003a,b) has focused on mechanisms by which the therapeutic relationship can alter the neurobiological processes related to affect regulation, building on his seminal work in understanding how affective regulation patterns originally developed in the context of early attachment relationships. From his understanding of the neurobiology of early development of affect regulation structures in the brain, he has linked neurobiological research to the remediation of affect regulation structures in psychotherapy, emphasizing the importance of micro-second right-brain to right-brain communications between therapist and patient.

This interpersonal neurobiological perspective has utilized research on the brain to understand how psychotherapy helps to change the brain function and structure in the direction of greater neural integration, affect regulation, and more secure attachment (Badenoch, 2008). IPNB applies neuroscience research in excogitating how to deliberately enhance the impact of psychotherapeutic processes on neuroplasticity and neural integration.

Models of the brain

Although summarizing the research bases of interpersonal neurobiology is beyond the scope of this chapter, it is useful to describe basic models of brain function that are relevant for our discussion. One long-standing model divides the brain into three areas: brainstem, limbic, and cortex. The oldest region in terms of phylogeny is the brainstem, which manages the physiological state of the body, for example, heart rate, breathing, arousal. Next is the limbic area, the emotional–motivational centre in the brain, which includes the amygdala, hippocampus, and hypothalamus, among other structures. In new situations, the amygdala makes a rapid judgement about safety. This judgement then motivates action—to stay present and engage if there is safety, or to defend or flee if there is danger. The amygdala encodes these experiences as implicit memories. For the first 12–18 months of life, this is the only kind of memory available. Implicit memories are encoded as behavioural impulses, bodily sensations, emotions, perceptions, and, sometimes, fragmentary images. When activated, we experience these implicit memories as "the way it is" (Badenoch, 2009) in the present, rather than recalling it as a past experience. These implicit encodings form the basis of our "taken for granted" assumptions, perceptions, and beliefs about ourselves, our relationships, and our sense of how trustworthy the world is. Understanding this is especially important in group therapy, as implicit relational assumptions always influence members' relating without explicit awareness of that influence. At about 12–18 months, the hippocampus matures and explicit memory gradually develops. The hippocampus integrates implicit memories into a coherent memory with a timeframe. I can then know, "I was frightened yesterday", instead of feeling fearful with no context. Responding to the perception of safety or lack of safety, the hypothalamus and the pituitary control the neuroendocrine system, which prepares our body to remain in connection if safe, or fight, flee, or freeze if not safe. The limbic region adjoins the middle prefrontal region of the cortex, which, when integrated with the limbic, provides for emotional and relational regulation. The cortex, the outer layer of the brain, receives sensory information (occipital, parietal, and temporal lobes) and integrates it with information from the body and limbic areas into a fully formed experience.

Another perspective highlights the right and left hemispheres. Each lobe is considered a specialized processing system, with the left biased toward linguistic processing and the right toward emotional and bodily experiences (Cozolino, 2006). The right brain dominates early development (the first two years), and is strongly involved in stimuli appraisal, holistic and emotional understandings, and mapping body awareness. The right brain has stronger limbic connectivity, is more inward-looking, and more oriented to withdrawal. The left brain is more linear, logical, literal, and language-dominated (Siegel & Hartzell, 2003), and more outward toward the world, with an approach orientation.

Other research has generated models that describe integrated neural networks. IPNB has focused on the "social brain" (Cozolino, 2006) that includes both the limbic (amygdala, hippocampus, hypothalamus) and the middle prefrontal regions of the cortex, mostly in the right hemisphere (Badenoch, 2008) that work together in processing and integrating inner emotional and bodily experience and social information. The IPNB paradigm has also emphasized the importance of integrating the linguistic left hemisphere that creates meaningful narrative with the input from the holistic right hemisphere. Resonance circuitry includes the mirror neuron system (Iacoboni, 2007), the insula, superior temporal cortex, amygdala, and the middle prefrontal areas. Siegel (2006, 2007) has synthesized the research on the middle prefrontal area and identified nine functions that emerge as these circuits integrate with the limbic region: regulation of the body, attuned communications, regulation of emotion, response flexibility, empathy, insight, fear extinction, intuition, and morality. Importantly, he has recognized that the first seven of these functions correspond to the outcomes of secure attachment. This has led Siegel to emphasize fostering integration between the middle prefrontal cortex and the limbic regions in working with attachment issues in psychotherapy.

A theory of living human systems and systems-centred therapy

The idea of a "group mind" comes from thinking about a group as a living human system. A theory of living human systems (TLHS) and its systems-centred therapy (SCT) were developed by

Agazarian (1997). TLHS defines a hierarchy of isomorphic systems that are energy-organizing, goal-directed, and system-correcting.

Hierarchy defines a living human system as a set of three systems, where each exists in the context of the system above it and simultaneously is the context for the system below it in the hierarchy. Living human systems always exist in context, never in isolation. This hierarchy of interdependent systems organizes the flow of energy and information towards the goals of survival, development, and transformation. For example, a psychotherapy group can be conceptualized as a set of three systems, schematized as three concentric circles. The innermost circle is the person system, the source of energy for the hierarchy. In the middle circle, member systems, which emerge from the person system, organize to form transient subgroup systems. In turn, the group-as-a-whole, the outermost circle, emerges from the subgroup organizations of energy and information. Organization of energy and information in each system has an impact on the other systems in the hierarchy, and each system influences the development of the system above and below, and is simultaneously influenced by them.

The systems in a defined hierarchy are isomorphic (defined as similar in structure and function). Structure is defined as boundaries that open or close to the flow of energy/information. Living human systems function to discriminate and integrate information in the service of survival, development, and transformation. Thus, whatever one understands about the flow of energy/information in one system in the defined hierarchy of three will be useful in understanding the other systems. For example, with a psychotherapy group, understanding something about how the subgroups in a group are discriminating and integrating information informs us about the people, members, and the group-as-a-whole.

Defining the group mind

Mind, defined as an embodied and relational process that regulates the flow of energy and information (Siegel, 1999), is a characteristic of every living human system. Building on isomorphy, this process will function at all system levels in the hierarchy. Thus, we conceptualize the group mind as the interdependent processes within and between the person, member, subgroup, and group-as-a-whole that regulate the flow of energy and information within the system of the psychotherapy group.

Our version of group mind builds links between interpersonal neurobiology and group therapy. In this schema, the function of group psychotherapy is developing a group mind that provides an experiential context that regulates the flow of energy and information in which the minds and brains of its group members can develop. As members develop their minds (by discriminating and integrating information in the direction of increasing neural integration), more and more potential energy/information for the group mind is released. In turn, as people contribute more energy/information, this adds still more resources for developing the group mind, and, as the group mind develops, it again changes the brains and minds of group members. This recursive process supports the primary goal of every psychotherapy group.

In making this proposition, we are not excluding the potential for groups to become mind-numbing and closed-minded instead of mind-developing. For example, "group think" (Janis, 1972), social conformity (Asch, 1951), and obedience (Burger, 2009; Haney, Banks, & Zimbardo, 1973; Milgram, 1963) research all point to how group norms can dominate the individual. Berns (Berns et al., 2005) has replicated Asch's study using functional magnetic resonance imaging of the brain, and identified the "distortion" from social pressure as activating the parietal and occipital regions, which suggests that the social context actually impacts the neurophysiology of perceptions.

Clearly, group therapists must work explicitly to develop a group mind that not only potentiates problem-solving, but also creates experiences that develop the minds and brains of the group members. From an IPNB view, this means that we must consider how our groups do or do not create environments that increase the potential for neural integration. Maximizing neuroplasticity requires that we create an experiential group environment that provides a secure relational context, where moderate levels of emotion can be experienced with the containment that enables modulation and integration. This facilitates the integration and reintegration of cognitive and emotional elements of human experience that, in turn, increases access to the range of human experience and capacity for regulating one's experience with one's self and with others.

Functional subgrouping

Using this IPNB framework, we posit that the systems-centred method of functional subgrouping contributes to developing a group mind with the kinds of experiences that enhance neural integration: functional subgrouping contains emotional arousal and facilitates emotional modulation in the flow of energy/information, creates a secure relational context, and fosters a group mind that potentiates the integrative systems in brain function toward greater integration capability.

Functional subgrouping is a conflict resolution method implementing the theoretical idea that living human systems survive, develop, and transform through the process of discriminating and integrating differences, both the differences in the apparently similar and the similarities in the apparently different (Agazarian, 1997). Information is the energy of living human systems. However, as human beings, we react to information that is too different from what we know as though we are endangered (activation of the "fear" systems and sympathetic nervous system arousal), and we often close our minds to these differences. By organizing communications so that the reactions to differences in energy/information can be modulated and contained, functional subgrouping enables differences to be used in the service of the group's development.

For example, functional subgrouping interrupts typical group phase communication patterns that fixate group development by avoiding differences (flight phase) or attacking them (fight phase) (Agazarian & Gantt, 2003). In the flight phase, members often try to advise or help others, frequently creating the roles of "identified patient" and "helpers", as when a member describes being anxious while other group members speak up to reassure or sympathize or ask about the member's anxiety. In this communication pattern, the flow of energy/information is from "helpers" to "identified patient". Neither the information contained in the "helpers" nor the "identified patient" subsystems is explored. In the fight phase, group members typically refute differences with "yes, but's" and elect a scapegoat to contain the differences the group has not yet explored (Agazarian, 1997; Horwitz, 1983). Functional subgrouping interrupts these typical group phase patterns by changing the communication patterns. In the flight phase example, the subgroup of "helpers" explores together their impulse of "wanting to help" and in a separate subgroup, all those "wanting to be helped" explore their impulse.

Functional subgrouping interrupts these stereotyped group patterns by introducing an alternative communication pattern: training group members to ask, "Anyone else?" when they have finished with what they are saying. For example, Doris begins by saying, "I'm anxious. Anyone else?" The phrase "Anyone else?" lets others know Doris has finished *and* wants to be joined. Donna joins, saying she is anxious, too, and then builds by adding, "I am all fluttery, not knowing how this is going to go. Anyone else?" Members are trained to join and build with their similarity and resonance. In this way, functional subgrouping builds resonant subsystems as members join and explore together. In these subsystems of relative similarity, boundaries are more open and small differences more easily tolerated. Thus, without the sympathetic reactivity to differences that triggers survival roles at the expense of development, energy/information can be more easily discriminated and integrated and neural integration fostered.

As each subgroup works in turn, within their subgroup environment of comfortable similarity, members begin to notice and accept "just noticeable differences" in what was apparently similar. When a member introduces a difference that is "too" different from the working subgroup, the leader validates the importance of this difference, and asks the member to start a new subgroup when the working subgroup has finished its exploration. This enables exploration in the context of subgroups of similarity and resonance. For example, as mentioned earlier, a therapy group working in the flight phase would often have one subgroup exploring the impulse to help and "make things right", and the other exploring the wish to be helped and "taken care of". These subgroups contain and explore the human experiences of anxiety and dependency that are inevitable in early group life. This same process is applicable to the exploration of any human experience.

When a subgroup pauses and the group is ready for a difference, the "different" subgroup forms with members who resonate with this difference. In this example, once the anxious subgroup paused, the "excited" subgroup explored. And again, in the "excited" subgroup, members worked in resonance, enabling an openness to discovering "just noticeable differences" with each other within their similar experiences. In their shared resonance with activated mirror neurons and resonance circuits, the subgroup climate supports neural integration. Over time, group members discover similarities between what were initially two different subgroups (in this example, both discovered relief), and integration takes place in the group-as-a-whole.

Containing emotional arousal and facilitating emotional modulation in the flow of energy and information

Porges (1995, 1998, 2007) has identified three levels of autonomic nervous system circuits that operate hierarchically. These circuits activate differentially depending on "neuroception" of the level of safety or danger in a situation. The myelinated ventral vagal branch activates to neuroception of safety and is the highest and the only uniquely mammalian level of the three. This circuitry links the heart to the striated muscles in the face, and inhibits sympathetic activation of the heart. Porges calls this ventral vagal circuit the social engagement system, in that its activation orientes to facial expressions, vocalizations, and listening, which allows for interpersonal regulation and experiences of calm, relaxation, and openness. The middle level of autonomic activation involves the sympathetic branch and activates with perceived threat. Sympathetic activation prepares us for fight or flight and diminishes social engagement. The lowest level system, the unmyelinated dorsal vagal, takes over with severe threat and initiates a death-feigning, dissociating freeze response.

Creating groups that foster interpersonal neural integration then requires developing group contexts that are experienced as "safe-enough" to activate the social engagement circuits that support "brain to brain" neural modulation. Complexity theory introduced the idea of near-to- or far-from-equilibrium as descriptors of "systems function". To the extent that a system functions near-to-equilibrium, it approximates a closed system and approaches entropy. To the extent that a system functions far-from-equilibrium, it approaches chaos (Kossmann & Bullrich, 1997).

Functional subgrouping creates a "mid-from-equilibrium" condition (Gantt & Agazarian, 2004), activating the brain's social engagement system. "Mid-from-equilibrium" creates a stable-enough context for system containment while simultaneously introducing the conditions for system change through discriminating and integrating differences in an ongoing process of system development.

Right-brain processing is specialized towards bodily and emotional experience and biased towards negative or avoidance emotions, for example, there is a right-brain bias in anxiety disorders (Canli, Desmond, Zhao, Glover, & Gabrieli, 1998). The left hemisphere is biased toward positive or approach emotions (Cozolino, 2006).

Applying these perspectives, an "anxiety subgroup" is more typical of right-brain processing with sympathetic activation in response to neuroception of danger (often referred to as flight/fight). The left hemisphere orients to making meaning of the right-brain input. The anxiety is then "explained" by left-brain analysis ("this group will not work out for me and is not the right context for me"). The explanation itself creates additional anxiety.

SCT discriminates "explaining" from "exploring". "Explaining" is similar to what Siegel (2007) calls "top-down" thinking that maintains a "usual" view. "Explaining" generates familiarity that pre-empts attention to new or current experiences. In contrast, functional subgrouping supports exploration of the new. Joining on resonance and similarities activates the social engagement system. Moreover, functional subgrouping emphasizes looking at, talking to, and making eye contact with the members of one's subgroup. In the earlier example, as the "anxious" subgroup worked together, members felt relieved as they discovered others felt anxious, too. Thus, the social engagement system was activated in the subgrouping process, lowering the sympathetic mobilization to the "threat" of the new, or the "unknown", as SCT terms it, that is inevitable in every new group. Neuroception of safety activates the social engagement system, which deactivates the sympathetic mobilization to threat (Porges, 2007).

The considerable research on anxiety and the brain's "fear system" is also relevant (cf. LeDoux, 1996). Those brain subsystems that are most relevant for anxiety and fear are the amygdala, the orbital prefrontal cortex, and the sensory thalamus. The amygdala is located in the limbic system, the middle part of the brain involved in emotional processing. The amygdala is closely connected by neuronal pathways to both the vagal and sympathetic nervous systems, and potentially has strong connections to the prefrontal cortices. In many ways, our brains are primed to be alert for threat (Cozolino, 2006). A sensory "alarm" is relayed through the sensory thalamus that sends signals to both the amygdala and the cortex. The amygdala processes the sensory input and serves as the fast-track alarm system (Goleman, 1995). The cortex receives signals from the thalamus as well, but is a slower and more precise response system that discriminates details of the stimulus, makes a more accurate assessment of danger, and can then modulate the amygdala response (LeDoux, 1996). LeDoux gives an example of seeing a coiled object in the woods. The amygdala reaction is to run from the "snake", the cortex "collects" more data, recognizes a coiled vine, and then sends signals to the amygdala to relax. Depending on the integration in that moment between the prefrontal cortex and limbic regions, the amygdala's activation of an immediate fear response might or might not be inhibited by the slower cortical assessments. Research with post traumatic stress disorder (PTSD) patients (Shin et al., 2004, 2005) pointed to the interplay in the fear circuitry between an under-functioning orbital medial prefrontal cortex and an overactive firing in the amygdala. When the fast-track amygdala is highly sensitized by previous fearful experiences without enough cortical modulation, the result is the kind of chronic anxiety and fear seen in PTSD and generalized anxiety disorder (GAD) patients. In addition, the amygdala, with its fearful associations (including out-of-awareness implicit memories), can send ascendant alarm signals, which the left hemisphere organizes into fearful narratives at the expense of the cortex collecting data and modulating amygdala arousal.

In groups, differences that are "too" different are often experienced as threats. By teaching group members to deliberately join on similarities, members learn to shift their attention away from their "fast-track" responses to differences. Thus, functional subgrouping not only activates the social engagement system, but also supports cortical assessment and modulation. Once functional subgrouping is established, the "anxious" subgroup's task is to check the reality of their fears in the here-and-now. This next step in systems-centred groups is implemented by asking the subgroup members to talk together to identify the source of their anxiety: "Find out if your anxiety is coming from a thought, a feeling, or the edge of the unknown" (Agazarian, 1997). This kind of question stimulates cortical activity in the brain and group members learn to shift their attention away from the limbic/amygdala firing (middle brain), which further modulates their anxieties. Learning to shift one's attention de-escalates habitual fear priming.

Early in a group's development, members often identify their anxiety as coming from a thought, typically a negative prediction about the future. As Sally put it: "This group might not be good for me", a common negative prediction in new groups. Having identified the specific thoughts that are making them each anxious, subgroup members are asked to "turn on their researcher" to find out if they believe they can tell the future. This further engages cortical processes and continues restoration of the neural balance in the fear system. Doing this work in the context of the subgroup maintains the social engagement system activation, fostering the possibility of ongoing mutual regulation of emotion. Typically, subgroup members answer "no" and feel calmer still. SCT thinks of this as restoring reality-testing. The next step is asking how each person feels for themselves about having been caught up in thoughts that created anxiety. This is often answered with "I feel compassion", or "sad for me", linking an emotional experience to anchor the cognitive work, an important neural integration, and activating the highly integrative middle prefrontal region. Thus, the security in the subgroup, with its activation of the social engagement system, lowers the mobilization to threat, deactivates the fast-track amygdala responses to difference, and facilitates vertical integration, activating the prefrontal cortex to check reality and modulate the amygdala.

A secure relational context

The heart of functional subgrouping is learning to build on similarities and resonance. This creates a context of attuned communication *within* the subgroup, while simultaneously building a group-as-a-whole that organizes its emerging differences in resonant subsystems. This enables all members to increase their attunement to others and develop the ability to accommodate a wider range of different experiences in themselves. Siegel (1999) calls this resonant attunement "contingent communication" with alignment of "states of mind". Within the subgroup, each person's experience shapes and is shaped by the experience of others as members feel "felt" by one another. The subgroup is emergent, and in this emergent system, new experiences unfold as members build on resonance, amplifying the subgroup's capacity to hold these emotions. In fact, subgroup members discover that each person will explore places in the process of subgrouping that they are unlikely to explore alone.

Joining on resonant similarities is an emotional communication, an exchange of emotional energy/information. The subgroup provides a secure emotional and relational context. Members learn to hold their differences and direct them to another subgroup. This develops the environment *within* the subgroup of cohesive alignment in similarities, and the environment *within* the group-as-a-whole of making room for all differences. Tronick (Cohn & Tronick, 1989; Tronick, 2006) demonstrated that in interactions between adults and infants, moving from matching to mismatching affective states with infants generated stress in the infant that was "resolved by the reparation back to matching states" (Tronick, 2007, p. 389). In effect, the emphasis in functional subgrouping on joining on similarities ameliorates distressful mismatching that comes from differences that are too different. There is little reason to suppose the distress is any less for adult–adult interactions, since responses to differences in groups often precipitate "fight" communication patterns replete with blame and attack.

Functional subgrouping develops a secure context in which the typical human reaction to difference is regulated both by the sense of feeling understood and the sense of security that develops in the subgroup system. McCluskey (2002) has suggested that functional subgrouping increases the potential for attunement and creates an environment in which early attachment failures can be explored and remediated as internal models are modified at the intuitive, non-verbal, and sensory levels. Building on McCluskey's work, SCT suggests that the secure-enough environment of the subgroup system provides the context for activation of the exploratory drive, so essential to human development (Heard & Lake, 1986, 1997). It is the exploratory drive, or "curiosity", as SCT names it, that enables the essential process of discriminating and integrating differences in the service of development. In effect, a functional subgroup approximates a secure-enough attachment system in the here-and-now experience that may begin to affect implicit memories of how things are.

In functional subgrouping, "joining" and feeling understood generates a positive emotional state. As the subgrouping continues, members discover small differences in their experience (which might lead to mild sympathetic activation). In the subgroup environment of similarity and resonance, small differences are more easily accepted without distress or fear. In this way, the subgroup development creates a secure system that contains the aligned *and* slightly different communications, the matches, and the increasingly tolerable mismatches. In this way, functional subgrouping may increase the "window of tolerance" that balances the autonomic activation in an integrative pattern (Siegel, 1999, p. 182), both within a subgroup and between subgroups for the group-as-a-whole. Schore (1994), in fact, described a secure attachment as a balance between sympathetic and parasympathetic activations.

Eye contact is emphasized in functional subgrouping. This also facilitates mirror neuron firing. Observing others' emotions, especially the facial expressions of those emotions, activates mirror neuron firing just the same as if we were making the facial expression ourselves. Iacoboni (2008) detailed this automatic process of mirror neuron firing in response to others' facial expressions: as the mirror neurons fire, they send signals via the insula to the limbic system, particularly the amygdala, and on to the prefrontal cortex. This process allows us to "feel" the feelings and experience the intentions of others.

As the group develops, the subgroups that emerge reflect the conflicts in each phase of group development and the members' challenges related to these human conflicts (Agazarian & Gantt, 2003). In the early phases of flight and fight in a group, the main challenges, reflected in the subgrouping, are commonly related either to anxiety, fear activation, or emotional arousal. The "flight" subgroup described earlier sounds very different than a subgroup exploring "fight" energy: "Hot and full of energy . . . big . . . feel like an angry bull . . . want to ram . . . me too, want to paw and charge and want to snort. . . . Freer as we work. . . . Stronger."

Attachment issues are also reflected early in a group in the tendencies to join subgroups quickly or slowly. For example, someone with an avoidant attachment style will tend to see every subgroup as "too different" to join, while someone with an ambivalent attachment might lose his or her own experience by "subgroup hopping". The in-depth exploration of attachment issues is not sustainable until, and unless, the group develops to the intimacy phase. In the intimacy phase, subgrouping centres on the exploration of the attachment roles that influence how members subgroup and join in resonant communications with others, often linked to implicit memories. The early attachment issues are then explored in the security of functional subgrouping, with its "good-enough" attachments. In fact, once members have learned the basics of functional subgrouping, they then learn a more nuanced process of subgrouping: the first step is to attune to the last person who has spoken, and then either to join in emotional resonance or paraphrase in attunement. This is reminiscent of the imitation that Iacoboni (2008) sees as essential to the development of mirror neuron functioning. The second step is to separate, rejoin one's self, and then individuate by adding one's own "build" to the group, which will introduce some difference. The third step is to look around the group-as-a-whole and ask "Anyone else?" furthering the individuation and fostering the attunement with the larger group. Schore's (2003a,b) work suggests that the micro-attunements that occur in such a secure environment directly rewire early implicit attachment patterns in the direction of greater security. Since implicit memories are not easily accessible through the usual process of remembering, but instead show themselves in automatic, out-of-conscious-awareness relational patterns, the possibility of rewiring through the experiences of connecting and being understood represents an important aspect of the group process.

Developing the group-as-a-whole and neural integration

Previously, SCT has emphasized using functional subgrouping to integrate the conflicts inherent in each phase to facilitate the group through its phases of development (Agazarian, 1997). IPNB enables the additional view of functional subgrouping in the service of developing the group mind. From a group mind perspective, functional subgroups are differentiated emergent subsystems that influence group functioning and maturation by regulating the flow of energy and information within and between members, subgroups, and the group-as-a-whole. Within the group, functional subgroups contain differentiated functions for the group-as-a-whole in its development as a complex adaptive system. As the subgroups develop functionally by discriminating and integrating information, integration occurs in the group-as-a-whole, and the dynamic subgroups then dissolve. Functional subgrouping can then adaptively contain any number of splits in human experience that reflect current neural integration at the level of person/member, and foster integration in the mind of the group-as-a-whole.

The integration of cortical and sub-cortical structures is easily illustrated by looking at the fear-activation system. As discussed, the right-brain role in fear activation via the amygdala is moderated by the orbital frontal cortex. It is not uncommon, for example, for an anxious subgroup to emerge in the group when a "fight" subgroup is exploring. From the group dynamics perspective, the two subgroups contain the two polarities that characterized the group's phase of development, fight and flight. From an IPNB view, both subgroups reflect sympathetic mobilization. Functional subgrouping contains each experience by activating the ventral vagal circuitry that modulates the sympathetic mobilization. This then enables cortical involvement with the potential for greater vertical integration and restoration of neural balance between the cortical and limbic responses.

In addition, within each subgroup, exploration increases, and differences and novelty emerge. Novelty is a condition for neurogenesis (Badenoch, 2008). This is particularly important for "memories" or emotional responses that originally occurred under conditions of stress or trauma that were encoded in the amygdala (implicit memories), but not organized by the hippocampus into explicit memories. These implicit "stress" responses are often triggered by a here-and-now group event. In fact, it is common for fear-related implicit memories to be triggered in response to anger, and for group members to be frightened without knowing why. Functional subgrouping provides the containment and contingent communication in which these implicit responses can be explored and new links built to higher level cortical processing.

"Right-brain subgrouping" promotes horizontal integration across modalities of experience. Functional subgrouping, with its emphasis on exploring rather than explaining, creates a "right-brain rich" environment that develops the capacity of members for images, right-brain to right-brain communications, polysemantic understandings, analogic communications, and an increased awareness of sensation and bodily experience. The "fight" subgroup, with its experience of "feeling like a bull", exemplifies how functional subgrouping supports exploration of bodily experience and analogic knowing. In the security of a subgroup, members are more open to exploring human experience.

Directing attention to the "fork-in-the-road" between "exploring" one's experience instead of "explaining" it (Agazarian, 1997) develops the capacity for subgrouping by focusing attention through intention. Recent research (Lazar et al., 2005) has demonstrated that consciously focusing the mind (as in meditation) increases cortical thickness, supporting development of neural connections between the middle prefrontal and limbic regions. Deliberately attending to the energy and information coming from the body strengthens vertical integration—drawing body, limbic, and cortex together. Identifying and describing the experience in one's limbs and facial muscles changes/fires the somatosensory cortex, while attending to visceral shifts in the body fires the orbital frontal cortex and anterior cingulate, predominantly on the right side (Siegel, 1999). Exploring these body experiences in attunement with subgroup members who are observing similar experiences builds neural capacity for a coherent experience of body knowledge. The attuned resonance in the subgrouping allows members to feel "felt" (Siegel, 1999, 2007) and to feel others in the process of exploring bodily experience.

"Left-brain subgrouping" provides a context for exploring left-hemisphere constructions and verbal communications that may be misattuned or out of date with right-brain input. This process supports members detecting and assessing previously invisible and habitual "top-down" influences, like negative predictions, that are sometimes rooted in implicit memory. For example, functional subgrouping can be used to explore the ambiguities, contradictions, and redundancies in communications (Shannon & Weaver, 1964; Simon & Agazarian, 2000) that represent a left-brain adaptation to right-hemisphere dysregulation. Subgroup exploration follows this pattern: first, identify the thoughts that are generating the worry; second, say aloud to each other the specifics of the thoughts; and third, test and compare the thoughts to the actual observable external reality (Agazarian, 1997). All of this happens in resonant attunement with others in the subgroup who are having similar thoughts.

It is not unusual for one subgroup to work with the left-brain exploration and a second with the right-brain experience. For example, one subgroup might voice and explore the right-brain experience of anger involving somatosensory experience, images, and metaphors, and thus strengthens the subgroup's access to right-brain processing. The second subgroup, activated by the anger of the other subgroup, voices and explores the left-brain worries related to fears generated by the past or speculations about the future. These thoughts translate the anxieties of the right-brain fear arousal in response to the anger into thoughts or explanations that generate and maintain fear arousal. The group's challenge is to contain both human propensities, providing sufficient safety to regulate the response to the differences. When there is good-enough containment, the exploration of both the anger and anxiety can occur with left- and right-brain processing that is sufficient for an integration of the two. A new neural integration can then be established between the left- and right-brain processing systems. In effect, functional subgrouping then develops the group mind through stimulating vertical integration (the middle prefrontal better regulating the limbic circuits) and horizontal integration (the left hemisphere providing a new narrative based on here-and-now reality).

Describing one's experience to each of the members of a subgroup also promotes horizontal integration of left and right hemisphere functioning. Verbalizing and describing one's emotions enhances emotional regulation by creating more of a balance between left and right hemisphere activation (Badenoch, 2008).

Functional subgrouping contains unintegrated splits that reflect a lack of neural integration in differentiated subsystems. Exploring both sides in the containing context of similarity enables each component of brain processing to do the work necessary for the group mind to develop, and to integrate differentiated systems and modes of processing. As each subgroup develops by discriminating differences in what was initially a similar experience, each begins to notice the similarities in what was initially different (Agazarian, 1997). This fosters integration in the group mind of the splits in the group-as-a-whole and isomorphically in its members. Splitting is evidence of lack of integration in a system at all system levels; functional subgrouping organizes splits in a way that promotes neural integration.

Summary and conclusions

We have discussed how functional subgrouping can lead to "feeling felt" as members resonate with experiences shared by other members. This creates a secure context and strengthens our social engagement circuitry, allowing for deepening self-awareness. Functional subgrouping is typically introduced in a group whenever there is a conflict or difference that is too different to be easily integrated. Conflict almost always results in some kind of neurophysiological arousal that is then contained in the subgrouping process, lowering the reactivity that, when unmodulated, leads to personal and interpersonal distress at the expense of neural integration. Thus, using functional subgrouping to resolve group conflicts and integrate differences constitutes the very combination of moderate arousal and the experience of closeness and understanding with one's subgroup that is similar to the conditions that promote neural plasticity (Badenoch, 2008; Cozolino, 2006; Siegel, 1999).

In systems-centred groups, functional subgrouping is often focused on the experience in the present. Paying attention to the present moment stimulates neural firing of here-and-now sensory input, enabling a shift away from the "known explanations" or "invariant cortical representations" that have been encoded by repeated experience (Hawkins & Blakeslee, 2004). This increases the capacity for exploring the "unknown" in one's experience. Building with others in exploring experience creates a heightened sense in the present moment with the containment and attunement of the subgroup. Within the experiential process of functional subgrouping, each person's mind is shaped by, and shapes, others in the direction of bodily and emotional regulation. This has a strong potential to create new neural activation patterns that support exploring "novelty" (the unknown) without disabling fear. Novelty, that is, differences, is essential to the development and transformation of living human systems.

This paper offers hypotheses that link functional subgrouping to neurobiological research. We have hypothesized first, that functional subgrouping develops the group mind, and second, that it is the group mind that regulates the flow of information and energy. In effect, functional subgrouping regulates affect at all levels of the group system: within the subgroup through attuned communications, within members who are contained within subgroups, and within the group-as-a-whole. This process of regulation meets Siegel's definition for mind: an embodied and relational process that regulates the flow of energy and information. Further, it may be that linking to the IPNB models will enable us as group therapists to more fully implement de Maré's (de Maré, Piper, & Thompson, 1991) idea that mind is *between* brains rather than *in* them and that group mind is culture and a living system of dialogue is required to link the individual with the group mind.

Note

Much appreciation to Rich Armington, Marianne Bentzen, and Paul Cox for their careful reading and helpful suggestions, to Bonnie Badenoch for her most excellent editing and suggestions, and to Roll Fellows for his reading and support of this paper. Some of the ideas here were first presented at the annual meeting of the American Group Psychotherapy Association in 2007 in Austin, Texas, USA.

References

Agazarian, Y. M. (1997). *Systems-centered Therapy for Groups*. New York: Guilford Press (reprinted in paperback, 2004, London: Karnac).

Agazarian, Y. M., & Gantt, S. P. (2003). Phases of group development: systems-centered hypotheses and their implications for research and practice. *Group Dynamics: Theory, Research and Practice, 7*(3): 238–252.

Asch, S. E. (1951). Effects of group pressure upon the modification and distortion of judgments. In: H. S. Guetzkow (Ed.), *Groups, Leadership and Men: Research in Human Relations* (pp. 177–190). Pittsburgh, PA: Carnegie Press.

Badenoch, B. (2008). *Being a Brain-Wise Therapist: A Practical Guide to Interpersonal Neurobiology*. New York: W. W. Norton.

Badenoch, B. (2009). Personal communication.

Berns, G. S., Chappelow, J., Zink, C. F., Pagnoni, G., Martin-Skurski, M. E., & Richards, J. (2005). Neurobiological correlates of social conformity and independence during mental rotation. *Biological Psychiatry, 58*(3): 245–253.

Burger, J. M. (2009). Replicating Milgram: would people still obey today? *American Psychologist, 64*(1): 1–11.

Canli, T., Desmond, J. E., Zhao, Z., Glover, G., & Gabrieli, J. D. E. (1998). Hemispheric asymmetry for emotional stimuli detected with fMRI. *NeuroReport, 9*: 3233–3239.

Cohn, J. F., & Tronick, E. (1989). Specificity of infants' response to mothers' affective behavior. *Journal of the American Academy of Child & Adolescent Psychiatry, 28*(2): 242–248.

Cozolino, L. (2002). *The Neuroscience of Psychotherapy: Building and Rebuilding the Human Brain*. New York: W. W. Norton & Co.

Cozolino, L. (2006). *The Neuroscience of Human Relationships: Attachment and the Developing Social Brain*. New York: W. W. Norton.

de Maré, P. B., Piper, R., & Thompson, S. (Eds.) (1991). *Koinonia: From Hate Through Dialogue to Culture in the Larger Group*. London: Karnac.

Durkheim, E. (1966). *Suicide*, J. A. Spaulding & G. Simpson (Trans.). New York: Free Press.

Gantt, S. P., & Agazarian, Y. M. (2004). Systems-centered emotional intelligence: beyond individual systems to organizational systems. *Organizational Analysis, 12*(2): 147–169.

Goleman, D. (1995). *Emotional Intelligence*. New York: Bantam.

Haney, C., Banks, W. C., & Zimbardo, P. G. (1973). Study of prisoners and guards in a simulated prison. *Naval Research Reviews, 9*: 1–17. Washington, DC: Office of Naval Research.

Hawkins, J., & Blakeslee, S. (2004). *On Intelligence: How a New Understanding of the Brain Will Lead to the Creation of Truly Intelligent Machines*. New York: Times Books.

Heard, D., & Lake, B. (1986). The attachment dynamics in adult life. *British Journal of Psychiatry, 149*: 430–439.

Heard, D., & Lake, B. (1997). *The Challenge of Attachment for Caregiving*. London: Routledge, Chapman & Hall.

Hebb, D. O. (1949). *The Organization of Behavior*. New York: Wiley.

Hopper, E. (2009). Building bridges between psychoanalysis and group analysis in theory and clinical practice. *Group Analysis, 42*(4): 406–425.

Horwitz, L. (1983). Projective identification in dyads and groups. *International Journal of Group Psychotherapy, 33*(3): 259–279.

Iacoboni, M. (2007). Face to face: the neural basis of social mirroring and empathy. *Psychiatric Annals, 37*(4): 236–241.

Iacoboni, M. (2008). *Mirroring People: The New Science of How We Connect With Others*. New York: Farrar, Straus & Giroux.

Janis, I. L. (1972). *Victims of Groupthink: A Psychological Study of Foreign-policy Decisions and Fiascoes*. Boston: Houghton Mifflin Co.

Kandel, E. R. (2006). *In Search of Memory: The Emergence of a New Science of Mind*. New York: W. W. Norton & Co.

Kossmann, M. R., & Bullrich, S. (1997). Systematic chaos: self-organizing systems and the process of change. In: F. Masterpasqua & P. A. Perna (Eds.), *The Psychological Meaning of Chaos* (pp. 199–224). Washington, DC: American Psychological Association.

Lazar, S. W., Kerr, C., Wasserman, R. H., Gray, J. R., Greve, D., Treadway, M. T., McGarvey, M., Quinn, B. T., Dusek, J. A., Benson, H., Rauch, S. L., Moore, C. I., & Fischl, B. (2005). Meditation experience is associated with increased cortical thickness. *NeuroReport, 16*: 1893–1897.

Le Bon, G. (1896). *The Crowd: A Study of the Popular Mind*. London: T. Fisher Unwin.

LeDoux, J. (1996). *The Emotional Brain*. New York: Simon & Schuster.

McCluskey, U. (2002). The dynamics of attachment and systems-centered group psychotherapy. *Group Dynamics: Theory, Research, and Practice, 6*(2): 131–142.

McDougall, W. (1920). *The Group Mind: A Sketch of the Principles of Collective Psychology With Some Attempt to Apply Them to the*

Interpretation of National Life and Character (2nd edn, revised). New York: G. P. Putnam's Sons.

Menning, H., Roberts, L. E., & Pantev, C. (2000). Plastic changes in the auditory cortex induced by intensive frequency discrimination training. *NeuroReport: Auditory and Vestibular Systems, 11*(4): 817–822.

Milgram, S. (1963). Behavioral study of obedience. *Journal of Abnormal and Social Psychology, 67*(4): 371–378.

Porges, S. W. (1995). Orienting in a defensive world: mammalian modifications of our evolutionary heritage: a polyvagal theory. *Psychophysiology, 32*(4): 301–318.

Porges, S. W. (1998). Love: an emergent property of the mammalian autonomic nervous system. *Psychoneuroendocrinology, 23*(8): 837–861.

Porges, S. W. (2007). The polyvagal perspective. *Biological Psychology, 74*(2): 116–143.

Schore, A. N. (1994). *Affect Regulation and the Origin of the Self: The Neurobiology of Emotional Development*. Hillsdale, NJ: Lawrence Erlbaum Associates.

Schore, A. N. (2003a). *Affect Dysregulation and Disorders of the Self*. New York: W. W. Norton.

Schore, A. N. (2003b). *Affect Regulation and the Repair of the Self*. New York: W. W. Norton.

Shannon, C. E., & Weaver, W. (1964). *The Mathematical Theory of Communication*. Urbana, IL: University of Illinois Press.

Shin, L. M., Orr, S. P., Carson, M. A., Rauch, S. L., Macklin, M. L., Lasko, N. B., & Pitman, R. K. (2004). Regional cerebral blood flow in amygdala and medial prefrontal cortex during traumatic imagery in male and female Vietnam veterans with PTSD. *Archives of General Psychiatry, 61*(2): 168–176.

Shin, L. M., Wright, C. I., Cannistraro, P. A., Wedig, M. M., McMullin, K., Martis, B., & Rauch, S. L. (2005). A functional magnetic resonance imaging study of amygdala and medial prefrontal cortex responses to overtly presented fearful faces in posttraumatic stress disorder. *Archives of General Psychiatry, 62*(3): 273–281.

Siegel, D. J. (1999). *The Developing Mind: Toward a Neurobiology of Interpersonal Experience*. New York: Guilford Press.

Siegel, D. J. (2006). An interpersonal neurobiology approach to psychotherapy: awareness, mirror neurons, and neural plasticity in the development of well-being. *Psychiatric Annals, 36*(4): 247–258.

Siegel, D. J. (2007). *The Mindful Brain*. New York: W. W. Norton.

Siegel, D. J., & Hartzell, M. (2003). *Parenting From the Inside Out: How a Deeper Self-Understanding Can Help You Raise Children Who Thrive*. New York: Tarcher/Putnam.

Simon, A., & Agazarian, Y. M. (2000). The system for analyzing verbal interaction. In: A. Beck & C. Lewis (Eds.), *The Process of Group Psychotherapy: Systems for Analyzing Change*. Washington, DC: American Psychological Association.

Song, H., Stevens, C. E., & Gage, F. H. (2002). Neural stem cells from adult hippocampus develop essential properties of functional CNS neurons. *Nature Neuroscience, 5*(5): 438–445.

Terrazas, A., & McNaughton, B. L. (2000). Brain growth and the cognitive map. *Proceedings of the National Academy of Sciences, 97*(9): 4414–4416.

Tronick, E. (2006). The stress of normal development and interaction leads to the development of resilience and variation. In: B. Lester, A. Masten, & B. McEwen (Eds.), *Annals of the New York Academy of Sciences*, Vol. 1094, *Resilience in Children* (pp. 83–104). New York: Wiley.

Tronick, E. (2007). *The Neurobehavioral and Social-Emotional Development of Infants and Children*. New York: W. W. Norton.

PART III

THE RELATIONAL AND INTERPERSONAL PERSPECTIVE

Introduction

Robi Friedman

Accepting that people are influenced by their "unconscious" is difficult enough; to acknowledge that they are constrained by their "social unconscious" is quite a challenge. But this differentiates group analysis from other therapies. In fact, understanding the social unconscious may be crucial for the future of our trade, and an appreciation of the intersubjective helps us to rethink these concepts. Weegmann points to the development of our understanding of intersubjectivity as a result of self-psychology and the relational perspective; Lavie depicts aspects of the influence of the sociologist Norbert Elias on the thinking of the group analyst S. H. Foulkes.

Making space for the appreciation of both sympathy and empathy in the study of human relations, Husserl (1931) introduced his concept of intersubjectivity within the context of a general discussion of phenomenology. This enabled a more complete conceptualization of the experience by one person of another person who is both a subject and an object of this experience. Moreover, from this perspective, the experience of oneself is defined in terms of how one has been experienced by another, and, thus, in terms of an internal world of relations which are almost entirely shared.

The recognition of intersubjectivity has created a new psychological paradigm in which the individual is regarded by definition as a "person-in-relation" (e.g., Hopper, 2003). Although the famous dictum that ". . . there is no such thing as a baby. . ." (Winnicott, 1958) refers to the fact that in the beginning of life the newborn is totally dependent on his mother, this statement has come to be a metaphor for the social–psychological interdependence and inter-relation of mother and child throughout their lives, or at least throughout infancy and childhood. The baby is not a passive being, unilaterally controlled by his genetic, instinctual, and even his experiential fate, but a "competent newborn" (Friedman & Vietze, 1972). This active baby co-creates his human environment, and is reciprocally co-dependent on mutual responses from and with other subjects. These two intersubjective aspects reflect a central paradoxical perspective of human existence: on the one hand, the insult of the individual's dependency on society and of his mind's permeability, and on the other hand, the individual's power over others and his ability to co-create relational situations which may be a burden to him.

Affects are embedded in a history of relations in which reciprocal (though asymmetrical, at least in the beginning) mirroring and dialoguing govern the development of communication in general, not only with the mother, but with all others, including, of course, the father. The principle of intersubjectivity is that partners in relationships influence each other mutually by permeating one another's conscious and unconscious lives. However, it is often impossible to recognize the unconscious influence of the mind of another on one's own mind, and on the shared space in which and by which a mind is defined. Nevertheless, such unconscious interpersonal influence is an essential element of the human condition, and is the essence of the nature of socio-cultural "constraint" (Hopper, 1981).

Martin Weegmann has stressed that from an intersubjective perspective both healthy and unhealthy psychological developments are, in essence, irreducibly relational. Contributions to the formation of this perspective have been made by many psychoanalysts, especially those who have emphasized the importance of projective and introjective processes in human relations, for example, Ferenczi, Klein, Fairbairn, Winnicott, and Balint, and, more recently, self-psychologists, such as Stolorow, Atwood, and Orange (2002). It also seems important and natural to include Bion in this list of psychoanalysts who have helped to define this relational frame of reference, especially with respect to his (Bion, 1963) model of container–contained, described as a mutual thinking, exchanging, and elaborating process.

Yet, socio-cultural systems are constructed on the basis of what modern psycho-dramatists and socio-dramatists call the "co-conscious" and the "co-unconscious" (Weinberg, 2007). Persons in co-conscious and co-unconscious relationships co-create a shared "third space" (Ogden, 1994) in which and through which they construct "social facts" such as societies and cultures and social systems more generally. Group analysts conceptualize such social systems in terms of what they call "dynamic" and "foundational" matrices, which Lavie would describe as intersubjective notions. They are based on the idea that social systems are both more than the sum of their parts and more than the sum of their participants. The socio-cultural communicative structures of social systems, ranging from families to organizations to nations, are derived from these co-constructed relational phenomena. Of course, over time, these processes become recursive: co-conscious and co-unconscious processes can only be understood in the context of their dynamic and foundational matrices.

The term "intersubjective" presupposes that the classical therapeutic dyad is indivisible—that we can no longer speak of the patient or the therapist as "individuals", as though they were not always in relation to one another. However, this is also true of the multi-personal relations of groups who meet for the purpose of psychotherapy. Group therapy is about close contact between participants in an emotional "field" which will be unconsciously and consciously pulled and pushed in such a way that personal and interpersonal characteristics ". . . like an assumption, will be co-created, maintained and worked through inter-subjectively by the linking objects . . ." (Billow, 2003, p. 40).

Through tracing the notion of the relational person implicit in Foulkes's (1973) work to the influence of Norbert Elias, Joshua Lavie has emphasized that Foulkes and group analysis in general have contributed significantly to the passage from thinking about people as closed individuals to thinking about them as open relational persons. In fact, group analysis created a new therapeutic paradigm by asserting that the therapist is not the exclusive therapeutic factor, and that all persons-in-relation-in-a-group are mutually healing. Although "... the concept of mental processes ... [as] ... multi-personal seems hard to accept ..." (Foulkes, 1964 p. 253), it was the conceptualization of these unconscious emotional movements as "transpersonal" that turned group analysis into one of the sources of intersubjective thinking:

> The truest account of what I do is that I analyse in the interest of each individual, but in the group context. For this purpose I use not only the processes as they reach me but as they reach everyone, that is to say, the total processes operating in the group context. To do justice to the fact that this mental field of operation very much includes the individual but also transgresses him, I have used the term "transpersonal processes". These processes pass through the individual, though each individual elaborates them and contributes to them and modifies them in his own way. Nevertheless, they go through all the individuals—similar to X-rays in the physical sphere. [Foulkes, 1973, p. 229]

Lavie has called for a renewed combination of psychogenic and sociogenic aspects in the group analytic perspective. Weegmann believes that as a result of intersubjective understanding of group analysis, the conductors of therapeutic groups will have to develop a "particular sensitivity", and hints of new directions in the conductor's technique. Emphasizing Foulkes's (1964, p. 287) suggestion that we should "leave things unresolved, in mid-air, incomplete ('no closure')", he also highlights the conductor's complex position within the context of intersubjective approaches to clinical work.

The relational perspective also lends new social meaning and insights into the unconscious configuration of dreaming, dreams, and dreamers. It influences the appreciation of the transformative influence of dream-telling on human relations (Friedman, 2008) and the role of social unconscious communication. Understanding the relational dimensions of dreams and dreamtelling also furthers our understanding that the essence of psycho-pathology is relational. In so far as people even dream for one another, dream processes are not only a source of insight into the intersubjective nature of personal and social identities, but also changes them. Dreaming is both a co-creation of mind and society, and co-creator of them. Unconscious communication though? Dreamtelling may be the intersubjective mechanism for this shared transpersonal creation. Further, social dreaming (Lawrence, 2007) may be a perfect example of the manifestation of intersubjectivity in the group as-a-whole. While being a method for identifying cultural knowledge, it may also be understood as a way of finding "the social truth" represented in dreams.

References

Billow, R. M. (2003). Relational variations of the "container–contained". *Contemporary Psychoanalysis, 39*: 27–50.

Bion, W. R. (1963). *Elements of Psycho-Analysis*. London: William Heinemann [reprinted London: Karnac].

Foulkes, S. H. (1964). *Therapeutic Group Analysis*. London: Allen and Unwin.

Foulkes, S. H. (1973). The group as matrix of the individual's mental life. In: E. Foulkes (Ed.), *S. H. Foulkes Selected Papers* (pp. 223–233). London: Karnac, 1990.

Friedman, M., & Vietze, P. (1972). The competent infant. *Peabody Journal of Education, 49*(4): 314–322.

Friedman, R. (2008). Dream telling as a request for containment – three uses of dreams in group therapy. *International Journal of Group Psychotherapy, 58*(3): 327–344.

Hopper, E. (1981). *Social Mobility: A Study of Social Control and Insatiability*. Oxford: Blackwell.

Hopper, E. (2003). *The Social Unconscious: Selected Papers*. London: Jessica Kingsley.

Husserl, E. (1931). *Cartesian Meditations, an Introduction to Phenomenology*, D. Cairns (Trans.). Dordrecht: Kluwer, 1960.

Lawrence, W. G. (2007). *Infinite Possibilities of Social Dreaming*. London: Karnac.

Ogden, T. (1994). The analytical third: working with intersubjective clinical facts. *International Journal of Psychoanalysis, 75*(1): 3–20.

Stolorow, R. D., Atwood, G. E., & Orange, D. M. (2002). *Worlds of Experience: Interweaving Philosophical and Clinical Dimensions in Psychoanalysis*. New York: Basic Books.

Weinberg, H. (2007). So what is this social unconscious anyway? *Group Analysis, 40*(3): 307–322.

Winnicott, D. W. (1958). Anxiety associated with insecurity. In: *Through Paediatrics to Psycho-Analysis* (pp. 97–100). London: Tavistock.

CHAPTER SIX

Working intersubjectively: what does it mean for theory and therapy?*

Martin Weegmann

O ne of Freud's favourite quotations was from the poet, Heinrick Heine, who derided the philosopher thus:

> With his nightcaps and the tatters of his dressing-gown,
> he patches up the gaps in the structure of the universe.
>
> (in Freud, 1933a, p. 161)

Classical philosophers have been prone to the belief that they could arrive at a state of certainty or discern an irreducible principle, in full control of what they have conceived, a principle personified by Plato's "philosopher king" and present in Descartes' notion of knowledge being like a house needing a secure foundation, beyond doubt. Part of this omnipotent thinking stemmed from the idea that one can indeed comprehend an explanatory principle or totality, a "state" which is without gaps and fully coherent. Freud knew this to be an illusion, which is why he resisted trying to

---

*An earlier version of this chapter was published in 2001, in *Group Analysis*, 34(4): 515–530 and is reproduced with some changes by permission.

convert his psychoanalysis, which he saw as a science, into a new fabricated "view of the universe" or *Weltanschauung*; in fact, Freud believed that psychoanalysis could find its place within the "scientific *Weltanschauung*" that already existed. It could be argued, however, that Freud fell into a different, but related, trap, that he thought he had discovered the irreducible principles of mental life, the ultimate structuring principles of "the unconscious", "repression" and "infantile sexuality". The analyst, by virtue of his training, was in a privileged position and, with his interpretations, could patch up the gaps in the structure of the patient's mind, so to speak. In other words, he conceptualized an isolated mind, a "one-body psychology" and the analyst, who could feel secure once guided by this new branch of medical science.

This chapter uses contemporary analytic ideas from Robert Stolorow's intersubjectivity theory and from group analysis to convey an impression of what it might mean to move decisively away from the "myth of the isolated mind" and one-body psychology. A significant tilt towards the "relational" is apparent in several areas of modern psychoanalysis: self psychology (self-object matrix), attachment theory, empirical psychoanalysis (Stern et al., 1998, and other infant research), relational, perspectivism (Aron, 1996; Mitchell, 1988; Orange, 1995), to name a few, which are, arguably, compatible with many of the ideas of Foulkes: contextualism, the figure/ground dynamic, the "meeting of minds" in group and a dynamic concept of location (Behr & Hearst, 2007). Foulkes (2003, p. 316) also exposed the myth of "mind" or self as self-enclosed entity and looked forward to a time when thinking could "get beyond the metaphysics of psychoanalysis". In this reading, Foulkesian group analysis is one version of a relatively more communicative, relationally bound unconscious, notwithstanding inconsistencies in theorization (Stacey, 2001). "Intersubjectivity" is, therefore, a concept within an emerging paradigm in psychoanalysis and group analysis, sharing a common emphasis on conceiving complex relational fields and organizing principles, within which psychological processes come together and through which experience is continually shaped and reshaped. There is a move away from postulating a traditional dynamic unconscious as the only form of unconscious mental life, and from formulaic or universal explanations of particular conflicts: development and pathology are seen as irreducibly relational, embedded in many intersubjective contexts. We agree with Stolorow's idea (Stolorow & Atwood, 1979) that psychoanalytic ideas, too, are profoundly influenced by the personal, subjective worlds of their creators, and that treatment can only be conceived as an "intersubjective field", involving reciprocal principles and influence, an intersection of two differently organized subjectivities—that of the analyst and that of the patient. As just one instance of this, he claims that "Not only does the patient turn to the analyst for self object experiences, but the analyst also turns to the patient for such experiences . . ." (Stolorow & Atwood, 1992, p. 396).

I suggest that this broad approach not only helps us to understand psychoanalysis in a new way, but also helps us to comprehend more about the historical context within which Freud's "discoveries" were made: in fact, I think it is important to see psychoanalysis as both discourse and discovery. Something of Freud's attitude or relationship to his ideas was mirrored, for example, in his stance towards the fledgeling movement he created, to the early circle of analysts and the organizational structures which functioned to contain the new doctrine.

I contend that intersubjectivity theory illuminates group as well as individual processes, whether that of historical groups, like Freud's circle or the International Psychoanalytic Associations, or groups of individuals who come together with the aim of seeking therapy and personal change (see Schulte's article (2000), which touches on some similar areas, but which is clinically focused). I will begin, however, with a brief description of some of the features of a classical psychoanalytic orientation.

Classical theory

During the 1890s, many of the cornerstones of Freud's "discovery" were set in place: Freud moves away from his interest in hypnosis and cathartic techniques to encouraging "free association" and listening. Through his researches in treating hysterics (all the early patients of "psychoanalysis" were hysterics and, by the definition of the time, female), a new method emerges and a new significance becomes attached to a "phantasy", often seen as coterminous with

Freud's abandonment of the "seduction hypothesis" around 1897. Within these changes, we have the formation of the new domain of psychoanalysis, christened "the talking cure" by Anna O, the "first patient" of psychoanalysis (Weegmann, 1982). For our purposes, in this brief excavation of psychoanalysis, we shall refer to Freud's topographical understanding of the mind and the metaphor of archaeology, his notion of resistance and the transference and, by extension, the stance adopted by the analyst.

The archaeology metaphor

An archaeological metaphor is used frequently by Freud to describe mental life: psychoanalysis of "depth", whereby later stages of development are overlaid on earlier ones, just as the archaeologist unearths traces of earlier civilizations beneath later ones. History, in Freudian theory, is governed by endogenous drives, with treatment aiming to resolve the deeper "infantile neurosis", thus restoring the patient and "fill[ing] the gaps in memory". The reality produced by psychoanalysis is "discovered" or "recovered" in the archaeological metaphor; Wolberg (1976) has likened the classical view of treatment to that of a mining operation, that of reaching a psychic core or latent content. There are two points to emphasize here. First, the Freudian "self" was based on the idea of a self-enclosed subject, organized around intrapsychic structures and driven by instincts. Second, the perspective is a vertical one, from top to bottom, with the analyst presiding over the treatment, over the patient, as it were.

Stolorow and colleagues indicate, "The inter-subjectivity concept is in part of a response to the unfortunate tendency of classical analysis to view pathology in terms of processes and mechanisms located solely within the patient" (Stolorow, Brandchaft, & Atwood, 1987, p. 3).

The resisting patient

"I had explained the idea of 'resistance' to him at the beginning of the hour . . ." (Freud, 1909d, p. 166).

The concept of resistance appears early on in the formation of psychoanalysis and becomes integral to understanding treatment and the obstacles to it; overcoming resistance is a "law of treatment" (*ibid.*) and failure to do so is the factor that "finally brings treatment to a halt" (Freud, 1905e). Importantly, and this fact may help throw light on Freud's own subjectivity, not only did he use the term to refer to obstacles in gaining access to the unconscious, but he used it also to refer to resistance to psychoanalysis by its critics, those who had encircled his "embattled science". It linked into Freud's own myth of the isolated hero.

The concept of transference becomes tied up with the concept of resistance. Freud writes, "This transference alike in its positive and negative form is used as a weapon by the resistance; but in the hands of the physician it becomes the most powerful therapeutic instrument" (1923a, p. 247).

In the case of Dora, Freud makes several references to the "incompleteness" of that case, what was left unanalysed, its omissions. In his postscript to the case, we are told of the one central omission to explain this incompleteness, this being the concept of transference. In a phrase that might reveal a lot about Freud's own desire and position, he writes that in the case of Dora, "I did not succeed in *mastering* the transference in good time" (1905e, p. 118, my emphasis). In psychoanalysis, from that time on, what was apparently the biggest obstacle to treatment (the "un-welcome" factor to which Joseph Breuer (Breuer & Freud, 1895a) alluded) now becomes "its most powerful ally", if sufficiently mastered. Transference is the "carrying over" of the past, stimulated, but not invented by, the treatment. Linked to libido theory, it is understood in conflictual terms, with the analyst as the figure on to whom libidinal wishes are transferred, the focus of a transferred, internal "battleground".

Freud, in 1919a, distinguished "the pure gold of analysis" from the "copper of direct suggestion" what distinguishes pyschoanalysis from other psychotherapies is the role of interpretation and, increasingly important, of interpretation of resistance and the transference. The vertical perspective is again clear, with the analyst making the interpretation (because he is in charge) *to* the patient (who resists). In Strachey's (1934) famous contribution, he argues that only transference interpretations have this mutative power. Hearst has commented on the language of trench warfare in Strachey's paper; she summarizes the outlook then as one where "it is the task of the analyst to penetrate step by step through the minefield of the analysand's resistance to the source of the neurosis. The analyst's weapon is the correct, and correctly timed, transference interpretation" (2000, p. 2).

In intersubjectivity theory, by contrast, the situation is viewed as one of mutuality, where the patient is seen as co-constructing his own treatment, and as certainly "interpreting" the analyst as much as the analyst interprets him/her.

> The concept of transference as displacement (or regression or projection) has perpetuated the view that the patient's experience of the analytic relationship is solely a product of the patient's past and psychopathology and has not been determined by the activity (or non-activity) of the analyst. [Stolorow, Brandchaft, & Atwood, 1987, p. 33]

It now becomes possible to think that some of the very concepts used by the early analysts, and the treatment ambience they fostered, helped to create some of the resistance they claimed to have discovered. And, far from being neutral, the stance of the analyst entailed an assumption of a superior point of view or epistemology—an assumption which did, in fact, permeate the culture and style of many early analysts. Many others, influenced by postmodern ideas, have commented on this kind of silence, meta-narrative truth and power in psychoanalysis (e.g., Foucault, 1978).

The surgical metaphor

"I cannot advise my colleagues too urgently to model themselves during psychoanalytic treatment on the surgeon, who puts aside all feelings . . ." (Freud, 1912e, p. 115).

Consistent with Freud's topographical model and archaelogy stance, he believed in the essential exteriority of the analyst (of which sitting behind the couch might be seen as one expression), who caries out treatment "in abstinence" (this idea being based on the instinct mode). His recommendation was that the analyst "should be opaque to his patients, and, like a mirror, show them nothing but what is shown to them" (*ibid.*, p. 118). There is a theme of surgical detachment in classical psychoanalysis and this fitted well with Freud's identification with the scientist and the idea of an objective treatment.

Because of this model and the vertical perspective, the authority of the analyst is enshrined. Although we have little direct sense of how Freud worked in practice (and he certainly did not advocate coldness), the tone of writing and interpreting in his case studies often appears as one of "explanation", "pointing out", "demonstrating to". Foulkes comments on the term *Deutung*, and suggests that the interpreter in the Freudian conception has "a specific knowledge . . . by no means open to everyone, but only to the select few who have been initiated on the strength of a quite peculiar ability" (1975, p. 114). There are implications of infallibility, or at least of an incremental notion of the truth: the good analyst is in an increasing relationship of truth to his patient. We know that later, analysts such as Ferenczi began to question this and found their ideas got them into increasing trouble with more "loyal" analysts.

Perhaps the surgical metaphor, then, is tied up with the *power* of the physician (the early generation of analysts were all physicians, and Freud uses the terms interchangeably). The historical context in which this occurs is important: a culture that enshrined a strict hierarchy and authority of the physician over the patient.

On history and the psychoanalytic movement

"This is not psychoanalysis" (Freud, quoted in Eisold, 1997, p. 97).

The history of the psychoanalytic movement is of considerable interest to the student of groups. I have suggested some parallels already between some of the theoretical concepts and metaphors of psychoanalysis (like archaelogy and surgery) and Freud's own stance as the leader of the movement he founded. As with all movements, we see the creation of "foundation" myths, legendary aspects that become attached to the ideas and individuals involved. Perhaps, in Freud's own preferred myth of isolation and resistance to his discoveries, he comes close to identifying with his boyhood idol, Hannibal, who challenged an empire and conquered Rome.

In the early years, with the creation in Freud's apartment of the "Wednesday Evening Society", the early psychoanalytic ethos was reflected in some aspects of the proceedings. Kanzer observes, for example, that "Freud always presided, so that a distance was established between himself his followers", and that, following presentations, he "alone had the privilege of intervening at will" (1983, p. 8).

The relationship of Freud to the psychoanalytic movement that unfolded and to the organizational structures devised is a complicated one, and we know that in many ways Freud was a reluctant leader. A complex co-relationship existed with the creation in 1910 of the International Psycho-Analytic Association, between Freud and those to whom he turned to safeguard and to continue the enterprise of psychoanalysis. Eisold's (1997) fascinating research suggests that Freud gravitated towards becoming, in Bion's (1961) terms, a "fight leader', with him and his Viennese followers needing a culture of allegiance (the members being still dependent on Freud as well as needing to promote the professional aspirations of the membership). An "unconscious pact" resulted, argues Eisold, "in which they sought and rooted out 'enemies' within the movement . . . who questioned his basic concept of childhood sexuality and would lend support to the 'external' enemies of psychoanalysis" (1997, p. 87). Hence, the notion of resistance to psychoanalysis from both outside and within.

The notion of an "orthodoxy" is also an important one in understanding the behaviour of groups. Who has the power to sanction an orthodoxy and what is the shibboleth that distinguishes the adherents of a movement from its opponents? Also, if we use a self-psychological and intersubjectivist viewpoint, how might we understand the self-object needs of the members of such a movement or emergent orthodoxy? In many ways the fledgeling or fragile movement reflects the fragile self: for example, Freud's own anxieties about what he had discovered, the dependence of his colleagues on his support, his dependence on friendly allies and a host of other narcissistic needs, for recognition and admiration and for the consolidation in this first generation of analysts of a new "analytic identity" (see Bergmann, 1997, for a valuable account of the historical roots of orthodoxy).

Therapy

The philosophical and theoretical influences upon, and implications of, intersubjectivity theory are manifold, and would certainly have a linkage to many developments in late nineteenth-century and twentieth-century philosophy: the ideas of Nietzsche, Husserl, Heidegger, to name a few (*Group Analysis*, 1996; Orange, Atwood, & Stolorow, 1997). Postmodern thinking is similarly relevant (e.g., Goldberg, 2000). Zeddies (2000a) observes that

> Traditional psychoanalytic concepts such as neutrality, interpretation, free association, and the unconscious have been dramatically reshaped over the last several decades. This "reshaping" has provoked a crisis of sorts, leaving many analysts scrambling for a stable mooring to ground their identities as analysts. [p. 521]

It seems clear, then, that there needs to be a reconceptualization of the role and assumed and ascribed authority of the analyst or conductor as a member of wider groups, including particular training traditions as well as diverse cultural locations.

A changing view of interpretation

With Foulkes's basic encouragement of psychotherapy *by* the group, not just between the analyst and the group, an important divergence emerged from that of the more classical psychoanalytic stance. As is well known, Foulkes also encouraged the conductor in many capacities besides making interpretations, such as confrontations, clarifications, acknowledging/receiving contributions, etc. (Foulkes, 1990a). Furthermore, by getting away from the idea that group analysis was "a hunt for unconscious meaning" (1990a, Chapter Twenty-one), the power of communication was opened up with it and the ever widening and deepening of a communicative "matrix". A horizontal perspective conjoined with the more traditional vertical perspective of individual psychoanalysis.

In spite of these advances, when it came to an understanding of the patient's *individual* pathology, Foulkes remained a committed Freudian, keeping the pre-eminence of the psychosexual stages as universal psychic contents. In recent debates, this fact, among other aspects, has been referred to as the "Orthodox Foulkes", contrasting with a "Radical Foulkes" (Dalal, 1998). Locked into concepts of libidinal development and repression, some psychoanalysts have been slow to adapt to naturalistic and detailed empirical understanding of child development. To name but one example, Daniel Stern (Stern et al., 1998), working from a more practical, interpersonal, and intersubjective perspective, has recently explored "non-interpretive mechanisms" in therapy. This exploration has, of course, a pre-history and echoes in other work of the Independent School of psychoanalysis in Britain, for example (see Stewart, 1990, for an excellent discussion of interpretation and other agents of psychic change). Stern talks about the notion of a "something more" than interpretation during treatment and that patients often recall, after treatment, not only "key interpretations" which might have affected psychic change, but also special "moments of meeting", the latter involving what they term "implicit relational knowing" and complex "affect attunement", ideas which stem from contemporary infant research. According to intersubjectivity theory, a good interpretation (or a bad one) *is* a relational process and not a disembodied observation *about* the patient, as in a vertical perspective. In the traditional epistemology of psychoanalysis, the "word" (the voice, the interpretation) was seen as different from the "act": it was conceived as informative rather than performative (see Aron, 1996, Chapter Seven for a discussion of this; Pines, 1996 offers a clarification of interpretation as an act of revelation—of the therapist *and* patient and as part of an unfolding dialogue, drawing on Bakhtin's work). This takes us away from some of the insularity of the Freudian conceptions of development. Schain (1989) has tried to show what implications these ideas around child development, particularly notions of responsiveness and reciprocity, might have for the group therapist. There are also some clear parallels here in the Kohutian concept of empathy, and to the importance of knowing the patient—and the group—"from within" as an essential component of the interpretive stance. This view challenges the assumed detachment and exact objectivity of the analyst.

From analyst to conductor

Let us for a moment consider the possible impact on a group of adopting a classical stance, taking as our example the work of some clinicians working at the Tavistock Clinic during the 1950s. The work of people like Ezriel and Sutherland took inspiration from the ideas of Bion, which had been developed with training groups, and applied these to therapy groups.

Ezriel (1950) described efforts to apply a "strictly psychoanalytic technique" to group therapy groups, with, among other things, a "rigorous technique of transference interpretation". Building on the tradition of Strachey and Rickman before him, Ezriel assigned over-riding importance to transference interpretation in the "here-and-now" of the group session. The task of therapy is universalized by Ezriel as to do with the resolution of infantile, Oedipal conflicts, and so the material is always viewed in this light. To quote Ezriel, all the material "is considered as the idiom used by the patient to give expression to his need in that session for a specific relationship with the therapist" (1952, p. 120).

The Foulkesian approach was quite different, but here we would like to isolate some key aspects of Ezriel's approach with respect to the role of the analyst–conductor.

The analyst ultimately centres the communications of the group to him/herself and, by extension, to the analyst's overarching framework. Ezriel even goes so far as to contend that the other members of the group are reducible to co-present "stimuli", there to attract the projection of internal defences.

It might be argued, as Brown (1979) suggests, that this type of analyst-centred mode fosters another kind of "'basic' assumption dependence", and infantilizes the patient. It also reduces the importance of understanding and engagement from and by other members, as an end in itself.

As with Freud's idea of abstinence and neutrality, the analyst's own organizing principles (including theory and training) are bracketed out of the equation, with the therapist viewed as being external to the setting. The framing of all material in terms of, for example, unresolved infantile conflicts, is, from an intersubjective viewpoint, already a structuring and organizing (and thereby constraining) viewpoint contributed by the analyst, and is thus far from being "neutral". In Malan's (1976) important empirical evaluation of the Tavistock groups, he points to the resentments often encountered among patients to an unduly impersonal psychoanalytic approach, and to the emphasis on conflictual object relations alone. In a surprisingly mild recommendation, he says, "it does seem possible that therapists ought to feel less constrained by what they have learned from their classical psychoanalytic train-ing" (1976, p. 1315). I would add that, by using an understanding of groups afforded by self psychology, we might see some of these resentments as expressions of protest at the imposition of a "tech-nique" and as a reaction, in some cases, to a felt undermining of the total self by an exclusive attention to a part of the self. Perhaps some of the patients felt that the legitimacy of *their* ideas and relation-ships with each other were not sufficiently appreciated. People and patients need to know they are having an effect on others.

The transference: an intersubjectivist view

There are several drawbacks with the classical view of transference and its role in treatment. One of these difficulties was that the early generation of analysts (and many who came later) tended to see themselves as representing a position of objective truth, *vis-à-vis* the patient, with their own *conceptions* of the main contents of mental life and conflict taken as already valid. This resulted in some extremes, easier to recognize with the benefit of hindsight. Ferenczi, for example, challenged the prevailing epistemology of his time by disagreeing with the implied infallibility of the analyst and in taking the patient's criticisms as valid. This led him into severe dif-ficulties with his peers and with Freud himself (see Eisold, 1997). Another extreme was the failure to recognize how dependent the patient was on the acceptance of the analyst and, and through this, the patient's dependence on seeing "reality" through the basic con-cepts that organized the *analyst's* observations and interpretations. We know that Ferenczi's pupil, Balint (1968), took up this theme in his warnings against the dangers of "over-insistent interpreting" and the "obtrusive analyst" Stolorow (Stolorow & Atwood, 1992) expresses the dilemma in the following way: "this is the require-ment with which patients often felt compelled to comply as the price of maintaining the vitally needed tie to the analyst" (*ibid.*, p. 91).

If we take the uncertainty principle of physics seriously, then modern analysis—be it in groups or with individuals—has to incor-porate fully the idea of the analyst as being a subjectivity in his/her own right and to acknowledge the essential indivisibility of observer and observed. Interestingly, the word "understanding" has different connotations to the terms "interpretation", and might convey this indivisibility more clearly: as Orange (1995, p. 5) describes it, "The term 'understanding' thus refers to both person and process, to both self and relation". It may be the case that it is easier to convey intersubjectivist concepts around multiplicity, mutuality of understanding and interpretation, and radical openness with respect to group treatment, which, by definition, is a multi-body situation. The radical inclusion of the conductor within the process of change is wonderfully described by Foulkes's famous notion of analysis "by the group, for the group including the conductor" (1986, p. 3).

We are indebted to Kohut for a systematic attempt to clarify different kinds of transference and for broadening the concept away from an exclusive emphasis, as with Freud or Klein, on intrapsychic conflict (and this narrowly conceived in sexual and aggressive terms). Through his work with narcissistic patients, Kohut discovered so-called "selfobject" transference, where the individual attempts to find an experience which will help him to have or to maintain a basic sense of cohesion and well-being (Kohut, 1977). These transferences stem from areas of unmet need, particularly around the formation and cohesion of the self. So, in addition to what the person might wish for, the area of repressed desire, there is also the question of what the patient *needs*, the area of "developmental deficit". As Stolorow and Lachmann put it, "experiences that the patient legitimately needed but missed or prematurely lost are understood in the transference in order to assist the patient in his belated psychological development" (1981, p. 309). Kohut postulated a variety of basic narcissistic needs and a relationship to the analyst as a "selfobject", which is distinct from the analyst as an object of instinctual conflicts. Symptoms and fears can be understood more widely, and perhaps more affirmatively, as "developmental and restorative necessities" and not merely as compromise formations based on psychic conflict, as Freud believed (Lachmann, 1986). Within a group, other members also continually evoke and respond to these selfobject needs, creating a new matrix from which new development might proceed, if all goes well. The group creates a complex spatial and temporal reality within which recurring, restorative, emergent, and new experiences unfold.

The relationship of selfobject to other dimensions of the transference is usefully framed in terms of a continually shifting figure–ground relation, with different constellations at different periods. It could be argued, for example, that until a person is assured through a selfobject experience that his/her self is supported or cohesive enough, it is unlikely he/she will be able to tackle psychic conflict in a safe manner. Furthermore, selfobject needs are not confined to the overtly "narcissistic" patient, but apply to areas of narcissistic need in *all* individuals.

There are rich implications for the understanding of groups, although the literature in this area is still relatively new (Harwood & Pines, 1998). The group conductor is faced with the complex task of responding empathically at different levels, both between different members of the group and also within the same individual at different times (even within the same session). Bacal (1998) has suggested the term "optimal responsiveness" to describe this flexible capacity in the therapist, replacing the traditional notion of neutrality, which was sometimes confused by analysts with a minimal response. The group therapist also helps to foster spontaneous reactiveness and responsiveness taking place unconsciously, and preconsciously, between the members at all times.

The irreducible subjectivity of the therapist

In 1919, Freud distinguished the "pure gold of analysis" from the "copper of direct suggestion" in his effort to distinguish psychoanalysis from other forms of psychotherapy and suggestion. This was linked to the concept of the "neutral analyst" and the idea of fostering the "transference neurosis" of the patient. However, as Gill contends, when the analyst does intervene, or even when he does not, "he may be experienced as suggesting a direction for the patient to pursue" (1982, p. 171).

Orange, Atwood, and Stolorow (1997) have questioned what they term the "myth of neutrality" in psychoanalysis. They argue that "each time the analyst offers an interpretation that goes beyond what the patient is consciously aware of, he or she invites the patient to see things, if ever so slightly, from the analysts' own theory-rooted perspective" (p. 39). In the intersubjectivity model, by contrast, the analyst has no "objective position" from which he/she is able to approach the patient, and what is crucial is the ability of the analyst to be reflective in a way that includes an awareness of the values and theoretical frameworks which guide him/her. In this sense, "theory" can be understood not only as a model of thinking, but also as an internal selfobject, so to speak, helping the analyst to feel secure and coherent in his/her functioning. Criticizing the notion that neutrality helped to create an "uncontaminated transference", intersubjectivists draw attention to the unavoidable organizing principles of the therapist, including the proposal that transference can be understood as an "organization" to which analyst and patient both contribute (Fosshage, 1994). Perhaps this is similar to Aron's (1996) insistence that the treatment is mutually constituted, but asymmetrical.

What of the conductor's or analyst's contribution? Orange (1995) argues that the term "counter-transference" needs to be replaced by "cotransference". In her view, the cotransference is defined as the analyst's perspective on "what is going on", a shared impression, with the argument being that it is often impossible to quite know what is "counter" to the patient's material, as if each partly were independent of the interaction (see McLaughlin, 1981). An apt question raised by Goldberg (2007), relevant to such arguments, is that of "who owns the countertransference"? Although Goldberg is specifically addressing publishing and dilemmas surrounding the writing up of case experience, it can be seen as representing a wider philosophical question, once "mind" is no longer seen as independent substance, encased within someone's skin. Not only this, but the analytic dyad, and the therapy group, do not exist in isolation from a wider organizational and social context, which also nourish and influence that relationship (Zeddies & Richardson, 1999). Orange (1995), thus, declines the temptation to ground some ultimate objectivity in the lone authority of the analyst. A group analytic and certainly sociological view might be that the authority of analysts (individual or group) is simply a product of specific historical networks of relations.

Beyond the particular theory that the analyst or conductor might hold—and it is interesting to speculate why different therapists gravitate towards a preferred model—are the wider (or deeper) values which influence conduct and thinking. All clinical exchanges involve some communication of values between the patient and therapist, expressed by verbal and non-verbal means. Lichtenberg (1983), in his valuable contribution, argues that the point is not that the analyst can ever become *value*-free (or theory-free), but that he/she can become more *value sensitive*. In terms of group analysis, this is where the concept of the "social unconscious" has an important role, reflecting, as Zeddies (2002, p. 381) ably puts it, "a complex, historically woven tapestry of moral and ethical values, beliefs, and assumptions". And, from an experiential point of view, membership of a large or median group can be of considerable help to members in locating themselves within the larger cultural matrix which produces them.

Metaphors and models of unconscious life

Stolorow and Atwood (1992) offered a building and house metaphor with which to encapsulate their proposed "three realms of the unconscious" (dynamic unconscious, pre-reflective unconscious, and the unvalidated unconscious). They incorporate the Freudian, dynamic unconscious (associated with repressed, intolerable impulses, wishes, etc.) below ground within the dwelling, consistent with an image of mind as rooms within a house, locating the unconscious, as one might expect, in the basement. The pre-reflective unconscious, by contrast, has no physical place as such in Stolorow and Atwood's metaphor, but corresponds to something like the "architect's plan" from which the building has been erected. As organizing principles, they inform the construction of the building and the relationship between the various parts of the building, so, while not "seen" as such, their influence is all around. In this regard, the Stolorow metaphor is already an improvement on Freud's, in so far as the house is not a once and for all structure, but involves an ongoing process (design, building, improvement, etc.). The unvalidated unconscious is represented by the "bricks, lumber, and other unused materials" left lying around, "materials which were never made part of the construction but that could have been" (Stolorow & Atwood, 1992, p. 35). In psychological terms, the latter are not (to date) articulated or integrated into mainstream psychic life, but might so do at some future stage; they represent potential and possibility.

Is, however, the building and house metaphor too static, given the penetrating insights of relational psychoanalysis and modern group analysis? The house, representing mind, is a detached dwelling image, after all, separate from a neighbourhood. To displace the detached house corresponds to displacing the detached Cartesian subject, the independent, "punctual" self (Taylor, 1989). In similar vein, Foulkes (1990b, p. 277) argued that mind is not simply a quality "inside the person as an individual". Theorizing a "multipersonal" dimension, Foulkes (*ibid.*, p. 280) said that there cannot be a "conventional, sharp differentiation between inside and outside. . . . What is inside is always also outside, and what is outside is inside as well". One solution, therefore, is to improve the metaphor, to make the dwelling a terraced house within a street, within a neighbourhood, and so on.

Foulkes (1990b) proposed a traffic analogy of psychic and social life, as distinct from that of the house, involving networks, regions, movement, and so on. In emphasizing such notions of interconnection and transpersonal process, Foulkes pointed out that "The traffic (i.e. 'transpersonal processes') is not an isolated fact and closed system"; there are other towns, other road users, many routes and differing ways in and out.

The group analytic concept of "social unconscious" traverses the repressed unconscious, the pre-reflective unconscious, and the invalidated unconscious, in so far as these can be separated at all; it constitutes the transpersonal "traffic", the rich tapestry of influence through which individuality is formed, maintained, and transformed.

Conclusion

"I do not think we should always try to understand . . . In this connection I tend to leave things unresolved, in mid-air, incomplete ('no closure')" (Foulkes, 1964, p. 287).

I have tried to demonstrate some of the obstacles and defensiveness arising from the more classical analytic tradition, whether applied to an individual or to groups. This does not imply that intersubjective theory is non-analytic, discards the transference, or erases the difference between the therapist and patients. Instead, I would suggest that intersubjectivity is an important development, related to, but not identical with, self psychology, and that it is about developing a particular *sensitivity* to the work of therapy rather than a new "technique" as such. As argued, one of the limitations of, particularly, earlier versions of intersubjectivity was that although it challenged the "myth of the isolated mind" and "myth of neutrality", it concentrated on the analytic partnership or dyad in isolation (Zeddies, 2000b); this over-emphasis has been subsequently corrected by Stolorow, Atwood and Orange (2002). Greenberg (1999a,b) helpfully explores the embedded dimension of analytic treatment and how definitions of therapeutic authority invoke the cultural milieu in which they operate, although group analysis provides even wider analytic resources by which to conceptualize the co-constructed nature of therapeutic work, whether with individuals or in group.

Foulkes's notion of "incompleteness" takes us far away from Heine's image of the philosopher. There are many unexplored links between fallibilism and radical perspectivisim of intersubjectivity theory and the Foulkesian tradition of group analysis, taking us well beyond the analytic closure and desire for certainty in the early generation of analysts.

References

Aron, L. (1996). *A Meeting of Minds: Mutuality in Psychoanalysis*. Hillside, NJ: Analytic Press.

Bacal, H. (1998). Notes on optimal responsiveness in the group process. In: I. Harwood & M. Pines (Eds.), *Circular Reflections* (pp. 175–180). London: Jessica Kingsley.

Balint, M. (1968). *The Basic Fault*. London: Tavistock.

Behr, H., & Hearst, L. (2007). *Group Analytic Psychotherapy: A Meeting of Minds*. Chichester: Wiley.

Bergmann, M. (1997). The historical roots of psychoanalysis orthodoxy. *International Journal of Psychoanalysis*, 78: 69–89.

Bion, W. (1961). *Experiences in Groups*. London: Tavistock.

Breuer, J., & Freud, S. (1895d). *Studies on Hysteria. S.E.*, 2. London: Hogarth.

Brown, D. (1979). Some reflections on Bion's basic assumptions from a group-analytic viewpoint. *Group Analysis*, 12(3): 203–210.

Dalal, F. (1998). *Taking the Group Seriously*. London: Jessica Kingsley.

Eisold, K. (1997). Freud as a leader: the early years of the Viennese society. *International Journal of Psychoanalysis*, 78: 87–103.

Ezriel, H. (1950). A psychoanalytic approach to group treatment. *British Journal of Medical Psychology*, 23: 59–74.

Ezriel, H. (1952). Notes on psychoanalytic group therapy: interpretation and research. *Psychiatry*, 15: 119–126.

Foucault, M. (1978). *The History of Sexuality, Volume 1: An Introduction*. Harmondsworth: Penguin.

Fosshage, J. (1994). Towards re-conceptualising transference: theoretical and clinical considerations. *International Journal of Psychoanalysis*, 75: 265–280.

Foulkes, S. H. (1964). *Therapeutic Group Analysis*. London: Allen & Unwin.

Foulkes, S. H. (1975). *Selected Papers of S. H. Foulkes*, E. Foulkes (Ed.). London: Karnac.

Foulkes, S. H. (1986). *Group-Analytic Psychotherapy: Methods and Principles*. London: Maresfield.

Foulkes, S. H. (1990a). My philosophy in psychotherapy. In: *Selected Papers* (Chapter 21). London: Karnac.

Foulkes, S. H. (1990b). The group as a matrix of the individual's mental life. In: *Selected Papers* (Chapter 22). London: Karnac.

Foulkes, S. H. (2003). Mind. *Group Analysis*, 36(3): 315–321.

Freud, S. (1905e). *Fragment of an Analysis of a Case of Hysteria*. S.E., 7: 3–122. London: Hogarth.

Freud, S. (1909d). *Notes upon a Case of Obsessional Neurosis*. S.E., 10: 153–249. London: Hogarth.

Freud, S. (1912e). Recommendations to physicians practising psychoanalysis. S.E., 12: 109–120. London: Hogarth.

Freud, S. (1919a). Lines of advance in psycho-analytic therapy. S.E., 17: 157–168. London: Hogarth.

Freud, S. (1923a). Two encyclopaedia articles. S.E., 18: 233–260. London: Hogarth.

Freud, S. (1933a). *New Introductory Lectures on Psychoanalysis*. S.E., 22. London: Hogarth.

Gill, M. (1982). Psychoanalysis and psychotherapy: a revision. *International Review of Psycho-Analysis*, 11: 161–179.

Goldberg, A. (2000). Postmodern psychoanalysis. *International Journal of Psychoanalysis*, 82: 123–128.

Goldberg, A. (2007). *Moral Stealth. How 'Correct Behaviour' Institutes Itself in Psychotherapeutic Practice.* Chicago: University of Chicago Press.

Greenberg, J. (1999a). The analysts' participation: a new look. *Journal of the American Psychoanalytic Association, 49*(2): 383–391.

Greenberg, J. (1999b). Analytic authority and analytic restraint. *Contemporary Psychoanalysis, 35*: 25-41.

Group Analysis (1996). Special Issue on Philosophy, *29*(3).

Harwood, I., & Pines, M. (Eds.) (1998). *Self Experiences in Groups.* London: Jessica Kingsley.

Hearst, L. (2000). Power—where does it reside in group analysis? (unpublished lecture).

Kanzer, M. (1983). Freud: the first pyschoanalytic group leader. In: H. Kaplan & B. Sadock (Eds.), *Comprehensive Group Psychotherapy* (2nd edn) (pp. 8–14). Baltimore, MD: Williams and Williams.

Kohut, H. (1977). *Restoration of the Self.* New York: International Universities Press.

Lachmann, F. (1986). Interpretation of psychological conflicts and adversarial relationships: a self-psychological perspective. *Psychoanalytic Pscychology, 3*(4): 341–355.

Lichtenberg, J. D. (1983). The influence of values and value judgements on the psychoanalytic encounter. *Psychoanalytic Inquiry, 3*: 647–664.

Malan, D. (1976). Group psychotherapy: a long-term follow-up study. *Archives of General Psychiatry, 33*: 1303–1315.

McLaughlin, J. (1981). Transference, psychic realty and counter-transference. *Psychoanalytic Quarterly, 20*: 639–664.

Mitchell, S. (1988). *Relational Concepts in Psychoanalysis.* Cambridge, MA: Harvard University Press.

Orange, D. (1995). *Emotional Understanding: Studies in Psychoanalytic Epistemology.* New York: Guildford Press.

Orange, D., Atwood, G. E., & Stolorow, R. D. (1997). *Working Intersubjectively.* Hillsdale, NJ: Analytic Press.

Pines, M. (1996). Dialogue and selfhood: discovering connections. *Group Analysis, 29*(3): 327–341.

Schain, J. (1989). The new infant research: some implications for group therapy. *Group, 13*(2): 112–121.

Schulte, P. (2000). Holding in mind: intersubjectivity, subject relations and the group. *Group Analysis, 33*(4): 531–544.

Stacey, R. (2001). What can it mean to say that the individual is social through and through? *Group Analysis, 34*(4): 457–471.

Stern, D., Sander, L., Nahum, J., Harrison, A., Lyons-Ruth, K., Morgan, A., Bruschweiler-Stern, N., & Tronick, E. (1998). Non-interpretive mechanisms in psycholanalytic therapy. *International Journal of Psychoanalysis, 79*: 903–921.

Stewart, H. (1990). Interpretation and other agents for psychic change. *International Journal of Psychoanalysis, 17*: 61–69.

Stolorow, R., & Atwood, G. (1979). *Faces in a Cloud: Subjectivity in Personality Theory*. New York: Jason Aronson.

Stolorow, R., & Atwood, G. (1992). *Contexts of Being: The Intersubjective Foundations of Psychological Life*. Hillsdale, NJ: Analytic Press.

Stolorow, R., & Lachmann, F. (1981). Two psycholanalyses or one? *Psychoanalytic Review, 68*(3): 307–319.

Stolorow, R., Atwood, G., & Orange, D. (2002). *Worlds of Experience*. New York: Basic Books.

Stolorow, R., Brandchaft, B., & Atwood, G. (1987). *Psychoanalytic Treatment: An Intersubjective Approach*. Hillsdale, NJ: Analytic Press.

Strachey, J. (1934). The nature of the therapeutic action of psychoanalysis. *International Journal of Psychoanalysis, 15* (reproduced in Vol. 50, 1969): 127–159.

Taylor, C. (1989). *Sources of the Self: The Making of Modern Identity*. Cambridge: Cambridge University Press.

Weegmann, M. (1982). *The Emergence of the Psychoanalytic Domain* (unpublished).

Wolberg, L. R. (1976). The technique of short-term psychotherapy. In: L. R. Wolberg (Ed.), *Short-Term Psychotherapy* (pp. 128–189). New York: Grune and Stratton.

Zeddies, T. (2000a). Psychoanalytic praxis and the moral vision of psychoanalysis. *Contemp. Psychoanal., 36*: 521–528.

Zeddies, T. (2000b). Within, outside and in between – the relational unconscious. *Psychoanalytic Psychology, 17*(3): 467–487.

Zeddies, T. (2002). Historical experience in social and historical context. *Group Analysis, 35*(3): 381–389.

Zeddies, T., & Richardson, F. (1999). Analytic authority in historical and critical perspective. *Contemporary Psychoanalysis, 35*(4): 581–601.

CHAPTER SEVEN

The lost roots of the theory of group analysis: "interrelational individuals" or "persons"*

Joshua Lavie

This chapter combines a micro-historical analysis of unpublished drafts of work by S. H. Foulkes—intended to be part of his "Theory Book" on group analysis—with my reading of published writings by Norbert Elias that are especially relevant to group analysis. (My reading is a "historical reading" taking into account both the cultural–historical climate that prevailed at the time Elias and Foulkes thought and acted, and a "micro-historical analysis" of documents which were discovered in the Archives.) I will focus on two lost roots of the theory of group analysis: one, Elias's innovative conceptualization of the simultaneous and interdependent process of individualization and socialization; two, Foulkes's attempts to conceptualize the mind as a multi-personal (or transpersonal) phenomenon. The main argument is that the theory of group analysis is based on the notion of interrelational individuals (in the plural) or persons (Hopper, 2003) rather than the

*This chapter is based on extensive interdisciplinary research that I am conducting for a doctoral thesis with The Cohn Institute for the History and Philosophy of Science and Ideas, Faculty of Humanities, School of Philosophy, Tel-Aviv University.

reified "individual" as opposed to the nominalized "group". It is proposed that Foulkes's conceptualization of the individual mind as a multi-personal and transpersonal phenomenon is compatible with Stephen Mitchell's much later work on "multiple selves"; in fact, several contributions from group analysis, such as those of Hopper (1977) and Pines (1986) in connection with the notion of the self as a group and the group as a self, might have contributed to the early development of relational psychoanalysis. It is also proposed that, for Foulkes, the social unconscious was a transpersonal phenomenon, both forming and being formed by multi-relational persons (Weinberg, 2007).

The legacy of the work of S. H. Foulkes and of Norbert Elias has helped us to avoid a twofold problem in the social psychological study of group dynamics: the idealization of the individual and the denigration of groups, and the opposite, the denigration of individuals and the idealization of groups, each tendency representing different facets of modernity. The representations of this false dichotomy can be found in the social sciences, political ideologies, philosophies, literature, etc., for example, as seen in the perennial and virtually archetypical discussion of nature vs. nurture.

Throughout the mid-1930s, Elias conducted comprehensive research in order to study the psycho-social historical origins of modern individuals in the course of what he termed the "civilizing process". Furthermore, he enquired into the specific historical and ideological conditions underlying the establishment of modern psychologies—especially psychoanalysis—which were based originally on the conception of "The Individual" (in the singular) as a closed entity, that is to say: the model of the "closed man" (or "Homo Clausus"). Elias argued for a different, more realistic and more scientific conception of individuals (in the plural) as, in his own words, "open entities with open valences of bonding to other individuals", and as "Homines Aperti" or "open people" (Elias, 1969).

The sociologist Eric Dunning, who worked directly with Norbert Elias, and who was a very close friend of Earl Hopper's, wrote, "I like to think of Elias as sociology's equivalent to Copernicus . . . correcting what he called the *homo clausus* view of humans and replacing it with an orientation towards *homines aperti*, pluralities of open people" (Dunning, 1997, pp. 477–478, my italics). There is no doubt that this new paradigm was based on one of the earliest interdisciplinary studies carried out in the twentieth century, attempting to study the individual (psychology) and the social (sociology) within their generationally and historically specific conditions.

Foulkes (1938) was fascinated by Elias's discoveries and revolutionary conceptions of modern individuals, and wove them into his own new revolutionary psychotherapeutic practice. His simple basic idea was: if people live from birth as interrelational open entities with open valences of bonding, if they are thoroughly both socialized and individualized at the same time, and if during this process they are liable to produce psychopathological conditions, then we *not only might, but also must*, assemble them in a therapeutic group in order to treat them.

Elias stands on Freud's shoulders in his magnum opus The Civilizing Process: Sociogenetic and Psychogenetic Investigations

The fundamental essence of Elias's project, which is the complex, interdisciplinary enquiry into the *individuals* of our modern era, was to explore the course by which people in the West became *more and more individualized* during the civilizing process.

This is the reason why Elias's starting point sprang from the discoveries of Sigmund Freud, which dealt primarily with the mental structures of modern individuals. In fact, one can see Elias's studies as a "footnote" to, or "correspondence" with, Sigmund Freud. Actually, in a footnote in *The Civilizing Process* in connection with the socio-genesis of the superego, Elias (2000) writes,

> it scarcely needs to be said, but is perhaps worth emphasizing explicitly, how much this study owes to the discoveries of Freud and the psychoanalytical school. The connections are obvious to anyone acquainted with psychoanalytical writings, and it did not seem necessary to point them out in particular instances, especially because it could not have been done without lengthy qualifications. Nor have the not inconsiderable differences between the whole approach of Freud and that adopted in this study been stressed explicitly, particularly as the two could perhaps after some discussion be made to agree without undue difficulty. [p. 527]

For Elias and Foulkes, the main issues derived from problems concerning the freedom and well-being of modern individuals in the 1920s and 1930s facing fascism and its mass psychological phenomena. Even if Foulkes named his new method "group analysis", which discovered and explored specific group-analytic factors, it was, in essence, a method for treating individuals (in the plural), not "the individual" (in the singular) and not "the group" (as a whole). In other words, it was an attempt to make a space and manner of practice for healing individuals who lost their individuality and personal identity in the tangle of their psychopathology and life crises. To recall the paradox suggested by the closing words of the *Introduction to Group-Analytic Psychotherapy* (Foulkes, 1948, p. 170),

> Group Analysis is thus an ingenious device . . . Collectively they (the patients) can do what individually they fall short of, acting as each other's therapist . . . The better the individual is or becomes, the more free and integrated, the better he becomes as a member of the group. The better its members the better the group becomes. A good group, however, breeds and develops, creates and cherishes that precious product: *the human individual.* [original italics]

The simultaneous interdependent process of "individualization" and "socialization": the first root of group-analytic theory

The very title of Elias's (1991) book, *The Society of Individuals*, tells the whole story. It is not "Society *and* Individuals", it is not "Individuals *in* Society", and it is not, even as group analysts tend to say, "Society *in* Individuals"; it is "Society *of* Individuals" (Babylon Dictionary: "OF" = belonging to; characterized by), and in the original in German, *Die Gesellschaft der Individuen* (1987). The usual prevailing thinking and expression in group analytic circles is: "Society inside individuals", as in the notion, "The individual is social through and through". It is difficult to go beyond the opposition between individual and society, and to understand modern society as a "society *of* individuals", a society which consists of ever-growing individualization of its members. This book has an unusual and peculiar history, on the verge of being a detective story. Roger Chartier, the eminent French historian, director of the Ecole des Hautes-Etudes en Sciences Sociales, Paris, wrote in his book, *On the Edge of the Cliff: History, Language, and Practices* (1997),

> *The Society of Individuals* was written as part of a lengthy summary that concludes Elias's major work, *The Civilizing Process*, published in Basel in 1939. For reasons he never explained, however, Elias removed this text when his book was in the proof stage, sent to a Swedish journal to be published separately, the text instead remained unpublished and the review never saw the light of day. It was not until 1983 that it was revised and reproduced and circulated at the University of Stockholm, and not until 1987 that it became easily accessible. Its importance within Elias's work is nonetheless capital, because it outlines the theoretical bases for his analyses in *The Civilizing Process*. [p. 107]

Bauman (2000) grasped the essence of Elias's paradigmatic revolution, so essential to the understanding of the first root of the theory of group analysis:

> . . . the title given by Norbert Elias to his last, posthumously published study, *Society of Individuals*, flawlessly grasps the gist of the problem which has haunted social theory since its inception. Breaking with the tradition established since Hobbes and reforged by John Stuart Mill, Herbert Spencer and the liberal orthodoxy into the *doxa* (the unexamined frame for all further cognition) of our century, Elias replaced the "and" or the "versus" with the "of"; and by so doing he shifted the discourse from the *imaginaire* of the two forces locked in a mortal yet unending battle of freedom and domination, into that of *"reciprocal conception"*: society shaping the individuality of its members, and individuals forming society out of their life actions while pursuing strategies plausible and feasible within the socially woven web of their dependencies. Casting members as individuals is the trade mark of modern society. That casting, however, was not a one-off act: it is an activity re-enacted daily. Modern society exists in its incessant activity of "individualizing" as much as the activities of individuals consist in the daily reshaping and renegotiating of the network of mutual entanglements called society. [pp. 30–31]

Bauman (2001) used the same text in his Foreword to Beck and Beck-Gernsheim's (2001) book *Individualization*, titling it: "Individually, together". Although this title sounds paradoxical, in fact it grasps the group analytic and the relational character of the process of the individualizing process.

In *The Society of Individuals* (exactly as in the *Civilizing Process*), Elias did not criticize Freud for not having a social theory of people, neither did he disavow him for focusing on individuals. On the contrary, he honoured Freud for his discoveries concerning the individual psyche. Yet, he saw his own work as emphasizing its social-historical origins. Definitely, Elias's vision was a challenge to Freud, yet its aim was not to put society or groups as alternatives to the human individual, but to study further, comprehensively and more deeply, the phenomenon of individualization. Elias indicates that individualization is a process embedded in society with a specific history, and that every child in our evolving society is "thoroughly individualized and socialized at the same time".

In order to contextualize the basic argument of *The Society of Individuals* and its essential role in the theory of group analysis, I will quote from a conversation between Dennis Brown (1997) and Norbert Elias, which took place in November 1989, in Amsterdam. Elias was then ninety-two years old, a year before his death.

Dennis Brown: Tell me, in what way do you feel your expertise in sociology influenced Foulkes? Were there ideas of yours that he took over directly?

Norbert Elias: From early days on I tried to overcome the language which forced us to speak as if individual and society, individual and group are different and opposed entities. I don't know whether you know the book *Die Gesellschaft der Individuen*—it has not yet appeared in English but it is about to be translated.

DB: No. Unfortunately I don't speak German. Your book *The Civilizing Process*, as it was called in English, is of course well known.

NE: Yes, that is *the theoretical interest which Foulkes was interested in* [my italics]. It comes out indirectly, that is to say *the very idea of the civilizing process implies that the individual is thoroughly socialized and individualized at the same time* [my italics]. What was for me a new discovery was that I could show how the social norms change and if one translates this from the abstract to social norms in human terms, *one must also say that the individuals change* [my italics], individuals in different generations grow up with somewhat different social rules, you can see it in the freedom of the younger generation today compared to that with my youth. So I think it was this knowledge that *individuals can only be understood in groups and groups only as groups of individuals* [my italics] . . . I do not know to what extent even today is still in group-analytic theory used, that one sees the individual and the group as two levels in the group. That was one of the things which I brought in, as it were, and later turned out in group-analytic treatment wanders from the group level to the individual level and from the individual level to the group level, both having roots in the focus of one's attention.

DB: A sort of foreground/background dialectic . . .

NE: Yes, *I am not quite clear whether I would see it foreground/background but I want to have it on an equal level so there are two levels of equal weight* [my italics]. And thoughts of this time can be found in the first part of *The Society of Individuals* . . .

DB: I look forward to reading it.

NE: We [Foulkes & Elias] were very much at one, that *we did not want to reduce one to the other, nor did we want to dissolve* [my italics], so that was, I think, even before we earnestly talked with similar inclination. [Brown, 1997, pp. 518–519]

. . .

DB: . . . It was quite striking, even ideas like the individual as a nodal point, a sort of intersection in a web, like a neuron in the nervous system.

NE: Yes, I had already at that time developed instead a concept of figuration in one of my first books, *What is Sociology?* Human beings form figurations. *If one says "a group" one has difficulties to say "a group of individuals" and I was looking for a word which would make it possible just to say that. A figuration of individuals, or if you prefer to say, configuration of individuals* [my italics], that came very near to what Foulkes needed . . .

I have in *What is Sociology?* a slight picture which shows the naïve perspective of the individual in which she or he is in the center of the group and then an act of detachment or distancing is necessary

in order to see oneself as one among others, and that is what I
wanted to express with the term figuration. [*ibid.*, p. 520]

I refer now to the diagrams (Figures 1 and 2) to which Elias drew
our attention. (The diagrams illustrate the new paradigm Elias so
eagerly initiated and promoted: a paradigm, which conceives the

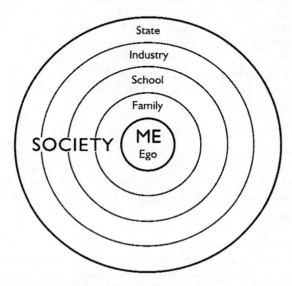

Figure 1.   Basic pattern of the egocentric view of society. From Elias 1970.

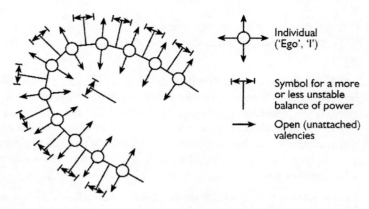

Figure 2.   A figuration of interdependent individuals ("family", "state",
"group", "society", etc.).

human world not in the language that separates "Individuals" and "Society", but as a human world of interdependent individuals forming figurations ("web structures") with each other. Note the metaphoric use of the concept of "valence", derived from chemistry, to point to the attachment characteristics of individuals towards each other. Elias used this concept as early as 1937, years before Bion (1961) used it to denote the group dynamics of the basic assumptions. It is the same metaphoric concept for different ideas. However, the use of the chemical concept of valence in the human sciences deserves more elaboration for another occasion.) I reproduce these diagrams, which Elias called "pictures", in order to give us the full feeling of Elias's new paradigm in the human sciences, as expressed in the old saying: "a picture is worth a thousand words".

> NE: I think that was the basic attitude which we [Foulkes and Elias] shared where, as I say, I think I could help a good deal, because I was quite clear that in society at large the separation of individual and society was in part due to the fact that different parties accentuate differently. The right the individual, and the left the group and *one carries these values of a partisan conviction into the theory* [my italics], which is not very good ... I was very much interested in ideologies and this is the item I brought into our community—that as long as society at large is split in terms of the basic views giving individual and society different values, one speaks and thinks as if individual and society had a different existence, and that is beginning I think to change.

> One can at least hope that it is now nearing the end of this division ...

Actually, the idea of the social unconscious is clearly depicted in the interview above. When Elias says: "I could show how the social norms change and if one translates this from the abstract to social norms in human terms, one must also say that the individuals change, individuals in different generations grow up with somewhat different social rules", he is referring to the impact of the social restrictions on their daily behaviour of which people are unaware, and also to the different constraints in different generations which facilitate (or restrict) individualization, of which people are unaware.

Foulkes's innovative conception of the mind: the second basic root of group-analytic theory

In an attempt to uncover the second lost root of group-analytic theory, let us now turn to a micro-historical analysis of Foulkes's unpublished documents. Parenthetically, we should not forget the fact that Foulkes intended to write a "Theory Book" together with Norbert Elias. He was aware of his need for Elias as far as theory was concerned. Foulkes not only had theoretical difficulties in establishing an explicit theory, he also had political difficulties as a result of his being part of the therapeutic disciplines. Elias, as opposed to the other founding fathers–mothers of the "Group Analytic Society", was the only one who came from a different discipline, that is, the social sciences, and a "continental" sociology in particular. This fact helped him to go beyond the boundaries of the traditional division between the disciplines of psychology, sociology, anthropology, and history, which deal with human beings from different perspectives. Foulkes brought Elias into the Society and, with him, the fertile spirit of interdisciplinary thinking and research.

Foulkes's literary "remains", kept in the Wellcome Archives for the History and Understanding of Medicine in London, illustrates the intellectual struggle that Foulkes had with the concept of the "individual mind". Foulkes was really interested in the topic of mental structures of individual people and not predominantly the themes of group dynamics. Foulkes improvised with his ideas while writing journal articles or books relating to the community of group psychotherapy. He managed to blur his primary concern with individual minds by emphasizing primarily the mediatory concept of the "Matrix", although the concept of the "matrix", or the "communication in the group matrix", has a theoretical and, particularly, a clinical and therapeutic significance of its own.

The following material has been extracted from drafts that Foulkes wrote in 1969 for the planned "Theory Book", which was in preparation when he died in 1976. The extracts are printed in their original form. I will present the transformations of the title in different drafts and then part of the content itself, looking into the significance of the small changes made before the final product.

Stage 1.

22.10.69

Drafting

Some Notes on my Concept of the Mind as a Multi-personal
or better still transpersonal phenomenon.

S. H. FOULKES

Stage 2.

*The group matrix. In
Wolberg + Schwartz (eds) Group
Therapy 1973*

October, 1969.

Some Notes on my Concept of the Mind as a Transpersonal
Phenomenon.

---

by S. H. FOULKES

Stage 3.

CHAPTER TWENTY-TWO

The group as matrix
of the individual's mental life

Chapter in L. R. Wolberg and E. K. Schwartz (eds.), *Group Therapy
1973—An Overview* (New York: Intercontinental Medical Book Corpora-
tion, 1973).

As late as 1973, Foulkes was reluctant to publish his theory of
the mind, which was so essential to the theory of group analysis.
For, if the human mind is from the outset "multi-personal", and if
you assemble people in a group, then a multi-personal "group

matrix" is generated as an indispensable outcome of the characteristics of the mind of each of the participants in the group.

It is important to note that in the published version, Foulkes
(1973) accentuated "the group as matrix of the individual's mental life", and not "the mind as a multi-personal/transpersonal
phenomenon". In a way, this speaks for itself. However, he utilized
part of the material in the published version, as can be seen in his
post factum remark on the draft from 1969 written in his handwrit-
ing in step 2: "*used in 'The gp as matrix'* . . . *In Wolberg & Schwartz
(eds) Group Therapy 1973*". This *post factum* remark, written after
1973, indicates that Foulkes was dealing with these drafts during
the three years preceding his death, preparing them for his book on
theory. And, nevertheless, Foulkes's (1973) published article, "The
group as matrix of the individual's mental life", became a keystone
in later attempts to widen the scope of the theory of group analysis
(see, for example, Brownbridge, 2003; Stacey, 2001a,b).

Let us now delve more deeply into Foulkes's theoretical moves
concerning: one, the strong conception of the mind as belonging to
an individual and his body; two, the strong conviction that our
minds are embedded in the outside world, and have been constituted through introjecting the experience we accumulate during
our lives. Is it possible to read Foulkes as a relational, intersubjective thinker? Well, maybe yes, maybe no! We can assume that, in the
early 1960s, Foulkes was very much in contact with the rigorous
method of infant observations developed and carried out in
London by Esther Bick. Consider the paragraph from the 1969 draft:

> After all, there is hardly any internal experience possible which has
> not been stimulated from outside and by other people—even the
> experience of our own bodies has from the first been imbued with
> the influence of our mothers. There is no "outside" (reality) experi-
> ence which is not containing us and all our reactions—including
> even phantasies and distortions . . .

Certainly, Foulkes regarded the skin as embryonically at both
the core and the boundaries of the body, and possibly of the mind.

It is well known that Foulkes was preoccupied with the phenomenon of "introjection" in connection with what the infant took
in from the external world. This was a theoretical direction in line
with Esther Bick's findings, and the opposite from the centrality

of "projection" that prevailed in Melanie Klein's theories. As Hinshelwood (1989) writes with regard to the work of Esther Bick:

> Bick's most significant observation concerned the infant's passive experience of being held together by an external object sensed through the skin sensations . . . this first object binds the personality together and has to be introjected in order to give a sense of space into which introjections can be put. The view that the experience of an internal space is one that is acquired, through adequate experience, contrasts with the idea of an innate experience of internal space implied in Bion's theories. [pp. 230–231]

Moreover, as Hopper (2006) has written, Foulkes acknowledged that he was especially influenced by the idea of the "relational individual" as "a person who, by definition, has been suffused and infused with the social, and vice versa". However, Foulkes "always [acknowledged] the continuing importance of the constraints of the body on the mind, and vice versa" (p. 423).

Hopper (2006) also reports that Foulkes very much agreed with a few lines from his PhD thesis (later published as *Social Mobility: A Study of Social Control and Insatiability*):

> it is self evident to the sociologist that a human being develops only through social interactions. Human beings draw their personal boundaries from the social relationships and cultural patterns of their society at all phases of life cycle. Each person differs from others, but each person also differs from the human organism in which his personality is rooted. In brief, the brain exists with the cranium, but the mind exists among interacting individuals.

> Personality and character have a social basis, and society and culture have a personal basis in terms of the mediating actions of persons who have emerged from socialized organisms . . . [Hopper, 1981, p. 5]

Although Foulkes acknowledged the "mind" as an aspect of the "cherished and precious individual human being", he understood that the constitution, development, and preservation of the mind was a multi-personal process. The phenomenon of "mind" is multi-personal. Becoming an "individuated self" is a complicated and sophisticated progression based on sociogenetic and psychogenetic complementary processes. Clearly, then, the intertwinement of Elias's and Foulkes's discoveries about human beings, their minds, personality structures, and selves, are a *sine qua non* for building a coherent theory for group analysis.

Networking, interweaving, relationality, and relational matrix

I would like to delve into the depths of Norbert Elias's text written as early as 1939. This prophetic text was part of Elias's Sisyphic endeavours to overcome the prevailing dichotomous way of thinking and talking and to create a new Network Language (and after seventy years we can also say a new Interrelational Language) for the human sciences. Elias's prophetic words speak for themselves:

> So each gesture and act of the infant is *neither* the product of his *"inside"* nor of his *"environment"*, nor of an *interaction* between an "inside" and an "outside" which were originally separate, *but* a function and *precipitate of relations*, and can be understood—like the figure of a thread in a net—only from the totality of the network. Likewise the speech of others develops in the growing child something which is entirely his language, and at the same time a product of his *relation* to others, an expression of the *human network* within which he lives. In the same way, ideas, convictions, affects, needs and character traits are produced in the individual through *intercourse with others*, things which make up his *personal "self"* and in which is expressed, for this very reason, the *network of relations* from which he has emerged and into which he passes. And in this way this self, this personal "essence", is formed in a continuous interweaving of needs. It is *the order of this incessant interweaving* without a beginning that *determines the nature and form of the individual human being*. Even the nature and form of his solitude, even what he feels to be his "inner life", is stamped by the history of his *relationships*—by the structure of the *human network* in which, as one of its *nodal points*, he develops and lives as an individual. [*The Society of Individuals*,1939, p. 33]

Elias's essay, *The Society of Individuals* (which was characterized above), was written in 1939, just before the start of the Second World War, in Stockholm, where he briefly taught and studied. It was written in order to clarify certain of his findings in his magnum opus, *The Civilizing Process*, which was completed the year before. However, *The Society of Individuals* went into oblivion, and was not discovered again until 1982 in the archives of the University of Stockholm. None the less, Foulkes, who was one of the first reviewers of *The Civilizing Process* (together with Franz Borkenau and Raymond Aron), knew about Elias's theoretical conceptions, in particular his figurational-process sociology, which had been derived from his socio-psycho-historical findings in his investigations of the civilizing processes in the modern era in the western world. Foulkes later acknowledged that the fact that he never reified either "*the* group" or "*the* individual" was based on the intellectual influence of Elias. Foulkes always looked at the "group-analytic situation" composed of "interrelational individuals" who came to treat their psyches, conceptualized as "multi-personal minds" (or "multiple selves", see below). For Foulkes, as we could see in Elias's conception of the nature of the personal self, a healing process must involved both *individualization* and *socialization* in the same place, at the same time.

It is noteworthy that it was not until the late 1990s that Stephen Mitchell introduced the concept of "multiple selves", devoting an entire chapter, entitled "Multiple selves, singular self", to the subject in his book, *Hope and Dread in Psychoanalysis* (Mitchell, 1993):

> There is no hidden chamber . . . Self is woven into reciprocal interactions between the subject and others . . . The very terms and categories, in which we experience ourselves, embody a social history, a family history, a complex interpersonal history . . . People organize their experience into both *multiple and integral configurations.* [p. 95, my italics]

Mitchell also wrote about the "relational matrix" in his theoretical book *Relational Concepts in Psychoanalysis* (1988): "The most useful way to view psychological reality is as operating within a *relational matrix* which encompass both intrapsychic and interpersonal realms" (p. 9, my italics).

Furthermore, in his last book, *Relationality*, Mitchell (2000) acknowledged the importance of the ideas of the psychoanalyst Hans Loewald in foreseeing the relational turn in psychoanalysis. It is worth noting the similarities between the ideas of Loewald and those of Elias and Foulkes, who were part of the same generation of German-Jewish scholars who fled from Nazi Germany around 1933 and spread throughout Europe and the USA. As Loewald wrote much later in 1970,

> Psychic development takes its beginning in a psychic matrix which comprises—mother and infant . . . This matrix is a psychic field from which the infantile psyche gradually becomes differentiated as a relatively autonomous focus of psychic activity, by process of internalization and externalization . . . The concept of internaliza-tion, as essential process in intrapsychic structure formation or, to put it differently, in individuation, presupposes neither the subject object split nor the assumption of a separate psychic apparatus or organization, however primitive, from the beginning. What becomes internalized—to emphasize it again—are not objects but interactions and relationships . . . I am saying that instinctual drives are formed by interactions within the original matrix . . . the rela-tional character of drives becomes to a various degree internalized . . . [Loewald, 1970, p. 284]

In other words, Loewald delineated the relational character of the unconscious, stemming from the original matrix between the infant and the mother, as the first representative and agent of soci-ety. Although Loewald did not talk directly about the "social unconscious", but of the relational character of the unconscious, his emphasis on fields and matrices points to his wide cultural and social orientation. His later work "Man as moral agent" (1975, in Loewald, 1978) and "Comments on religious experiences" (1976, in Loewald, 1978), refer beautifully to Freud's book *Civilization and Its Discontents* (1930a), seeing Freud's ideas about "oceanic" feelings as stemming from the original relational matrix of the infant–mother field.

Sociogenesis and psychogenesis: dual basic processes constituting the social unconscious in group analysis

Elias's and Foulkes's sociogenesis and psychogenesis of human minds are the two bedrocks on which the theory of group analysis stands. Pines grasped this intuitively in his article "The coherency of group analysis" (2002) (a term that is slightly elaborated in this work, referring to Elias and Foulkes): "The coherency of group analysis is both internal and external. Formation of *individuated selves* is fundamentally a social-historical process (Elias, 1978, my italics) affected by caregiver interaction constituted through language (Bakhtin, 1981: Vygotsky, ref. Wertsch, 1991)" (Pines, 2002, p. 13).

We are closing a circle. Elias gave Freud's meta-psychology a spin by introducing the process of "psychogenesis" recapitulating the process of "sociogenesis". As a continuation and critique of Freud's hypotheses about the mythological genesis (Oedipus) as being recapitulated in the psychogenesis of the superego, Elias's discoveries extended Freud's ground-breaking way of thinking to the whole psycho-social-historical genesis of modern individuals, comprising their entire psyche structures, including ego functions, self images, emotions, the unconscious, etc. Elias created this paradigmatic revolution at the end of Freud's life with the inspiration of Foulkes, who was one of the first psychoanalysts to give culture and society a fundamental place in the formation of the human self.

The legacy of group analysis was, is, and always will be "to take *interrelational individuals* seriously", not the reification of "*the individual*" nor the abstract concept of "*the group*". What happens in group-analytic psychotherapy derives directly from the gathering of these individual minds, which are multi-personal or transpersonal from the outset, before they assemble into a group. However, Foulkes developed this therapeutic situation before he formulated a coherent theory of the mind in health and in sickness.

The sociogenesis and psychogenesis of human individuals and human groups; the simultaneous processes of socialization and individualization of human individuals (in childhood, adolescence, and through adulthood) which produce human *relational persons* (as Hopper (2006) phrased it); the individualization of social institutions: it is these processes in which the social unconscious originates, and, thus, the social unconscious is both relational and personal simultaneously. Foulkes warned us against the belief that somehow our individuality is natural and that our relationality and sociality are artificial, in his speech in 1965 at the Hebrew University (Lavie, 2003):

Social psychologists and cultural anthropologists have made us familiar with an abundance of observations showing beautifully how all individuals are conditioned to their community . . . There is quite a considerable *resistance* against such a perspective, that the ego and the superego, the very core of the personality, are socially conditioned. As soon as it becomes real and concrete in our daily lives and profession!; modern man *clings anxiously* to his individuality and identity, and quite *erroneously assumes* these [his individuality and identity] to be threatened by such observations; instead of realizing that they are *threatened*, on the contrary, by the rift between the group and its individuals in our culture. This *transmission* [of the rift] from generation to generation is an unconscious process. The individual tends to *remain unconscious* of it [of the above erroneous assumption] in his own person, and *well defended* against its recognition. I have called this [the above combination of processes] the "Social Unconscious". The ego cannot see itself, just as one cannot look into one's own eyes, except in a mirror. [Discovered in Foulkes's archives at the Welcome Institute for the History and Understanding of Medicine; first published in Foulkes, 2003, pp. 85–86, my italics]

In sum, according to Foulkes, this combination of feelings, anxieties, false-beliefs, defences, inversions, and misconceptions all constitute the modus operandi of the social unconscious. Moreover, although this definition of the social unconscious was not very clear and perhaps not widely known, it serves to illustrate how the social unconscious is simultaneously both personal and relational, based on interrelated processes of sociogenesis and psychogenesis.

A lesson from the past and a glance to the future

As I mentioned earlier, Foulkes (1938) was among the first to review Elias's work when it appeared in the late 1930s. He pleaded with his colleagues, the psychoanalysts, to take into consideration the historicity and the social and cultural foundations of the human psyche. But they remained mute. Now, after seventy years, following the "relational and intersubjective turn" in psychoanalysis, based primarily on the "cultural and linguistic turn" in post modernity, we can see that Foulkes was ahead of his time. Foulkes internalized but did not completely digest Elias's findings and insights, which helped to precipitate this "cultural turn" in the human sciences (the new paradigm based the primacy of culture and language over the subject), culminating in the second half of the twentieth century. In his prophetic and perhaps revolutionary Chairman's address to the Medical Section of the British Psychological Society in 1961, published as "Psychotherapy in the sixties" (1964), Foulkes wrote,

> The work of Freud and of psychoanalysis in the broad sense, has dominated the first half of this century. Its contributions will remain of paramount importance for all future progress. . . . Modern research shows [however], that much of what appeared to be biological inheritance is in fact cultural inheritance transmitted socially. . . . *I have stressed the existence of a network of interaction, in which everybody tries to solve the conflicts common to all in interdependence with the others* . . . our work is indeed difficult, but is intensely rewarding. All signposts—unless there is total destruction—point to such rapid development that, *looking back from the year 2000,* the first half of the twentieth century might well appear as remote as do the middle ages to us. [pp. 153–154, my italics]

Acknowledgements

I express my gratitude to the Wellcome Institute for the History and Understanding of Medicine for being so kind in welcoming me and assisting me in my research. The majority of the personal documents belonging to S. H. Foulkes were deposited in the Contemporary Medical Archive Centre by his widow, Elizabeth Foulkes, in 1991, for the purpose of scrutiny, study, and research.

References

Bakhtin, M. (1981). *The Dialogic Imagination: Four Essays by M. M. Bakhtin,* M. Holquist (Ed.). Austin, TX: University of Texas Press.

Bauman, Z. (2000). *Liquid Modernity.* Cambridge: Polity Press.

Bauman, Z. (2001). Individually, together. In: U. Beck & E. Beck-Gernsheim (Eds.), *Individualization* (pp. xiv–xix). London: Sage.

Bion, W. R. (1961). *Experiences in Groups and Other Papers.* New York: Basic Books.

Brown, D. (1997). Conversation with Norbert Elias. *Group Analysis*, 30(4): 515–524.

Brownbridge, G. (2003). The group in the individual. *Group Analysis*, 36(1): 23–36.

Chartier, R. (1997). *On the Edge of the Cliff: History, Language, and Practices*. Baltimore, MD: Johns Hopkins University Press.

Dalal, F. (1998). *Taking the Group Seriously*. London: Jessica Kingsley.

Dunning, E. (1997). Sport in quest for excitement: Norbert Elias's contribution to the sociology of sport. *Group Analysis*, 30(4): 477–487.

Elias, N. (1969). Sociology and psychiatry. In: S. H. Foulkes & G. S. Prince (Eds.), *Psychiatry in a Changing Society* (pp. 117–144). London: Tavistock.

Elias, N. (1978). *What Is Sociology?* London: Hutchinson [originally published (1970) as *Was ist Soziologie?* Munich: Juventa Verlag].

Elias, N. (1991). *The Society of Individuals*. Oxford: Basil Blackwell [originally published (1987) as *Die Gesellschaft der Individuen*. Munich: Suhrkamp Verlag].

Elias, N. (2000). *The Civilizing Process* (revised edn). Oxford: Blackwell [originally published (1939) as *Über den Prozess der Zivilisation*. Basel: Hans zum Falken].

Foulkes, S. H. (1938). Book review of Norbert Elias's *The Civilizing Process*. In: E. Foulkes (Ed.), *S. H. Foulkes, Selected Papers*. London: Karnac, 1990.

Foulkes, S. H. (1948). *Introduction to Group Analytic Psychotherapy*. London: Heinemann Medical [reprinted London: Karnac, 1983].

Foulkes, S. H. (1964). *Therapeutic Group Analysis*. London: George Allen and Unwin.

Foulkes, S. H. (1973). The group as matrix of the individual's mental life. In: E. Foulkes (Ed.), *S. H. Foulkes, Selected Papers* (pp. 223–233). London: Karnac, 1990.

Foulkes, S. H. (2003). New psychoanalytic contribution to interpersonal dynamics: theoretical considerations and applications in therapeutic group analysis (first publication). *Mikbatz—The Israeli Journal of Group Psychotherapy*, 8(1): 79–86.

Freud, S. (1930a). *Civilization and Its Discontents*. S.E., 21: 59–145. London: Hogarth.

Hinshelwood, R. D. (1989). *A Dictionary of Kleinian Thought*. London: Free Association Books.

Hopper, E. (1977). Correspondence. *Group Analysis*, 10(3): 24.

Hopper, E. (1981). *Social Mobility: A Study of Social Control and Insatiability.* Oxford: Blackwell [excerpts reprinted in Hopper, E. (2003). *The Social Unconscious: Selected Papers.* London: Jessica Kingsley].

Hopper, E. (2003). *The Social Unconscious: Selected Papers.* London: Jessica Kingsley.

Hopper, E. (2006). The relational perspective in psychoanalysis and group analysis: a comment on the exchange between Dalal and Lavie concerning "the lost roots of the theory of group analysis: "taking interrelational individuals seriously"!' by Joshua Lavie. *Group Analysis, 39*(3): 421–431.

Lavie, J. (2003). Foulkes in Israel. *Mikbatz—The Israeli Journal of Group Psychotherapy, 8*(1): 87–88.

Loewald, H. (1970). Psychoanalytic theory and psychoanalytic process. In: *Papers on Psychoanalysis.* New Haven, CT: Yale University Press, 1980.

Loewald, H. (1978). *Psychoanalysis and the History of the Individual.* New Haven, CT: Yale University Press.

Mitchell, S. A. (1988). *Relational Concepts in Psychoanalysis.* Cambridge, MA: Harvard University Press.

Mitchell, S. A. (1993). *Hope and Dread in Psychoanalysis.* New York: Basic Books.

Mitchell, S. A. (2000). *Relationality: From Attachment to Intersubjectivity.* New Jersey & London: The Analytic Press.

Pines, M. (1986). Coherency and disruption in the sense of the self. *British Journal of Psychotherapy, 2*(3): 180–185 [reprinted in M. Pines (Ed.), *Circular Reflections* (pp. 211–223). London: Jessica Kingsley, 1998].

Pines, M. (2002). The coherency of group analysis. *Group Analysis, 35*(1): 13–26.

Stacey, R. (2001a). Complexity and the group matrix. *Group Analysis, 34*(2): 221–239.

Stacey, R. (2001b). What can it mean to say that the individual is social through and through? *Group Analysis, 34*(4): 457–471.

Weinberg, H. (2007). So what is this social unconscious anyway? *Group Analysis, 40*(3): 307–322.

Wertsch, J. W. (1991). *Voices of the Mind. A Socio-Cultural Approach to Mediated Action.* London: Harvester Wheatsheaf.

PART IV
THE MIND OF THE SOCIAL SYSTEM

Introduction

Felix de Mendelssohn

These two intriguing papers that comprise the section entitled "The mind and the social system" explore the largely uncharted territory at the confluence of individual developmental psychology with specific structures and functions of social systems. Through the use of extensive but pertinent international literature, the authors bring to us a plethora of original insights gathered from their formidable and formative clinical experiences in Eastern Europe under the workings of totalitarian regimes and ideologies, and the sudden, often traumatic, collapse of these extreme forms of "social order".

Helena Klímová, from Prague, in her astute and moving paper "The false we/the false collective self", takes us with patience and high descriptive power through the stages of individual and collective psycho-social development that underlie the pernicious, all-pervading processes of life under totalitarian dictatorship.[1]

Klímová registers the effects of these projections of the individual self on to and into the collective life in terms of "parallel processes", although it must be said that one could also think here of a kind of reciprocally incremental feedback effect. Her use of some small but well-chosen case vignettes is helpful in illustrating not only theoretical, but also empathic qualities in her understanding of these complex processes.

From the outset, Klímová is concerned with language: its connotation of the symbolic order and usage, its connection with a specific "style of thinking/feeling", its central role in the development of subjectivity and its subsequent fate when unconscious individual and social processes of disintegration/incohesion and aggregation/massification take place. This section, which also introduces the "pronoun" as a decisive ordering principle of individual subjectivity and social discourse, is beautiful in its concision and clarity.

Moving on to a discussion of "Collective subjectivity: is there such a thing?", I find myself somewhat at variance with the author in her terminology, perhaps due to my still unresolved critical stance toward the Kohutian School of Self Psychology, while remaining convinced and enlightened by her description of the phenomena. I still find the idea of the collective self to be a somewhat reductionist misnomer, and prefer greatly the stance, quoted by Klímová, of Karterud and Stone (2009) who declare: "Groups do not contain any supraindividual mind, but a supraindividual project. The project consists of certain ambitions, ideals and resources embedded in *a specific history (similar to the individual self)*" (my italics). In my view this "group project" is constantly liable to being tested according to the reality principle by the individual subjectivity of the different group members.

Thus, I am also loath to embrace her idea of a "collective subjectivity": I believe it to be impossible, except when enforced under totalitarian conditions as a "False Self", or, rather, as a destructive and self-destructive "impossible project", as elaborated by Hopper (2003), concerning trauma and fusion, and by Strenger (2002) concerning the struggle for individuality. My personal view is that collective mourning is never more than partially possible because collective subjectivity can never be totally obtained (perhaps Thank G-d!). I (de Mendelssohn, 2010) have seen evidence of this in small and large analytic groups and refer here to my recent publications on this topic.

In a touching and clear sequence of personal vignettes, Klimova guides us through the developmental aspects of the individual "false self" in the interaction of a small girl with her mother and the identification with the aggressor which initiated it. When she expands this concept (which could be taken rather as a metaphor) to collective processes, she can delineate in a most illuminating way how the structure of collective life under communism in Czechoslovakia was fraught with traumatophilic aspects of the social unconscious—a "parody of mothering" manifesting quasi-religious attitudes towards a "Mother Party", a perverse "language of confused pronouns", an intrusion on human intimacy and spirituality, a "politically correct" concept of the "Kolektiv", as opposed to the "Group" as a dirty word, all demonstrating the fundamentally perverse character of the totalitarian programme of massification and "group-think" in its worst sense (as −K?).

This leads one to consider another aspect of Winnicott's thought, which we could append to Klímová's lucid account. Winnicott holds that when the individual "false self" has become weakened through the analysis of the defences involved, what is first to emerge is not "the true self", which he more or less defines as the "spontaneous gesture", but intense and immense rage, rage above all over the past life consumed and, to some extent, wasted by living under the dominance of the "false self", thus betraying both oneself and others. Only after this rage has, to some extent, been worked through can the "true self" begin to emerge.

If this could remain true for individual analysis, it could be reversed in collective processes. My own memory of brief visits to Prague in 1967 and 1969 were illuminated by what seemed to me, from several gifted and unconventional people I was privileged to meet, expressions of immediate authenticity and spontaneity, which I was hard put to find in the West. Later, as we now know, when the system finally crumbles, rage can emerge in the collective and be dealt with first, in this case, by splitting processes (the division into the Czech Republic and Slovakia) and displaced by frustrated "losers in the new deal" on to Roma minorities and others.

I find the gripping character of Helena Klímová's exemplary paper to lie in its combination of two intertwined approaches: a highly original and serious attempt to apply theoretical concepts of early ontogenetic psychic development to social processes, and a basic empathy and clarity of insight, perhaps only possible to one who has experienced these phenomena at first hand. Helena Klímová has lived through what she describes and has survived to enlighten us with a deeper and more differentiated understanding of collective processes. Hers is truly an "informed heart" (Bettelheim, 1960).

The author of the second paper, "Some manifestations of psychic retreats in social systems", Marina Mojović from Belgrade, also writes from first-hand knowledge, not only of the totalitarian aspects of collective life in former Yugoslavia, but also of the traumatic effects of its disintegration through civil war into the subsequent political calamities endured in the new republic of Serbia. Like the previous author, Mojović is concerned to research the applicability of specific ontogenetic developmental positions in understanding social structures and the unconscious processes that underlie them, and she does so in a quite brilliant and highly structured account, creating a kind of new language or symbolic "grid" for ordering these phenomena, while constantly illustrating these concepts with often short but always sharp examples which make them come alive. Mojović's theoretical approach is impressively cogent in her use of Bionian "binocular vision" in her application of developmental psychology to the study of group dynamics and social systems. She meets various "cross-over" problems with considerable sophistication when she writes, "This phenomenon is often discussed in terms of 'parallel processes', but 'equivalence' allows for the assignment of importance and priority to various causal processes". This example shows how careful the author is to choose her terms of reference, and this is matched by the care she has taken in categorizing the structures and functions of psychic retreats in the individual mind and in the social collective.

Mojović has a profound scholarly knowledge of the complex and cross-fertilizing psychoanalytic literature involved. She also shows herself to be an original thinker who has new things to tell us. This quality may come from her hard-won ability to digest and make sense of the symptoms of war, collective trauma, and social disruption while living in their midst, herself subject to their immediate influence. This is pointed up by two compelling factors in her presentation: first, the wide range of highly pertinent associations to her themes, from all realms of social activity, that highlight the bizarre aspects of traumatophilia in individuals, groups, and society at large. Second, and what impresses most from the clinical point of view, is her willingness to discuss the direct implications of her findings on her own clinical work in treating individuals and groups and in consulting for organizations. Her case examples here illustrate the extreme difficulties a therapist or consultant may encounter in dealing with severe cases of psychic retreat and suggest a model for the basic approach and conduct to be considered.

An aspect on which one might elaborate in future work on this theme is the role of somatic disorder as a mode of concretization of the psychic retreat. As Steiner has elucidated, certain classic organic disorders of the respiratory or excretory functions, such as asthma or chronic colitis, are somatic "equivalents" to the psychic retreats of autistic or borderline states of mind. My experiences in the supervision of therapies of survivors of massacre and torture in Bosnia, Kosovo and other areas of former Yugoslavia who are now present in large numbers in Austria—many of whom receive treatment at the Outpatients Department at the SFU in Vienna—would seem to confirm that this form of somatization into chronic physical ailments is often the chosen and most impregnable fortress against the unbearable tragedy of insight which might otherwise erupt.

I will not attempt here to recapitulate the fine work Mojović does in differentiating such concepts as "encapsulation" and "psychic retreat", especially in regard to our clinical understanding of the treatment problems involved, but I would highlight one aspect of it that could become central to future work: the question of prenatal, intrauterine experience as a matrix for such later mental phenomena. Our increasing knowledge of neurobiological factors involved in the growth of the foetus in the womb, along with the expertise of new technical methods such as ultrasound and neuroimaging, will give us ever greater insight into the importance of prenatal life. Recent discussions of the roots of aggressive behaviour in traumatogenic intrauterine or perinatal experiences have indicated just how fruitful such studies may become (Piontelli, 1992; Thomashoff, 2009).

If, in this Introduction, I have strayed into areas of not totally unrelated disciplines, it is only because I believe it is important for group analysts to stay in contact with findings or hypotheses from the neurosciences and from evolutionary biology, and even from the more dubious and simplistic notions of an "evolutionary psychology" derived from it. This is but testimony to the fact that these two authors, both writing from an authentic position of "learning from experience", and, thus both contributing original and helpful ideas and concepts for our group analytic work, have said the principal things that needed to be said about developments in the inner world of the mind of the human being and how these are reflected in groups and societies, in the collective processes that form them and are formed by them. My own comments and associations exemplify how these two papers can start one thinking on one's own personal journey, which is just what good writing should do.

Note

1. While reading this paper, I found myself thinking about *Wenn das der Fuehrer wuesste* ("If the Fuehrer heard of this . . .") by Otto Basil. This novel was first published in 1966, but has recently been republished in Austria. Basil began his career before the *Anschluss* (annexation of Austria) in 1939, was under *Schreibverbot* (prohibition to publish) during the Third Reich, and then, after its collapse, proceeded to rejuvenate Austrian literature in remarkable fashion. His novel is a "counterfactual history", describing a world in which Hitler and the Japanese had won the war and how Europe might have been faring under a Nazi dictatorship—with Hitler's death (here over twenty years later than it actually occurred) a series of cataclysmic splits and schisms brings global civilization to the point of utter disintegration. One of the finest qualities of the novel is its ability to conjure up that curious mixture of hi-tech jargon, coded speech copied from state-of-the-art military weaponry and strategy (organizations and institutions have only cryptical names, such as an assembly of initials or a mythical figure) merged, or, better, fused with a host of obscure esoteric belief systems, pseudo-mythological rituals, and etymological nonsense. DNA plus SS creates an ordered pandemonium of brutality engineered by a racist pseudo-scientific phantasma that undercuts all levels of society.

References

Basil, O. (2010). *Wenn das der Fuehrer Wuesste*. Vienna: Milena Verlag.
Bettelheim, B. (1960). *The Informed Heart: Autonomy in a Mass Age.* Glencoe, IL: Free Press.

de Mendelssohn, F. (2010). *Das Psychoanalytische Subjekt*. Vienna: SFU Verlag.

Hopper, E. (2003). *Traumatic Experience in the Unconscious Life of Groups*. London: Jessica Kingsley.

Karterud, S., & Stone, W. N. (2009). The group self: a neglected aspect of group psychotherapy. In: *Contributions of Self Psychology to Group Psychotherapy, Selected Papers* (pp. 19–33). London: Karnac.

Piontelli, A. (1992). *From Fetus to Child*. London: New Library.

Stone, W. (2009). *Contributions of Self Psychology to Group Psychotherapy: Selected Papers*. London: Karnac.

Strenger, C. (2002). *Individuality—The Impossible Project*. New York: Other Press.

Thomashoff, H.-O. (2009). *Versuchung des Boesen*. Munich: Koesel Verlag.

CHAPTER EIGHT

The false we/the false collective self: a dynamic part of the social unconscious

Helena Klímová

A task for group analysts has emerged: to interpret the social unconscious in connection with recent historical experience, especially in the context of totalitarian societies, or, rather, those societies who have lived through totalitarian regimes. The two totalitarian systems in Europe have gone, yet we are presented with two ubiquitous dangers that are properties of our foundation matrices: the transmission of trauma over generations, and the compulsion to repeat traumatic experience.

> The predisposition both to experience events as traumatic and actually to seek traumatic experience, is known as traumatophilia (Abraham, 1907). It involves both libidinal and aggressive wishes, including the desire for punishment as well as for revenge on others. It is based on the compulsion to repeat traumatic experience that has been encapsulated in the context of attempts to master the original experience ... [Hopper, 2003a, p. 56]

These patterns actually can be detected in the roots of the totalitarian regimes, in their historical reappearance.

Understanding totalitarian dynamics draws on several theoretical contributions to group analysis, but especially important are those taken from self psychology and from the study of systems of communication, especially of language. Language serves as a means of communication and it is laden with a symbolic function, not only when transformed into art (poetry, drama, literature). Language and communication play a decisive role in connection with self-development, but also as a central dimension of the structure of human groupings.

In his theory of the fourth basic assumption, Hopper (2003b, p. 71) distinguishes several features which are characteristic for the state of incohesion and which differ according the actual state of either aggregation or massification. These are: interaction, normation and communication—under communication, two phenomena are meant, language and style of thinking/feeling. The way of communication (language and style of thinking/feeling) is both the instigator and indicator of the state of incohesion, of either aggregation or massification, which are both marks of totalitarian tendencies.

The difference among various ethnic or social groups, generations, and social levels is symbolized in the language differences. The totalitarian society uses these symbolic phenomena as tools, as signs of obligatory identification. (This use of language and certain terms was even predicted by Orwell in his book *1984*.)

> . . . in social systems characterized by massification, people tend to be "Membership Individuals" who define their identities by using cult-speak and by speaking in tongues. Words and catch-phrases have nuanced meaning only to the core-members of the group. Rumour abounds. Communication is laden with references to their common history, which must have been shared in order for statements to be fully understood . . . people use jargon in order to indicate their group identity. [Hopper 2003b, p. 72]

The phenomena of massification, including special unauthentic communication, are characteristic for fundamentalistic movements as well as for the groups characterized by oppression, scapegoating, or by obligatory preferences in taste, fashion, life-style, music, etc.

The totalitarian regime may develop when cult-speak (and other massification phenomena) become obligatory in the size of the whole system and when the ruling taste or choice of values turns into ideology which is proclaimed as only acceptable on the scale of the society at large. Thus, the phenomenon of totalitarianism could be explained with the help of the fourth BA theory and its frame of reference.

Our understanding of the social unconscious in the context of the foundation matrix can be deepened by drawing on some ideas from self psychology and from some ideas about the functions of language and communication in general.

Human subjectivity is shaped and reflected through language

Starting from individual psychology, the self, first of all

> is a structure within the mind since (a) it is cathected with instinctual energy and (b) it has continuity in time . . .The self, then, quite analogous to the representations of the objects, is a content of the mental apparatus, but is not one of its constituents, i.e., not one of the agencies of the mind. [Kohut, 1971, p. xv]

Second, as the infant becomes able to distinguish between me and not-me, the primal unconscious unity gives way to his ability to relate to others as objects as well as to himself. This is necessitated by the need for mere biological survival (to feed himself, a child needs to obtain something from somebody: usually, two sorts of objects are present). This ability precedes his recognition of subjectivity, both his own and that of others, which is discovered and created in the process of unending mutual communication:

> The infant's cries obtain appropriate responses, physical gestures elicit reciprocal gestures, cries and gestures are interwoven into narratives and plays and the infant begins to enter into human culture. What is important is the acquisition of "mentality", the sense of possessing a mind of one's own in a world where meaningful contact can be made with other minds. This is the world of intersubjectivity, not simply of object relations. [Pines, 1996, p. 188]

The developmental process is reflected, too, in the use of language. In the beginning, when addressing others and when speaking about himself, the child does not use pronouns, because this would require recognition of his own and the other's subjectivity.

Vignette 1

Otík (twenty months) is especially interested in tools and in musical instruments. He creates sentences with grammatical subject, predicate, several objects, and adverbs. He announces "baba has a real big drum at home". He asks, too, "Mum gives yogurt to Otík quickly—quickly", or "Daddy gives key to Otík—garden—to run, to run." He is able to grasp intellectually the objects, and people, for him, seem to belong into the same category. He does not recognize his own face in the mirror (he says, "It is a baby") and he uses only an indirect third person when he speaks of himself and when he addresses others. He is not mature enough to create the idea of subjectivity.

The grammatical subject is a building bloc without which the sentence cannot be created, but is not identical with subjectivity in the psychological sense. The child is able to understand intellectually that the objects are moved, created, destroyed, etc., by a subject, but still, for the baby, this grammatical subject is not inhabited by psychological subjectivity, by the human soul. The culture of mothering (indeed, there is such a culture) is able to respect this development. Mothers turn to their babies, too, in the grammatically third person ("Now, Mummy will give some nice yogurt to Otík.").

The experience of subjectivity is a matter of emotional development, but it is reflected in the child's ability to use the pronouns "I" and "Thou", probably towards the third year of age. (This gradual discovery of subjectivity may be just one more step on the way to how ontogeny is copying phylogeny.) The psychological subjectivity, then, is a developmentally high achievement; it may be one of the steps by which the child crosses over from the animal into the human world.

The art of subjectivity is more the task, the ideal attributed to emotional maturity, and might lead to human spirituality (Martin Buber: I and Thou). No wonder that this high achievement of conscious mind and of mature feelings is often prone to regression.

Some of these developmental steps are ritualized and have become rooted in culture as a matter of etiquette. In the ritual distance, the subjectivity of the other is addressed neither directly nor personally but often enlarged into the plural, "You, Vous, Vy", in place of "Thou, Tu, Ty". In another context, one's own subjectivity may have been ritually altered (enlarged): the royals used to speak in the first person plural ("we, the king . . ."). In various cultures, the subordinates used to address the authorities only by the third person singular (just as if imitating the situation of a helpless child, or in order not to touch directly).

To address each other as "I" and "Thou" can be compared to what it means to gaze directly into one other's eyes: it means to see the other, to let oneself to be seen by the other, "in a deeper level" (Weinberg, 2009). It is a sign of intimacy, of trust, of challenge; it means the dissolution of boundaries between two highly estimated subjectivities.

The conscious creation of subjectivity is not only a rather decisive step in the evolution of the individual, as well as of the species, subjectivity is seen, too, as delicate, as fragile, not easy to be touched, safer to be avoided under some cultural or psychological conditions.

The real intellectual and emotional mastery of conscious subjectivity, however, even if once attained, is not granted forever. It is more one of the variations of the human existence, which is being left aside in various situations: for the sake of both pleasurable and protective regression, people dissolve their boundaries and merge with others in dyads, in groups, in masses, etc., inspired, for example, by music, by sports, by sex, by narcissistic admiration, or by religion.

And, for the sake of omnipotence (and through its omnipotent ways), the totalitarian system, too, deprives the citizens of their individual subjectivity and makes them merge in one big and *false collective self*.

Collective subjectivity: is there such a thing?

A human being develops into the image of the species not only through the unconscious building of his individual body, but also through the creation of the group—the social way of existence. As Winnicott would have put it, the individual becomes a person by creating the group and by being created by it, which is, of course, an essential element of the concept of the transitional object and transitional phenomena in general, including language itself. The group is as characteristic of the human species as the upright walk, the use of language, or the naked skin. The inborn model, the "foundation matrix" is based on the biological and on the socio-historical cultural setting. According to Foulkes (1990, p. 228)

> even a group of total strangers, being of the same species and more narrowly of the same culture, share a fundamental, mental matrix (foundation matrix). To this their closer acquaintance and their inti-mate exchanges add consistently, so that they also form a current, ever-moving, ever developing dynamic matrix.

From the concept of the foundation matrix and the dynamic matrix the idea of *group subjectivity, based on the concept of the group self,* logically follows: ". . . if there is an essential element of 'group' in the constitution of the individual, as indeed group analysis affirms, then it becomes more possible to consider that there is a value in regarding 'the group as a Self'" (Pines, 1996, p. 183), and "Another contribution from early development to the 'Self as a group' comes from recognition of the essential 'we-ness' of human beings" (*ibid.*, p. 188).

When addressing their infants, mothers use not only the third person singular, but, sometimes, too, the first person plural—we: "How have we been sleeping? Let us make something good to eat, shall we? Come, little baby, let us eat . . ." Such a baby-talk is produced by mother for the sake of the baby, who is the protag-onist, while mother is the one who is enabling. The child, however, does not use this manner of speech (of the first person plural), still not being able to acquire the position of any subject. So, when expressing her own "we" mood, the mother discovers for the child something new: she names the first dyad. This first "we-ness" or "we-go" is the model for the later we-ness—or self—of the group.

The concept of the group self is enriched by the idea of the "collective project":

> whatever the reasons are for people being together, they will neces-sarily construct meanings and purposes for their togetherness . . . the purpose of togetherness is . . . a fundamental quality of the group self . . . this purposeness of being together is part of a larger phenomenon, of a collective project. . . . Groups do not contain any

supraindividual group mind, but a supraindividual project. The project consists of certain ambitions, ideals and resources embedded in a specific history (similar to the individual self), and the project can be carried out on all levels of sophistication ... [Karterud & Stone, 2003, p. 7]

The first basic idea, "the group as a self", thus becomes filled with new contents. The new terms, group self or collective project, however, do not reveal their creative or destructive potentials. The collective project in the context of psychotherapy is supposed to be a creative one: to create the group self, which enables the individual members to become more authentic and healthier, to search for their true needs and goals. However, under certain circumstances, a group (any group) may develop as well a rather destructive or self-destructive collective project: the group self may be used for alien purposes. In fact, in the same way that an individual person may develop a false self, so, too, can a group develop a false collective or group-self.

Individual self might be true or false

According Winnicott (1960), the individual self of an infant may develop in two ways: the true self may emerge when the natural basic needs of the child are recognized instinctively by the "good-enough mother", who gives the child her care and loving. In the opposite case, when the care-taker is a "not good-enough mother", then the false self is likely to develop.

Vignette 2

Carla seeks psychotherapy (as the somatic treatment was in vain): she suffers from recurrent painful inflammation. Carla is an admired beauty: she performs perfectly in studies, sports, in money-earning. However, she is not able to enjoy a love relationship. In therapy, she suggests that her mother never really loved her: she praised Carla, but never hugged or kissed her. Carla grew into her mother's ideal: she became perfect in all respects. As an adult, however, as soon as she cares for a man, she becomes obsessed by panic. Instead of enjoying physical intimacy, she falls ill with genital inflammation.

During the treatment, Carla revealed, too, that her mother used to complain of having been neglected as an infant: Carla's grandmother used to put her daughter, from when she was very young, into whole-day-long institutional care (as was expected by the totalitarian regime).

And when Carla as a child was hugged by her grandmother, her own mother became enraged with a childish envy.

In the search for love from her mother during childhood, Carla suppressed and split off part of her feelings, those that for her mother would not be acceptable: she was never allowed to show her anger or her longing for physical contact. She developed her personality not according her true emotions, but as a fulfilment of her mother's wishes: she developed mainly her false self, which became the leading principle of her behaviour and of her self-perception. She accepted herself only after having performed perfectly.

As an adult, Carla started to hope anew. Her underdeveloped authentic part, her true self, woke up, tried to live, to take the leading role in the search for an unconditioned love relation. Then the challenge of a mighty inner conflict between hope and the horrible fear of the unknown, of failure, arose, and could be met only on a deep bodily level in the form of a psychosomatic disease.

> When a child tries to adapt to the desires of a mother who fails to be good enough, and has to suppress his/her spontaneity and his/her desires in order to obtain love and safety, then the structure of the false self is built and strengthened . . . when the needs of true-self are met by the good enough mother she reinforces the infant's feelings of his/her power, but a compliant child using a false self adaptation experiences only strong parental power. Thus the power problem . . . which is present in hidden or manifest form in all dyadic or triadic forms of human relationship, can be traced through the development of the true self and the false self. [Šebek, 1994, p. 23]

Both the true self and the false self are represented dynamically, as patterns of an individual's behaviour and his emotional life. Moreover, once these patterns are formed, they tend to be reinforced and even transmitted over generations.

Vignette 3

During the group session, Lili mentions her occasional half-conscious fits (in such cases, she says, her husband treats her by his kind talk and gentle physical contact). At one of the next group sessions, the thing happens: Lili falls down to the ground, yells in horror about guards hunting prisoners, about a prisoner who is going to die. The therapist takes her into her arms, lulls her like a baby, asks her to watch the therapist and other group-members, to return to reality. Lili gradually recovers and starts to talk about her mother.

In Lili's childhood, her mother suffered of uncontrollable fits of anger followed by self-accusations, tried to commit suicide several times, and Lili used to live in constant horror. Instead of enjoying protection and mothering, Lili had to provide this service for her mother, who, as a teenager, had survived a Nazi concentration camp, although she never disclosed this experience fully to her daughter. Lili tried to discover the details in her phantasy.

As a married woman, Lili developed the fits. With the help of the group, she discovered the pattern: she used (unconsciously) the fits when she needed to be helped or just to be listened to. She had grown up in the belief that her own emotions were of no importance compared to her mother's. So, in her adult life, she allowed herself to show some needs, but only under the disguise of what she thought was her mother's inner world.

Lili is haunted by her false self, which cruelly dominates her behavior. The false self originated as an identification with her mother, whose role in the family actually was that of an aggressor. As a child, in order to be accepted by her mother, Lili had to give up her own true emotions and, instead, she had to stay with her mother during her mighty emotional storms; Lili had to provide the balance. In this process, Lili's own emotional needs stayed undernourished, unrecognized: her emotions stayed entirely or partly unconscious because they had not been previously recognized and respected by her mother.

Later, when Lili, as an adult, was moved by her needs, she first used to suppress them (as she was used to doing in her childhood), but when she was no longer able to contain them, the suppressed energy blew up in a seizure. Lili was lacking her own words, images, and frame of reference to name her feelings (as this part of her personal development had not been earlier supported by her mother), and so her seizures were accompanied by versions of her mother's frame of reference, even when the actual images (because of the lack of ordinary communication with mother) might have been the product of Lili's phantasy.

Identification with the aggressor as the trigger of the false self

In the preceding vignette, the patient had to split off some of her needs in order to accept her mother's needs in their place, and to identify with them, to feel them, and to proclaim them as her own. Her true self stayed underdeveloped, unrecognized, unnamed. Thus, the patient's false self was created in the process of identification with the aggressor. The process has been described as follows:

> faced with an external threat . . . the subject identifies himself with his aggressor. He may do so either by appropriating the aggression itself, or else by physical or moral emulation of the aggressor, or again by adopting particular symbols of power by which the aggressor is designated . . . [Laplanche & Pontalis, 1973, p. 208]

However,

> what is classically referred to as identification with the rival in the Oedipal situation . . . it is situated in the context not of a triangular but of a dual relationship—a relationship whose basis . . . is sado-masochistic in character. [*ibid.*, p. 209]

From a group analytical point of view, *the development of the false self is likely to have begun at least one generation earlier with exchanged roles*: in both vignettes it was the mother, who was the original victim, before she acquired, later, the role of an aggressor towards her child. The phenomenon of the false self, as well as the pattern of identification with aggressor was transferred over generations as a decisive part of personality, *as a way of coping with abuse of power*. The phenomenon may develop into a serious personality disorder, it may become the way (as seen in both vignettes) how the cultural or societal problems are transmitted on to the private personal level—and how they are solved there in a miserable, deplorable way. In other words, the dynamics of the false self may seem to be located primarily in the infant–mother dyad, but this dyad itself exists within the context of triangulation and Oedipal configuration within the context of the dynamic and foundation matrices of the wider society.

The issue of power, as formulated by Šebek (1994) is the crucial one. The same factor is decisive on the formation of the group false self, too.

The group self: true or false

Vignette 4

It was shortly after the Second World War. The group consisted of young volunteers, mostly students, who sacrificed their holidays for "brigade-work", temporary unpaid work for some big industrial or agricultural projects. Their daily task was simple, the highest possible work efficiency, and they used to fulfil this task with complete enthusiasm. Not so long ago, some of them returned from the Nazi camps, from the forced labour camps or from concentration camps. All of them were still recovering from traumata of the war: in their childhood, a mighty pattern of violence was imprinted on their minds as a model of social behaviour. Being caught up in this pattern, they were desperately longing to beat any enemy and to build the so-called New World. They were filled with deep understanding for all the suppressed, exploited, victimized people of all times. They were longing for unity and sameness and felt proud to be part of "the masses".

The group was one of many that belonged to the generation of "blue blouses", the protagonists of the onset of communism in Czechoslovakia after the Second World War. The boundaries between the group and the outer society, and between various roles within the group, were not supposed to exist. The leadership of the group was projected on to the authorities high above. In another time or place, such people would become the true believers of some religion, or even sect (Weinberg, 2009); here, they became the true believers of the ideology turned into religion, named Marxism–Leninism.

The independent development of individuals or groups was neither possible nor desirable. Both individual and group identities were kept underdeveloped and lacking in true selfhood. The "we" of group members was the false we, or the false collective self, without any awareness, without any consciousness.

The developmental pattern of the false collective self was comparable to that of the individual false self:

- the needs, qualities, uniqueness and boundaries of the subject (here, of the group) were suppressed, not permitted;
- in their place other needs (here, in the form of ideology), were substituted, then identified with, supported, nourished by group members;
- although the process was enforced, it was experienced as the genuine wish of the subject because the subject had identified with the aggressor.

The phenomenon of the false collective self could not be reduced to the prevalence of those noted for the false self (even if such a case might be apparent): the false collective self is a group phenomenon. The group project (Karterud & Stone, 2003) was the one of the whole society—the project of "building communism, struggling for the New World". It was meant to unite all social forces and to dominate them. While the individual group members were supposed not to differ, but to enjoy their sameness, the real differentiation was reserved for social classes. Class origins (the inborn quality) determined individuals, and class hatred was a legitimate, desirable force for organizing the society.

The phenomenon of the false collective self (false we) was triggered by identification with the aggressor, and the process was set into motion by sadomasochistic impulses. The truly sadomasochistic nature of the impulses was reflected, too, in terms of the proclaimed values: the eternal cruel suffering of the proletarian masses was adored, was worshipped. In fact, such a victim was needed in order to justify the search for an enemy to be hated, to be hunted, to be murdered.

Even when the verbal content of the ideology seemed to be the opposite from the previous disastrous Nazi regime, the patterns of behaviour, the patterns of the power struggle, of the violent enforcement, resembled those that were used under the Nazis.

Within traumatized societies, people tend to repeat traumatic experience within their families, schools, military, political and religious
institutions and organizations, and within their groups generally
... Immigrants, refugees, and survivors of social trauma are especially likely to recreate their previous traumatic experiences in their
new societies. [Hopper, 2003a, p. 63]

After the Second World War, the whole nation was traumatized,
but the youngsters of the "blue blouses generation" had experienced the Nazi way as the first and only one in their sensitive age
between childhood and young adulthood. No wonder that for
many of that generation the identification with the aggressor has
become a general pattern. With all their conscious effort, the "blue
blouses" were fighting and working for the "New Better World".
Unconsciously, however, many were using these violent patterns
that had been imprinted on their minds by the previous aggressor:
they identified with "him"—especially when they were fighting
against a chosen enemy. Actually, they segregated people into
ready-made, innate categories, although this time not according to
race, but according to class origins. The group hatred was again
used as a legitimate and even legalized form of enforced social
development and social control.

The "blue blouses" naively disavowed the sadistic murderous
inclinations that they had internalized from the past regime, and
the feelings of their opponents who had been effectively silenced.
Thus, as soon as one totalitarian system was over, that of the Nazis,
the totalitarian Communist system began to grow, despite the
conscious intentions of many. The imprinted structures and social
behaviour were easily associated with new content, new ideology,
and new words.

The process of massification involving homogeneity and a
developing sense of oneness (Hopper 2003b, p. 66) was an element
of this process. A special language was developed which reflected
the forced reorganization of human subjectivity.

The language of the confused pronouns

The false "we", the redundant "Thou", the missing "you", the
monstrous "they" appeared as a result. Similar to other languages,

in Czech, usually the second person singular (Ty = Thou, Tu/Toi) has been reserved for intimate situations: for family members, friends, lovers, for praying and for swearing. In other situations, people for centuries addressed each other in the second person plural (Vy = You, Vous), as an expression of politeness and of boundaries. Under totalitarianism, however, a forced change was introduced: people had to address each other in the manner of the familiar "Thou". This enforced "sibling" identity was intended to manifest the matching attitudes of proletarian brotherhood, comradeship, and sameness, but, more often, this general use of Thou was experienced as improper among those who felt better within their natural personal boundaries.

With the attempt to destroy the independent identity of mature, individuated citizens (Hopper, 2000) by misusing the intimate pronoun, another shift of identity occurred: the use of the second person plural seemed to decrease in frequency. This happened in two interrelated contexts: among individuals and among groups. Natural boundaries among various groups were suspended, and all citizens were supposed to merge into one big, all-embracing, collective self.

Even if the use of the second person plural was only natural in the inter-group connection, it would be seen, however, as a sign of differentiation among groups, which was not supposed to exist: the position of a different group was reserved for the class enemies only. Then strange cases occurred.

Where the authentic "you" should be, the false "we" is there

Vignette 5

In the second half of the 1960s, major attempts were made by citizens to turn the totalitarian system into democracy. The group was a team of the editors of a literary weekly. Every week the brush-proof pages had to be brought to the press inspection; the censors read the proofs and confiscated some of the articles. The editor-in-chief tried to defend the confiscated content to obtain the imprimatur. He was using the Marxist terms and the "we" which included both editors and censors. He said such things as, "We, the

Marxists, are following Lenin, who proclaimed . . .", and here, under the guise of a pretended Lenin quotation, he tried to smuggle in some independent ideas. But, as soon as he returned to his team, he expressed a different identity. Then the group with whom he identified truly was the team of his colleagues: here, the "we" meant the team. And the censors, the representatives of power, in their absence, were labelled as "they".

In the dialogue with the censors, the intellectuals were using the "we" modality instead of distinguishing "we" from "you", which would be proper, but suicidal. In other words, the false we was used by both groups—the editors as well as the censors—and, for that matter, by the whole communist society.

Such behaviour was a bizarre parody of the original culture of mothering. The pronoun "we", which mothers sometimes use to express the mother–child dyad as an intimate unity, was used to express the lack of boundaries in the fear that distinctions of this kind were dangerous. This actually involved a kind of linguistic topsy-turvy, a perversion of communication through language.

The group members in Vignette 5 were actually the "blue-blouses" generation, except that they were almost two decades older. Meanwhile, their original ideology-turned-into-religion was tested by the reality principle. They became "reform communists", asking for "socialism with a human face". When speaking with the representatives of power, they used the original false we, which continued from the time of the original all-engulfing unity and sameness (cf. Vignette 4). However, in the small group of their team, they developed the new intimate sort of "we"—the emerging true we.

This "true we" was born in the process of reality testing. The more it became conscious and justified, the more the substance of the original "false we" was shifted from an unconscious error into a conscious pretence, still enforced by power and by fear of the persistent aggressor. It would be difficult, however, to find the breaking point between the unconscious false we and the conscious pretence. The transformation went step by step (as might happen with the false self of an individual).

None the less, at the very beginning, at the onset of totalitarianism, there was the emptied, disordered, violated identity: in the place of authentic "you" not only the false "we" developed.

Instead of the authentic "you",
the monstrous "they" appeared

Indeed, was there any way left in which to express inter-group difference? While the authentic "you" was unacceptable, while "we" lost its natural boundaries and served to hide many inter-group differences, "they" remained as a container for all that did not match, for all the rejected rubbish. "They" was the position to which the "different" group was removed. The use of "they" could be seen as the basis of an objectification process. "They" became seen as inhuman objects (Klímová, 1990).

Verbal dialogue is a human prerogative that distinguishes humans from animals. Those who were deprived of the possibility of sharing the direct dialogue, being neither "we" nor "you", those were the ones who tended to turn (in the subconscious of the dialogue owners) into animals. Or into monsters—devils, in fact. Then, the only method of direct communication between "we" and "they" was a non-verbal destruction of "they'. This was what was happening during the 1950s and 1960s, on a massive scale, and it was supposed to justify the "class struggle". The class enemies were doomed to the position of "they", to the existence of an eternally silenced object without subjectivity.

The shift of pronouns, however, was a phenomenon of the system at large. It was used by all involved, by the opponents of the regime too, only with the opposite meaning. Thus, the pronoun "they" became synonymous for "enemies" in general. In the secret intimacy of their team, the editors in Vignette 5 used "they" to name the power-holders with whom they officially shared the false we.

For the majority of the population, "they" meant the totalitarian authorities. In this case, the monstrous "they" were not murdered physically, but symbolically: they were seen as "having lost their human face". They were seen as having committed "character suicide", which is a parallel to "character assassination" (Hopper, 2003b, pp. 82, 89).

Thus, a society developed, inhabited by citizens who were lacking in truly mature subjectivity, by people who were objects to each other, and by monsters.

"Mother party" as a complement to the false collective self

In art, as well as in the common language, a metaphor of an ant-hill, or of a bee-hive, traditionally was used to imply a strange form of identity: one subject dwelling in multiple collaborating bodies. Sometimes, the metaphor is attributed to the totalitarian system. Is such a case—one subject dwelling in multiple bodies—indeed possible among humans? The idea is horrifying. It contradicts the very basis of natural development. Both phylogeny and ontogeny are aiming towards the conscious individual subjectivity as the main attribute of humans.

Before reaching this developmental peak, however, some preparatory steps are made.

Let me remind the reader of the essential elements in a culture of mothering. Before the child is able to pronounce consciously "I, myself", he lives in a different modality. He is not aware of his own self, but enjoys experiencing the self of his mother. Actually, it is not the mother's self, but the self of the dyad. The child accepts the signals from the outer world as well as from his own body and from his awakening soul. The mother feels those signals as if they belonged to her, and she reacts with her body language and with her human language. The child becomes aware of mother's reactions and is thus invited into consciousness and subjectivity. In other words, one subject dwells in two collaborating bodies. A mother symbol was also used by the totalitarian system. It was the "Mother Party", the official pet name for the communist party. She was endowed with godlike epitheta: she was omnipotent (her leading role was guaranteed by the state constitution), she was to be everlasting (her hegemony was legally anchored for eternity), and she was omniscient (she was the embodiment of the infallible truth and, too, the shrine of all information, supplied by the secret police). "Mother Party" was the only real one, and a paradox as a political body in a modern society. (The system originated in the former Soviet Union under the tradition of Byzantine spirituality and was alien to the sceptical Czech mind.)

The Communist Party was introduced as a dominant matriarch, and another official pet name for her (in Czech, "rodná", in Russian, "rodnaja") had the meaning of "inborn, of one's own blood", which can be compared to the Orwellian "Big Brother", another intimate family member.

The perverse tendency of the totalitarian system to intrude into human intimacy and spirituality was based on an attempt by those in power to dominate not only the economic, social, and political affairs, but also to possess human souls, to become the only model for identification, the only source of subjectivity. While citizens allowed (under regression) the boundaries of their selves to be loosened, their subjectivity was shared and transformed in a way which reminded them of the primary times of the child–mother dyad. The omnipotent maternal archetype seduced citizens into the role of children. Mother Party then offered mighty pleasures: protection against any outer enemy and the bliss of undifferentiated merger with Her.

The subsequent metamorphosis of society involved the loss of mature faculties of decision making, of independent thinking, of free choice; the decline of adult differentiation, the dissolution of group boundaries, the identification with powerful authorities. Rationality, clear, conscious mind, freedom of choice, activities of the work group, all were suppressed. The Big Mother took their place. In other words, the work group was exchanged for the basic assumption group and enforced massification took place. The word "masses" even got a positive connotation. Actually, masses were seen as a positive sign of undifferentiated identification with the Mother Party. Under totalitarianism, this homogenization was induced wilfully as an attempt to abolish class differences.

In the state of homogenization, the subjectivity of individuals, of groups, was projected, was delegated on to the Mother Party. She was experienced as the only real subject gifted by real life. She used to be loved and hated: in both ways her subjectivity was acknowledged. She was dominating the system as one subject dwelling in multiple bodies: some obedient ones, some dysfunctional ones, but all of them as part of the system.

In such a society what was the position of the human group?

"Group" as a dirty word, and "kolektiv" as the proper word

The term "group" involves a rich structure and complex dynamics. The group is a kind of social organism, with its own boundaries, able to live an independent life and possessing its own subjectivity.

These functions are in clear contradiction to the situation that was permitted under totalitarianism, in which all sorts of boundaries and role differences were dissolved; the identities were removed, destroyed, the decision-making was elevated to the higher system, the natural group leaders were castrated as soon as they appeared.

Even the word "group" was understood as something suspicious, alien to the masses. It was used in expressions like "anti-state group", or "anti-socialistic group", or "group of conspirators". In some cases, the "group" was used to refer to a certain number of people who were unknown to one another, but who were assembled by the secret police and put on political trial.

The group identity was reserved for the class enemy. For the official totalitarian language, the word "kolektiv" was the proper one. A "kolektiv" was a number of people who came together in the same school or place of work, or by serving as staff members or crew members: they were put together institutionally. The "kolektiv" was run from above, in secret ways, without any self-determination. The word implies the image of those who were collected, passively put together, thus resembling a collection of beetles or of butterflies pinned into immobility on some matrix. The word was used, however, in a positive connotation, as a true expression of the proletarian brotherhood and sameness. Thus, a "kolektiv" might have included members who were aggregated originally as a variety of isolated individuals, but were supposed to merge into an undifferentiated mass as soon as possible. Although these phenomena were the passive outcomes of incohesion, they were actively supported by the totalitarian power. The totalitarian system behaved as though it were a living creature, gifted by subjectivity, aware of its own interests, able to act in one's own favour. Is it possible that the subjectivity that was denied to groups was somehow projected above, to the level of society, to the system itself?

Did the totalitarian system have a subjectivity of its own?

The Mother Party was the dyadic partner of the false collective self. Analogous to the not-good-enough mother, in relation to the false self of an individual child, was the Mother Party in relation to the false we of collective entities, which I hesitate to call groups. Authentic subjectivity was actually subverted. The "Mother Party" personified the system. She was introduced and accepted as a "super-being", possibly in a similar manner to that of idols of ancient times and distant cultures, as a mighty archetypal symbol that was to be accepted in a religious way. As an ancient goddess, she truly dominated the life and death of citizens.

Her vitality, however, was absorbed from her worshippers (and from her victims as well). Her power was based on the reintrojection of what people had originally projected into her: while projecting some contents on to the Mother Party, people endowed her with qualities of a powerful living creature. Thus, projective identification occurred between two partners, one of whom was merely a product, an object, a piece of workmanship, which was endowed with life by the other.

From the beginning of time, people have tended, under certain conditions, most probably those of traumatic experience, to create idols: by endowing these objects with their own vital forces and by worshipping them later, they colluded in this parasitical transfusion. Such behaviour had been named and forbidden already by the Decalogue:

> 4 Thou shalt not make unto thee any graven image, or any likeness of any thing that is in heaven above, or that is in the earth beneath, or that is in the water under the earth:
>
> 5 Thou shalt not bow down thyself to them, nor serve them: for I the Lord thy God am a jealous God, visiting the iniquity of the fathers upon the children unto the third and fourth generation of them that hate me;
>
> 6 And shewing mercy unto thousands of them that love me, and keep my commandments. [Exodus 20: 4–6]

However, the temptation to make idols is an anthropological constant, and an eternal danger. The source of these products and processes (including the transmission over generations) is the collective false self. As a result of its origin in some traumatic experience, under some forced and unauthentic identification, the collective false self tends to recreate anew an inauthentic artificial partner to identify with: to make "likenesses", artificial objects such as ideologies, to give them false life and power and the god-like epitheta, to worship them, until these idols, finally, might destroy the authentic life.

Thus, the two totalitarian systems of the twentieth century were nourished from the psychological resources of the collective false self, by the false we; in spite of their political defeat, the danger of any new form of totalitarianism has not vanished, as long as the phenomenon of the false collective self is viable, ready to reappear as a social force.

Group analysts would argue that idolatry originates in the basic assumption group of incohesion associated with traumatic experience, which can only be prevented by the development of a democratic work group whose citizen-members are able to enjoy independence, collective subjectivity, boundaries and mutual respect.

References

Exodus (1611). In: *The Holy Bible*. London: Cambridge University Press.

Foulkes, S. H. (1990). The group as a matrix of the individual's mental life. In: *Selected Papers* (pp. 223–233). London: Karnac.

Hopper, E. (2000). From objects and subjects to citizens: group analysis and the study of maturity. *Group Analysis, 33*(1): 29–34.

Hopper, E. (2003a). The fear of annihilation and traumatic experience. In: *Traumatic Experience in the Unconscious Life of Groups* (pp. 53–65). London: Jessica Kingsley.

Hopper, E. (2003b). The fourth basic assumption: incohesion:aggregation/massification or (ba) I:A/M. In: *Traumatic Experience in the Unconscious Life of Groups* (pp. 66–90). London: Jessica Kingsley.

Karterud, S., & Stone, W. N. (2003). The group self: a neglected aspect of group psychotherapy. *Group Analysis, 36*(1): 7–22.

Klímová, H. (1990). "I" and "you", "we" and "they": thoughts of a psychotherapist in Prague. *Group Analysis, 23*(3): 317–322.

Kohut, H. (1971). *The Analysis of the Self—A Systematic Approach to the Psychoanalytic Treatment of Narcissistic Personality Disorders*. New York: International Universities Press.

Laplanche, J., & Pontalis, J. B. (1973). Identification with the aggressor. In: *The Language of Psychoanalysis* (pp. 208–209). London: Hogarth Press and The Institute of Psychoanalysis.

Pines, M. (1996). The self as a group: the group as a self. *Group Analysis*, 29(2): 183–190.

Šebek, M. (1994). The true self and the false self: the clinical and social perspective. *Journal of the British Association of Psychotherapists*, 26: 22–39.

Weinberg, H. (2009). Personal communication.

Winnicott, D. W. (1960). *Ego Distortion in Terms of True and False Self*. London: Hogarth.

CHAPTER NINE

Manifestations of psychic retreats in social systems

Marina Mojović

Introduction

This chapter will consider the manifestations of "psychic retreats" (Britton, 1998; Grotstein, 2009; Steiner, 1993) in social systems ranging from dyads to societies in the context of traumatogenic processes, especially in connection with the theory and concept of the social unconscious (Hopper, 2003a; Weinberg, 2007). These manifestations are usually troublesome, but obscure, which may be one reason why they have rarely been explored and discussed. However, they underlie much social pathology and social trauma, including their transgenerational repetition, through unconscious co-creation of specific social–psychic formations within social systems, which I call "social–psychic retreats'.

According to Steiner, psychic retreats are internal "pathological organizations" involving highly structured and closely knit systems of defences and object relations. Formed initially out of desperation, these sabotaging, self-protecting, and self-organizing internal subsystems are actually sub-personalities, which provide alternative shelters from human relationships and from reality in general. In their very essence is a paradox: they both protect and imprison the vital parts of the self. They could be located on the continuum that ranges from taking over almost the whole of the personality (as in the cases of some psychotic and severely borderline patients) to only small parts of it (as in the cases of some slightly neurotic or normal individuals). Discovered first as resistance to treatment, they are found to cause serious difficulties in various interpersonal relations, functioning as obstacles to many life processes, to their free flow and joy.

Since early psychoanalytic writings, phenomena similar to psychic retreats have been described under various names: "internal saboteurs" (Fairbairn, 1952), "fantasizing" (Winnicott, 1971), "internal gang" or "Mafia" (Rosenfeld, 1971) "claustrum" (Meltzer, 1992), "encapsulations" (Hopper, 1991; Klein, 1980; Tustin, 1987), among others. In the post-Kleinian literature, which includes the work of Steiner, such phenomena are always regarded as pathological. However, it still remains debatable whether in certain circumstances, especially in connection with trauma, some of them might be considered as "normal" defensive organizations, which are helpful for survival because they protect the person from greater regression and provide a sort of transient arrest or moratorium to development until the capacities for growth recover. In fact, the work of those who have considered the possibility of "normal" versions of these sets of psychic phenomena may be located in another mainstream of psychoanalytic thinking, in which are those authors who also take into consideration the involvement of the fears of annihilation and autistic anxieties and defences against them arising within a developmental position that is prior to the paranoid–schizoid position, such as Ogden's work on the autistic–contiguous position (1989), various studies on "encapsulations", "autistic features" (Klein, 1980), "autistic retreats" (Barrow, 2008), among others. Hopper (1991) clearly emphasized their positive aspects within his concept of "positive encapsulations" and their positive manifestations in social formations, especially in traumatized societies. Therefore, the links between Hopper's concept of encapsulations and psychic retreats are of particular relevance for this discussion.

"Social–psychic retreats", unconsciously formed within groups, families, organizations, and societies, might also be more positive or more negative, as well as partial or total. Transiently or permanently, they become properties of the dynamic and foundation matrices of these social systems. The members of these social systems tend to be unconscious of their social-psychic retreats, as they are of their personal psychic retreats. Thus, we may discuss these phenomena in terms of the social unconscious.

Many similarities between intra-psychic pathological organizations and social pathological organizations have been noted, but this has been mainly in order to convey the nature of the internal organization, rather than the other way around. The *locus classicus* of this is Rosenfeld's (1971) description of Mafia-like internal organizations:

> The destructive narcissism of these patients appears (to be) highly organized, as if we are dealing with a powerful gang dominated by a leader, who controls all the members of the gang . . . so that they will not desert the destructive organization and join the positive parts of the self. [p. 175]

It is argued that the life of the Gestapo and other terrorizing organizations tends to reflect this terrifying and life-sabotaging internal drama.

Possibilities for linking these internal prisons with social–psychic formations are offered by Bion's theory of "reversible" and "shifting" perspectives for achieving binocular vision in order to enable the perception of individuals within the context of their groups, and can similarly be found in Foulkes's discussions of the *gestalt* of the figure and ground of an observer's perceptions, and in Pines' (1998) discussion of frames of reference. However, these discussions pertain to the elucidation of psychic life as distinct from its manifestations in social systems in general, and do not pertain to psychic retreats and social–psychic retreats specifically. Neither do they address the aetiology of either. However, in common with many other writers on these subjects, I suggest that the manifestations within the external world of these unconscious psychic phenomena that are beneath symbolization and associated with profound anxieties are a matter of projective and introjective processes, and other forms of internalization and externalization, including projective and introjective identifications. The motives for the recreation of internal life in the external world are many, but the most important include the compulsion to control, to evacuate, and to attack, and, above all, to enact in the service of communication: that is, to engage in an unconscious narrative process in which people are seduced into the internal drama. Traumatophilia would seem to be central to such processes (Hopper, 2003b).

Unconscious intra-psychic processes are not the only sources of social–psychic retreats, which must be understood within their social, historical, and political context. Social–psychic retreats are recapitulated within component subsystems of larger, more total social systems, and vice versa. In other words, it is necessary to take an open-systems perspective. This phenomenon is often discussed in terms of "parallel processes", but "equivalence" allows for the assignment of importance and priority to various causal processes.

It should be noted at the outset that I am not able to discuss the aetiology of profoundly painful anxieties or of specific defensive processes by which psychic retreats are constructed. Neither am I able to discuss the structures and functions of the social–psychic retreats and how they might, in turn, cause further fear of annihilation. However, I do provide numerous examples of social–psychic retreats, and discuss possibilities for healing processes ranging from psychotherapy to the political activities of citizens.

More about "psychic retreats"

The literature

The roots of the concept of psychic retreats can be traced to many early psychoanalytical studies, mainly in connection with chronic obstacles to treatment, including negative therapeutic reactions. The professional literature on the subject involves an almost infinite network of ideas, as if mirroring the very image of the phenomenon itself, ranging from Abraham's (1927) "narcissistic resistance" and Reich's (1933) "character armour" to the work of Kleinian authors such as Segal, Joseph, and O'Shaughnessy, who have described patients who are trapped in powerful defensive systems. Especially important are Klein's (1980) study of autistic phenomena and Meltzer's (1992) discussion of the "claustrum". Grotstein (2009) holds that psychic retreats are a hidden source of all analytical resistance.

The actual terms "psychic retreat" and "pathological organization" were introduced by Steiner (1993) on the basis of his clinical
experience with "borderline patients":

> a psychic retreat provides the patient with an area of relative peace
> and protection from strain when meaningful contact with the
> analyst is experienced as threatening . . . serious technical problems
> arise in patients who turn to a psychic retreat, habitually, exces-
> sively, and indiscriminately. [p. 1]

For Steiner, it is a family of defensive systems and object relations,
which facilitate the escape from difficult feelings through the avoidance of contact with people and "reality". Such retreats help people
to tolerate the pain of the vicissitudes of the paranoid–schizoid
and the depressive positions by providing a "slip" into a third,
intermediate and default, position. In these asylums, they feel
protected, yet often still in pain. According to Britton (1998), regres-
sive movement into this position of non-development and non-
object relating may take place from any level of the continuum
between the two positions, whereby he distinguishes retreats organized as "quasi-paranoid–schizoid positions" or as "quasi-depres-
sive positions'.

By the term "retreats", Steiner refers to withdawal into states
that are often experienced spatially as if they were places in which
the patient could hide. They may appear consciously, or, in unconscious fantasy, as literal spaces: a cave, an island, a desert, or take
an interpersonal form, usually as an organization of objects or part-
objects which offer to provide security and which may be represented as a business organization, a religious sect, a totalitarian
government, or a Mafia-like gang.

Thus, the internal pathological organization "contains" the
anxiety, offering itself as a protector, but at the same time dominating the personality. The equilibrium is reached at the cost of
a developmental stasis. Actually, the person is trapped in an omnipotent organization, from which there is no escape, but in which,
in a perverse way, one finds narcissistic and masochistic gratifi-
cations. Steiner argues that psychic retreats can be found in
both neurotic and more normal persons, although always pathological.

Sisyphus and mimicry of the alternative world

Everything is *difficult* about psychic retreats. Repetitive, endless difficulty is their essence, and Sisyphus might be their logo. First, they were discovered by "difficult patients", and so psychic retreats themselves are difficult to understand, to cope with, and to change. Anyone who tries to help a person who is caught in the throes of a psychic retreat is likely to be sucked into it, and sooner or later is likely to feel stuck, robbed of vitality and a sense of meaningful motivation. This is accurately described in Sartre's *No Exit* and in Beckett's *Waiting for Godot*. The negative power of these systems is based on perfidious and continuous "attacks on linking" with good external and good internal objects. Psychic retreats may appear to be "transitional spaces" (Winnicott, 1971), which are essential for human development, but actually they are obstacles to progress. Although, they seem to be creative spaces for dreaming, in fact they are fantasizing, static, and energy absorbing. They are spaces for perverse mimicry, tending to distort and misuse good objects, truth, and reality. They are like the rocks on which mermaids appear in an effort to lure lost and starving sailors in *The Odyssey*. Psychic retreats are not ontologically grounded, in that they lack power and energy in their own right, but take their power parasitically from the selfhood of the person. They exist on the edges, margins, and peripheries, from where they convey their repetitive circles of simultaneous acceptances and disavowals, endless agreements and disagreements, back and forth, in and out, fantasizing and in touch with reality, invisible and visible . . . all of which generate vagueness. At best, we see only parts of this internal drama, and only a few of the main roles within it, rarely more than a glimpse of their figurations.

The basic scenes of the internal drama

The basic scenario: the victim, the oppressor, and his terrorizing regime. The central role of the victim is taken by the authentic self, or part of it, unreachable, imprisoned in frozen pain and terror. The *politics of the internal regime* is characterized by expertise in manipulation, especially around barriers and boundaries between relations inside and outside its territory. Although this "hidden self" may be visible, at least faintly, the "ruling establishment", which organizes the pathological system, is even more invisible. Its Emperor always has new clothes! The primitive internal society sketched by Bion and elaborated by Rosenfeld operates in, and at the depth of, human minds. The drama of the internal world is a political one in which an internal establishment seeks to maintain its control by using lies and, ultimately, violence. The boundaries between the victim and the oppressor are kept blurred by self-regulating aspects of the drama, in that the subjects are always willing to be "taken-in" by the system (Hoggett, 1998).

The role of the superego is significant, because it is likely to be a "destructive superego", and the "bad" object is very often placed there. The dynamics around the "bad" object is certainly especially important: for example, how it conducts its power and organizes its relationships, and the areas in which it operates. Thus, in some cases, the "bad" object might be a destructive omnipotent object that becomes an internal totalitarian dictator. This may also be seen in what appears to be an opposite formation, that is, a figure of a child in a coffin, or a Snow White or Sleeping Beauty who has been anaesthetized or poisoned. When the good objects are unable to contain the self, attachments break down. The self is directly exposed to a "nameless dread", and, left without alpha-functions, the "alpha function in reverse" occurs. An agglomeration of unmetabolized beta-elements and its half products, so-called "balpha-elements" (Ferro, 2005) occur, and form a beta-screen around those split-off contents, thus holding the psychic retreat together (Grotstein, 2009). It is often difficult to distinguish the capsule/screen from the "bad" object itself. "Negative containment" and the "parasitical type of container–contained relationship" (Bion, 1970) keep the imprisoned self inside a totally diverted perspective of the world. −K dominates over the space, turning the logic on its head in often bizarre ways.

Encapsulations and psychic retreats

Following the work of Fairbairn, Bion, Winnicott, and especially Tustin's (1987) elucidation of autistic defences and encapsulations,

Hopper (1991) reformulated a theory of encapsulation in the context of traumatogenic processes, defining them as: "a defence against annihilation anxiety through which a person attempts to enclose, encase and to seal-off the sensations, affects and representations associated with it", such that the entire traumatic experience is encysted or encapsulated, producing "autistic islands of experience". The fears of annihilation are linked to intra-uterine and birth experience, thus, originating before the paranoid–schizoid position takes root. The key parts of the self are trapped in repetitive movements in non-developmental processes within the autistic chamber. This is the basis for their formation as prototypes or moulds for their formations associated with traumatic experience later in life.

They can be "negative", primarily in order to seal off horrendous experience and bad objects, or "positive", primarily in order to seal off the essentially healthy parts of the self and the good object from overwhelmingly bad experiences. Hopper also suggests that negative encapsulations are manifest in various kinds of social formation, especially in traumatized societies, such as enclaves and ghettos, which may be voluntary but which reflect splitting and scapegoating processes in the wider society. Positive encapsulations are also manifest in various kinds of social formation, especially in the social systems of traumatized societies, and this can be seen in the subgroups that attempt to hold more hopeful and resilient possibilities, partly for themselves and partly for the wider society.

In connection with his theory of the fourth basic assumption in the unconscious life of traumatized social systems, which he terms Incohesion: aggregation/massification or (ba) I:A/M, Hopper suggests that massification processes are, in effect, attempts to encapsulate the total social system. This is not only an expression of fusionary and confusionary interpersonal relations, but also an expression of wishes to merge with the hallucinated mind and body of the mother. Such wishful dynamics is based not only on the assumption of original bliss, but also on traumatophilia in search of the original trauma and the compulsion to repeat it.

An integrated version

Integrating these two concepts with my clinical experience, I would suggest that encapsulations, in Hopper's terms, are either a version of pathological organizations or an integral part of it: as such, existing either on their own, or as part of a larger and more complex pathological organization. The most terrorizing anxieties, the annihilation fears, are lodged and enclosed within the encapsulation, whereas paranoid–schizoid and depressive anxieties are placed more in the wider area of the pathological organization. It is most difficult to reach the contents of the encapsulation. The pain is lodged in the chamber, but not suffered (Bion, 1970; Symington, 2000). There are many variations concerning internal relations of these phenomena, such as the devastating experience of the "black hole" placed either in the self (Tustin, 1987) or in the object (Pecotic, 2002), or the location of the internal barriers, etc. We often discover multiple functions of the barriers: both to keep *in* the trauma and to keep *out* the annihilating persecutor, or to avoid contact and to make adhesive contact with the barrier itself, or a defensive function and a retreat as pleasure. Hopper used a metaphor of a nest of internal Russian dolls in order to convey the sense of encapsulations within encapsulations, some of which are positive and some of which are negative. In such complex cases, to understand empathically the position of "in" and "out" concerning the traumatiz*ing* and traumatiz*ed* parts requires Bion's "shifting" perspective.

As an equivalence phenomenon, we also find that in social encapsulations within social–psychic retreats there are many variations concerning what is kept inside or outside the barrier, the position of the bad (traumatiz*ing*, persecut*ing* or annihilat*ing*) social object, as well including encapsulation within encapsulation. From the open-system perspective, these may be considered as variations of component subsystems of larger systems and complex dynamics between them. In the unconscious life of such a social system ba I:A/M operates, tending to expand and take over whole systems, creating obstacles to mourning and reparation processes, but enforcing traumatophilia as a repetition compulsion.

Examples of social–psychic retreats

Persons who have developed psychic retreats tend unconsciously to externalize them into their relational fields and thereby to engage other people into sharing these alternative worlds. Such social–psychic retreats are co-constructed within dyads, families, informal and formal groups, organizations, and whole societies.

Dyads and families

Social–psychic retreats are created in dyads, such as partnerships, marriages, parent–child relations, friendships, therapist–client relations, etc., which, of course, always exist within their contextual social systems.

Example 1. A positive partial family social–psychic retreat

In a dysfunctional family, a histrionic mother and an alcoholic father aggressively abused and neglected their children. Three siblings supported and protected each other in practical and emotional matters, and even helped their parents as much as they could. "Once, when we opened the door, two threatening men entered asking for a huge sum of money from us, which our mother had borrowed from them. In a matter of seconds we had to transform into a perfect team of liars, united in holding together all the terror of the situation, although dying from fear at same time." However, this was accomplished with a lot of denial and idealization of the family reality, anaesthetizing themselves against the pain, perhaps as the only possible survival manoeuvre. Images of super-orphans or myths of super-sisters often emerged in their dreams. Later, it was difficult to abandon that idealized retreat, which then became an obstacle for their further individual development. "We were one soul in three bodies, so beautiful, strong and untouchable! I can't imagine anybody between us", said one sister during her therapy for problems that she had in her partnership.

Example 2. Positive whole family social–psychic retreat

A refugee family with rigid, fortress-like family boundaries manifested strong bi-cultural splitting between their inside and outside functioning. The threatening enemy was kept alive in fantasy for years after the threat was over, continuously re-fixing the encapsulation. There was an unconscious agreement never to mention their burned village in Croatia. One member, after a series of dreams about the lost house from his childhood, decided to travel and visit the village, for which other members indirectly accused him of a betrayal. However, healthy mourning began for him, and then for the whole family, followed by a slow dissolving of the encapsulation.

Example 3. A negative whole family social–psychic retreat

A family in which the father was a militant nationalist with an anti-social personality disorder who abused his anxious wife, her parents, and three children. Terrible ethnic conflicts in their small town enabled him to abuse the situation by exaggerating information and presenting himself as a protector from ethnic enemies. Important contributing factors for the persistence of the retreat included the mother's internal persecutors colluding with her husband's aggression.

Informal and formal groups

Example 1. A positive whole group social–psychic retreat

A transient informal group of neighbours, friends, and relatives, who gathered during the bombing of Belgrade in a "real" sanctuary in the cellar of a building for many weeks, comes to mind. They supported one another to survive huge anxieties in maintaining various primitive defences, such as denial of dangerous reality, group idealization, manic omnipotence, even projection of all weakness paradoxically to enemies. Mothers with small children and the elderly received extra support, which helped them to manage their suffering.

Many of these groups formed during the bombing.

Example 2. A negative whole group social-psychic retreat

During the same period of bombing, another group evinced hyper-manic behaviour of dancing and singing on bridges, led by a person who projected his own psychotic pathological organizations on to the whole group, inducing others into transient psychotic states of mind, as a sort of counter-phobic escape from enormous fears. The fears were, in fact, entirely realistic, as seen in a group of young employees of Belgrade Central TV station who had to go on night duty, expecting that the station might be bombed. It actually was bombed, and they all died.

Organizations

Pioneers in the field of the psychoanalytic work with organizations, Jaques (1955) and Menzies-Lyth (1959), within their concept of "social defences", proposed that organizations function as containers for primitive anxieties, which appear in the organization's structure and culture. Yet, only recently (2005), Armstrong described difficulties caused by psychic retreats in organizations and how they may be mobilized as "illusory containers", serving as structured retreats when the internal or external situation of the organization threatens the limits of its capacity to function. Such retreats are likely to be built into the organization from the very outset of its formation.

Example 1

A positive, whole organizational social–psychic retreat was experienced by the author herself when working as a psychiatrist at the psychotherapy ward in the Psychiatric Day Hospital of the University Clinical Centre, Belgrade, when the regime of Milosevic intruded and diverted even some basic ethical principles of the medical profession, which never had occurred before, even during Tito's regime. The ward encapsulated itself in order to keep alive the therapeutic community, which had been developed at the ward for decades, and ignored the demand to apply some new rules and to participate in many wider staff meetings. It isolated itself from many contacts with other colleagues. The traditional ward setting became a bit rigid, especially in the three-times-a-week large group, which had been run for more than twenty years as a space where different contexts were democratically brought together for joint reflection and insights, and which was especially under attack from the outside.

Example 2. Negative whole organizational social–psychic retreat

At the same time, in other units of the Clinical Centre, there were some wards in which the head identified with, and was corrupted by, the regime. The staff was put in the position of either submitting to the new way of functioning or leaving.

If focusing on these two examples from the perspective of the Clinical Centre, these wards could be perceived as partial organizational social–psychic retreats, serving the whole large health organization to hold opposite aspects: the former encapsulating positive values for protection from external damage, the latter manifesting its immediate threatening environment, which was identified with the corrupted values from the more general environment. Both dynamically influenced the arrangements within the larger organizational matrix, also recreating patterns of wider social dynamics.

Countries and regions

1. *Positive partial societal social–psychic retreats.* Minority groups (ethnic, racial, or other) threatened by majority groups often protect themselves in enclaves and ghettos.
2. *Negative partial societal social–psychic retreats.* Some enclaves and ghettos that were originally formed for self-protection, even if they were for "as-if" protection, can be transformed into formations in which the population stagnates or becomes extinct, like some Indian tribes in reservations in the USA and Canada, or African-American inner city neighbourhoods based on formal or informal real estate laws and customs.
3. *Positive whole societal social–psychic retreat.* In the spring of 1941, the citizens of Serbia decisively rejected any pact with Hitler through huge demonstrations, shouting "Death rather than slavery!", and became an isolated country surrounded with countries that either surrendered or joined with Hitler and his Axis. There are many narratives about the atmosphere of high enthusiasm from this brief period, ended by Hitler's total bombing of the country.
4. *Negative whole societal social–psychic retreats* may be found in totalitarian regimes, which disseminate their perverted patterns throughout the social web. The victimized population,

over time, more or less, submits to the regime, unconsciously enabling its self-maintenance. Psychic retreats, internal and social, are core agencies of such social unconscious processes.

Serbian citizens experienced two totalitarian communist regimes, Tito's after the Second World War until his death, and Slobodan Milosevic's during the 1990s. Both created prominent forms of social–psychic retreats, the latter building on patterns already established by the former. Here, I outline a few characteristic features of the latter.

During the 1990s in the Federation of Yugoslavia (called also Tito's Yugoslavia), there occurred successive secession of its six republics into new independent states through multi-ethnic and religious conflicts and war atrocities. A large part of the international community, especially the Western world, considered the regime of the Serbian leader, Milosevic, to be responsible for those wars, and therefore imposed on Serbia sanctions for many years, which meant severe isolation of the country in economic, political, cultural, traffic, medical, mass media, and other social issues. That isolation of Serbian citizens was amplified and misused by Milosevic's regime in order to stay in power, enabling him to control the media, further disseminate ethnic fears, nationalism, and arguments about the "anti-Serbian politics of the Western world", and thus to continue malignantly to control communications and interactions between people inside and outside of the encapsulated country. Many images of social reality were diverted by propaganda, contributing also to perverse twists towards idealization of the regime with widespread illusions about its protection of the citizens, in spite of its destructiveness and the fact that it was one of the major sources of this. Those traumatic social processes mobilized in people various defence systems, including psychic retreats. Isolation and self-isolation of the population were recursive processes, inducing various sorts of destructive and self-destructive vicious circles in persons, groups, and organizations.

Larger regions

Groups of countries and their governments submitting to a higher regime, like the previous Eastern Bloc set up by Stalin's dictatorship, were walled off from other parts of the freer world (behind the Iron Curtain). We might consider many aspects of their politics in respect to global social–psychic retreat dynamics contributing to their lasting for decades.

Healing of psychic retreats

Unlike the vast literature about treating patients with individual psychic retreats in one-to-one psychoanalytic settings, there is little literature concerning their healing in human groups. According to Armstrong, "although all groups can function as psychic retreats they have not extensively been drawn on, including group relation practitioners, perhaps because the number of those with direct experience of analytic *and* group work is relatively small" (2005, p. 78, original italic).

It should be said that apart from my roles as a psychiatrist and individual psychoanalytic therapist, my clinical work as a group analyst has led me to believe that group analysis provides a unique space for observing, understanding, and treating both individual and social–psychic retreats, and also for elucidating processes of transformation of one into the other and vice versa. The work in group analytic settings (within ongoing groups and experiential workshops) is useful for understanding the dynamics of social–psychic retreats in larger systems, and for developing skills for engagement in their healing, which includes applying psychoanalytic and group analytic approaches to organizational consultancy, as well as attempts to entangle and remove complex obstacles to democratic social changes (Mojović, 2007a,b).

Through immediate experience, it might be discovered how the processes of equivalence concretely operate: for example, of the characteristic psychic retreat drama of the vital self paralysed under the domination of some dictator and his establishment; how exactly the recreation of such patterns occurs, both horizontally over systems or vertically between levels of systems and their subsystems; how internal dictators lodged within the destructive superego are linked to real dictators and pathological political systems; how they have an impact on personality development, adapting citizens to their images within collectivistic cultures; how totalitarian states take over the role of symbolic parents from individual parent figures, being perceived by the self as powerless and miserable, etc. Šebek (1996), a psychoanalyst who lived in Communist Czechoslovakia, conceptualized the "totalitarian object" as a highly bullying superego figure. According to Žižek (1984), Kafka's "Castle" is among the best representations of the post-liberal bureaucratic versions of internal and external totalitarianism. Totalitarian aspects of cultures imprisoning and self-imprisoning human relations in such ways are certainly much easier to see within communist regimes than in officially democratic ones, in which attacks on the transitional spaces and true selves of citizens are more sophisticated and invisible (Žižek, 1984; Western, 2008; Amado, 2009).

It might further be learnt that the "emancipation of the ego from the domination of superego" (Britton, 2003), or from its representations in social groups within social–psychic retreats, is very often part of the evolution of the healing process. In my experience, a sort of revolutionary period involving the overthrow of internal or external dictators seems to be inevitable, ideally with minimum wounding and "casualties". Fairbairn's (1952) concept of "divided loyalty" is relevant, as is Grotstein's (2009) notion of the "'double agent', in which the patient fearfully and sometimes collusively and disingenuously maintains an alliance both with the analyst *and* pathological internal objects within the psychic retreat" (p. 195), as if being then put to choice. Such periods of significant choices for persons or social system are important aspects of psychic retreat transformations (Mojović, 2007a). Dissemination of their transference throughout the levels of systems can sometimes be followed.

Analytic groups

The common shared ground of the dynamic matrix of the analytic group is a medium in which such "autistic islands of experience", the persecuting, victimized, and other parts of psychic retreats might be discovered more easily than in dyadic settings, especially with regard to the co-creation of social–psychic retreats in the matrices of their social systems as "collective transference phenomena" (Hopper, 2007). These formations recursively emerge and hide and fluctuate in unpredictable rhythms, being more or less exposed to shared group experience, mutual mirroring, and various individual and group-as-a-whole reactions. There are indefinite variations and phases in these processes. From time to time, two or more personal psychic retreats merge into complex combinations of partial and/or whole group social–psychic retreats. In clinical work, such processes lead either towards elucidation, more comprehensive understanding and transformative integration, or in the opposite direction, towards greater confusion, group incohesion, fragmentation, and other sorts of group stagnation. Oscillations also occur, as do negative therapeutic reactions, so that it is usually difficult to be sure about the main trends (Mojović, 2007b).

Example 1. Oscillating between a positive and negative whole group social–psychic retreat

In one group, a stiff, paralysed atmosphere lasted for more than a year, culminating in three sessions of almost total group silence. Among the first images to appear was a dream of a group that was crouching for years in a submarine that was floating under water, with the dreamer trying to open its round door, but with the pressure of the water immediately pushing her back. The dream stimulated fantasies and reflections about whether the dream represented collective escape from facing personal problems, hiding from circumstances of war in the group's environment, or a sort of unconscious suicidal submarine journey. "Do we know what kind of a journey this is?"; "The parents of this country were crazy and didn't care at all!"; "Maybe we can learn not to be collectively suicidal!"; "Is it dangerous to break our silence?", were some of the associations. Such group discussion illustrates how the fluctuation between the positive and negative sides of this group retreat became approachable for mentalization for the "work group". The positive side of the submarine (as a protective object from anxieties and pain pouring too fast from internal and external reality), as well as the negative side (as a cold "as-if" protective object keeping the group in an underworld prison) could be considered, putting it also into a position of more mature choice. As the song "Yellow Submarine" was mentioned, unconscious links to the therapist's name and blond hair were probably there, too, offering further options for interpretations.

Example 2. A negative whole group social–psychic retreat

A tortured girl from Kosovo, very inhibited and depressed, revealed through dreams that her "buried self" was fused with mass grave images and centuries-long nations' suffering: in fact, being dominated by a large group of internal dead objects. Merging of personal, family, and societal/social unconscious was revealed, the socio-historic drama as a significant building material for her retreat. For a long time, the group was soothing her pain through its warm presence. However, when the dismantling and abandoning of her morbid retreat started, she cried out, "If I wished to belong to this group, I'd betray them all forever!", meaning her abused/dead family and national objects. Massive projective identification of dead objects on to the group-as-a-whole occurred, transiently transforming it into a "mass-grave-place", shared group state of mind, which could only later be verbalized. It was not experienced by the girl as helpful, requiring her to face her ghosts as a punishment for attempting to escape the rules of the retreat to which she had been adapted for years, and she left the group in psychotic anxiety.

Example 3. A positive whole group social–psychic retreat

A student refugee from Croatia carried massive transgenerational war and concentration camp traumas. He fled his burning home and escaped immediate death in the massacre, together with his father, in their old car. In the group, over the years, his emotionally detached attitude softened. Once, he even shouted, "Please, don't let me stay in this internal concentration camp any longer!" and he finally came to approach his most painful internal zone. For several sessions, he induced others into temporarily shared terror and frozen states: "Don't you all see that we are dead, just simulating life!", and the group was indeed paralysed, impotent for any reflective work. Only later did it become apparent that it was an enclosed-in-the-cellar-waiting-to-die-atmosphere (transferred to the group from his immediate childhood experience when fascists were nearby, coming to massacre the family). During that process, an obsessive older member with a sort of mirror psychic retreat, originating also in family war tortures, was, paradoxically, scapegoated by the group as a cold racist. There was a shared group belief that the student's infantile tortured self would never be rescued if "the racist" were not exiled from, actually put behind the walls of, the group. This emotional journey of the group inside his retreat was possible due to the group's well-established containing capacities, so that the scapegoating did not provoke a further destructive anti-group.

The following two examples illustrate a high activity of disintegrative forces when healthy needs for dependency on good objects (internal, external, group) are exposed to sarcasm, contempt, envy, toxic diversion of meaning, with preference for addictive or perverse bands. Negative partial group social–psychic retreats (especially their omnipotent bad objects) are striving to defeat the work group, to make it submerge and to give up faith. Sarcasm, social traumas, and merging with external traumatizing bad objects are used for their triumphant propaganda.

Example 4. Negative partial group social–psychic retreat

The official name of NATO operation of bombing Serbia was "The Merciful Angel". The term was used few times in derision, when some beams of faith in humanity would emerge: "In our group we started to believe in the goodness of the Merciful Angel. Don't you all see how we get involved in this seductive play! It's better to be drunk!"

Example 5. Negative and positive partial group social–psychic retreat

Another image, once used for laughing down tendencies to happiness in a group, was a large building in the centre of Belgrade, totally burned out by bombs, which one morning emerged clothed in bright colours with a huge Coca-Cola advertisement, "Cheerful and happy with Coca-Cola!" Then, sudden pain of memories exploded into the matrix, immediately blocking mentalizing processes, even by the conductor for a while. The wounds pulled towards another positive group retreat as a transient arrest. However, as soon as people recovered their capacity to think, this experience actually loosened important knots within the social unconscious.

Analytic family therapy

The family from Example 3 came into therapy. Due to danger of retaliation from the father, the therapist had to be very cautious in his strategy in approaching such a malignant family retreat, which was slowly, step-by-step, elucidated in a presence of a relatively secure institutional setting. The mother decided to consider divorce, but her husband decided to start intensive therapy in the ward for personality disorders. Those processes enabled family members to take back some of the projections they were holding for each other as component parts of the shared family retreat.

Organizational consultancy

Example 1

A professional organization, Group Analytic Society Belgrade, within its study group for understanding organizational and social dynamics, revealed an early "conception trauma" of its own organization, due to war circumstances (Mojović & Despotović, in press). This was helpful in setting up a healing process for the sequels of traumas, which included isolation as an aspect of an organizational social-psychic retreat. The healing process involved coming into contact with deep wounds through large group processes during regular and special trauma workshops, which enabled mourning to begin and develop, as there are indeed so many losses to be mourned.

Healing of society

Healing of a large country social–psychic retreat within totalitarianism, like the one described during Milosevic's regime in Serbia, certainly involves complex democratization processes and changing the relations with the international community. Usually, both are inevitable: long evolutionary and brief revolutionary periods, and, in the aftermath, further struggles with remnants of the old regime, which are often lodged in various negative social–psychic retreats.

Long before the fall of Milosevic, throughout the social web covertly behind the scenes of the regime, the rising up of democracy was going on. Positive social nuclei were kept alive in many areas: positive psychic retreats in persons and social units and democratic nets between them, which, step-by-step, gathered into larger and more open units: democratic political parties, NGOs, and many other civil-society nuclei. For many months, every day hundreds of thousands of citizens gathered on the streets, blowing their whistles against the regime within the Belgrade Peace Protest, which happened during the 1990s a few times, lasting many months, until the last one finally toppled the dictator.

The fall of the regime happened on the 5th October 2000, often called the day of the Revolution, and was paradoxically peaceful without casualties. This might be linked to the fact that the "bad" object of that retreat, the ruler and his establishment, at that point became so obvious in their malignancy, their manipulation and corruption so vivid to most people, the falsified elections not legitimate in the eyes of the citizens, the whole of the police, the army, and even special forces, together with all their officers, absolutely refused (effectively deserting) Milosevic's order to turn their guns on the citizens in the streets, when on that day the masses were taking over the Parliament. Milosevic admitted losing the elections.

In the following years, complex healing processes developed on the way to a more mature democracy, which permits and encourages dialogue and mature citizenship. Unlike in communist times, when mainly positive social–psychic retreats were walled off from the threatening environment, in the post-communist time, while those slowly dissolve, just the opposite occurs: many social areas remain identified with the previous regime and keep their power by creating negative social–psychic retreats, co-operating with each other by way of hidden and often criminal networks, including international ones, even abusing the positive retreats and creating malignant obstacles to healthy processes. In such fights to regain power and effect retaliation, they attack in many ways. One attack, in 2003, tragically assassinated the new Serbian Prime Minister, Dr Djindjic, who was the proponent of democratic change. Immediately after that, strong government and police action against criminal networks was accomplished, quite successfully, but thereby almost stopping democratic freedom, which was probably one of the aims of the assassination. During transition, the pendulum often oscillates backwards to authoritarian trends, because the disappointments and disillusionments in the new order are open to exploitation by remnants of the old regime.

The development towards "mature citizenship", meaning, among other things, the people's ability and willingness to take risks to change deviant social circumstances and to transcend the limits of their own parochial cultures (Hopper, 2000), inevitably goes through many ebbs and flows, overcoming obdurate obstacles again and again. The analogy of Sisyphus is always present. Civil society networks persistently have to struggle with the hate and contempt of democratic dialogue that are lurking in −K areas of social–psychic retreats, ready to attack and dismantle their meaning.

Concluding remarks

Social–psychic retreats (equivalence phenomena of internal psychic retreats) are specific social–psychic formations taking place below the surface of various social systems co-created by recursive externalization and internalization processes, which occur in both directions: from persons and smaller systems towards larger systems, and vice versa. They involve highly structured systems of social defences and object relations, which create alternative shelters from many macro- and micro-social mainstreams. They covertly influence a lot of arrangements and dynamics of social–political power relations. In their negative versions, they indirectly disseminate totalitarian patterns/styles over social discourses and practices, whereas positive versions may protect from those. The social unconscious operates on a vast scale through them.

Social–psychic retreats are often the "hidden destructive rulers" behind chronic resistances to change and obstacles to various social healing processes, such as the efforts to entangle unconscious patterns of transgenerational transmission of "traumatophilia", "chosen trauma", and other paradoxical human phenomena. It is important to cultivate operational fields in which they can be elucidated and related to systems and cultures through immediate experience. The analytic groups, especially large and median, provide unique spaces for learning about mature citizenship by humanizing and transforming the hate of democratic dialogue, much of which is camouflaged in social–psychic retreats, and in general *making the social unconscious conscious*. Further development of similar psychosocial spaces may bring more hope of ending the absurdities and negative power of much social destructiveness.

References

Abraham, K. (1927). *Selected Papers of Karl Abraham*. London: Hogarth Press.

Amado, G. (2009). Psychic imprisonment and its release within organizations and working relationships, *Organisational and Social Dynamics*, 9(1): 1–20.

Armstrong, D. (2005). "Psychic retreats": the organizational relevance of a psychoanalytic formulation. In: D. Armstrong (Ed.), *Organization in the Mind* (pp. 69–89). London: Karnac.

Barrow, K. (2008). *Autism in Childhood and Autistic Features in Adults*. London: Karnac.

Bion, W. R. (1962). *Learning from Experience*. London: Karnac.

Bion, W. R. (1967). *Second Thoughts*. London: Karnac.

Bion, W. R. (1970). *Attention and Interpretation*. London: Karnac.

Britton, R. S. (1998). *Belief and Imagination*. London: Routledge.

Britton, R. S. (2003). *Sex, Death and the Superego, Experiences in Psychoanalysis*. London: Karnac.

Fairbairn, R. (1952). *Psychoanalytic Studies of Personality*. London: Routlege & Kegan Paul.

Ferro, A. (2005). *Seeds of Illness, Seeds of Recovery*. Hove: Brunner-Routledge.

Grotstein, J. (2009). *. . . But At The Same Time and On Another Level . . . Volume I*. London: Karnac.

Hoggett, P. (1998). The internal establishment. In: P. Bion Talamo, F. Borgogno, & S. Merciali (Eds.), *Bion's Legacy to Groups* (pp. 9–24). London: Karnac.

Hopper, E. (1991). Encapsulation as a defense against the fear of annihilation. *International Journal of Psychoanalysis*, 72(4): 607–624.

Hopper, E. (2000). From objects and subjects to citizens: group analysis and the study of maturity. *Group Analysis*, 33(1): 29–34.

Hopper, E. (2003a). *The Social Unconscious: Selected Papers*. London: Jessica Kingsley.

Hopper, E. (2003b). *Traumatic Experience in the Unconscious Life of Groups. The Fourth Basic Assumption: Incohesion: Aggregation/Massification or (ba) I:A/M*. London: Jessica Kingsley.

Hopper, E. (2007). Theoretical and conceptual notes concerning transference and countertransference processes in groups and by groups, and the social unconscious: Part III. *Group Analysis*, 40(2): 285–300.

Jaques, E. (1955). Social systems as defences against persecutory and depressive anxiety. In: M. Klein, P. Heimann, & R. E. Money-Kyrle

(Eds.), *New Directions in Psycho-Analysis* (pp. 448–498). London: Tavistock, 1955.

Klein, S. (1980). Autistic phenomena in neurotic patients. *International Journal of Psychoanalysis, 61*: 395–402.

Meltzer, D. (1992). *The Claustrum: An Investigation of Claustrophobic Phenomena*. Worcester: The Ronald Harris Trust.

Menzies Lyth, I. (1959). The functioning of social systems as defence against anxiety. In: *Containing Anxiety in Institutions. Selected Essays Volume I*. London: Free Association Books, 1988.

Mojović, M. (2007a). "Psychic retreats" as defences from the ugliness of war gorgons and the power of the analytic group. Paper presented at the Regional IAGP Barcelona.

Mojović, M. (2007b). The impact of the post-totalitarian social context on the group matrix. *Group Analysis, 40*(3): 394–403.

Mojović, M., & Despotović, T. Group analysis in Serbia within major changes in the social context. Early social trauma inscribed into the 'Field's Social Unconscious'. *Clinical Social Work Journal* (in press).

Ogden, T. (1989). On the concept of an autistic-contiguous position. *International Journal of Psychoanalysis, 70*: 127–141.

Pecotic, B. (2002). The "black hole" in the universe. *Journal of Child Psychotherapy, 28*(1): 41–52.

Pines, M. (1998). *Circular Reflections. Selected Papers on Group Analysis and Psychoanalysis*. London: Jessica Kingsley.

Reich, W. (1933). *Character Analysis*. New York: Farrar, Straus & Giroux, 1972.

Rosenfeld, H. (1971). A clinical approach to the psychoanalytic theory of the life and death instincts: an investigation into aggressive aspects of narcissism. *International Journal of Psychoanalysis, 52*: 169–178.

Šebek, M. (1996). The fate of the totalitarian object. *International Forum Psychoanalysis, 5*: 289–294.

Steiner, J. (1993). *Psychic Retreats: Pathological Organizations in Psychotic, Neurotic and Borderline Patients*. London: Routledge.

Symington, J. (Ed.) (2000). *Imprisoned Pain and its Transformations. A Festschrift for H. Sydney Klein*. London: Karnac.

Tustin, F. (1987). *Autistic Barriers in Neurotic Patients*. London: Karnac.

Weinberg, H. (2007). So what is this social unconscious anyway? *Group Analysis, 40*(3): 307–322.

Western, S. (2008). *Leadership. A Critical Text*. London: Sage.

Winnicott, D. W. (1971). *Playing and Reality*. London: Tavistock.

Žižek, S. (1984). *Birokratija i uživanje*. Beograd: SIC.

PART V

THE MATRIX OF
THE SOCIAL SYSTEM

Introduction

Gerhard Wilke

A t the core of these two chapters are questions about linkage: how does an individual relate to society and fit into a group; how does the body relate to the mind; how do nature, culture and social structure interlink; in what sense is the "We" greater than some of its parts; and in what sense do social systems have minds of their own? However, these questions define the perimeters of a permanent academic building site—open for construction, deconstruction, and reconsctuction.

The founder of group analysis, S. H. Foulkes, was inspired by the psychoanlytic writings of Sigmund Freud and the sociological theories of Norbert Elias. Freud (2000) showed that the mind of an individual and the culture in which this individual lives out a lifespan are shaped by biological drives and unconscious psychological defences against socially unacceptable desires. In a brilliant theoretical conjuring trick, Freud reduced the interaction between the individual and society to a one-to-one relationship that he believed could ultimately be explained in terms of individual psychology. Foulkes (1986, 1990) broke from this way of thinking by placing patients face to face in a group, and claiming that it had become clear to him that the minds of all group members are connected in a web of relationships through which unconscious material flows. It followed from this that the small group also has a "mind" open to the transference from its members of cultural, social, and historical information and undigested psychic feelings that mostly originate from within the wider social system. The transference of information—verbal or emotional—is always an exchange, involving at least the self and the other. The mutual influence goes both ways and system and subsystem can transfer unconscious information and tasks to each other, depending on the context and the function that the object of exchange serves for the individuals and the whole social system. Foulkes tried to capture the interactive, relational, and interdependent nature of human interaction in and between groups by referring to the "mind" matrix of the small group in terms of its dynamic matrix, and to the "mind" matrix of a society/culture in which the smaller group is located in terms of its foundation matrix.

Regina Scholz quotes Foulkes's explanation of what he means in her chapter:

> I have accepted from the very beginning that even a group of total strangers, being of the same species and more narrowly of the same culture, share a fundamental mental matrix (*foundation matrix*). To this their closer aquaintance and their intimate exchanges add consistently so that they form a current, ever moving and ever developing *dynamic matrix*. [Foulkes, 1990, p. 228]

This way of seeing the relational and interactive nature of social order and group relations overlaps with the ideas propounded by the Symbolic Interactionist School of Sociology, which turned away from structural explanations of social order and cohesion. Its proponents began to see social structure as an accomplishment of social actors in everyday and small group interactions. This is also the theoretical approach of the American anthropologist, Clifford Geertz (1993), who discourages us from seeing culture as something with a capital C and out there, separate from human agency and pulled over us through socialization in childhood, never to be changed thereafter. He saw culture with a small c as a kind of foundation matrix, a web of interconnected smaller groupings that weave themseleves together and into a larger whole through continuous interaction. With each social contact and exchange, the groups that make up a larger whole culture generate the confirmation of the order of things, necessary adaptations, and might also reinvent and change what is there.

This book reminds us that it was Erich Fromm who started a long line of politically conscious social scientists who argued that social order rests on the repression of individual human desire and knowledge of the full truth about how social structure works, putting some in an advantaged position and others in a disadvantaged one. What is defined as undesirable truth by those who hold the power in a society is made socially unconscious. This privileged subgroup, or class, wants those who must be subjected to their rule, albeit in an unconscious way, to remain ignorant of the full picture. This kind of evaluation of power as abusive and in the service of a privileged minority involves the Utopian vision that if we make all humans equal and abolish the social hierarchy as abnormal, everyone will have full consciousness and the end of history and suffering is nigh. This is quite a widespread way of thinking among group analysts throughout Europe.

I prefer Norbert Elias's (1974) portrayal of power as relational, something that is generated during the interaction of privileged insiders and underprivileged outsiders. Through interaction and altered external circumstances, their respective positions change. When a role reversal occurs between insiders and outsiders, the disempowered behave in the same way as those who oppressed them.

We need to resist simple and correct answers to the questions of how individual, group, and social minds are correlated. The choice of a theory has the most power to convince a community of doubting scholars, because any reasonable explanation depends on the context and the historical juncture of the debate.

Fahad Dalal's contribution to the study of the social unconscious and ideology takes as significant that psychoanalysts now have to argue for the social, and that they find it difficult, because most psychoanalysts see the social as born of the psychological, as a symptom, not a cause. In part, psychoanalysts have done this in order to comply with the demands of the traditional scientific world, so that the observer is the subject who studies things, not other subjects, especially patients! This makes it hard for psychoanalysts to see the world in relational and social terms, but, perhaps more importantly, it traps the observer in a linear universe and in an ideology that puts the individual and not the group at the centre of the social universe. However, Dalal suggests that we put the social before the psychological, and, as a result, we get a radically different picture of the relationship between the individual and society. He writes,

> What becomes clear is that as each particular individual is born into the social milieu, he or she cannot help but imbibe the dominant discourses that are embedded within that milieu, and these must become fundamental and integral to the developing individual self. . . . What we are now faced with is a *social apriori*. One name for the social *apriori* is the Foulksian one of the social unconscious.

Of course, the danger in this persepctive is that it is simply a repetition of Durkheim's (1947) much criticized idea that social order is made possible by it being there before a baby is born and after the adult dies and leaves this world. It is the initiation into the culture, its shared vales and norms and its shared collective consciousness, that makes the individual a social being and liable to resist becoming a deviant. Why? Deviants get singled out, punished, shamed, and excluded, and it is this double reinforcement system of behaviour modification which gives a social system cohesion and coherence.

I agree with Dalal that all anwers to the conundrum of social cohesion and order must be ideological, based on implicit assumptions and, therefore, remain questionable and incomplete. Progress lies, according to him, in thinking like a group analyst in a more radical and uncompromising way. He opposes any idea that the social can emerge from the "asocial internal world of asocial individuals . . . human life begins and continues in the plural and has never been in singular". But what does not follow from this is that there is an equivalence of the I and the We, and neither can both We and I be collapsed into each other.

Regine Scholz has built on the work of Earl Hopper (2003a,b) and Vamik Volkan (2004) who have argued that collective trauma results in a time collapse in which the I and the We, the group and the social system, are seen as equivalent—their difference is lost. What Volkan calls "chosen traumas" act as memory markers for a group and unify it in the retelling of the story of suffering and heroism when facing an external enemy, who reminds the one that brought the trauma upon the group. In this way and in this sense, the creation of a group mind generates rage, fear, and phantasies of extinction and pollution on contact with the enemy. Earl Hopper distinguishes among the processes of societies, groups, and persons, and argues that in the presence of trauma and, thus, the loss of a state of normal social reality, the shared mentality of the group is mistaken for that of the contextual social system, and/or participants in this process. The members of a traumatized social system (or, for that matter, a group analytic supervisor of it) tend to get sucked into generalizing from the person to the group to the system, and generate metaphors and hypotheses that revert to the analytic tradition which Dalal criticizes.

In Dalal's portayal, analysts see society as reducible to an individual mind, whereas group analysts tend, according to Hopper, to reduce the societal social system to a group process. In neither paradigm is the social seen as variable in its own right, and is implicitly reduced to a secondary phenomenon. If we are serious about the psycho-social genesis of a human being, we need to construct a mental bidge between the I, the We, and the Social System. The authors of these two contributions share this view, and imply that there are no individuals, groups, or society without a relationship between them in time and space and without language, habits, ideologies, and rituals.

We do not know much about the social unconscious of the foundation matrix of a group or of the foundation matrix of a societal social system when they are not constrained by traumatogenic processes, and, thus, by the collapse of time and generational and other boundaries. Dalal tries to make sense of what is already on the theoretical map, and reorders this under the heading of "radical group analysis". Similarly, Scholz moves towards a theory of what holds ordinary groups together and what enables the sharing of language within them. She shows how the group unconscious draws on stories and shared collective memories to give its members a sense of identity and cohesion in both normal and abnormal times. This is achieved by filtering other symbolic traces of memory out of the narrative of the genesis myth of the group. The excluded memory elements are made unconscious and excluded from the dialogue in the group through the process of unconscious collusive selection. The group unconscious is, therefore, connected to forms of "symbolic violence", in terms of what can be told and what cannot be told. The dialogue in the group and a sense of belonging to it depends on this process of making unconscious that which is unwanted.

The way of looking at this phenomenon might be to argue that social order rests, at least in part, on "make believe". This is true at the level of a conversation, during ritual enactments of the ideal social order, such as on holy days or during scientific symposia, when the collective memory of a community is reconstructed for another time period. No society is as well integrated and stable as it appears. Ideologies, myths, and rituals are always a source of both cohesion and incohesion.

In my own writing, I have begun to take a stand on the issue of a shared group "mind" and the foundation matrix (Wilke, 2001, 2002; Binney, Wilke, & Williams, 2005) and I feel uneasy about theories that tie the social unconscious to schemes of repressing and supressing the unwanted truths that some hold and others are denied. The truth lies somewhere in between Durkheim's concepts of the collective consciousness and Marx's imposition of false consciousness by those in power over those out of it. There are such things as a shared mentality or a framed classification system that signify the ways that particular cultures are both the same as, and different from, others. Shared beliefs and systems of mental classification are linked to social systems, but are not identical with them. They are properties of the matrices of social systems. Thus, there is room for individuation, variation, deviation, and differentation. Perhaps if we looked at how social order is made possible as much as how it is defended against and deviated from, we would find it easier to acknowledge the existence of a confusion of words used to describe the same phenomenon, indicating that we cannot do without a concept of a collective consciousness and unconsciousness, but have not yet found a shareable language for discussing this. The authors of the following two chapters invite us to continue searching for such a language.

References

Binney, G., Wilke, G., & Williams, C. (2005). *Living Leadership, A Practical Guide for Ordinary Heroes*. Harlow: Financial Times and Prentice Hall.

Durkheim, E. (1947). *The Division of Labour in Society*. London: Glencoe.

Elias, N. (1974). *Die Gesellschaft der Individuen*. Frankfurt: Suhrkamp Wissenschaft.

Foulkes, S. H. (1986). *Group Analytic Psychotherapy*. London: Maresfield Library, Karnac.

Foulkes, S. H. (1990). *Selected Papers*. London: Karnac.

Freud, S. (2000). *Massenpsychologie und Ich-Analyse*. In: *Sigmund Freud, Studienausgabe, Fragen der Gesellschaft und Ursprünge der Religion*. Frankfurt am Main: Fischer.

Fromm, E. (Ed.) (1967). *Socialist Humanis*. London: Allen Lane.

Geertz, C. (1993). *The Interpretation of Cultures*. London: Fontana.

Hopper, E. (2003a). *The Social Unconscious: Selected Papers*. London: Jessica Kingsley.

Hopper, E. (2003b). *Traumatic Experience in the Unconscious Life of Groups*. London: Jessica Kingsley.

Volkan, V. (2004). *Blind Trust: Large Groups and Their Leaders in Times of Crisis and Terror*. Charlottesville, VA: Pitchstone.

Wilke, G. (2001). *How To Be a Good Enough GP, Surviving and Thriving in the New Primary Care Organisation*. Abingdon: Radcliffe Medical Press.

Wilke, G. (2002). The large group and its conductor. In: M. Pines & R. Lipgar (Eds.), *Building on Bion* (pp. 70–105). London: Jessica Kingsley.

CHAPTER TEN

The social unconscious and ideology: in clinical theory and practice

Farhad Dalal

Introduction

Let me begin with two questions: why is it that in the psychoanalytic world, we find ourselves in this curious position of *having to* argue *for* the social? And why is it that the argument tends to have a defensive quality about it, of having to justify something that seems to go against the grain?

In part, this is because of the established norm in the psychoanalytic mainstream, this being that the social is secondary to, and born of, the psychological. It is perhaps not surprising to hear Klein say, "the understanding of [the individual's] personality is the foundation for the understanding of social life" (Klein, 1959, p. 247). Neither is it surprising to hear Bion say,

> I think that the central position in group dynamics is occupied by the more primitive mechanisms [of] . . . the paranoid–schizoid and depressive positions . . . [It] is necessary to work through . . . *the more primitive anxieties of part-object relationships* . . . [as] I consider [them] . . . to contain *the ultimate sources of all group behaviour.* [Bion, 1961, p. 189, my italics]

Both Klein and Bion have their genesis in the later Freud. But, unlike them, Freud does grant the social an actual presence in the psyche in the shape of the superego. The Freudian superego is, in part, constituted by internalized elements of authority figures (in contrast, the Kleinian superego is constituted by elements of the death instinct). But one of the primary reasons that it comes into existence is to do the work of repressing primitive impulses: for example, incestuous desire. Thus, ironically, a part of the work of the representative of the social in the psyche (the superego) is to *increase* the dominion of the unconscious through its activity of repression. However, when humans gather in groups, then the superego loses its grip:

> when individuals come together in a group all their individual inhi-
> bitions fall away and all the cruel, brutal and destructive instincts,
> which lie dormant in individuals as relics of a primitive epoch, are
> stirred up to find free gratification. [Freud, 1921c, p. 79]

Freud also says, "how well justified is the identification of the group mind with the mind of primitive people" (*ibid.*).

But, surprisingly, even the relationists like Fairbairn and Winnicott, despite their best efforts, also ultimately collapse back into individualism: Fairbairn's claim that "all sociological problems are ultimately reducible to problems of individual psychology" (Fairbairn, 1935, p. 241), finds an echo in Winnicott's "the clue to social and group psychology is the psychology of the individual" (Winnicott, 1958, p. 15).

This, then, is the dominant view in psychoanalysis: that the internal *primitive* psychology is prior to the individual, who, in turn, is prior to the social. The social itself is an expression of a *pre-existing* psychology within the individual. In other words, the psychological is the "cause" and the social is its "effect". Thus, the social has little status since it comes third in order of importance: first, the internal psychology, then, the individual, and finally, the social. And it is because this is the context that we are speaking into that the tone taken by the arguments which seek to privilege the social is defensive; it is an argument against an established, taken-for-granted norm, an argument against the grain.

The positivist schema

This norm arises out of a particular positivist world-view, a world-view that continues to dominate not only psychoanalysis, but many other disciplines. It is also the basis of the thinking of policy makers in the UK, permeating all territories from mental health to the economy to ecology.

The positivists hold that the objective world-of-things exists before individual humans, and individual humans exist before society. In this view, society is not just secondary, but *tertiary*, since it arises because of individuals joining together with other individuals. It can be depicted as shown below (Figure 1).

In this "picture", there are two distinct regions. The space between the individual and the world of things is where objective science is said to happen. Science, in this account, is the activity of the individual studying the world of things. Meanwhile, it is supposed that it is in the other space, between *the* individual and society, is where politics happens, politics being the various (problematic) engagements and struggles individuals have with each other in their attempts to join together and form society.

From this depiction, it would appear, then, that the two regions—science and politics—have nothing to do with each other, as they each occupy different "spaces". This is the basis of the claim that politics has nothing to do with science, and so politics ought to be kept out of science (and art, and sport, and everything else).

This schema is *linear*. And it is this very linearity that allows it to seem that politics and science are very different *kinds* of activities that have nothing to do with each other. One of the points I want to flag up at this early stage is that the diagram and the way of thinking that it illustrates is already an expression of a certain ideology,

(autonomous rational)

First, the world of things ➔ then *The* Individual ➔ then the social world

λ

Region of Scientific Activity	Region of Politics
The individual investigating the workings of the world. **Clear and rational.**	Individuals engaging with each other. **Messy and confusing.**

Figure 1. The positivist world view.

an ideology that privileges the individual over the social. I will say more on ideology and related matters as I proceed. But, for now, I want to make the point that the apparent "obvious" division between the objective world and that of human interaction only appears to be so obvious because of the premises utilized in constructing the diagram. The diagram is not a straightforward description of the natural state of things (which is how it looks on first impression), but a division generated by a particular ideology, an ideology that serves particular ends. As we will see shortly, there are other ways of representing and thinking about the situation, and these give rise to other "outcomes", other ends.

Anyhow, it is on this kind of basis that politicians claim that, although they are in the business of politics, the decisions they take are fully rational because they are made on the basis of scientific evidence.[1] However, there is no discussion as to what constitutes scientific evidence, as this is a part of the taken for granted. The taken for granted always pushes in certain directions, always towards certain ends, *but always surreptitiously*. A case in point is the current reorganization of psychological therapies in the UK. The government demands that psychological therapies ought to be "evidence based". But what *counts* as evidence privileges a certain kind of therapy (the cognitive) over other kinds. It is not surprising, given that the scientific methodology being used to gather this "evidence" is positivist, that it ends up finding in favour of a psychological modality that is also positivist. The *ends* are already present in the *means*. The ends that are being served are manifold: a great many people are apparently treated, rapidly and cheaply, and the government is seen to be doing something helpful, while, at the same time, managing to "save" money. And the entire enterprise is legitimated by apparently being "scientific". The sting in this particular serpent's tail will, no doubt, be felt in the not too distant future.

Anyway, let me return and attend more directly to the positivist schema. According to the rationales of this schema, it is possible to figure out how the world-of-things works, because it works according to the rules of cause and effect. These rules can be worked out through the rational individual doing objective science. However, what constitutes science is not a given, although the way the situation is set up, it appears that this is so, and that, therefore, there is nothing here to be questioned.

This kind of understanding of science arises from the positivist world-view in which there is the priority of "things" over "ideas about those things". You see what you see because what you see is real and plainly there to see. It exists as itself, before you see it. You speak what you see. Observation is direct, unproblematic, and value free.

So, on the left hand side of Figure 1, above, we have the possibility of clarity and predictability, while on the right hand side, in the region of politics, humans seem to behave in ways that appear irrational and, therefore, unpredictable.

(Let us note one other thing: although this linear story begins with the world of things, *agency* is located in the autonomous rational individual.)

So, on one side of the picture we have clarity, and on the other side, confusion. The question we are now faced with is why, despite their rational capacities, do humans behave in seemingly irrational ways? As we have seen, some of the psychoanalysts above (in particular, Bion) have answered that they behave in these irrational ways because of the eruption of the primitive in the psyche. I will sketch Freud's version of events.

The Freudian schema

Freud (1930a) famously gave an explanation for the irrationality of humans through a description of the way the mind comes to be structured. In his view, the mind was as it was because of the residue of two histories, the first history being that of the human species (the primal horde and so on). The effects of these primitive and powerful themes from the dawn of humankind are laid down in the psyche in the form of the instincts. The second history is that of early childhood and of psychological development. This is the story of what happens when the first history (in the shape of the primitive instincts) are confronted with other people and objective reality in the present.

Although the developmental process is mostly and more or less successful, human rationality during adulthood is always compromised by the residue of both histories, that of a particular developmental story, as well as that of archaic primitive processes. Both of these continue to have a life in the unconscious, from where they come to have an invisible role in our seemingly rational life. It follows then that our *rationales* for doing things are always, to some degree, *rationalizations*.

The Freudian model is akin to that of Kant in the following sense. Kant (1999) thought that humans were born with certain categories of logic already present in the mind, and said that humans experience the world through these categories. So, Kant is called an idealist, because he privileges these *a priori* ideas (categories) over things. In this context, what *a priori* means is innate knowledge, which is to be contrasted with knowledge gained through lived experience. This *a priori*, innate knowledge not only exists prior to experience, it also forms that experience. The categories inform what we are able to see and the way we see it. The Freudian equivalent of Kantian categories (Figure 2) is that of the instincts. Freud would say that we come to experience the world and others in the ways that we do because our experiences are mediated and permeated by the instincts (Klein calls these, innate unconscious phantasies).

When it comes to *classical* psychoanalytic treatment, the situation is complicated (I am oversimplifying the situation to tease out the points of interest). On the one hand (as Freud himself proposed), the psychoanalyst is conceived of as a scientist, a scientist capable of objective rational thought and observation. The patient, however, is a Freudian creature, in that the patient's rationality is subject to, and permeated by, unconscious processes. The patient is placed on the side of things—an object being investigated by the rational psychoanalyst. The purpose of the investigation is to expose and understand the workings of the two histories within the unconscious, so that the patient has more possibility of operating rationally. In this world-view, the analyst is confident that his observations and deductions are value free and objective. The methodology is "scientific", consisting of observation, hypotheses formation, testing the hypotheses, and so on.

World of things ➔ *The* Individual ➔ The social world
(Freudian) patient ⬅⬅⬅ *(rational)* psychoanalyst

Figure 2.   Classical treatment according to the positivist/Freudian schema.

In sum, the psychoanalytic method is the use of scientific methodology, drawn from the left hand side of Figure 1, to bring more clarity and understanding to the messy right hand side of Figure 1, human motivation and behaviour.

The Eliasian/radical Foulkesian schema

But what if we come at this scenario from the opposite direction and redraw the picture? In this case, the social precedes individuals and we will arrive at a radically different understanding of human motivation (Figure 3).

The first thing to note is that the social, by definition, *is* the domain of the political. The political is an eternally conflicted field, generated and constituted by power relations, of which it is an expression.

What is important about this "picture" is that it makes clear that *as* power struggles and politics are there at the beginning of the picture, they *must* permeate all that follows. This includes not only the psyches of the individuals that are born into the social, but also the relations that take place between them. But most importantly for our purposes, the logic of the picture exposes the fact that politics and power themes must necessarily permeate the *activity* of science—the study of how things work.

This picture is also linear, and so, as a representation of the processes of human existence, it, too, is an over-simplification. But, despite this obvious limitation, its virtue resides in the fact that it shows how and why the activity of science is, of necessity, imbued with the agendas of the human beings that engage in it.

First, the social world ➔ The Individual ➔ Then the world of things
(permeated by the social)

Region of Politics Of power relations	Region of Scientific Activity Necessarily permeated by the field of power relations— the social.

Figure 3.   The Eliasian/radical Foulkesian schema.

The developmental story

There is a critical consequence for the developmental story in this scenario.

What becomes clear is that, as each particular individual is born into the social milieu, he or she cannot help but imbibe the dominant discourses that are embedded within that milieu, and these must become fundamental and integral to the developing individual self.

What is *prior* to the newborn infant in this scenario is what is written into the fabric of the social, thus effectively reversing the previous statements of the psychoanalysts:

> the understanding of *social life* is the foundation for the under-standing of [*the individual's*] personality (from Klein).

> all problems of *individual* psychology are ultimately reducible to *sociological* problems (from Fairbairn).

> the clue to the psychology of the individual is social and group psychology (from Winnicott).

What we are now faced with is a *social a priori*. One name for the social *a priori* is the Foulkesian one of the *social unconscious*. There are two dangers here. The first we have already noted, that this picture, being so linear, does not capture the complexities of human existence; the picture is a one-way street beginning in the social and driving right through everything that follows it. This, then, leads into the second danger that we now fall into: the error of social determinism, what Wrong (1962) has called the over-socialized conception of "Man". Both these dangers give rise, quite rightly, to the following objection.

An objection and a confession

Surely, the individual infant is not a complete *tabula rasa* at the point of birth, entirely at the mercy of the social, with the individual being written on and into by discourse and ideology? Surely, humans are more substantial than that? What of human autonomy and responsibility? Another way of putting the objection is this: what is the source of the *individuality* of individuals? If everyone were simply formed by discourse, then we would expect people to be much more regimented than they actually are; this is clearly not the case: individuals vary enormously, each individual is, indeed, unique. So, what is the basis of this uniqueness?

I agree with the objection, and am interested in the questions that it gives rise to, but do not agree with the ways that the questions are often answered.

The territory that this question is engaged with is that of the moment of birth. The question becomes one of what is already present at birth, and how is one to think about it? Or, to put it another way, what is the nature of the clay that is to be moulded by the psycho-socio-developmental processes, and how plastic or resistant is it to being moulded?

And here is the thing: the answers to these questions cannot help but be ideological, in support of this or that world-view. If the radical direction is right, then it has to be the case that the answers to these questions cannot ever be purely scientific, objective and neutral, but will have all sorts of other functions and purposes, some of which are known and knowable, and others not. In other words, this issue is already an explication of the theme of this chapter: that one cannot ever reside outside the ideological and, therefore, the politica, even in the clinic. This, however, is not to suggest that the only possibility before one is docile submission to the prevalent world order. This is because the methodology of Foulkesian group analysis has the potential to subvert and deconstruct ruling ideologies, even as it inevitably promotes alternative ones.

This is also true of me, of course, as well as of this paper—neither is ideology-free. So, let me come clean about where I stand, or at least as much as I know about it: I want to argue against the individualism and internalism endemic to much psychoanalytic discourse—the viewpoint that says that the source of all human life, as we know it, emerges from the asocial internal world of asocial individuals; a viewpoint in which introjection is the poor cousin of projection; a viewpoint that supposes that there can exist such a thing as "the" individual in the singular.

In saying this, I do not wish to claim that there are no such entities called individuals *per se*. I want, instead, to advocate for something similar to Hannah Arendt when she chastises Karl Marx, no less, of getting it wrong when he speaks of "Man". She says that "the human condition [is that] of plurality . . . the fact [is] that men, not Man, live on the earth and inhabit the world" (1998[1958], p. 7). Human life begins and continues in the plural and has never been in the singular.

In my view, if we begin the story not with *the* individual (e.g., Klein, Freud), or with *the* individual-in-relation with another individual (e.g., Winnicott, Fairbairn), or with individuals-in-relation (e.g., Foulkes, Mitchell), but with individuals-in-*social*-relation (e.g., Elias), then we find ourselves in a new paradigm, in which not only the theory of human interaction, but also the practice and technique of psychoanalysis/psychotherapy is considerably different (Dalal, 1998, 2002).

Let me return to the objection itself, and the way it is often answered. The answer begins with the truism that the infant comes into the world already formed to some degree. The moment of birth is often described as one where a new psycho-biological being is born into, and, *for the first time*, is confronted with an established social order. This newborn is a unique body, certainly, and, being body, it is thought of as pure biology. This infant also has its own unique responses to its environment and carers, which, being unique, is described as its character. And being there right at the beginning of its life, before the social has had any chance of doing its work, it would seem that this uniqueness *is* its true nature—a unique nature that is personal, because it is prior to, and unsullied by, the social. To this way of thinking, the true self resides in the domain of Nature, a domain that is continually being threatened and distorted by the domain of Culture.

There are several points of disagreement here.

The first disagreement is with the wish to fix what is present at the moment of birth as "true character". Given that character continues to change right through one's life, what are the grounds on which it is claimed that it is at this moment that the individual's personality is at its truest and purest? In saying this, I do not wish to fall into the alternative error of claiming that this moment—of birth—is of no more significance than any other. That, too, would be nonsense. Birth is obviously a highly charged and significant moment when family and infant meet each other face to face for the first time. It is also the case that much experience has already taken place in the womb. Where are we to insert "the beginning"? In this discussion, the Vitalists might perhaps use the language of "soul" and "the spark of life" to capture the unique mystery that is individual human aliveness.

We should also note, in passing, the claim made by some psychoanalytic schools that those suffering from character disorders cannot change, while those suffering from neurotic disorders can.

My second point of disagreement is with the Humanistic claim that the shape of the character at birth is the "true self" and the changes that take place through the psycho–social–developmental process constitute a dilution and contamination of this true self. I would also disagree with the classical psychoanalytic formulation in which the psycho–social–developmental processes are conceived of as consisting of modulating something primitive in the shape of instincts or drives into something civilized.

My ethos would find affinity with *aspects* of the psychoanalytic schools of relationality (e.g., Winnicott and Fairbairn), attachment (e.g., Bowlby and Holmes), and most closely, intersubjectivity (Mitchell), *but with the following important caveat:* that the processes of relationality, attachment, and intersubjectivity take place in a sociological milieu, and that their shapes and forms are driven by the discourses that prevail. What this means is that power relations are intrinsic to relational, attachment, and intersubjective processes: it is this that is the essence of what the social unconscious.

The body, being body, is readily thought of as a biological entity. It is. But it is also a sociological entity. Over the aeons, our physical bodies have evolved always in relation to other bodies. In other words, sociological themes have always been present throughout the biological evolutionary processes and so are embedded in the structure of our bodies, into our biology. Thus, the newborn's biological body is already social. The birth of an individual is not the first occasion on which biology meets society. As Elias says: "Human society is a level of nature" (Elias, 1991, p. 85). He continues, "humans are *by their nature made* for a life with each other, *a life which . . . includes* interpersonal and inter-group struggles and their management" (*ibid.*, p. 91, my italics).

So, something about what Kant and Freud say is right after all, but not quite in the ways that they meant them. The infant does come into the world knowing something, but not exactly with Kantian categories.[2] It does already "know" something about spatial and temporal relationships, cause and effect, and so on. The infant comes into the world not just ready to relate, but *already involved* in the process of relating. And, most dramatically, the inter-subjectivists tell us that the sense of self itself comes to be consti-tuted through the processes of relating. What radical group analysis has to add to this is the reminder that intersubjectivity and the pro-cesses of relating are always a *social* process, and this necessarily involves power relations, and so power relations necessarily come to have a formative role from the beginning in the constitution of the developing individual.

Let me now return to the main subject of this paper: the social unconscious.

The social a priori

Foulkes is not the first, or the last, to come up with the idea of a social *a priori*; a great number and range of scholars have proposed some version of it. Hopper (2003, p. 159) tells us that "although Karen Horney was the first psychoanalyst to apply the [notion of] the social unconscious to clinical work ... the concept was intro-duced by [Erich] Fromm". Foulkes, however, makes no mention of Fromm. Hopper suggests that this is because Foulkes thought Fromm too left wing (personal communication).

The question being engaged with is this: how is it that (broadly and not without contestation) in particular times and places, humans (in the plural) come to *share* a view (more or less) of what is right, what is wrong, of the way things are, and so on? And that this is the case despite the range and variety of individual personal histories. In other words, how do we (in the plural) come to take certain things for granted, things that are not only outside the scope of our consciousness, *but the basis of it*?

And variously, the scholars all answer that the basis of these attitudes are to be found in the unreflected conventions that we are each born into, that we each imbibe, and that we each repro-duce and reinforce, all without knowing that we are doing so (Table 1).

Perhaps the most well known of these scholars is Marx. In his view, the ruling classes deliberately (that is, consciously) promul-gated a *false ideology* that the working classes were unable to resist,

Table 1.   Varieties of the social *a priori*.

Scholar	Variety
Foulkes	Social unconscious
Marx	Ideology (conscious)
Althusser	Ideology (unconscious)
Hegel	Zeitgeist, categories
Barthes	Mythology
Lacan	Unconscious like language
Elias	Symbol, habitus
Foucault	Epistemes, discourse
Kuhn	Paradigms
Bourdieu	Habitus
Leyton	Normative unconscious processes

the purpose of the ideology being to convince the oppressed that there was no alternative to their exploitation because they were participating in the natural order of things.

Althusser (1969) went further, saying that ideology is unconscious, and unconscious not only to the oppressed, but also to the oppressors, with each genuinely believing that the status quo is an expression of the natural order of things.

Hegel (before Marx) had proposed that individuals came to think in similar ways to each other through participation in, and absorption of, the *Zeitgeist* (the spirit of the times). Hegel (1979), too, thought that there were *a priori categories* that existed prior to individuals, categories through which individuals experienced themselves and the world. But Hegel's categories differ from Kant's, in that they are to be found in the social that the individual is born into.[3]

Barthes talks of these social conventions as *mythology*. He says,

> myth has the task of giving an historical intention a natural justification, and making contingency appear eternal ... [myth] has turned reality inside out, it has emptied it of history and has filled it with nature ... *myth is depoliticized speech.* [Barthes, 1984, p. 142, my italics]

Elias (1991) says that we come to think alike because, through language, we all participate in a dimension he calls *symbol*; he also puts forward a notion of *habitus* to account for the unreflected consensual. Foucault (1972) has two terms for these habituated ways of experiencing and perceiving the world: *epistemes* and *discourses*. Kuhn's (1962) term is *paradigms*. Then there is Bourdieu (1986), who also speaks of *habitus*.

It is also the case that there are many scholars from within the psychoanalytic tradition itself (e.g., Marcuse, Habermas, Fromm, and Sullivan, among many others) who have also struggled with this sort of question. It has to be said, however, that mostly they are not considered to be significant and remain at the margins of contemporary mainstream psychoanalytic conversation. Perhaps best known is Lacan's (2007) explanation for the commonality of perception, this being that the individual's unconscious is structured like a language, and language is always communal, and prior to the birth of any individual. There are many others in the psychoanalytic field engaging with this kind of question, for example, Cushman (1994) and, most recently, Leyton (2006) has spoken to these themes through her notion of *normative unconscious processes*. Not to be forgotten is the work of Hopper (2003), and the other voices included in this volume.

This, then, is a way of thinking about the social unconscious: in any period, one or other particular world-view comes to prevail and extensively dominate one's faculties, and leads to particular ways of experiencing events. During these times, there seems no sensible alternative to these world-views. To the flat-earth way of thinking, the idea of a spherical earth is not only implausible, but incredible, and obviously wrong. The spherical alternative belies their *actual experience* of flatness. These unreflected world-views are the basis of the phenomenon that we call *common sense*. It is a *sense* that is *common* to all, and is so obvious that, in the main, it does not even occur to one to question it. In the positivist schema (Figure 1), it is made *obvious* that politics can have nothing to do with science, and those that think otherwise are plainly mistaken, as is evident in the diagram.

These seemingly all-powerful world-views are not eternal, however. They are continually being interrogated by other options residing on the margins, and through this process, over time, the dominant world-views come to mutate into new shapes; on occasion the shift is not gradual, but sudden and cataclysmic. In other words, even in the time of the flat earth, there are others who are able to have alternative conceptions and theories as to the shape and nature of the earth—not all of them correct of course—and, depending, the other options are either treated as errors, ignored as idiotic, or attacked and repressed as heretical.

My purpose in listing these thinkers (and by no means does the list pretend to be a complete one) is not to tease out the differences in each of their conceptions of the social *a priori*. Rather, the purpose is to make the point that the idea that humans are both formed and constrained by the social orders they inhabit is hardly a novel one, although it appears to be so to many of those inhabiting some quarters of the psychoanalytic world. And they believe this, despite the fact that much before Marx, Arendt, or Elias, even someone like Thomas Aquinas (hardly a revolutionary left-wing radical) had already said that "man is by nature political, that is, social".[4] The only way to explain how it is that this kind of tunnel vision continues to hold sway within certain psychoanalytic circles is to say that they are blinded by, and in the grip of, an ideology, an individualistic and internalist ideology.

Not all psychoanalysts and group analysts think like this, of course, as exemplified by those mentioned above. But they can hardly be construed as mainstream, particularly in the British context.

The clinic: implications

To begin with, let me summarize where I have come to and, in the process, say something about the relationship (as I understand it) between the two terms I have been using, ideology and discourse.

Ideology is unconscious. It is the taken for granted that is utilized in formulating ideas and experiences. It provides the categories we use in our thinking: ideology is the basis of what we call common sense. It legitimates the interests of interest groups, but in ways that are hard to recognize. This is because the work of ideology is to give the historical and contingent the appearance of the natural and inevitable.

As Harland says,

The individual absorbs language before he can think for himself: indeed the absorption of language is the very condition of being able to think for himself . . . Words and meanings have been deposited in the individual's brain below the level of conscious ownership and mastery. They lie within him like an undigested piece of society. [Harland, 1987, pp. 12–13]

Elias shares this view. Language, according to Elias, is not a passive means of representing the world; it actively informs the sort of world one experiences. He says that language provides people with "the means of orienting themselves *far beyond the field of their personal experience*" (1991, p. 125, my italics).

Here is the thing: the kinds of languages one is born into and absorbs both form and constrain thought, emotion, and experience itself. Note: I am speaking in the plural, of languages, not language, the significance of this being that the turbulent relationship between these languages/discourses opens up a space in which reflection becomes possible. This last point is critical. In itself, it is a description of group analytic methodology.

Discourse, on the other hand, is a more comprehensive notion. It includes ideology, that is, language categories and ideas, but also includes the forms of *practice* that are informed by that language. The theory and practice reinforce and support each other.

Discourses furnish the very criterion by which its results are judged successful. Discourses are self-validating. One cannot ask from within a discourse whether it itself is true or not, as it furnishes the basis on which we judge what is true and what is good. Discourses impose a taxonomy on the world and the mind. Taxonomies are systems of inclusion and exclusion, and the means by these are achieved are never value free.

It follows, then, that the theories and practices of psychoanalysis and group analysis can also never be value free.

Those who would defend the view that the activity of analysis inclines towards the objective do so by claiming that the theory of psychoanalysis is based on scientific evidence gathered in the clinic through the practice of psychoanalysis. The defence is positivist, in that it presumes that theory and practice are distinct from each other, and that neither is tarnished by politics and ideological agendas.

But, as the psychoanalysts Greenberg and Mitchell remind us,

There are no purely objective facts and observations which lie outside of theory . . . One's theory, one's understanding, one's way of thinking, *determine* what are likely to be taken as facts, determine how and what one observes. Observation itself is understood to be "theory laden". [Greenberg & Mitchell, 1983, p. 16, my italics]

This chapter, then, is a reminder of something already well established, but hard to remember: that the therapist's perceptions and interventions are *inevitably* compromised by the ideologies that the therapist unwittingly subscribes to, as well as the discourses that the therapist unknowingly participates in. This results in the therapist/analyst unthinkingly reproducing and reinforcing these ideologies and discourses through their activities, *despite themselves*. As Elias says, structures have histories and histories have structure. In other words, history is structured into the psyche, a history of norms and values. In fact this is exactly how Freud describes the contents of the superego. These taken-for-granted norms and values, born of a particular history in a particular time, privilege certain ways of thinking while they close off others. And this takes place so powerfully that mostly one is not even aware of what has been closed off.

The powerful thing about discourse is that even as it privileges a particular way of seeing and experiencing things, in the same moment it closes off other possibilities so much that it does not even occur to one that there are other possibilities there to be entertained. For example, if one conceives of human beings as ahistorical, differentiated, encapsulated entities, then it would seem that the only means for individuals to engage with each other are through the device of sending and receiving communications of various kinds. In psychoanalytic theory, these mechanisms are called projection, projective identification, and sometimes *massive* projective identification; they have become essential and key to understanding all clinical phenomena. The existences of these mechanisms are *givens* in psychoanalytic discourse. There is no discussion in mainstream literature about *whether* they exist; rather, the discussion is limited to how and why they take place, and their meanings and consequences. This is the dominant and prevailing view not only in psychoanalysis, but also in group analysis. This way of thinking also leads to the contemporary Kleinian premise that *all* the analyst's responses in the clinic are to be understood as countertransference, that is, in some way unconsciously provoked and *caused* by the patient's *projections* into the analyst. I would contend that it would be pretty much impossible for a candidate training to get through a psychoanalytic training while questioning the existence of these mechanisms. The trainee would be thought of as delusional or just foolish, certainly as someone not able to understand some fundamental things about the nature of human beings, and, therefore, not appropriate to become a psychoanalyst. What I want to make explicit here is that the workings of power privilege some ways over others, and that these are hard to resist swallowing whole. But these processes are not conscious, neither are they conspiracies contrived by the ruling elites (which is not to say that politicing does not take place on the committees of psychoanalytic trainings). The point I want to make is that, in the main, it does not even occur to many practitioners to question the taken-for-granted ground that their version of psychoanalysis stands on.

The notion of the social unconscious questions the individualistic premises of mainstream psychoanalysis and leads to other ways of reading clinical phenomena. What is being proposed here is that the analyst's responses to the patient are going to be informed by the discourses that the analyst inhabits as much as by anything else. And discourses, by their nature, are out of the scope of the analyst's consciousness as much as anyone else's. But, as I have been arguing, there are alternative ways of thinking about human beings, ways that privilege their sociality. This way of thinking provides alternative metaphors for human communication. For example, in my view, Foulkes's notion of "resonance" is a potent alternative to that of "projection". I do not wish to go into the notion of resonance itself in this essay; rather, what I want to emphasize is that the notion of resonance *presupposes* some sort of connectivity between agents for the resonance to take place. It is the nature of that connectivity that is being thought about by the scholars mentioned above. And, while each gives answers that not only differ but sometimes also contradict each other, what they all take for granted is the connectivity itself—the key word in the previous sentence being "presuppose". This taken for granted is, of course, also an expression of a particular ideology—one, it so happens, that I sign up to.

Ultimately, there is no comfortable, ideology-free zone for the analyst to retreat to, no place of scientific objectivity from which they can feel confident that things are indeed as they are being perceived and experienced. This, in itself, is no bad thing. As Foulkes (1986, p. 129) counsels, doubt is the very basis of the attitude of "basic modesty" that ought to be central to, and cultivated by, every therapist.

Acknowledgement

I wish to thank Earl Hopper for his thoughts on an earlier version of this chapter.

Notes

1. Take President Obama's recent reversal of George Bush's ban on stem cell research. Obama said that his decision was driven by scientific evidence, whereas Bush had made his decision "in consultation with God".
2. Although Klein thought that this was indeed the case, that the infant comes into the world with the categories breast, penis, and vagina already present in the mind (Hinshelwood, 1991, pp. 324–326).
3. I am aware that, in speaking of *the* social, I am in fact reifying the process of ongoing human interaction. And, in doing this, I am giving succour to the view that *the* social and *the* individual are different and antithetical to each other. My view follows that of Elias, which is that notions of individual and social are both abstractions and aspects of the same psycho–socio–genetic process of human interaction.
4. "homo est naturaliter politicus, id est, socialis" (quoted in Arendt, 1998 p. 23).

References

Althusser, L. (1969). *For Marx*, B. Brewster (Trans.). London: New Left Books.

Arendt, H. (1998)[1958]. *The Human Condition*.Chicago, IL: Chicago University Press.

Barthes, R. (1984). *Mythologies*. London: Paladin.

Bion, W. R. (1961). *Experiences in Groups*. London: Tavistock/Routledge.

Bourdieu, P. (1986). *Distinction: A Social Critique of the Judgement of Taste*. London: Routledge.

Cushman, P. (1994). Confronting Sullivan's spider—hermeneutics and the politics of therapy. *Contemporary Psychoanalysis, 30*: 800–844.

Dalal, F. (1998). *Taking the Group Seriously: Towards a Post-Foulkesian Group Analytic Theory*. London: Jessica Kingsley.

Dalal, F. (2002). *Race, Colour and the Processes of Racialization: New Perspectives from Group Analysis, Psychoanalysis, and Sociology*. Hove: Brunner-Routledge.

Elias, N. (1991). *The Symbol Theory*. London: Sage.

Fairbairn, R. (1935). The social significance of communism considered in the light of psychoanalysis. In: *Psychoanalytic Studies of the Personality* (pp. 233–246). London: Routledge, 1994.

Foucault, M. (1972). *The Archaeology of Knowledge*, A. M. Sheridan Smith (Trans.). New York: Pantheon.

Foulkes, S. H. (1986). *Group Analytic Psychotherapy*. London: Karnac.

Freud, S. (1921c). *Group Psychology and the Analysis of the Ego. S.E., 18*: 67–144. London: Hogarth.

Freud, S. (1930a). *Civilization and Its Discontents. S.E., 21*: 59–145. London: Hogarth.

Greenberg, J. R., & Mitchell, S. A. (1983). *Object Relations in Psychoanalytic Theory*. London: Harvard University Press.

Harland, R. (1987). *Superstructuralism*. London: Methuen.

Hegel, G. W. F. (1979). *Phenomenology of Spirit*. Oxford: Oxford University Press.

Hinshelwood, R. D. (1991). *A Dictionary of Kleinian Thought*. London: Free Association Books.

Hopper, E. (2003). *The Social Unconscious*. London: Jessica Kingsley.

Kant, I. (1999). *Critique of Pure Reason*. Cambridge: Cambridge University Press.

Klein, M. (1959). Our adult world and its roots in infancy. In: *Envy and Gratitude and Other Works 1946–1963* (pp. 247–263). London: Virago Press, 1988.

Kuhn, T. (1962). *The Structure of Scientific Revolutions*. Chicago: Chicago University Press.

Lacan, J. (2007). *Ecrits*. New York: Norton.

Leyton, L. (2006). Racial identities, racial enactments, and normative unconscious processes. *Psychoanalytic Quarterly, LXXV*(1): 237–270.

Winnicott, D. W. (1958). Psycho-analysis and the sense of guilt. In: *The Maturational Processes and the Facilitating Environment*. London: Hogarth Press, 1982.

Wrong, D. H. (1962). The over-socialized conception of man in modern sociology. *Psychoanalytic Review, 49*(B): 53–69.

CHAPTER ELEVEN

The foundation matrix and the social unconscious

Regine Scholz

Introduction

This chapter contains an attempt to conceptualize ideas on transpersonal, supra-individual processes, usually referred to as "the social unconscious", suggesting that it might be fruitful to revert to S. H. Foulkes's notion of the "foundation matrix". The concept understands individual and group as one single and inseparable process in which biological, social, cultural, and economical factors meet, based on ongoing communication. This chapter tries to work out these ideas without drowning the individual in the social or treating societies as though they were persons: in other words, to work on the endeavour of a group analytic idea of unconscious processes in which the multiple actors are constitutive.

After outlining dimensions of content that constitute the foundation matrix, I will enlarge the meaning of "communication" to include actions and the body as carrying meanings. I will also consider the time dimension of the "foundation matrix". The unconscious is not a reservoir of eternal topics, released from the laws of time and space. Unconscious life has a special relation to time and has its special media. I try to stress the role of embodied memories and values, the significance of family talks, and that of externalizations such as books, museums, and rituals, as well as places, making a distinction between communicative and cultural memory, emphasizing the fact that personal memories emerge from, and are based in, collective memories.

I also argue that the foundation matrix pertains to group cohesion, as shared memories, stored and passed on by different modes, are vital for the duration of social entities. This aspect is then discussed referring to collective traumata, identifying them as " hot spots" in a foundation matrix and as very powerful group markers, connecting people in shared emotions, unconscious fantasies, and defences. It could be an interesting question—and perhaps decisive in de-escalating international conflicts—to outline other factors of group cohesion and to which degree or in what situations individuals are dependent on it.

From Freud to Foulkes

The nineteenth century knew much about the idea of transpersonal unconscious processes, be it as a biological heritage of the species or as the divine spark in each of us. Ellenberger (1970) traced thoroughly how much Freud owed to these traditions of thinking while developing his own ideas. Although more than half of his work is dedicated to questions of culture, religion, literature, and arts (i.e., the role of the unconscious in transpersonal contexts) his ideas on the unconscious are essentially developed in the context of individual treatment and, thus, from the point of view of the individual. His understanding of the unconscious is linked to his instinct theory and to the notion that psychic development is deeply rooted in, and tied to, biological maturing processes of the body. The ingenuity of this idea is the formulation of a process integrating biologic, psychic, and, to a certain degree, even social aspects. Inseparably connected to it are a theory of psychopathology (neurosis as regression of libido to earlier stages of development) and a theory of therapeutic change. But this thinking is not easily—and, I think, not necessarily—transferred to group processes. I shall come back to this later.

For the given moment, I want to point out that the more psycho-analytic thinking developed along the lines of individual treatment, the more the unconscious became an individualistic concept: somat-ically based individual drive needs are inevitably in conflict with internalized social norms represented in the superego and/or in conflicts with demands of reality that have to be mediated by ego structures. If no adequate solution to the conflicts is found, the con-flicts become suppressed and repressed into the unconscious. This is the price to be paid for a more or less well functioning social life.

The first Freudian attempts to respond to the psychic dimension of mass phenomena—still along the lines of an individualized concept of the unconscious—were, after the First World War, mainly in Freud's idea of a death instinct (Freud, 1920g) and in his thinking on mass psychology, which assumed that each individual member of an organization (army, church) projects his ego-ideal on a leader (Freud. 1921c). The sheer amount of collective human aggression and cruelty, but also the incredible enthusiasm displayed in the context of the first "modern war", was deeply frightening. For the younger generation of psychoanalysts, the old answers soon were no longer satisfying. The question arose: how to deal with the obvi-ously shared psychic dimensions of these social phenomena?

The rise of fascism in the aftermath of the Great War added to the urgency for finding new theoretical concepts to explain the reactions of the masses. Maybe the best known of these notions was Reich's "Massenpsychologie des Faschismus" (1933). As, for example, Hopper has pointed out repeatedly (Hopper, 2003a,b and previously), the main problem with these early theories is the im-plication that society and culture can be treated as a body or as a person, in which the Freudian unconscious, which is inseparably linked to the somatically based instincts, is merely transferred to the realms of society. In itself, this idea is not without its own political implications.

The first person to make an explicit attempt to connect sociology and psychoanalysis on the basis of the concept of a social uncon-scious was Fromm (1930). In 1962, he summarizes his thinking on this topic:

> ... each society determines which thoughts and feelings shall be
> permitted to arrive at the level of awareness and which have to

remain unconscious. Just as there is a social character, there is also a *"social unconscious"*. By "social unconscious" I refer to those areas of repression which are common to most members of a society; these commonly repressed elements are those contents which a given society cannot permit its members to be aware of if the society with its specific contradictions is to operate successfully. [Fromm, 1962, p. 88]

Based on, and embedded in, these same historical developments of the first half of the twentieth century was the thinking of S. H. Foulkes, a German-born psychoanalyst of Jewish origin. Before emigrating to the UK, he had worked in Frankfurt, where he was intellectually attracted by the Institute of Social Research, which, at that time, housed the Institute of Psychoanalysis, of whose outpatient department Foulkes had been in charge. His experience still echoed in his later work, in which he began to treat his analytic patients in groups, founding what he later called "group analysis", a term first used at the end of the 1920s in Frankfurt by Karl Mannheim (1943). In reflecting on his experiences in groups, he made a crucial step towards a better understanding of unconscious processes as not something *inside* an individual, but more *between* people, being aware of the pitfall of understanding a plurality of persons as one unit with special psychic threats.

Like Freud, Foulkes's innovation was first a methodological one: he changed the setting from the couch to the circle, from the rule of free association to that of free discussion. Foulkes was very much aware of the fact that changing the setting required a change in theory. He had to integrate into his theoretical thinking the fact that, in his groups, unconscious material was communicated and understood. In the group setting, it could be seen that there is not a collection of several individual "unconsciousnesses" in the room, but a set of common unconscious meanings under construction by communication. In a first theoretical attempt, Foulkes put it like this:

... the group analytic situation, while dealing with the unconscious in the Freudian sense, brings into operation and perspective a totally different area of which the individual is unaware. Moreover the individual is as much compelled and modelled by these colossal forces as by his own *id* and defends himself as strongly against their recognition without being aware of it, but in quite different ways and modes. One might speak of social or interpersonal unconscious. [1964, p. 52]

Although quite clearly influenced by British objects relation theory, Foulkes did not go on with terms like "social unconscious" or "interpersonal unconscious". His genuine elaboration to conceptualize his findings was the term "matrix":

> The matrix is the hypothetical web of communication and relationship in a given group. It is the common shared ground which ultimately determines the meaning and significance of all events and upon which all communications and interpretation, verbal and non-verbal, rest. [*ibid.*, p. 292]

He later differentiated between "dynamic matrix" and "foundation matrix", the latter describing the common ground necessarily existing before any actual communication occurs and on which it is based. He put it as follows:

> I have accepted from the very beginning that even a group of total strangers, being of the same species and more narrowly of the same culture, share a fundamental mental matrix (*foundation matrix*). To this their closer acquaintance and their intimate exchanges add consistently so that they form a current, ever moving and ever developing *dynamic matrix*. [Foulkes, 1990, p. 228]

Thus, Foulkes can be seen as an early communicational theoretician of unconscious processes. But, as Dalal (1998) has stressed, after his death, not much emphasis was laid on elaborating a revolutionary sentence such as the following: "What we traditionally look upon as our innermost self, the intrapsychic against the external world, is thus not only shareable, but is in fact already shared" (Foulkes, 1975, p. 62). Here, no place is left for something "social" somehow added to something "individual". This is a different direction of thinking than that of Freud, who fundamentally doubted the human ability for culture, stating as the basis of culture and civilization the necessity of massive instinct repression (Freud, 1930a), thus constructing a sharp antagonism between culture and individual.

Foundation matrix

Dimensions of content

The "foundation matrix", as introduced by Foulkes, is based on biology, the anatomy and physiology of the human species, and includes language, culture, and social class. This list is clearly neither comprehensive nor systematic; what it shows is that Foulkes is trying to convey an understanding of individuals as well as of society *as units consistently under construction by communication.* He draws our attention to the fact that different communicational levels are connected to *different time rhythms,* ranked according to the speed—or, better, slowness—of the time needed for change. Including biology as a level of communication means considering the body as a biological–social unit. Biology is the slowest moving "level". Language is part of the slow-moving unit of "culture".

Foulkes does not explain what he considers to be part of a given culture. He just implies that the common biological base of all humans is worked out in different ways by different cultures. That, of course, refers to our overall bodily makeup. Furthermore, nowadays we know that although the expressions of basic affects, such as fear, anger, disgust, sadness, surprise, interest, and happiness, are innate, and can be communicated and understood very early in life and by all humans (Ekman & Friesen, 1978; Krause, 1983), there is a phylogenetic heritage of affect expressions indicating our basic capacity to relate and the necessity to do so. It is also well known that even our brains do not develop outside the context of the course of early interactions, and that the mutual attuning processes between mother and infant have a clearly physiological site (see Stern, 1985). The recent studies of the "mirror neuron" suggest that imitation is a very basic communication process in primates. Thus, from the very beginning, our biology is social, and we are born into a pre-existing culture.

Le Roy (1994), who worked in Africa, puts it this way: "This collective cultural basis has become part of our body and self" (p. 181). Different foundation matrices differ in how they spell out such basic dimensions as family systems, gender relations, the relationship between generations, and, moreover, the understanding of inside and outside the cultural group: who belongs to "us" and who is "not us". However, the categories mentioned by Le Roy probably cover the social structure of a simple society. In more complex societies, these categories have to be enlarged to cover the whole social structure, including social class, for example. And if we include these dimensions, which are relatively stable but clearly open to change, we have included history and power. The notion of the foundation matrix implies a communicative approach to biology as well as to culture. Culture, then, can be seen as a group achievement, as a historically developing set of shared rules and regulations, of shared systems of interactions and symbols, including the related patterns of thoughts, emotions, and unconscious meanings and fantasies. This cultural matrix always contains, in a condensed and fantasmatic form, the international history and its power relations—and, thus, a time dimension. However, at every level, we are again confronted with the following questions: how do groups or systems of groups, form and maintain themselves? How do the members develop a sense of we-ness, recognizing each other as—maybe in a contradictory way—belonging together and excluding others? This is an ever-ongoing process, but, at a given moment, it always has a specific shape, which can undoubtedly be described as an historical phenomenon.

Media

What media of communication are related to these dimensions of content? How are these basic dimensions conveyed and understood? Sometimes, the primordial level of communication (see Foulkes, 1964, Chapter X) is linked to the foundation matrix. It is not my intention to question the significance of primordial images, which, in my opinion and in accordance with modern Jungian thinking, arise as result of basic human situations, for example, birth and death, men and women, etc., at a basic level of symbolization (see Moore & Fine, 1990, p. 192). I would like here to focus on another direction, and argue in favour of a *broader understanding of communication*. Language is not the solution, but part of the problem to be explained.

To understand the forms of interaction into which a child is born, the notion of communication has to be enlarged beyond verbal language. The cultural matrix is transmitted already in the first months of life through holding, nursing, songs, rhythms, bodily contact, and games (Le Roy, 1994, p. 183). There is a level "in between" implicit action knowledge and verbal representation (Stern, 1985). Attuning processes between mother and infant, consisting of movements and actions very close to the body, are meaningful and communicative, even building up the infant's brain structures and, thereby, paving the way for all later elaborations of perceptions, categories, and evaluations. We have to consider our brains as open systems built and shaped in a process of social interaction. Culture is like an external store of collective memory and, at the same time, a source of an epigenetic programme for developing the brain of the infant, because the brain itself does not function symbolically (Donald, 1991).

In this context, the body is no longer understood solely in biological terms. From the very first moment on, an individual's body is perceived and constituted in all its dimensions at a social level. There is no gesture, no expression or attitude without a social meaning. Bourdieu calls this "Habitus" (Bourdieu, 1972). Habitus means more an order in the body than in the mind. Habitus means embodied social values inevitably acquired through early interactions carried out in a given social context by the body (e.g., the rituals of greeting that inform us about status and hierarchies), or near the body (e.g., the dress code that classifies us along different lines of gender, age, social class), which are connected to a whole bundle of emotions. Most of the phenomena referred to in this context are unconscious, not only in the meaning of unknown or suppressed, but deeply unconscious regarding all the meanings included in the actions, plays, rituals, and the use of space. *Here the body itself acts as memory*. Thus, the concept of the "Habitus" allows us to articulate at a social level the forms of interactions, the communication patterns and related emotions, ways of perceiving, etc., which are relevant when outlining the foundation matrix.

Biology directs us by basic affects towards the care-giver, who has already embodied the preferences and limitations of his/her social group and the culture to which s/he belongs. The findings from infant research concerning the relationship between mother and infant and the research of the ethno-methodologists (Garfinkel, 1967) concerning the interactive construction of seemingly natural rules on which mutual understanding is based open up the possibility for a theory of the unconscious which is based on group analytic thinking, integrating biology, psychology, and sociology. This implies that there is no place for a theory of the "social unconscious" separated from a theory of the so-called "individual unconscious".

Some further implications

Time

This conceptualization of the foundation matrix requires a reconsideration of the role of time in unconscious processes. Freud asserted that the unconscious does not know about time, it is timeless (Freud, 1915e). This was evident in the language of dreams, the typical language of the unconscious: the primary process, which allows us to be old and young at the same time, being here and there without moving, etc. (Freud, 1900a). It is a specific way of thinking with its own cognitive potential. Timelessness was also seen in unconscious material and in the well-known fact that nothing is lost in the psyche as long as it carries psychic energy (Freud, 1933a, p. 80). However, there is a variety of phenomena from therapy and everyday life that suggests an alternative approach. Freud's notion is not only based on his rich therapeutic experience, but is an integral part of his theory of culture and his anthropology, in which—to put it in a very reduced way—an ahistorical individual is civilized by "instinct abstention". Therefore, the unconscious—the place of the instincts—is, by definition, not able to know about the cultural achievement of "time". Assmann (2004) has outlined that, in effect, Freud's theoretical thinking leaves no real space for something like "cultural unconscious" or transgenerational transmission of cultural elaborations such as "time".

Elias (1991) argued that we should not think of time as a thing, but as the process of timing; that is, giving duration, phases, beginnings and endings to processes, actions, etc. He holds that our understanding of time (past, present, future), a continuum divided into days, weeks, months, and years, etc., measured by watches and clocks, is itself a cultural construct which took mankind some thousand years to develop. Boswood (2003, p. 192) concludes that "The development of an agreed calendar has been a huge and recent human achievement". Measuring time based on the movement of the sun and the stars, thus developing an abstract frame of reference for every event to occur, is a very special human achievement and has many implications. For example, in therapy, the way a person deals with the culturally achieved collective standards of time gives us precious hints about the kind and level of disturbance.

This so-called "objective" time is not identical with "perceived" time. Everybody knows that time feels very different if one is happy or sad, or if completely awake or in a dream. This has two implications: experienced time is, even on a conscious level, never identical with "objective" time, and lived time is different from calendar time, because it always means a lifetime: that is, biography at given places and times, constituting and, at the same time, being part of a specific historical period (see Scholz, 2004).

The psychic "fall-out" of historical periods is always at work, but is best seen in the transgenerational transmission of collective trauma. Within the framework of the classical Freudian theory, these phenomena are difficult to understand, though this understanding is needed, however, in a group analytic conceptualization of unconscious processes. Moreover, a theory of collective memory is necessary, because no group can sustain cohesion over time without a shared imagined history and its emotional (libidinal) loadings. Most of our memories come to us when parents, friends, or other people recall certain events for us (see Halbwachs, 1992, p. 20). In other words, some of our memories are "stored" in other people. Halbwachs also points out that the past does not just come up again, but is reconstructed from the point of view of the present. The idea that memory is constructed through group communication is actually both a modern psychoanalytical and a group analytical idea. The development of a theory of collective memory, which includes Halbwachs' ideas but transcends his rationalism, would be a decisive challenge for group analysis.

Group cohesion

The foundation matrix contains a time dimension in which the body is used as a "store" for shared values, etc. This implies a theory of group cohesion. The Freudian view of group cohesion is well known: group members are connected by identification with a leader, investing their libidinal energies into an ego-ideal that is projected on to the leader; they are connected through the love for this leader. However, I would add to this set of ideas that groups have to ensure their cohesion in space and time. Three realms of memory are connected to three distinct main media, which differ in their duration and the number of people who are reached at a given moment.

- The body carrying deeply unconscious material that is communicated and understood, and is only partly accessible to translation into verbal language, as implicit knowledge can never wholly be transformed into explicit knowledge. Group members with the same mimetic will recognize each other without words being necessary, for example, religious groups, soldiers, people of the same traumatic field of events, etc. Bodily communication needs proximity, and, thus, at a given moment, only reaches a limited number of people. The "advantage" of bodily represented knowledge and values is its stability due to its limited accessibility to thinking; the disadvantage is clearly to be found in its limited capacity to be transferred at longer distances in time and space. The time boundary is given by mortality.
- Language and narration which can bridge longer distances. A group, a family, talks. In this close emotional context, movements are accompanied by comments. Rules are first "done", but then more and more explained. The family members share memories and tell stories. In these repeated stories (e.g., "how it was when mummy (or daddy) was a child"), special events are less important than one might assume. It is more about how our "we" is constructed: The underlying message is: "That is how it was, before you were here. That is how it is done with us, we are like that and you—as a part of us—are like that". Thus, the child is made a member of the group and gets words for the already existing connections. Welzer (2002) spells out Halbwachs' notion of communicative memory, which is passed on in the families and is based on its "talks"— which means it has its limits in the oral tradition of the family. At most, this ranges for 80–100 years.

● Cultural memory (Assmann, 2004) mediated by bodily and oral tradition. Whereas communicative memory still needs physical presence and allows for disparate details, cultural memory represents the history in a highly condensed form. Its media are objects such as museums, memorials, monuments, and repetitive scenes, as in rituals, which can be seen as externalization of the material to be memorized. With these media, accompanied by written language, a group can pass on their traditions for round about 3000 years.

Example: collective trauma

This connection of feelings that influence experienced time and historical events in building up the psychic life of large groups and in constituting large parts of their foundation matrices is perhaps best seen in *collective traumata*. Traumata, at an individual level, are defined as situations that overwhelm a person's psychic coping capacities and, thus, evoke feelings of extreme helplessness and despair. At a group level, occurring as mass phenomena, traumata tend to disintegrate the whole social structure. Trauma brings together the powerful and the powerless in the same space of events, raising high emotions, breaking down the level of differentiation already achieved.

Especially important are "chosen trauma", in which, seemingly independent of time and space, a historical fact comes to define both the inside and the outside of a group, that is, its boundaries (Volkan, 1999). People to whom this event is meaningful and who participate in remembering it in a specific way, that is, how it is perceived and felt, are members of the given group, while those who do not are outsiders, or are in danger of being expelled from the group.

Traumata have a very special relation to time. They are always now. This statement holds true at a personal level of individuals suffering from post traumatic stress disorder (PTSD), who, in their flashbacks, behave as though they were still in the traumatic situation. But somewhat similar phenomena also can be observed in large groups, such as in nations or in ethnic groups. For example, the conquest of Constantinople (today's Istanbul) in 1452 still has its psychic relevance today. The partitions of Poland more than 200 years ago still mean something in that country, and for the Jews, the destruction of the second temple is still an issue. These events have become part of what Assmann (2004) and Assmann (1999) call "cultural memory", memories which date too far back to be part of the oral personal tradition, but which need holy books, places, ceremonies and rituals, that is, externalization, to be remembered again and again, thus becoming part of the mental representation of each member and of the we-ness of a group.

Volkan describes the process of chosen trauma as an intergenerational process, as a narration of a humiliating event passed down over many generations and, thus, becoming part of the psychic representation system of all members of a society or large group. However, in common with many others, Volkan does not distinguish between large groups and society, thus underrating the impact of institutions and other intermediate structures (Hopper, 2005). Neither does he differentiate cultural from communicative memory (that is, he does not distinguish between events which date too far back for any person of the community to have a personal knowledge of it) and between events that are still passed on in a personal way in a family. That is why most people read his books from the background of the Second World War in general and especially of the Holocaust, in spite the fact that Volkan does not consider the Holocaust/Shoah a "chosen trauma", explaining that, nevertheless, "it is on its way" (personal communication, Volkan, 2000).

Distinguishing between the two types of memory can help us to understand the processes in which a collective catastrophe shifts from the communicative memory of family talk (or silence) to the cultural memory of monuments and memorial days. These processes are not confined to the Jewish community. They occur throughout the entire world. As personal memories fade, libraries, memorials, and museums become necessary. And, during these processes, the meaning of events can change; for example, the meaning of the Holocaust has shifted from a horrendous war crime committed against a special group to the signifier of the ultimate humanistic catastrophe (Levy & Sznaider, 2001) setting overall moral standards.

The crucial point Volkan was the first to draw our attention to is that events from the very far away past can evoke intense feelings in the present, which can determine actions with consequences for the future. He calls this "time collapse":

> [E]motions and perceptions belonging to the past are experienced as coinciding with emotions and perceptions belonging to the present and are even projected onto the future. Memories, emotions and expectations coincide. [1999, p. 244, my translation]

Hopper, following Bion's sentence that the basic assumption group knows no time, refers to similar phenomena when he states that traumatized people tend to recreate traumatic situations (see Hopper, 2003b, p. 131) as a primal defence against the anxieties of helplessness which are often, but not always, associated with social trauma. These ideas, and especially the notion of time collapse, resemble the concept of timelessness of unconscious material, but there is an important difference. According to Volkan's concept of time collapse, well-known facts generated at a specific moment and at a given place are transformed into a myth. That is, they are treated and then experienced *as if* they were timeless. Having become part of the psychic life of a member of a given group, these events then contaminate every interaction and colour all feelings and behaviours of this individual, at very conscious and unconscious levels. Traumata then become part of the foundation matrix, reorganizing and homogenizing its material, as a pattern that generates patterns. Chosen traumata (traumata that, by unconscious choices, act as "group markers" for large entities such as nations and ethnic or religious groups), thus, are very strong in fostering group cohesion. They are also the most potent poison to intercultural understanding. If "activated" by a recent mass trauma and filled with other psychic material, they act as something like a nuclear bomb to constructive international relations. As Weinberg, who has an Israeli background, puts it,

> The mental representation of the past disaster becomes condensed with the issues surrounding current conflicts, magnifying enemy images and distorting realistic considerations in peace negotiation processes. [Weinberg, 2007, p. 319]

Volkan connects the chosen trauma to the inability of previous generations to mourn the experience of shared traumatic events. He believes that in the case of chosen trauma, the group has failed to heal a narcissistic wound and to overcome humiliation. Volkan shifts the centre of the trauma from cruelty and the consequential suffering and despair associated with it to the accompanying destruction of vital basic narcissistic illusions, such as:

- I am inviolable; nothing can happen to me;
- the world has a systematic order, and events are predictable. In other words, I can control them;
- good things happen to good people; bad things happen to bad people. If I live up to moral standards, I shall receive my reward;
- on a group level, even if I suffer and die, my group (nation, religion, ethnic group) will go on forever.

Trauma destroys these assumptions and confronts us with chaos. For individuals, transforming mass trauma into chosen trauma could be seen as a defence mechanism in order to counter these unbearable feelings, which include shame at being so vulnerable. On a group level, we could speak of the collapse and disintegration of the "group envelope", as discussed by Anzieu (1984). Trauma, thus, not only plunges us into feelings of helplessness and despair, but also elicits intense narcissistic rage, which protects us from experiencing the painful feelings associated with our vulnerability and finiteness. The transformation of mass trauma into chosen trauma is a very powerful tie keeping a group together, possibly even forming it, a magic defence against the fear of annihilation (Hopper, 2003a).

That transformation's dangerous potential is related to the narcissistic rage that is also encapsulated in this "choice", for rage is a feeling that tends to foster revenge and, hence, new traumata. The potential for a vicious circle, which can start even after a long period of quiet, stems from the fact that a trauma, if transformed into a chosen trauma, will never end. One reason for this is that all the suppressed feelings associated with it are still present in the transmission of trauma, but they are not mirrored or answered. Another reason is that the trauma takes on a very special form in the course of transformation. Only some facts are officially remembered; others are left out. Some feelings are allowed; others are not.

Research on memory has informed us that memory is under permanent reconstruction. Current needs determine what is remembered and how. Thoughts and emotions that the group members are to feel in this context tend to be prescribed. Thinking or feeling anything different on the given topic puts the individual in danger of losing his or her status as a group member. The chosen trauma acts as a group marker and is, thus, linked to the identity of all members of the group.

Although connected to unconscious fantasies, the shaping of thoughts and feelings that a special trauma entails does not occur unconsciously at all levels. To understand how this process is imposed on a particular group and its members, it may be helpful to consider the social structure and distribution of social power in a group. In given situations, concrete actions are taken to suppress deviant ways of thinking and feeling. Press censorship, for example, is a rather brutal method for excluding thoughts and findings from public discourse and for preventing their public evaluation. Although press censorship does, of course, still exist, there are many other, more subtle ways to tell members of a group how to think and feel. The result is that large bodies of relevant emotional facts are banned from public communication by *symbolic violence*, and, at the same time, are prohibited from surfacing in the conscious psychic life of individuals. Thus, this material becomes part of what we may think of as a society's "dynamic unconscious", which is consistent with my thinking about the "social unconscious" and the "foundation matrix".

The trauma, thereby, becomes a form that can be filled with current material, stemming from perhaps quite different sources. The chosen trauma is trauma that can be used and abused. In other words, it becomes an empty signifier. This is important, together with the differentiation between traumata that are passed on through communicative memory, and chosen trauma as part of the cultural memory. Because, dependent on the type of trauma and their connection to the members of a group, different media will be needed to bring the trauma and the related feelings back into the scope of time and space through communication (Schlapobersky, 2000).

It is a different task to help survivors of a mass trauma to find their voice or to work with second generations. Another type of broad public discussion is needed at all levels in order to retrieve the excluded material of a chosen trauma, to regain or even develop one's own view on the topics concerned, and, thus, to broaden the communicational base, yet avoiding expulsion by the group and escaping the destruction of one's inner life. Intellectual discussion alone will not suffice. New rituals, new places, new ceremonies will be necessary, a shift in symbolization.

Assmann's notion of cultural and communicational memory provides an idea of what is at stake and what can be done. This hints at the importance of the time dimension, and the fact that different types of memories need to be stored in different ways. If we think of the body as storing these memories and the feelings and values associated with them, it becomes clear that these shifts are "time-consuming".

Some conclusions

A tentative answer to the questions about the definition of "unconsciousness" from a group analytic perspective can now be suggested. First, *the unconscious refers to all those phenomena on which the symbolically mediated communication of group members is not focused* (after Mies, 2007). This descriptive definition refers to economical limits of awareness. A shift of focus can bring up unconscious material easily. Only the term "symbolically mediated" hints that there are other, perhaps genuinely unconscious or non-conscious, modes of communication, such as body movements, smells, etc., that deserve attention, especially if one wants to understand affect attunement and directedness in groups. Here, we approach the field of unconscious emotionally loaded processes that serve as cognitive functions. They are non-conscious and vital in building up individual psyche as well as groups. To transfer this knowledge in our ideas about groups is still a challenge.

The classical idea of the unconscious as Freud saw it was suppressed and repressed material, that is, material that by severe resistance is not allowed to become conscious. Freud constructed this idea along the social phenomenon of political censorship, in that he refers, in his description of an inner psychic mechanism, to a blockade of communication in the public area. But political

censorship is too rough a metaphor for the description of unconscious processes from a group perspective. Instead, we might use
the term "symbolic violence" (Bourdieu & Passeron, 1973) to
describe the equivalence of resistance on a group level. Symbolic
violence refers to the hidden dimensions and operations that make
the given situation seen and felt as the only one that is possible.
*From a group analytic perspective, the dynamic unconscious is related to
symbolic violence, and those scenes and communicational acts that are
excluded by these relations from the ongoing communicational process. By
symbolic violence, this exclusion appears as a condition of group membership and the capacity to communicate.* If the first mentioned areas of
the descriptive unconscious refer more to the overall adaptive function and, moreover, creative and facilitating characters of unconscious forces, the dynamical unconscious refers more to the
restraints that result from the naturalization of the social structure
in the context of structures of power.

For the same reason that led colleagues such as Hopper, Dalal,
and Knauss not to use the concept of the "social unconscious", I
prefer to use and spell out the notion of the foundation matrix
when referring to the genuine social nature of human beings: it is
primarily because "'social unconscious" implies that old opposition
of individual and group/society that Foulkes tried to overcome
when he said,

> Human beings always live in groups. Groups in turn cannot be
> understood, except in their relations to other groups and in the
> context of conditions in which they exist. We cannot isolate biolog-
> ical, social, cultural and economic factors, except by special abstrac-
> tion. Mental life is expression of all these forces . . . Rather, the
> distinction between group and individual psychodynamics is
> meaningless, except again by abstraction. We sometimes talk of a
> group or an individual separately, as we focus more on one or other
> aspect of what is in fact one single and inseparable process.
> [Foulkes, 1990, p. 252]

Yet, in trying to avoid using the concept of the social unconscious,
I do not wish to neglect the study of these important social, cultural,
and political restraints and constraints on personal and group
development.

References

Anzieu, D. (1984). *The Group and the Unconscious*. London: Routledge & Kegan Paul [published 1981 as: *Le Groupe et l'Inconscient*. *L'Imaginaire Groupal*. Paris: Dunot].

Assmann, A. (1999). *Erinnerungsräume—Formen und Wandlungen des kulturellen Gedächtnisses* [Spaces of Memory—Shapes and Changes of Cultural Memory]. Munich: C. H. Beck.

Assmann, J. (2004). Phylogenetisches oder kulturelles Gedächtnis—Sigmund Freud und das Problem der unbewussten Erinnerungsspuren [Phylogenetic or cultural memory—Sigmund Freud and the problem of unconscious memory traces]. *Freiburger literaturpsychologische Gespräche*, 23: 63–79.

Boswood, B. (2003). Marking time. *Group Analysis*, 36(2): 192–201.

Bourdieu, P. (1977). *Outline of a Theory of Practice*, Cambridge University Press. [published 1972 as: *Esquisse d'une Théorie de la Pratique*. Geneva: Droz. S. A.

Bourdieu, P., & Passeron, J.-C. (1973). *Grundlagen einer Theorie der symbolischen Gewalt. Kulturelle Reproduktion und soziale Reproduktion*. Frankfurt am Main: Suhrkamp [French: *La Reproduction. Eléments pour une théorie du système d'enseignement*. Paris: Minuit, 1970].

Dalal, F. (1998). *Taking the Group Seriously: Towards a Post-Foulkesian Group Analytic Theory*. London: Jessica Kingsley.

Donald, M. (1991). *Origins of the Modern Mind: Three Stages in the Evolution of Culture and Cognition*. Cambridge, MA: Harvard University Press.

Ekman, P., & Friesen, W. V. (1978). *FACS Facial Action Coding System: A Technique for the Measurement of Facial Movement*. Palo Alto.

Elias, N. (1991). *Time—An Essay*. Oxford: Blackwell, 1991 [published 1984 as: *Über die Zeit*. Frankfurt: Suhrkamp].

Ellenberger, H. F. (1970). *The Discovery of the Unconscious: The History and Evolution of Dynamic Psychiatry*. New York: Basic Books.

Foulkes, S. H. (1964). *Therapeutic Group Analysis*. London: George Allen & Unwin.

Foulkes, S. H. (1975). A short outline of the therapeutic process in group analytic psychotherapy. *Group Analysis*, 8: 59–63.

Foulkes, S. H. (1990). The group as a matrix of the individual's mental life. In: *Selected Papers* (pp. 223–233). London, Karnac.

Freud, S. (1900a). *The Interpretation of Dreams*. S.E., 4–5. London: Hogarth Press.

Freud, S. (1915e). The unconscious. *S.E., 14*: 166–215. London: Hogarth Press.

Freud, S. (1920g). *Beyond the Pleasure Principle. S.E., 18*: 7–64. London: Hogarth Press.

Freud, S. (1921c). *Group Psychology and the Analysis of the Ego. S.E., 18*: 67–143. London: Hogarth.

Freud, S. (1930a). *Civilization and Its Discontents. S.E., 21*: 59–145. London: Hogarth.

Freud, S. (1933a). *New Introductory Lectures on Psycho-analysis. S.E., 22*: 3–182. London: Hogarth.

Fromm, E. (1930). *The Working Class in Weimar Germany: A Psychological & Sociological Approach* [reprinted 1984, Cambridge, MA: Harvard University Press].

Fromm, E. (1962). *Beyond the Chains of Illusion.* New York: Continuum, 2001.

Garfinkel, H. (1967). *Studies in Ethnomethodology.* Malden, MA: Polity Press/Blackwell, 1984.

Halbwachs, M. (1992). *On Collective Memory.* Chicago, IL: University of Chicago Press Originally published in French in 1925 as: Les cadres sociaux de la mémoire. In: *Les Travaux de L'Année Sociologique.* Paris: F. Alcan.

Hopper, E. (2003a). *Traumatic Experience in the Unconscious Life of Groups.* London: Jessica Kingsley.

Hopper, E. (2003b). *The Social Unconscious: Selected Papers.* London: Jessica Kingsley.

Hopper, E. (2005). Response to Vamik Volkan's plenary lecture: Large group: identity, large group regression and massive violence. *Group Analytic Contexts, December* (30): 33–52.

Krause, R. (1983). Zur Onto- und Phylogenese des Affektsystems und ihrer Beziehungen zu psychischen Störungen [About onto- and phylogenetic development of the affect system and its relation to psychic disorders]. *Psyche, 37*: 1015–1043.

Le Roy, J. (1994). Group analysis and culture. In: D. Brown & L. Zinkin (Eds.), *The Psyche and the Social World* (pp. 180–201). London: Routledge.

Levy, D., & Sznaider, N. (2001). *Erinnerung im globalen Zeitalter—Der Holocaust.* Edition Zweite Moderne. Frankfurt: Suhrkamp Verlag [a shorter English version is: Levy, D., & Sznaider, N. (2002). Memory unbound: the holocaust and the formation of cosmopolitan memory. *European Journal of Social Theory, 5*(1): 87–106].

Mannheim, K. (1943). *Diagnosis of Our Time*. London: Paul Kegan, Trench, Trubner & Co.

Mies, T. (2007). Das Unbewusste in der Gruppenanalyse—Vorläufiger Versuch einer Begriffsbestimmung [The unconscious in group analysis—provisional trial of a definition]. In: *Arbeitshefte Gruppenanalyse (Hg): Die Gruppenanalytische Perspektive* (pp. 41–56). Psychosozial 107. Gießen: Psychosozial Verlag.

Moore, B. E., & Fine, B. D. (1990). *Psychoanalytic Terms and Concepts*. New Haven, CT: Yale University Press.

Reich, W. (1933). Die Massenpsychologie des Faschismus. Erweiterte und revidierte Fassung: Kiepenheuer & Witsch, Köln, 1971. English edition: *The Mass Psychology of Fascism* (3rd edn). New York: Farrar Straus Giroux, 1980.

Schlapobersky, J. (2000). Die Rückforderung von Raum und Zeit [The reclamation of space and time]. *Arbeitshefte Gruppenanalyse, 2000*: 61–86.

Scholz, R. (2004). Das Unbewusste kennt keine Zeit! Das Unbewusste kennt keine Zeit? [The unconscious does not know about time! The unconscious does not know about time?]. *Gruppenanalyse, 2*(4): 147–154.

Stern, D. (1985). *The Interpersonal World of the Infant*. New York: Basic Books.

Volkan, V. D. (1999). *Das Versagen der Diplomatie* [The Failure of Diplomacy]. Gießen: Psychosozial.

Weinberg, H. (2007). So what is this social unconscious anyway? *Group Analysis, 40*(3): 307–322.

Welzer, H. (2002). *Das kommunikative Gedächtnis*. [The Communicative Memory]. München: C. H. Beck.

PART VI

THE NUMINOUS AND THE UNKNOWN

Introduction

Amélie Noack

T he following chapters explore the connection between the social unconscious and the numinous, a topic that could be considered somewhat unusual in the context of a book like this. Gordon Lawrence, a former business consultant, and Stephanie Farris, a former solicitor who is now a Jungian analyst and group psychotherapist, each approach the subject from the angle of their own disciplines, which differ from Foulkesian group analysis.

Lawrence uses his experience of social dreaming, which is a method he discovered in 1982 when working at the Tavistock Institute in London, and which since has been widely applied in a variety of contexts, such as consulting to business and organizations, to explore the social dimension of dreaming, especially in connection with social trauma. Social dreaming looks at the thinking and cultural knowledge contained in dreaming and aims to elucidate political and social realities through a connection with the social unconscious, which "... comes into existence when three or more people relate through their individual unconscious ... and discover ... an added quality beyond the capabilities of their individual unconscious" (Lawrence, 2007, p. 6).

In his understanding of social dreaming, Lawrence here provides a definition of the social unconscious that is somewhat different from one derived from the work of Fromm (1962) and Dalal (1998), who tend to focus on the power-related restrictive and repressive aspect of social unconscious processes. Lawrence develops Hopper's (1996) view of a wider and deeper domain of the social unconscious through the invention of the social dreaming matrix. Contrasting the so-called objectivity and practical knowledge-based experience of the natural sciences with the subliminal knowledge of intuition and insight gleaned from social dreaming work, Lawrence emphasizes the realm of the infinite, the numinous, and the spiritual as part of the social unconscious. He muses that, if the self is rooted in the social unconscious with others in a relational web, perhaps all the dreams of the universe are lodged in the social unconscious, becoming available to dreamers attuned to the numinous. By quoting the German poet, Rilke, and reminding us that scientists tend to dream their discoveries first, he emphasizes the need for "quietness and sincerity of contemplation".

Reflecting on relativity, complexity, and uncertainty, social dreaming depends, he says, on a capacity for faith in tolerating unknowing and relinquishing the ego's claim to control. The dread of mystery and the awesomeness of the infinite, which can be encountered in social dreaming, mobilizes a mystic frame of mind through which dreams, by offering a multi-verse of meaning, can become the crucible of creativity.

Fariss comes from a totally different angle and asserts a basic Jungian principle, the refusal to dichotomize. She emphasizes the need to contain the tension of opposites between, for instance, religions or racial factions, and to move beyond them, because, she says, globalization makes us all intimates. This also applies to the study of culture, which derives from the culture-creating spirit in the human psyche and unfolds through a process aiming for wholeness, termed originally by Jung "individuation", and concerned with the production of meaning, which today also must be applied to the global field.

Fariss acknowledges the social unconscious as a group analytic term and refers to Foulkes's term of the "matrix" as the common shared ground. She distinguishes the foundation matrix related to the social or interpersonal unconscious, based on biology and the social, as well as culture, from the dynamic matrix as a network of relationships and communications in the present. In order to demonstrate that the individual psyche, too, is both organic and social, she offers a short overview of Jungian theory, in the course of which she differentiates the social unconscious from Jungian ideas about the cultural and the collective unconscious. The shadow, the tension of opposites, Jung's complex theory, and the various layers of the unconscious are mentioned. This is obviously an extremely brief overview of Jungian concepts, predisposed to her aim of connecting and delineating group analytic from Jungian concepts, and should not be taken as comprehensive.

Parallels between images, myths, and fairy-tales of people un-related in time or space, she tells us, allow Jung to describe an impersonal layer in the psyche, which he called the collective un-conscious. He understood this collective layer as *a priori* given, containing universally prevalent patterns and forces called arche-types, which have a numinous quality. Any particular cultural canon supersedes the previous by integrating in time the archetypes of the earlier one, and promoting in this way the development of human consciousness. The cultural layer of the unconscious can be imagined as situated somewhere between the personal unconscious (Freud) and the collective unconscious (Jung). A "cultural complex", that is, the historically or culturally shared trauma of a given people, constitutes a societal individuation task, which, in parallel to indi-vidual development, requires this group to hold the tension of opposites and move beyond it, since "we are human only through the humanity of others". Fariss postulates that only by valuing wholeness, unity, and freedom, and by holding the tension of opposing value systems, can a point of view in the service of expanding and developing consciousness emerge.

I found it interesting that Fariss and Lawrence do not refer to the principle of synchronicity (Jung, 1991), which often has been described as related to the experience of the numinous. The concepts of the social unconscious and the collective unconscious, as Fariss has shown, derive from two different disciplines and the differences are significant, in so far as the social unconscious belongs to a par-ticular social system, such as a hospital or any given society, while the collective unconscious belongs to the world at large and, as the home of the archetypes, can acquire a quasi-religious quality.

However, the social unconscious and the collective unconscious both interconnect with consciousness through the principle of synchronicity, which derives from the field underlying manifest reality. This field may have different layers, some of which are socially derived, while others are related to general qualities of humanity; however, in this field, everyone and everything is related in an unconscious matrix. This is an idea also found in Jung's notion of the *unus mundus*.[1]

A social dreaming matrix promotes the connection with the social unconscious in a movement based on synchronicity between consciousness and the unconscious, the finite and the infinite, and people often wonder how dreams not thought about for years can be remembered and even be related to the here and now. When things go even further and the dreams and the matrix dip into the collective unconscious, something which does not always happen by any means, a social dreaming matrix may become a numinous experience. A connection with the uncanny or the sublime may emerge, which can be fascinating as well as terrifying, because it touches on the *mysterium tremendum et fascinans*, which we usually attribute to the Divine and the Wholly Other. The accompanying feelings of impotence and anxiety of the ego may explain why some people find social dreaming matrices difficult.

Dipping into the numinous, or making a connection with the realm of the uncanny or the spiritual, can happen even in the course of a business consultation or in a weekly therapy session with either an individual or a group. These chapters, by Fariss and Lawrence, respectively, provided me with a valuable prompt and a useful stimulus for wondering about the connections between a necessary down-to-earth attitude in our work and the more sublime aspects of creativity manifesting in and through it.

Note

1.   "unus mundus" refers to Jung's (1974) idea of a unitary world, encompassing physical as well as psychological aspects and events, describing the eternal ground of all being.

References

Dalal, F. (1998). *Taking the Group Seriously*. London: Jessica Kingsley.

Fromm, E. (1962). *Beyond the Chains of Illusion. My Encounter with Marx and Freud*. New York: Simon & Schuster.

Hopper, E. (1996). The social unconscious in clinical work. *Group, 20*(1): 7–42.

Jung, C. G. (1974). The conjunction. In: *Mysterium Coniunctionis. CW, 10*. London: Routledge & Kegan Paul.

Jung, C. G. (1991). *Synchronicity: An Acausal Connecting Principle. CW, 8*. London: Routledge & Kegan Paul.

Lawrence, W. G. (Ed.) (2007). *Infinite Possibilities of Social Dreaming*. London: Karnac.

CHAPTER TWELVE

The social unconscious and the collective unconscious: the Jungian perspective

Stephanie Fariss

Introduction

In February 2006, European newspapers published several political cartoons, including a caricature of Islam's founder, Mohammed, as a terrorist with a bomb in his turban. Considered "blasphemous", the cartoons sparked violent protests in Muslim and Arab countries which resulted in several deaths. Europeans and Americans, who experience such satirical forms of expression as a legitimate cultural tradition, were nonplussed by the Muslim response. Around this time, an American Muslim named Eboo Patel told a story on National Public Radio that illustrated the dilemma of someone holding the tension of both views:

"Do you believe in free speech?" people asked him.

"To the teeth," he replied.

"Are you hurt by the ridiculing of the Prophet Mohammed in mainstream newspapers?"

"Deep in my heart."

Confused, they then say: "But your beliefs contradict each other; which do you choose, Western values *vs.* Muslim values? Free speech *vs.* cultural sensitivity?"

But Patel refuses to dichotomize the discussion or to be pushed to the point of polarization. As he sees it, viewing the world in such absolutes plays into the hands of those who are working to entrench the clash of civilizations and make it as bloody as possible. Some people, he imagines, are whispering into the ears of right-wing politicians in Europe, saying things such as, "True Europeans are ready to hear that we were not meant to live with these foreigners. Let's make Europe pure again." Their counterparts in the Muslim world, he imagines, are telling their people that if Muslims do not go to war with the West, then the West will continue to insult Islam. The two sides think they are battling with each other, Patel says, but their volleys serve mostly to destroy the dream of a common life together.

As he sees it, globalization makes us intimates.

"Who is flying the flag of coexistence on this planet," he asks.

"Who is telling the story of pluralism?

"Who is pointing out that They are Us?" (Patel, 2006).

This story illustrates several key concepts in analytical psychology, the branch of psychoanalysis developed by Carl Gustav Jung,[1] and introduces some of the tensions within individuals and social systems that I will explore in this chapter. Writing about the "social unconscious" and the "collective unconscious"—concepts that originate from two distinct analytic traditions, the Freudian and the Jungian, respectively—is not unlike attempting to speak two different languages to an audience whose members understand only one or the other. In such a situation, members of each group, indurated to their unique theoretical language, tend to miss the mark of truly understanding the other and instead might make intuitive leaps in the theory, distorting it to fit their own paradigm, or worse, might dismiss it altogether.

I hope, in this chapter, to avoid these pitfalls while promoting an interaction between the two groups of analysts who use these two different theoretical languages, and, like Patel, encourage a "globalization" of understanding in the study of the social unconscious among various analytic traditions.[2] I assume the majority of readers will be group analysts and other clinicians who speak the language of Freudian psychoanalysis. As a Jungian analyst who applies the theory of analytical psychology to individuals and a variety of social systems, including groups,[3] I hope to offer a selection of concepts in analytical psychology that may expand the purview of the study of the social unconscious, and illustrate the relevance of analytical psychology concerning collective issues such as race, gender, and politics by drawing on current political and societal issues.

Sociology, the cultural turn, and globalization

It is important to distinguish "social"from "cultural" and their respective academic schools of study, while noting the current move towards making connections between these two schools.[4] Modern sociology, especially in the USA, has tended to be "culture-resistant", leaving cultural sociologists no choice but to continue their work in the departments of cultural studies, cultural anthropology, and media studies. Gradually, with the emergence of postmodernism and global consciousness, there has developed a greater concern among sociologists with applying the study of culture to the global field.[5] Cultural phenomena—belief systems, symbols, and cultural values—are intimately linked to social interaction, political economics, and the functioning of organizations and societies (Robertson, 1992).

This new appreciation of the study of culture in order better to understand social interaction and structure, along with a more tolerant view of non-sociological treatments of cultural phenomena and a growing trend toward "interdisciplinarity", reveals several ways in which culture and cultural studies may resonate with the practice and theory of analytical psychology. The interdisciplinary nature of cultural studies highlights that culture is concerned with the production of meaning—the creation of cultural forms and how these inform social practices.[6] The making of meaning is not considered to be fixed or complete, but, rather, dependent on both context and particulars; it is a process, a "happening". While the importance of "material culture" continues to be recognized, there has been a call for making cultural analysis more dynamic, by shifting attention to the creative and transformative aspects of culture, with less focus on the static character of social products and the consumption of those products. Finally, the developing focus on the "practice of culture" encourages the study of performance and ritual in various cultures.

The development of the social aspects of the unconscious in psychoanalysis

The specific concept of the social unconscious does not exist in analytical psychology.[7] Jung tended to view groups negatively—as destructive rather than creative—in part due to his personal difficulty as a member of various professional organizations, and formed years before the development of group analytic theory and its appreciation for group dynamics. Jung did, however, study diverse cultures and their spiritual traditions, leading him to identify a "culture-creating spirit" in the human psyche, a way of creating meaning[8] and living life beyond the fixation to parental imagoes.[9] He also noted the limitations of the "dialectical process between two individuals" and, with faint praise, noted how "in a group we see operating all those psychic events which are never constellated by an individual, or may even be unintentionally suppressed" (Jung, 1970, par. 888).[10] Unlike Freud, who viewed the human organism as a "discrete individual entity each with its own mind, each with having a clearly defined boundary which separated an inside from an outside" (Zinkin, 1998, pp. 123–124), Jung regarded humans as perpetually incomplete, while viewing their incompleteness as pointing to a process of unfolding wholeness, which he called "individuation".[11] We could say that, theoretically at least, Jung valued a group perspective, but, unfortunately he limited his concepts of the social aspect of the unconscious to "the collective" and "the personal" within the individual.

Freud was not adept in groups either and tended to regard external reality as an invariant, focusing instead on the inner dynamics of individual patients (Brown & Zinkin, 2000).[12] But, a generation later, several Freudian psychoanalysts became intrigued with group dynamics, having made keen clinical observations in military treatment facilities following the world wars. S. H. Foulkes began treating his patients in groups, seeking to understand the unconscious processes *between* people. His emphasis was to recognize and analyse the social forces at the interpersonal and transpersonal levels and espouse that the individual psyche is both organic and social at birth (Hopper, 2003). Foulkes described multi-personal fields as a three-dimensional jigsaw puzzle where the individual is like one piece of the jigsaw (Brown & Zinkin, 2000). Foulkes's idea of a matrix as a network of relationships and meanings that impacts all participants within it parallels Jung's idea that even in individual analysis the "analytic container" is composed of psychic energies of the analysand *and* the analyst, with *both* being transformed in the process of their interactions.

Several generations of group analysts have continued to share an interest in the social unconscious—most notably Earl Hopper (2003), who published a collection of papers on the subject, and who defined the concept of the social unconscious as "the existence and constraints of social, cultural and communicational arrangements of which people are unaware" (Hopper, 2003, p. 127) including the intrapsychic representation of social forces and power relations in various other cultural phenomena (Weinberg, 2003, p. 198. This concept of the social unconscious resembles the concept of the cultural unconscious in analytical psychology. However, in analytical psychology, the cultural layer of the unconscious is not the end of the matter: Jung's *pièce de resistance* was his discovery of the "collective unconscious", the deeper layer of the unconscious inhabited by archetypes that underlies both the personal and cultural layers of the unconscious.

A foreshadowing of Jung's formulation of the collective unconscious and archetypes was first described in 1896 in a series of lectures he presented to his peers in a Swiss student fraternity while attending the medical school of Basel University. In one of the lectures, Jung describes his interest in Immanuel Kant's postulate of *ding-an-sich*, a concept which, in Jung's view, came to mean an "unconscious structure, unknowable in itself, which can be observed only in its manifestations as archetypal images, ideas and emotions" (von Franz, 1983). Indeed, it was Jung's deep immersion in philosophy that created a distinctly different cultural grounding in psychoanalytic enquiry from that of Freud (Kirsch, 2004).[13] This difference helps to explain why these two gifted men ultimately separated, each to travel his distinctive path. While recognizing the enormous contribution of Freud's discovery of the individual unconscious, I believe Jung's conception of the psyche—especially as it relates to the cultural and collective unconscious—has much to offer concerning the study of social systems and the members of them.

Jung's map of the psyche

Returning to the story at the beginning of this chapter: Eboo Patel's American friends are telling him that he cannot hold both Western and Muslim values, but must choose because there can be only one reality. This is an example of the all-too-human characteristic of making the reality of the individual ego the only reality, eschewing the possibility of an I–Thou encounter. Exploring the world beyond ego consciousness—beyond a choice of Western values or Muslim values—requires an attitude of humility and curiosity, an ability to be open to the unknown realms of the unconscious, a letting go of the belief that there is only one way of being, a willingness to confront what Jung called our *complexes*, those "splinter selves" that link us to the archetypal realm. It requires us to hold the *tension of opposites*—conscious *vs.* unconscious, outside *vs.* inside, us *vs.* them; to become aware of the undiscovered, detested, disowned parts of the psyche that Jung referred to as the *shadow*. It requires an ego strong enough to be receptive to what is present or emerging into the field of consciousness, such as knowledge experienced in dreams and synchronistic events, and information made comprehensible through feeling and intuition (Neumann, 1989). It also requires a developing ethical ego—an ego capable of reflecting on the symbolic messages from this tension-bearing to determine a legitimate standpoint and course of action. The process of this inner struggle, which Jung called *individuation*, can lead to what we often refer to as "character" and can introduce to the collective a new symbol, attitude, or idea.

One example of this may be what occurred in the USA on 4 November 2008, when an African-American man was elected President. In fact, President Barack Hussein Obama practically embodies all that Eboo Patel is struggling with—the ability to hold the tension of two ethnicities: one of white middle-class America, which is the heritage of his mother, and one of black Africa, the heritage of his father. Both the white majority and the black minority have struggled with Obama's "otherness", but, ultimately, due to his own ability to hold the tension of opposites and be "all about moving beyond" (Schaffer, 2007), Obama has led both groups to feel that he is "one of us", no matter his age, the colour of his skin, or his pedigree. Jung's map of the psyche provides tools for understanding how the process of holding the tension of ego consciousness and unconscious knowledge may lead to greater consciousness and wholeness for the individual as well as the social system of which he or she is a part. I will begin with Jung's conceptualization of complex theory.

Complex theory[14]

According to Jung, the ego is influenced by both external environmental stimuli, as experienced in a particular family and culture, and internal psychic stimuli, including those energies that originate from the archetypal realm of the collective unconscious. It is this process of differentiation by the ego that determines what stays in consciousness and what goes into the realm of the personal and cultural unconscious and ultimately leads to the creation of one-sided ego consciousness. Over time, the external environmental stimuli combine with the unfolding psyche of the child to create internal psychic stimuli in the personal and cultural unconscious called *complexes*.

Jung discovered these internal disturbances early in his career as a psychiatrist while conducting word association experiments with test subjects at the Burghölzli Hospital, the psychiatric clinic of the University of Zurich, under the tutelage of Professor Eugen Bleuler.[15] Jung began to see that certain stimulus words produced a disturbance in consciousness, even physiological reactions that could be measured using a psychogalvanometer, and he became curious about what was happening in the psyche of a test subject at those moments. Subjects would respond to certain stimulus words with nonsensical words, emotion, signs of anxiety, and defensive reactions that Jung considered to be *complex indicators*, that is, an emotionally charged signal that a personal or cultural complex had been constellated (Stein, 1998).

In analysing the patterns of response, Jung found that the words creating a disturbance were clustered around a theme that pointed to a common content. When subjects were asked to talk about their associations to these stimulus words, Jung found that the words had aroused painful and traumatic associations that had been buried in the unconscious. Jung concluded that these unconscious contents—the complexes—could interfere with conscious perfor-mance, will, action, and memory.[16] When a complex is constellated, a person may feel possessed by a strong force that cannot be willed away, or might feel as if he or she is coming "unglued". Known colloquially as "having one's button's pushed", complex reactions can also distort a person's reality, colouring it to fit an earlier ex-perience or trauma and producing a marked affective reaction that is "fuelled" by the *archetypal core* of the complex. Indeed, Jung referred to the complex as the "royal road" to the unconscious and the "architect of dreams". Through the concept, Jung was able to link the personal and archetypal elements of an individual's ex-periences. I would add that cultural complexes show the same kind of linkage, only between the cultural elements of a group's experi-ences and the archetypal realm. The complex enables us to envision how emotional experiences accumulate over a lifetime and why psychological life is more than a series of unconnected, meaningless events (Samuels, Shorter, & Plaut, 1986).

Multiple layers of the unconscious

The layer of the unconscious that contains repressed, infantile, personal experience is the level Jung explored during the word association test. He named this the *personal unconscious,* and found that mother and father complexes tend to dominate this field. But he discovered something else in the word association experiments that pointed to familial and cultural similarities in complex struc-tures. Some of the experiments tested family influences on the formation of unconscious contents in children and found evidence of similar patterns of complex formation among family members, especially mothers and daughters. These results led Jung to con-clude that a child's development is highly affected and patterned by close family relationships, at least until those structures can be modified through education and other cultural experiences (Stein, 1998). It also indicates that shared experiences or traumas in a group can lead to shared patterns of complex formation.[17]

Gradually, during this time, Jung began to notice parallels between images and myths of individuals and groups in unrelated historical periods and locations, as well as to identify myths, fairy tales, and religious images that appeared in the dreams and fantasies of patients who lacked exposure to such imagery. During a trip to the USA with Freud in 1909, Jung had a dream that led him "for the first time" to the concept of the collective unconscious (Jung, 1989). This dream, as described in his autobiography, was the source of his notion that the unconscious contained multiple layers of depth.

In the dream, Jung was in a house that had many levels—a house he called "my house" in the context of the dream. Throughout the dream, Jung explores the various storeys of the house from the "inhabited atmosphere" of the upper floor (that Jung believed represented consciousness), down to the "medieval furnishings" of the ground floor (that he believed stood for the first level of the unconscious), and beyond that down through several sub-cellars that led to a low cave cut into rock, where he encountered the remains of a primitive culture (which Jung thought represented the prehistoric and Paleolithic past). "The deeper I went, the more alien and the darker the scene became" (Jung, 1989, p. 160).

Jung thought the dream had a meaning beyond that of the realm of the personal.

> The dream pointed out that there were further reaches to the state of consciousness ... the long uninhabited ground floor in medieval style, then the Roman cellar, and finally the prehistoric cave. These signified past times and passed stages of consciousness. ... [M]y dream pointed to "the foundations of cultural history—a history of successive layers of consciousness" and "constituted a kind of structural diagram of the human psyche; it postulated something of an altogether *impersonal* nature underlying that psyche. [Jung, 1989, p. 161]

While Jung initially went along with the interpretation of the dream proposed by Freud—that it concerned Jung's secret death wishes toward his wife and sister-in-law—he believed that the dream had a fuller meaning. This particular dream became a "guiding image": "It was my first inkling of a collective *apriori* beneath the personal psyche", he said (Jung, 1989, p. 161). Jung eventually named this collective *a priori* level the "collective unconscious", and conceived of its contents as a combination of universally prevalent patterns and forces called *archetypes*. Jung discovered that we experience these archetypal patterns in the form of powerful imagery and emotion, and that these archetypal patterns or mythological motifs exist in all individuals and groups.

The cultural and collective unconscious

The archetype itself cannot be experienced directly; it needs the context of a particular culture in which to "clothe" the archetypal form, thereby creating an *archetypal image*, which *can* be experienced directly.[18] It is the cultural layer of the unconscious that actually provides this necessary "clothing". Although universal patterns may exist in all cultures, each has its own particular contextualization.[19] Despite his keen interest in diverse cultures and their sacred traditions, however, Jung focused on the archetypal level in his study of group life, and left such developments to the "second generation" pioneers whom he believed would have the "advantage of a clearer, if still incomplete, picture . . . [where] one now knows what must be known if one is to explore the newly discovered territory" (Jung, 1995, p. xiii).

While a student of Jung's in Zurich in the late 1920s, Joseph Henderson noticed in his peers a certain kind of transference to Jung that related to each person's particular cultural preference: for example, one student approved of Jung because "he was so Chinese", another approved because Jung was "so free of orientalism, so ruggedly western", as if each felt more at home with Jung's psychology if it could be linked to their own cultural preference (Henderson, 1962, p. 3). Over time, Henderson's curiosity led to further study, and in 1962 declared, "much of what has been called 'personal unconscious' is not personal at all but that part of the collective culture pattern transmitted through our environment before we were able to affirm its validity for ego-consciousness" (p. 9). He wrote that he:

> . . . found it useful to postulate the existence of a cultural layer of the unconscious existing somewhere between the personal unconscious which originated with Freud and the collective unconscious which is associated with Jung. [Henderson, 1992, p. 4]

Jung saw the collective unconscious as a container for the whole spiritual heritage of humankind's evolution born anew in the brain structure of every individual:

> To the extent that the archetypes intervene in the shaping of conscious contents by regulating, modifying, and motivating them, they act like instincts. [At the same time,] archetypes have ... a distinctly *numinous character* ... [that] mobilizes philosophical and religious convictions in the very people who deemed themselves miles above any such fit of weakness. Often it drives with unexampled passion and remorseless logic towards its goal and draws the subject under its spell, from which despite the most desperate resistance he is unable, and finally no longer even willing, to break free, because *the experience brings with it a depth and fullness of meaning* that was unthinkable before. [Jung, 1969, pars. 404–405, my italics]

The *numinous* experience of the archetype informs the ego that powerful spiritual energies exist in the psyche which are beyond ego awareness and control.[20] These unconscious forces and energies of the collective unconscious not only disturb consciousness, but provide contents that demand to be made conscious. Various analysts have described such momentous experiences as spiritual, religious, transcendent, "awesome", in the realm of the sacred, and—drawing on the influence of Goethe—a way of seeing things with the "eyes of the spirit" (Bishop, 2006, p. 129).[21] The numinous is experienced through the phenomenon of projection, whereby unconscious contents are located in sacred events, relationships, rituals, imagery, etc., and, through such experiences, link consciousness to the collective unconscious. These "hints" communicated by the collective unconscious could, through the process of individuation, provide a deeper and more meaningful perspective on life (Stein, 2006, p. 46). This aspect of the sacred in Jung's model of the psyche has, until recently, been dismissed on the basis of the positivistic views of the modern world, but since the advent of postmodernism the sacred might be gaining new credibility in connection with the scientific exploration of the psyche (Casement & Tacey, 2006).

Another "second generation pioneer" of analytical psychology who expanded the territory through research within the sphere of the cultural unconscious and its relationship to the collective unconscious was Erich Neumann, who introduced the ideas of the archetype of the cultural canon and the development of collective consciousness. As described by Neumann (1973), a continuous process of archetypal stages determines the creative evolution of consciousness in the life of humankind. Each stage maintains an organic relationship to the others, so that each successive conscious system absorbs more of the collective unconscious than the last, assimilating and integrating new unconscious contents in order to broaden the frontiers of consciousness. This process has been collectively embodied in mythology and is the template for the course every individual ego has to pass through in order to achieve psychic development. Neumann's presentation of these developmental stages through mythology—that is, the projections of the primordial images—shows how these archetypal stages are both the basis of psychic development *and* the result of previous development all through human history (Fariss, 2003, p. 59). Neumann viewed this creative evolution of consciousness as the "particular achievement" of Western culture.[22]

The cultural complex

Most recently, contemporary Jungian analysts Tom Singer and Sam Kimbles have applied Jung's complex theory to the cultural level of the psyche and introduced the concept of the *cultural complex* (Singer & Kimbles, 2004). The cultural complex functions like a personal complex and leads to unconscious, feeling-toned trains of thought that tend to overtake and stand in for the ego, blocking its ability to reflect on different ways of thinking or feeling. Cultural complexes often originate with a traumatic experience that is shared by the entire cultural group. These shared experiences of trauma lead to shared cultural complexes of the group-as-a-whole, as well as within the psyches of the individual group members. Tom Singer writes:

> Cultural complexes structure emotional experience ... Like individual complexes, cultural complexes tend to be repetitive, autonomous, resist consciousness and *collect experience that confirms*

their historical point of view . . . automatically take on a shared body
language . . . or express their distress in similar somatic complaints
and . . . *provide a simplistic certainty about the groups' place in the world
in the face of otherwise conflicting and ambiguous uncertainties.* [Singer,
2004, p. 21, my italics]

A contemporary example of a cultural complex is the proliferation and extremist teachings of Madrasahs, the religious schools that
educate millions of students in the Muslim world. These schools
have been blamed for brainwashing youngsters in the Middle East,
making them enemies of the West, but the trauma that led to the
anti-Western sentiment in these schools is overlooked. The Mad-
rasah system is a thousand years old, and was founded in eleventh-
century Baghdad to provide prestigious training schools for future
leaders and religious scholars in Muslim countries. The initial
curriculum included Islamic jurisprudence, philosophy, logic, and
the rational disciplines. Later, however, when the British took
control over South Asia, that all changed: Muslims were forced
to defend Islam against the onslaught of Christian influence—
English replaced Persian as the official language and Christian
missionaries set up English-speaking religious schools (Evans,
2006). The cultural complex created from this attack on Islamic
culture led to a closing of doors to modern knowledge in the
Madrasahs. "Modern knowledge" came to be viewed as polluting
young minds because of its association with the traumatic experience of attack on their cultural integrity. It is possible to conclude
that non-Western cultures' resistance to the secularization of education may mean that the cultural complex has been constellated,
helping us to understand how these cultures could experience the
foreigner's request for secularization as an archetypal declaration of
war on their cultural identity and resulting in all of the affective,
defensive, and aggressive reactions that the archetypal image of war
entails.

The cultural complex and the individuation of a social system

The experience of the cultural complex, fuelled by the energy of its
archetypal core, can affect individuals as well as a variety of social
systems—families, organizations, religious groups, nations. One

way to understand Jung's concept of individuation is to consider the process as a gradual working through and eventual integration of a person's or group's core complexes over a lifetime, even over generations. A good example of a civilization that has struggled for centuries with the cultural complexes of racism and colonialism is Africa. Considered to be the "cradle continent", Africa established well-organized states and prospered for significant periods of time (e.g., 300–1500 AD) before Europeans began their "scramble" to colonize the continent and establish the slave trade (Berg, 2004, p. 240). The tribal people of Africa were overwhelmed by the technical strength of the white Europeans and their defeat came to represent the overall supremacy of their conquerors—"whiteness" became associated with superiority and the continent became gripped by the cultural complex of racism, fuelled by the "archetypal fear of the unknown other" (ibid., p. 242). In South Africa, the white superiority complex became institutionalized as apartheid, prohibiting the interplay or bridging of the two race groups. With no synthesis of ideas and culture, severe power imbalances, and a total lack of respect for the "other", the positive complex of Black Consciousness emerged, forcing a revolutionary "interplay" (Berg, 2004). Ever since the defeat of apartheid, the individuation task for South Africa has been to contain the tension of opposites of black and white and move beyond racism.

Two deeply rooted complexes in South Africa that have promoted human evolution since ancient times are the *reverence for the ancestors* and the *spirit of ubuntu*—the profoundly integrated sense that "we are human only through the humanity of others" (Berg, 2004, p. 247). The South African belief in *ubuntu*, as articulated and promoted by Archbishop Desmond Tutu, led to the establishment of the Truth and Reconciliation Commission by the African National Congress in July 1995, in order to build a new democracy following decades of gross apartheid violations (Battle, 1997):

> [Ubuntu] means my humanity is caught up, is inextricably bound up, in theirs. We belong in a bundle of life. We say, "A person is a person through other people." It is not "I think therefore I am." It says rather: "I am human because I belong." . . .[23] [It] comes from a knowing that he or she belongs in *a greater whole* and is diminished

when others are humiliated or diminished when others are tortured or oppressed, or treated as if they were less than who they are. [Tutu, p. 31, my italics]

The cultural complex and the individuation of the individual and the group

The autobiography of Barack Obama, the President of the USA, *Dreams from My Father: A Story of Race and Inheritance*, chronicles his own individuation journey—how he came to integrate his African heritage without the need to negate the values of his white family of origin. Obama grew up primarily in Hawaii with a white mother, grandmother, and grandfather. He began to confront his blackness in a real sense after he moved to Chicago between college and law school and started community organizing on the city's South Side. There he discovered a clash of cultures of which he was an integral part. Listen to the turmoil Obama experienced as he attempted to reconcile his conscious attitude with the cultural complex of racism in the USA:

> [Black] nationalism provided . . . an unambiguous morality tale that was easily communicated and easily grasped. A steady attack on the white race, the constant recitation of black people's brutal experience in this country, served as the ballast that could prevent the ideas of personal and communal responsibility from tipping into an ocean of despair. . . .
>
> It was a painful thought to consider . . . It contradicted the morality my mother had taught me, a morality of subtle distinctions—between individuals of goodwill and indifference. I had a personal stake in that moral framework; I'd discovered that I couldn't escape it if I tried. And yet perhaps it was a framework that blacks in this country could no longer afford; perhaps it weakened black resolve . . . Desperate times called for desperate measures. [Obama, 1995, pp. 198–199]

We could hypothesize that, at that time in his life, Obama had to address both the personal father complex created by the absence of his African father throughout his life—which was manifest in an intense desire to belong to and be accepted by the black community—and the cultural complexes of the black nationalists to whom he was introduced in Chicago, which was manifest in black rage and the demonizing of whites. Gradually, Obama began to find his way:

> It was this unyielding reality—that whites were not simply phantoms to be expunged from our dreams but were an active and varied fact of our everyday lives—that finally explained how nationalism could thrive as an emotion and flounder as a program ... What in the hands of Malcolm [X] had once seemed a call to arms, a declaration that we would no longer tolerate the intolerable, came to be the very thing Malcolm had sought to root out: one more feeder of fantasy, one more mask for hypocrisy, one more excuse for inaction ...
>
> The continuing struggle to align word and action, our heartfelt desires with a workable plan—didn't self-esteem finally depend on just this? It was this belief which had led me into organizing, and it was that belief which would lead me to conclude, perhaps for the final time, that notions of purity—of race or of culture—could no more serve as the basis for the typical black American's self-esteem than it could for mine. *Our sense of wholeness* would have to arise from something more fine than the bloodlines we'd inherited. It would have to find root ... in all the messy, contradictory details of our experience. [*ibid.*, pp. 202–204, my italics]

Conclusion

I began this chapter with a story told by Muslim American Eboo Patel, who describes his frustration when dealing with the dichotomous views of his Muslim and American friends, views he believes fly in the face of "the dream of a common life together". I have ended with two examples of Jung's concept of individuation and how the valuing of wholeness, unity, and freedom—"hints" from the collective unconscious acquired in the process—became the lodestar for Desmond Tutu in South Africa and Barack Obama in the USA. My desire in writing this chapter was to describe major concepts of analytical psychology that I believe add value to the study of the social aspects of the unconscious. It was also to emphasize the critical element of Jung's formulation of the psyche that calls for holding the tension of opposing points of view in the service of expanding and developing consciousness.

Jung thought that cultural history of the past two thousand years could be viewed as a pattern of unfolding consciousness with an underlying archetypal structure and that each of us carried a bit of the consciousness of the underlying archetypal images unfolding in history. He believed that as human beings we participate in the order of the universe by making patterns of that order available to consciousness. The physicist David Bohm also believed in the unbroken wholeness of the universe. His theory of implicate order—that a generative field underlies manifest reality, and the emerging whole manifests locally—is congruent with the investigative approach of Goethe, who worked to achieve an authentic wholeness by *dwelling in the phenomenon* and relying on *intuitive perception* to arrive at knowledge (Bishop, 2006; Bortoff, 1996).

Modern positivism has only been interested in approaching the whole by studying the parts, as if it were "a thing among things". Postmodern culture is interested in *moving beyond* the "mechanical philosophy" of the European Enlightenment and its accompanying emphasis on the Cartesian dualism of spirit and matter: valuing parts in preference to the whole, and individuals in preference to their collective; of unreflective scientific enquiry that believes itself to be objective; and an ambition to control the universe instead of relating to it. Globalization and the postmodern/post-9/11 world are calling for a more integrated, holistic approach.

Notes

1. Jung coined the term "analytical psychology", but it has often been used interchangeably with "Jungian psychoanalysis" (Kirsch, 2004).
2. I believe the editors, Earl Hopper and Haim Weinberg, are, in fact, encouraging such bridging by inviting a Jungian analyst to contribute to this text on the social unconscious. Another example of such an effort is *The Psyche and the Social World: Developments in Group-Analytic Theory*, a comprehensive collection of views concerning the group-analytic model edited by Dennis Brown and Louis Zinkin (Brown & Zinkin, 2000).
3. See Hopper and Weyman (2003) who distinguish between groups and social systems: "Whereas all groups are social systems, not all social

systems are groups. . . . In fact, a group is a social system with definite properties of its own . . ." (p. 56).

4. As has been made clear by Hopper in various articles, an important distinction has been made by social scientists between the terms "social" and "cultural" (Hopper, 2003).

The adjective "social" originated from the Latin socialis "united, living with others", from socius "companion, associate (originally follower)", and akin to sequi "to follow". The meaning, living or liking to live with others, disposed to friendly intercourse was first used in 1729, and the meaning pertaining to society as a natural condition of human life was first used in 1695 by Locke. http://www.etymonline.com/index.php?l=s&p=30

The adjective "cultural" is related to the noun "culture", which originated from the Latin cultura "care, culture, an honoring", and from the stem of colere "to tend, guard, cultivate or till". Although there are a variety of definitions for "culture", the one pertinent here refers to "all knowledge and values shared by a society" and "the customary beliefs, social forms, and material traits of a racial, religious, or social group". http://www.etymonline.com/index.php?term=culture. http://www.merriamwebster.com/dictionary/culture?show=0&t=1296426748 http://wordnetweb.princeton.edu/perl/webwn?s=culture.

Hopper defines sociology as "the scientific study of social systems which results in public, communicable, systematic, reliable and valid knowledge about them" (Hopper, 2003, p. 42).

"Cultural studies" is an interdisciplinary academic field that studies how a society creates and shares meaning. Richard Hoggart and Stuart Hall created the term in 1963/1964 upon the founding of the University of Birmingham Centre for Contemporary Cultural Studies. See http://www.gseis.ucla.edu/faculty/kellner/kellner.html.

Sociologists in the USA have been primarily concerned with their standing as a discipline among the hard sciences, i.e., applying positivistic methods, embracing objectivism (treating social facts as things), and arriving at a goal of explanation rather than interpretation. Sociologists in European countries have played a greater role in attending to the cultural in order to understand power relations in social systems. For instance, British sociologists were active participants in the development of the Birmingham School, located at the Centre for Contemporary Cultural Studies (Calhoun & Sennett, 2007).

5. The use of the term "global" became more prevalent beginning in the late 1980s. Initially, it meant "worldwide" or "whole", but, in 1991, the

Oxford Dictionary of New Words included it as a "new word" and defined "global consciousness" as a "receptiveness to and understanding of cultures other than one's own" (Robertson, 1992, p. 8).

6. One criticism of the field of cultural studies has been its intellectual and literary analytic approach. Similarly, a criticism of the sociology of culture has been its reductive approach (Calhoun & Sennett, 2007).

7. However, many British Jungian analysts who trained in the more developmental tradition of analytical psychology, as developed by Michael Fordham, are also group analysts.

8. Jung proposed a meaning-making function of the psyche, which he called the "religious function", as a "mythopoetic instinct reflected in humankind's inherent tendency to create myth. This function manifests wherever people make culture and try to find meaning" (Stein, 2004).

9. Jung believed that people need a wider community than the family in order to grow spiritually and morally. In Jung's volume on the development of the personality, he describes the necessity for a gradual separation from the parents, possible only when the person is capable of stepping "on to the next level" and becoming part of the spiritual organization of society, that is, "in place of the mother, there is substituted the wisdom of a doctrine. . . . Man needs a wider community than the family, in whose leading-strings he will be stunted both spiritually and morally" (Jung, 1954, par. 158).

10. In the "Introduction to Toni Wolff's 'Studies in Jungian psychology'". He continued: "[Dyadic treatment] gives results which are necessarily one-sided from the collective and social point of view" (Jung, 1970, par. 888).

11. See Chapter VIII in Jung's autobiography, *Memories, Dreams, Reflections*, where he acknowledges the relevance of the "social atmosphere" to the disturbances in the individual psyche, to wit:

> A collective problem, if not recognized as such, always appears as a personal problem, and in individual cases may give the impression that something is out of the order in the realm of the personal psyche. *The personal sphere is indeed disturbed, but such disturbances need not be primary; they may well be secondary, the consequence of an insupportable change in the social atmosphere.* The cause of the disturbance is, therefore, not to be sought in the personal surroundings, but rather in the collective situation. Psychotherapy has hitherto taken this matter far too little into account. [Jung, 1989, pp. 233–234, my italics]

Indeed, it was the encounter with cultural and collective psychic images that inspired Jung's development of the concept of the process of individuation, which he recorded in his visionary text, *The Red Book* (Jung, 2009).

12. Freud evidently tolerated groups that could function as "a sounding board for his ideas", so long as they fully supported these ideas, but in general, disliked groups and dreaded direct confrontation (see Grosskurth, 1991).

13. Particularly relevant are Leibniz's idea of *unconscious perceptions*, Kant's *dark representations* and *ding-an-sich*, Schopenhauer's idea of the "tendency of the unconscious material to flow into definite molds", and Nietzsche's idea of "going under" in *Thus Spake Zarathustra*.

14. The importance of this concept in analytical psychology is so great that Jung struggled with whether to call his theory "complex psychology" instead.

15. Jung's work on word association experiments at the Burghölzli led him to search out Freud, believing that Freud's investigation of the unconscious was crucial to understanding the results of his own research. So Jung began to write Freud in 1906, and an initial meeting of the two men occurred in 1907 (Kirsch, 2004).

16. Jung described complexes as "splinter psyches" that "behave like independent beings":

> My findings in regard to complexes corroborate this somewhat disquieting picture of the possibilities of psychic disintegration, *for fundamentally, there is no difference in principle between a fragmentary personality and a complex.* . . . . Complexes are psychic fragments which have split off owing to traumatic influences or certain incompatible tendencies. [my italics]

17. Jung's contemplation of this finding resonates with both the idea of the cultural complex and Foulkes's concept of the foundation matrix, which he defined as "inherited biological properties" and "culturally embedded values and reactions". Foulkes's concept of the dynamic matrix—"the theater of operation of ongoing change"—resonates with how the modification of those patterns of complex formation may occur through education and other cultural experiences, including individual and group analysis (Foulkes, 1986, pp. 131–132). An example of the cultural complex will be provided in another section of this chapter.

18. It is important to note that Jung's understanding and use of the term "archetypal image" represents much more than imagery:

> [Image] undoubtedly does express unconscious contents, but not the whole of them, only those that are momentarily constellated. This constellation is the result of the spontaneous activity of the unconscious on the one hand and of the momentary conscious situation on the other. . . . The interpretation of its meaning, therefore, can start neither from the conscious alone nor from the unconscious alone, but only from their reciprocal relationship. [Jung, 1971, par. 745]

19. In *Cultural Attitudes in Psychological Perspective*, Henderson describes how throughout the world tribes have evoked archetypes through ritual observances that are particular to them:

> Although absolutely pure cultures no longer exist, we can reconstruct many of the tribal chant-ways or dance-dramas from ceremonials still in use, where far from the urban centers of civilization, they still maintain some of their original integrity. If we were to attend a Navaho healing ceremonial, or a Bushman rain dance, an Australian initiation rite or an Eskimo hunting ritual, we would find that the meaning of the entire culture is evoked in each one. [Henderson 1984, pp. 77–78]

> Henderson goes on to describe how such ceremonies are *religious* because they invoke the presence of gods, *social* because the well-being of the tribe is bound up with them, *aesthetic* by virtue of their performance of dance and music, rock-drawings or carvings in sand, and *philosophic* in that the different strands of the tribal lore are woven together to explain the origin of the rites as related to a creation myth (*ibid.*).

20. The term "numinous" originates from the Latin *numen*, which is Latin for deity or divine will. German theologian Rudolf Otto first introduced a psychological and emotional component into the study of theology in his seminal text, *The Idea of the Holy*, and developed the use of the terms *numinosum*, numinous, and numinosity (Stein, 2006, pp. 38–39). Otto's description of a numinous experience includes aspects such as a sense of Terror, the All-Powerful, the Sublime, the Uncanny, the Void, the Wholly Other, Fascination, and Immensity. He describes the numinous paradoxically—as generating fascination on the one hand, and fear and dread on the other—producing feelings of

impotence and experiences of anxiety in the ego. Jung referred to the experience of the numinous as a "hint" to the ego that powerful non-ego elements exist in the psyche. For a comprehensive discourse on numinous experience, see *The Idea of the Numinous*, edited by Ann Casement and David Tacey.

21. Indeed, Goethe wrote about the necessity of "seeing with the eyes of the spirit" when encountering science. Bishop quotes Goethe:

> Because, in knowledge just as in reflection, no totality can be brought together, because the former lacks what is internal and the latter what is external, we must necessarily conceive of science as art if we are to expect any kind of totality from it. [Bishop, 2006, p. 126]

22. How archetypal images are ultimately experienced in this evolution of consciousness is interdependent with cultural context. Through the website of The Archive for Research in Archetypal Symbolism (ARAS) and its search engine, see how cultures from all over the world have lived the symbolic meaning of archetypal themes throughout the history of the evolution of consciousness. The ARAS website address is: http://aras.org/. ARAS has also published several texts: *An Encyclopedia of Archetypal Symbolism: Volume One*, and *An Encyclopedia of Archetypal Symbolism: Volume Two*. In November 2010, Taschen Books published ARAS's latest book: *The Book of Symbols: Reflections on Archetypal Images* http://www.taschen.com/pages/en/catalogue/art/all/06703/facts.the_book_of_symbols_reflections_on_archetypal_images.htm.

23. This is a quote from a 1997 address Mandela gave in Oxford on "Religious Heritage".

References

Battle, M. (1997). *Reconciliation: The Ubuntu Theology of Bishop Desmond Tutu*, (p. 1). Cleveland, OH: Pilgrim's Press.

Berg, A. (2004). Ubuntu: a contribution to the "civilization of the universal". In: T. Singer & S. Kimbles (Eds.), *The Cultural Complex: Contemporary Jungian Perspectives on Psyche and Society* (pp. 239–250). New York: Routledge.

Bishop, P. (2006). The idea of the numinous in Goethe and Jung. In: A. Casement & D. Tacey (Eds.), *The Idea Of The Numinous: Contemp-*

orary Jungian And Psychoanalytic Perspectives (pp. 117–136). London: Routledge.

Bortoff, H. (1996). *The Wholeness of Nature*. Barrington, MA: Lindisfarne Books.

Brown, D., & Zinkin, L. (2000). Introduction. In: *The Psyche and the Social World*. London: Jessica Kingsley.

Calhoun, D., & Sennett, R. (Eds.) (2007). *Practicing Culture*. New York: Routledge.

Casement, A., & Tacey, D. (Eds.) (2006). *The Idea Of The Numinous: Contemporary Jungian And Psychoanalytic Perspectives*. London: Routledge.

Evans, A. (2006). Understanding madrasahs: how threatening are they? *Foreign Affairs*, 85(1): 9–16.

Fariss, S. (2003). The resilience of a collective: A Jungian reflection on the American Democratic Republic. Unpublished diploma thesis, Analyst Training Program, C. G. Jung Institute of Chicago.

Foulkes, S. H. (1986). *Group Analytic Psychotherapy: Method and Principles*. London: Karnac.

Grosskurth, P. (1991). *The Secret Ring: Freud's Inner Circle and the Politics of Psychoanalysis* (pp. 36–45). Reading, MA: Addison-Wesley.

Henderson, J. (1962). Archetype of culture. In: A. Guggenbuhl-Craig (Ed.), *Der Archetyp: Proceedings of the 2nd International Congress for Analytical Psychology* (pp. 3–15). Basel, Switzerland: S. Karger AG.

Henderson, J. (1984). *Cultural Attitudes in Psychological Perspective*. Toronto, Ontario, Canada: Inner City Books.

Henderson, J. (1992). Cultural attitudes in light of C. G. Jung's psychology. Unpublished manuscript.

Hopper, E. (2003). *The Social Unconscious: Selected Papers*. London: Jessica Kingsley.

Hopper, E., & Weyman, A. (2003). A sociological view of large groups. In: E. Hopper (Ed.), *The Social Unconscious: Selected Papers* (pp. 42–71). London: Jessica Kingsley.

http://aras.org.

Jung, C. G. (1954). Analytical psychology and education. In: W. McGuire (Ed.) & J. van Heurck (Trans.), *C.W., 17*. Princeton, NJ: Princeton University Press [original work published 1926].

Jung, C. G. (1969). On the nature of the psyche. In: W. McGuire (Ed.) & R. Hull (Trans.), *C.W., 8*. Princeton, NJ: Princeton University Press [original work published 1946].

Jung, C. G. (1970). Introduction to Toni Wolff's "Studies in Jungian psychology". In: W. McGuire (Ed.) & R. Hull (Trans.), *C.W.*, *10*. Princeton, NJ: Princeton University Press [original work published 1959].

Jung, C. G. (1971). Definitions. In: W. McGuire (Ed.), H. G. Baynes (Trans.) & R. Hull (Rev. Trans.), *C.W.*, *6*. Princeton, NJ: Princeton University Press [original work published 1921].

Jung, C. G. (1989). *Memories, Dreams, Reflections*. New York: Vintage Books [original work published 1961].

Jung, C. G. (1995). Foreword. In: E. Neumann, *The Origins and History of Consciousness* (pp. xiii-xiv). Princeton University Press [original work published 1954].

Jung, C. G. (2009). *The Red Book*, S. Shamdasani (Ed. & Trans.), M. Kyburz & J. Peck (Trans.). New York: W. W. Norton.

Kirsch, T. (2004). History of analytical psychology. In: J. Cambray & L. Carter (Eds.), *Analytical Psychology: Contemporary Perspectives in Jungian Analysis* (pp. 5–31). New York: Brunner-Routledge.

Neumann, E. (1973). *The Origins and History of Consciousness*. Princeton, NJ: Princeton University Press [original work published 1954].

Neumann, E. (1989). *The Place of Creation: Six Essays*, H. Nagel, E. Rolfe, J. van Heurch & K. Winson (Trans.). Princeton, NY: Princeton University Press.

Obama, B. (1995). *Dreams From my Father: A Story of Race and Inheritance*. New York: Three Rivers Press.

Patel, E. (Speaker) (2006). A common life together. Radio interview in: M. Cunningham (Producer), *Eight Forty-eight*. WBEZ, Chicago, 13 February.

Robertson, R. (1992). *Globalization: Social Theory and Global Culture*. London: Sage.

Samuels, A., Shorter, B., & Plaut, F. (1986). *A Critical Dictionary of Jungian Analysis*. London: Routledge & Kegan Paul.

Schaffer, M. C. (2007). Hard to say "goodbye" (electronic version). *The New Republic*, 21 November.

Singer, T. (2004). The cultural complex and archetypal defenses of the group spirit: Baby Zeus, Elian Gonzales, Constantines's sword and other holy wars (with special attention to "the axis of evil"). In: T. Singer & S. Kimbles (Eds.), *The Cultural Complex: Contemporary Jungian Perspectives on Psyche and Society* (pp.13–34). New York: Routledge.

Singer, T., & Kimbles, S. (Eds.) (2004). *The Cultural Complex: Contemporary Jungian Perspectives on Psyche and Society.* New York: Routledge.

Stein, M. (1998). *Jung's Map of the Soul: An Introduction.* Chicago: Open Court Press.

Stein, M. (2004). Spiritual and religious aspects of modern analysis. In: J. Cambray & L. Carter (Eds.), *Analytical Psychology: Contemporary Perspectives in Jungian Analysis* (pp. 204–222). New York: Brunner-Routledge.

Stein, M. (2006). On the importance of numinous experience in the alchemy of individuation. In: A. Casement & D. Tacey (Eds.), *The Idea of the Numinous: Contemporary Jungian and Psychoanalytic Perspectives* (pp. 34–52). London: Routledge.

Tutu, D. (2000). *No Future Without Forgiveness* (p. 31). New York: Image Books.

Von Franz, M. L. (1983). Introduction. In: W. McGuire (Ed.) & J. van Heurck (Trans.), *The Collected Works of C. G. Jung* (Supp. Vol. A, pp. xiii–xxv). Princeton, NJ: Princeton University Press.

Weinberg, H. (2003). The large group in a virtual environment. In: S. Schneider & H. Weinberg (Eds.), *The Large Group Re-visited: The Herd, Primal Horde, Crowds and Masses* (pp. 188–200). London: Jessica Kingsley.

www.etymonline.com/index.php?term=culture

www.gseis.ucla.edu/faculty/kellner/kellner.html

www.merriamwebster.com/dictionary/culture?show=0&t=1296426748

www.taschen.com/pages/en/catalogue/art/all/06703/facts.the_book _of_symbols_reflections_on_archetypal_images.htm

http://wordnetweb.princeton.edu/perl/webwn?s=culture

Zinkin, L. (1998). The hologram as a model of analytical psychology. In: H. Zinkin, R. Gordon & J. Haynes (Eds.), *Dialogue in the Analytic Setting: Selected Papers of Louis Zinkin on Jung and on Group Analysis.* London: Jessica Kingsley.

CHAPTER THIRTEEN

Intuiting knowledge from the social unconscious with special reference to social dreaming

Gordon Lawrence

The working hypothesis to be explored in this chapter is that "personal knowledge" is enhanced through social dreaming because it goes beyond scientific enquiry by using the human capacity to recognize and acknowledge the "mystic", that is, any science the scientist does not understand. The mystic takes the person into the realms of the infinite, the numinous, and the spiritual, using insight to generate understanding, thinking, and knowledge.

Intellectual knowledge of the natural and organic sciences

Without consciousness, with its ability to think rationally, knowledge cannot exist. The natural and organic sciences have been brought into existence, and continue to emerge, through scientists observing natural phenomena, animal and plant life in the universe. These observations of phenomena are experienced through the senses to bring knowledge into being by means of the unique metaphors of the natural and organic sciences. Formal logic is applied to inanimate material phenomena, while dialectic logic is used for the organic sciences. Both use sophisticated measurement methods (Macmurray, 1935). This knowledge is accepted as being objective truth because it is verified by stringent proof. This knowledge is useful, acquired at school, and through higher education. Both natural and organic sciences are knowledge *about* the environment in which human beings live.

The personal knowledge of individuals

Personal knowledge, by contrast to the natural and organic sciences, is knowledge *of*, which the person accrues through intuition and insight.. It is derived from autobiographical experience, is tacit and subliminal, being created in both the conscious and unconscious mind. It is the highest form of knowledge, containing both the knowledge of the natural and organic sciences.

Knowledge *of* other human beings in the environment depends primarily on the use of emotions, feeling. Because emotions, and the resultant thinking, are infinite, non-linear, and complex in nature (Grotstein, 2007, p. 328), they are not amenable to the traditional methods of enquiry deployed in the sciences. Bion saw this knowledge as "mystical" because it respects relativity, complexity, and uncertainty, is numinous, and does not rely on the use of memory and desire.

This personal knowledge begins to be formed from infancy and have content in the relationship between mother and baby. They co-create a cultural space between them in which the baby feels and the mother responds though her feelings and *vice versa*, for the infant has no words to communicate (Winnicott, 1971, pp. 95–103). This cultural space of feeling is where the human ability to know is first fostered; this knowing is what Melanie Klein identified as the innate epistemophilic urge of humanity.

Within this initial cultural space, personal knowledge emerges from the use of the senses, but also by means of apprehending the non-sensual. The only instrument for gathering personal knowledge is the person in interaction with other persons. The method relies on intuition, which is the human capacity to apprehend emotionally to arrive at the truth. It is "gut feeling".

In doing this, we are pursuing an "act of faith" (Bion, 1970, p. 32), that is, operating on the assumption that the truth will be found, although it will be probable truth, never matching the scientific proof of the natural and organic sciences. This faith is to tolerate being in a state of unknowing by losing the ego through regression. It is from having the faith to be in uncertainty and doubt that the person comes to know, by experiencing the dread of mystery, the awesomeness of infinity and the unconscious.

It is through intuition and insight and by formulating working hypotheses, substituting another if one does not fit the evidence, that an accepted version of truth is formed. The non-sensually apprehensible is also intuited by accessing what is termed "mystic" science, which can cope with the uncertainties and the phenomena of emergence.

The acquisition of personal knowledge always takes human beings to the limits of their comprehension of traditional scientific methods, introducing them to the science that scientists do not understand, that is, the mystic (Adler, quoted in Wolf, 1995, p. 42). Intuition without emotional evidence and concepts is blind; concept without intuition is empty. The truth of this knowledge is tested against the signs and symbols matching reality as it is experienced. It is grounded in communicative reasoning and consensus formation to identify intersubjectively agreed, objective truth.

The search for truth is a collective enterprise, in which we can learn from each other. As a truth-finding strategy, this is objectionable on the grounds that it is vague and slow; as a political prescription, it can be criticized for "endorsing woolly minded community politics". But it has merits that, so far, have been insufficiently praised: it is humane, undogmatic, solidly rooted in tradition, optimistic, and, in effect, good for the individual who practises it and the society which benefits from it (Fernandez-Armesto, 1997, p. 222).

The twentieth century saw a revolution in the natural sciences because of the work of Bohr, Einstein, and their scientific contemporaries. They discovered quantum science, establishing that all material phenomena are composed of waves and particles. Waves cannot be seen, but particles can be observed. They reworked contemporary scientific notions by affirming that the visible world of the senses was composed of these invisible characteristics, that is, the non-sensually apprehensible.

They also discovered that the traditional idea of the scientist, derived from the Enlightenment, standing metaphorically behind a screen, calmly viewing and experimenting, was false. Now, the scientist and observer were seen as being intersubjectively related to what was being observed. The researcher participated in reality in the sense of partaking of it, became open to doubt and uncertainty because he was using his mind, capable of infinite possibilities of thinking, to understand phenomena. The same has always been a feature of psychoanalysis, in which observer and observed influence each other as they interact. The twentieth century saw a confluence of the methods of the natural and organic sciences with the methods developed in psychoanalysis, which deals with the complexity and uncertainty of humanity and infinity.

The I and the self

John Macmurray (1891–1976) was a Scottish philosopher who influenced Fairbairn and Sutherland, among others. He believed persons became mature through the experiences of being a person-in-relations, starting from infancy with the experience of a loving relationship with the mother. Each human being is unique and becomes so through relations with others, which realizes the self by being in community. He rejected Descartes's egocentric belief of the self-sufficient "I", and advanced the perspective that personal existence is constituted through relations with other persons. "The self is a dynamic organization of purposes and commitments whose behaviour is governed by conscious and unconscious motives, and whose developments and functioning are inseparably linked to the social environment" (Scharff & Scharff, 2005, p. 21).

The "I", if you will, is the private dimension of the self that is the public face of the "I", because this dimension is used to interact and relates to other selves. The independent "I" is the autonomous dimension of the "I and Self", with the "I" as the psyche of the species of humanity. It can be termed the Being of the person. "Self" is the psychic organization, which is in a semi-autonomous state, being mutually dependent on others, able to relate from a sense of integrated wholeness, able to take in feelings and emotions from others and transact their own with others. The "I" is "the universal form of psychic life, just as the Self is the universal matter of that form" (Deleuze, 1968, p. 260), which, to *become* a fulfilled person, must act and must relate to others as a "Self" capable of conceiving itself by having a continuity of self-feeling. Through self-reflection, it "can conceptualize, share, plan and negotiate" (Scharff & Scharff, 2005, p. 209). By keeping in balance the needs and wishes of the self and others, the self, existing in a web of conscious and unconscious relationships, has access to the social unconscious of others in the web.

The relationship between "I and Self" in the inner world is a symbiotic one mutually learning from each other. The "I" is the subjective experience of Being, but the "self" acts as an object in relation to others. This is how the person is able to differentiate between the states of subjectivity and objectivity. The "I" has its unique conscious and secret unconscious thinking of Being, but the "self", because it is always in semi-autonomous relationships, can embrace the thinking of the social unconscious. The "I-Self" is conceptualized imaginatively in the mind.

Thinking

The mind uses two modes of thinking: the principle of difference and that of sameness. The former mode is asymmetrical, recognized through consciousness. Asymmetrical thinking of differences is the root of intellectual thinking, relying on cultural rules expressing differences. Asymmetrical thinking is the basis of taxonomies and all the categories accepted by mankind as the basis of scientific thinking.

Sameness is symmetrical, arrived at through unconscious thinking, substantially through the dream. This is when everything becomes united and fused, is everything and nothing, is felt as uncanny, is derived from imaginative, symbolic experience that lies beyond immediate conscious knowing, and takes the individual into the unknown. As such, it represents the infinite, which has no number and is limitless. The (asymmetrical) infinite sets of the waking mind become, in sleep and dreaming the while, the (symmetrical) infinite sets. These two modes of thinking are mutually related, and are essential for differentiating consciousness from the unconscious, the finite from the infinite.

The unconscious: personal and social

The fact of the unconscious and the recognition of the infinite exist beyond the knowingness of the conscious, giving uniqueness to humanity. Freud saw the unconscious as a seething cauldron of destruction and negativity, but this an unfair formulation for the unconscious, because it represents the unknown and is the source of the bright idea of creativity.

The scientist develops knowledge that can be proved by accessing the unknown of infinity. Einstein started by thinking of images, then using words to describe them, and, finally, proving the rightness of his imaginative thinking mathematically. Similarly, the poet finds words to express the emotions of a unique experience, never before experienced. Chagall was able to paint the images of his childhood in Russia by reworking them in his unconscious, yielding surreal images of life as he was experiencing it in France and America.

The unconscious can be likened to the dark matter of the universe without which the known, visible universe would not exist. The phenomenon of dark matter, which is 90% of the universe, cannot emit light and can only be inferred from its gravitational effect. The miraculous is present in the cosmos just as the unconscious <> infinite surprises everyday conscious thinking and behaviour.

The value of the unconscious has been identified by Ehrenzweig with his discovery that

> Unconscious vision . . . [has] proved to be capable of gathering more information than a conscious scrutiny lasting a hundred times longer . . . the undifferentiated structure of unconscious vision . . . displays scanning powers that are superior to conscious vision. [cited in Gray, 2002, p. 63]

The individual unconscious is associated with creativity because the "I", as Being, has become aware of the unknown of the infinite. When one person as a self encounters others and establishes rapport, the "social unconscious" becomes pre-eminent as one person's unconscious resonates and "chimes" with the other. The unconscious perception of the reality by one person as a self can be checked against the other. Both are discovering independently from the infinite. They, then, can rework the idea, or artefact, or emotion, in terms of the known finite that can be communicated and understood by all.

When, however, the social unconscious is present in an organization, or system, it becomes far more difficult to check what is gleaned from unconscious thinking against others because the social unconscious is a feature of cultural reality. The distinction between conscious and unconscious thinking can always be tested to find out if thinking is in, or out of, touch with reality. The value of identifying unconscious thinking in organizations as systems is of critical importance because it can inform how the organization is not functioning as a purposeful system.

Bion was the first to map the place of the social unconscious in groups. He postulated that when any group met, there were two groupings present: the work group, there to fulfil the conscious purpose of the group, and another unconscious grouping in which the participants followed, at different times, what he called basic assumption behaviour to avoid the work and purpose of the group.

These basic assumption groups were dependency, flight/flight, and pairing. If the unconscious cultural assumption was dependency, participants would mobilize one person to be the source of satisfaction of their primitive needs for help and protection from the reality demands of the group and the idea of purpose was jettisoned.

Again to avoid the work purpose of the group, the participants might have a fight, ostensibly about the purpose, but really to take flight from it. Finally, two people would be mobilized to pair. Together, they symbolize a messiah, but they can never succeed in saving the group from the demands of reality and always fail.

When I was joint director of the Tavistock Institute's group relations programme, which focused on the unconscious functioning of groups and systems, I became interested in the function of dreaming in such conferences. Why wasn't dreaming used as an integral part of the data used to disentangle the role of the unconscious in conscious, rational life?

Social dreaming

Social dreaming (SD) was discovered at the Tavistock Institute of Human Relations in 1982. It is a method of accessing unconscious thinking through dreams. In contradistinction to one-to-one dream analysis, it is done with many simultaneously.

The purpose of SD is to transform the thinking and knowledge embedded in the dream narrative by means of free association and amplification so as to make links among the dreams and, in that process, be available for new thoughts and thinking. Because the focus was on dreaming exclusively, a context had to be devised for working with dreams while awake that would reflect the "matrix of the undifferentiated unconscious" (Ehrenzweig, 1967, p. 373) while asleep and dreaming. Whereas therapeutic dreaming focuses on Oedipus, whether in a dyad or group, SD takes the vertex of the sphinx on dreaming. Its interest is in the unconscious thinking, knowledge, and symbolism contained in the dream narrative, not the psyche of the dreamer.

The chosen context for examining dreaming with a large number was the matrix, a place from which something grows. This idea was derived from Foulkes (1973), who used the term matrix to represent the unconscious web of relationships subliminally present in any group formation. From the ground of matrix, the figure of group is born by using the rational, goal-orientated mind mainly. Groups tend to function on attaining a universe of meaning, but matrix, as has been discovered, can tolerate a multi-verse of meaning to a dream. The social dreaming matrix (SDM) exists to explore what only a matrix can explore, unencumbered by conscious, rational thinking. The founders of social dreaming had to make themselves "blind" to group phenomena in order to "see" (experience) the matrix as existing in its own right

There are differences in how dreams are perceived. There is the subject-centred mode of autocentricity. The dreamer asks, "What does the dream mean for me?" On the other hand, there is an object-centred mode of perceiving dreams, which asks, "What does the dream mean for humanity and its systems?" This is the mode of social dreaming because the focus is on the thinking, etc., embedded in the dream, which ceases to be a personal possession of any participants because, once voiced, it belongs to the matrix. This mode is object-centred, which Schachtel (1959) named the allocentric mode.

In the autocentric mode there is no objectification, for the emphasis is on how and what the person feels. Allocentric, on the other hand, has the emphasis on what the object is like. In the former, the emphasis is on how much pleasure, or non-pleasure, the perceived object can give and is physical as opposed to the allocentric mode, which is more intellectual and has a spiritual quality.

The mind, using the principles of difference and similarity, provides an "integrative reticulum" that constructs a mental schema of the completed object, even though there are gaps in the detail and information of the perceived object. "It is a combination of any or all of concepts, theories, hypotheses, and working notions or hunches. Unconsciously, it is a constellation of ideas-in-feeling, memories-in-feeling" (Jaques, 1960, p. 360). These are brought together and synthesized by being subliminally learnt.

In listening to a dream, there are felt gaps in the narrative. By regarding the dream in the allocentric mode, looking at it intellectually, the chances are the gaps can be filled by means of the non-sensually apprehensible by willing oneself into a mystical, spiritual, or numinous state to conjecture imaginatively what is not immediately visible. Schachtel offers a route to this:

> Rilke, who has given much thought to the conditions under which an object will reveal itself to the poet or the artist, writes: "In order to have an object speak to you, you must take it for a certain time for the only one that exists, the only phenomenon which, through your devoted and exclusive love, finds itself placed in the centre of the universe . . .," and on another occasion he writes about the "quietness and sincerity of contemplation" which enables the artist to see the objects in his own way and which is "more generous than he himself" ahead of and beyond all purposefulness he works to help it along. [Schachtel, 1959, p. 225]

The dreamer, once a dream is spoken, becomes an observer of the dream, but inextricably bound up with it and its potential meanings. The experience of dreaming draws the dreamer into attempting to understand the dream beyond cause and effect relationships. They can only be given meaning if the numinous, mystic frame of mind is mobilized. This is to heighten the emotions to register information by extending the personal bandwidth of consciousness to be aware of the uncanny of the unconscious.

The methods used for working with dreams in the matrix are free association to, and amplification of, the dreaming. The former is to say spontaneously what is passing through the participants' minds. Such associations are rarely voiced in group activities, which emphasizes the "I", or ego, being in control to achieve the primary task of the group. The latter method is amplification, which is to search for parallels to the dream: for example, a film, a novel, a memory to give the dream a context.

The domain of the social unconscious

Because there is the submergence of the ego, the participants are in the role of selves in the matrix relating subliminally and tacitly through the web of feelings present in the matrix. Also, since the subject of the matrix is dreaming, which is unconscious in origin, the method of working must use unconscious thinking to elucidate the knowledge and intelligence present in the dream.

The evidence of matrices, over the years, is that they rely on the social unconscious. In the context of social dreaming, there are inevitable resonances of the social unconscious as realized by persons-in-the-matrix-relations. A society of semi-autonomous relating selves gives rise to the social unconscious from which the autonomous "I" creates idiosyncratic intuitions. The idea of infinite is shared in a culture from which individual notions are derived. The truth of the infinite is established by the exchange of idiosyncratic individual notions to arrive at a consensus.

In harnessing the unconscious of minds in the matrix, a range of infinite possibilities of thinking are made available to the matrix. Spontaneity, free association, and divergent thinking are the hallmarks of thinking of dreams in a social dreaming matrix. There is no hierarchy of dreams. The matrix is democratic in the sense that no one is deemed superior to another. Hosts do not posses any quality other than the ability to explore social dreaming and pursue the unknown through reverie by willing themselves into a dreaming state while listening to the unconscious <> infinite of the dreams present in the matrix.

The multi-verse of meaning is revealed because it is freed from the demands of the ego and the wish for control. Instead of just one interpretation of a dream, participants make sense of a particular dream through insight and intuition or working hypotheses: that is, a sketch of the meaning of the dream. Truth is determined through the transaction of hypotheses, or intuitions. The act of social dreaming, thus, allows divergent thought processes to hold sway over the narrow, convergent processes of routine thinking. With divergence, the capability of intuition is enhanced, as is the recognition of the infinite to foster learning and creativity from the domain of the unknown.

The social dreaming project as a system

The diverse dream narratives of the individuals are carried into the matrix. When the dreams of participants are gathered for the experience of social dreaming they will be of stunning variety. When the dreamers come from an existing system, such as a commercial enterprise, the dreams will have commonality because of the shared experience of being in the system. Then the thoughts of the system that have never been voiced are likely to be articulated.

The purpose of the social dreaming matrix is to transform the thinking of the dreams presented to the matrix by means of free association to make links and connections between and among the dreams so as to be available for new thinking and thought. The task is always stated at the beginning of a matrix to help people manage themselves purposefully. They are then invited to offer their dreams.

The transformation process relies on the ability of the dreamers to free associate and to make connections, to use divergent thinking to plumb the potential meanings of the dreams. The events of the matrix are dream, free association, the linking of the two dreams, free association, perhaps amplification. No one is asked for a dream, and, indeed, a remembered dream is not required for participation in the matrix. But the experience of the matrix might cause a dream to be remembered. One example is of an Israeli who came to a matrix, saying he never dreamt. In the second session of the matrix he voiced that Israel in his dream was made of smooth marble. There were no cracks in the marble, so no dirt could collect and, therefore, nothing could grow. The resultant free associations and thinking were to the effect that Israel was barren and prevented the growth of political conditions that would be peaceful. One wonders if it is about the country of Israel or the people, or about the people who have historically been traumatized and wounded.

Again, someone dreamt in New York of two planes flying into a tower. At the time, no associations were offered because the event did not resonate with anyone's imagination. It took two years until the event was fulfilled in the bombing of the Twin Towers. It is known that Bin Laden forbade his followers from telling their dreams in case they alerted the enemy. Using quantum physics, dreaming could be seen as a universal phenomenon, with some persons dreaming and sending out waves unconsciously which are picked up by others whose minds are ready to register them. An event comes about through the encounter of responding and stimulating dreams of events. The bizarre thing is that these two dream events are required before an actual event can occur (Wolf, 1995, pp. 160–165) (Figure 1 below).

A matrix works most efficiently when the participants learn to temporarily "submerge their ego functions", which is a fairly recent development in psychoanalysis. This learnt ability allows them to be more open to dreaming and attunes them for listening to the unconscious messages of the dream content and the social unconscious operating in the matrix. Ego can always be rediscovered when the matrix ends.

Towards a theory of social dreaming

Freud informed dreaming through working with patients, that is, through the Oedipus perspective. Social dreaming starts from the sphinx vertex. It is not about the individual's intrapsychic and personal unconscious, but about intersubjective space and the social unconscious. It is not a matter of matching psychoanalytic discoveries to the findings of social dreaming; rather, these had to be made by using dreaming as a tool of social enquiry to check its findings against the existing knowledge of psychoanalysis and the social sciences. All that can be offered at this stage is a series of working hypotheses.

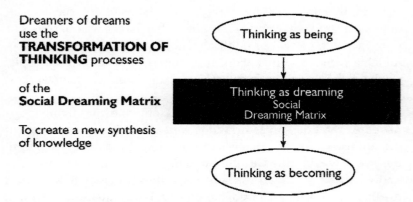

Dreamers of dreams
use the
TRANSFORMATION OF THINKING processes

of the
Social Dreaming Matrix

To create a new synthesis
of knowledge

Thinking as being

Thinking as dreaming
Social
Dreaming Matrix

Thinking as becoming

Figure 1.   A social dreaming matrix.

1. The possibility to dream socially was substantiated with the first social dreaming matrix convened at the Tavistock Institute in 1982.

2. If the dreams were received in a group rather than a matrix, the processes would be quite different. In a group, the study is of the relationships and relatedness of the participants. Transference and countertransference issues are dealt with appropriately face-to-face in the group. The technique in the social dreaming matrix is to focus on the dream as a transitional object, not the dreamers. The transference is the dream, with its knowledge and intelligence that is the subject of the matrix.

3. The existence of the matrix alters the nature of the dreams, compared to the classic situation. The matrix becomes a different "container" for receiving dreams, with the result that dream contents change. Participants are intelligent and can intuit from the stated purpose that some dreams are private and never to be offered in a matrix. However, in twenty-odd years, no dream has been offered that is demanding a therapeutic intervention, which may be a matter of participants intuitively or unconsciously adjusting and attuning themselves to the social context.

4. The matrix alters the nature of the thinking process and privileges the idea that we dream all the time, and free associate to the objects of our world. This is the basis of thinking, to be in touch with reality. The matrix deals with the personal knowledge intuited from the void and formless infinite.

5. The matrix questions the notion of the personal dream as a possession; my dream. Once voiced, dreams belong to the matrix.

6. Following on the planes crashing into the Twin Towers, it might be that all the dreams of the universe are lodged in its social unconscious mode, like dark matter parallel to life, becoming available for social dreamers attuned to the numinous.

7. The dreams of the matrix alert participants to the tragic and comic aspects of life. By privileging unconscious thinking, the horrendous of the unknown of the unconscious is intuited, as is the creative, joyful dimension of the unconscious. Social dreaming is realizing its potential as a tool of cultural enquiry in hospitals, with children in school, and firemen, for example,

showing that in a day's social dreaming, the issues of the system can be surfaced, which might otherwise take a month of interviewing.

8.   Unamuno argues that human beings are "a dream, a dream that dreams". This accords with the thinking of Bion and the contemporary insights of Bollas (Bollas, 2009). There is sufficient evidence to show that scientists and artists dream of their discoveries and artefacts. What we do in daily life will have been rehearsed in our dreams. The "dreamtime" of the Australian aborigines brings the landscape into being, but also furnishes a spiritual explanation of life itself.

9.   Because the contributions of thought to a matrix are ambiguous, with the result that the narrative of a matrix is "poetic", voicing uncertainties, playing with metaphors, and not reaching after fact or reason, a matrix symbolizes the "negative capability" of Coleridge.

Social dreaming and creativity

One purpose of social dreaming is to attain the "creative frame of mind". This frame of mind comes into force when we are not using rational thinking, but when we are willing our unconscious minds to be dominant, allowing ourselves not to be preoccupied with goal-orientated group thinking. In the process of transforming the thinking of the dreams, new thoughts and thinking become available to the matrix. The crucible of creativity exists both outside of us and inside us; outside, in the sense that the creative idea has never been thought before and is unenacted, inside, in the sense that it comes from the infinite possibilities of meaning to objects in our environment, that is, dream, within us. As the individual unconscious is given voice through the dream, it is received by the social unconscious of the people in the matrix to be enlarged by free association and amplification.

Hartmann writes,

In a broad sense, artistic creativity involves making new arrangements or connection, not randomly but picturing or expressing in some way the emotional state of the artist. In other words, artistic creativity, exactly like dreaming, involves making new connections, or making connections broadly guided by the dominant emotions. The work of art, much like the dream contextualizes the emotion or the emotional concern of its creator (Hartmann, 2000: 73).

The social dreaming matrix agitates or excites the unconscious, infinite sets of the mind by its processes of dreaming and free association to the dreams. Connections are always being made by the participants. In dreaming, connections between the events and happenings of the day become auto-associative, linking in diverse and surprising ways to make a sometimes bizarre narrative. The surreal narrative will contain the bright idea that eludes the dreamer while in wakeful consciousness. This can only be accessed through intuition, insight, and access to the mystical.

The benefits of the SDM in a system

An example of using the SDM is in organizations and systems. Using SDM in organizations helps in exploring the organizational unconscious and has the following merits:

1. Experientially, it fosters the *thinking capabilities* of the role-holders in the system.
2. The SDM allows for issues and problems to be addressed in a *lateral divergent way,* offering new solutions.
3. The SDM enhances the *creative capacity* of the organization to anticipate and respond to the environmental challenges of the business market.
4. The SDM uncovers the *emergent system* in the organization, that is, what it could *become.*

Some comments of participants on the experience of the SDM

*   It is a source of organizational intelligence;
*   it is an antidote to arrogance;
*   it is flexible, adaptive, and open;
*   it privileges insight and intuition;
*   it locates the present in relation to the past and the future;
*   authority is grounded in the dream narrative and not the dreamer;

- it is generative of learning;
- it provides space and evokes the skills for reflective enquiry;
- the SDM challenges existing mental modes of functioning;
- it builds high levels of trust and interdependence among participants;
- it develops creative potential by encouraging lateral and divergent thinking;
- it is a collaborative and dignified discourse;
- it is a mind-set based on the idea of play;
- the SDM is always speaking of, and addressing, experience that is of the numinous.

References

Bion, W. R. (1970). *Attention and Interpretation*. London: Tavistock.

Bollas, C. (2009). *The Evocative Object World*. Hove: Routledge.

Deleuze, G. (1968). *Difference and Repetition*. London: Athlone Press.

Ehrenzweig, A. (1967). *The Hidden Order of Art*. London: Weidenfeld and Nicholson.

Fernandez-Armesto, F. (1997). *Truth, a History*. London: Bantam Press.

Foulkes, S. H. (1973). *The Group as Matrix of the Individual Mental Life*. London: Karnac.

Gray, J. (2002). *Straw Dogs*. London: Granta Books.

Grotstein, J. S. (2007). *A Beam of Intense Darkness*. London: Karnac.

Hartmann, E. (2000). The psychology and physiology of dreaming: a new synthesis. In: L. Gamwell (Ed.), *Dreams 1900–2000*. Binghamton, NY: State University of New York.

Jaques, E. (1960). *Life*. London: Karnac.

Macmurray, J. (1935). *Reason and Emotion*. London: Faber & Faber,1995.

Schachtel, E. (1959). *Metamorphosis*. New York: Basic Books.

Scharff, J. S., & Scharff, D. E. (2005). *The Legacy of Fairbain and Southerland*. Hove, East Sussex: Routledge.

Winnicott, D. W. (1971). *Playing and Reality*. London: Tavistock.

Wolf, F. A. (1995). *The Dreaming Universe*. New York: Touchstone, Simon & Schuster.

INDEX

Abraham, K., 187, 212, 231
affect, 26, 28, 33, 75, 78, 81, 83, 85, 101,
    112–113, 119, 128, 142, 168, 171,
    216, 270, 272, 281, 302, 307
Agazarian, Y. M., xx, 73–75, 104,
    106–107, 109, 111, 113, 115–118,
    120, 123
aggression, xxix, xxxiv, 10, 15–16, 145,
    181, 183, 187, 195–196, 198–199,
    201, 218–219, 267, 307
Ahlin, G., xlv, liii
Alberdi, J. B., 50, 64
Althusser, L., 255, 261
Amado, G., 224, 231
Ancelin-Schützenberger, A., 24, 31, 41
Anthony, E. J., 4–5, 7, 12, 14–17, 20, 61,
    65, 81, 89, 97
anxiety, xxi, xxiv, xxix, xxxiv–xxxv,
    xxxvii–xxxviii, l–lii, , 36, 52,
    74–75, 87, 95, 106–111, 114–115,
    117, 140, 172, 210–213, 216–217,
    219–220, 225–226, 243, 278, 292,
    301, 316
Anzieu, D., 279, 283
archetypal/archetype(s), xlviii–l, 16,
    53, 63, 156, 204, 206, 291–292,
    299–302, 304–308, 311, 315–316
Arendt, H., 251, 257, 261–262
Armstrong, D., 220, 223, 231

Aron, L., xxxii, liii, 134, 142, 147, 150
Asch, S. E., 105, 120
Assmann, A., 277, 281, 283
Assmann, J., 273, 276–277, 283
Atwood, G. E., 129, 131, 135–136, 138,
    141, 144, 146, 148, 150, 152–153

Bacal, H., 146, 150
Badenoch, B., 100–103, 115, 118–120
Bakhtin, M., 142, 171, 173
Balint, M., 128, 144, 150
Banks, W. C., 105, 121
Bargh, J. A., 83, 96
Barrow, K., 210, 231
Barthes, R., 255, 262
Basil, O., 184
Battle, M., 308, 316
Bauman, Z., 159–160, 173
Behr, H., 134, 150
Bendix, R., 49, 64
Benson, H., 100, 116, 121
Berg, A., 308, 316
Bergmann, M., 140, 150
Bernfeld, S., xxvi, 9–11, 17–18
Berns, G. S., 105, 120
Bettelheim, B., 94, 96, 182, 184
Beuchot, M., 47, 64
Beuchot Puente, M., 47, 67
Billow, R. M., xxxii, 129, 131

Binney, G., 240
Bion, W. R., xviii, xxvii–xxviii, xxxiii,
    xl, xlviii, li, liii, 5, 15, 18, 74,
    95–96, 129, 131, 140, 143, 150, 163,
    167, 173, 182, 211, 215, 217, 231,
    243–244, 247, 262, 278, 322, 327,
    334, 336
Bishop, P., 305, 311, 316
Blackmore, S. J., 85, 97
Blakeslee, S., 119, 121
Bleger, J., 61–63, 65
Blomkvist, L. D., 37–38, 43
Bohm, D., xli, liii, 311
Bollas, C., 334, 336
Borkenau, F., 12–13, 16, 18, 169
Bortoff, H., 311, 317
Boswood, B., 273, 283
Bourdieu, P., 255–256, 262, 272, 282–283
Brandchaft, B., 136, 138, 153
Breuer, J., 137, 150
Britton, R. S., 209, 213, 224, 231
Brown, D., xxxvii, liii, 143, 151,
    160–162, 174, 298, 311, 317
Brownbridge, G., 166, 174
Bruschweiler-Stern, N., 134, 142, 153
Bullrich, S., 109, 121
Burger, J. M., 105, 120
Burmeister, J., 35, 41

Calhoun, D., 312–313, 317
Canli, T., 109, 120
Cannistraro, P. A., 110, 122
Carson, M. A., 110, 122
Casement, A., 305, 316–317
Cassirer, E., xxxiv, liii, 8, 16, 18–19
Castoriadis, C., 17–19
Chabris, C., xli, lvi
Chance, M., xli, liv
Chappelow, J., 105, 120
Chartier, R., 159, 174
Chartrand, T. L., 83, 96
Cohen, S., xxxvi, liv
Cohn, J. F., 112, 120
conscious see also: unconscious
    co-, xxxii, 23–24, 27, 32, 34–35,
        38–39, 129
    non-, xxiii, xxv, xl, 6–7, 281
Costa, L. F., 30, 43
Cozolino, L., liii–liv, 100–101, 103,
    109–110, 118, 120
Cushman, P., 256, 262

Dalal, F., xxi, xxxi, xxxvi, xlii, liv, 89,
    97, 141, 151, 174, 237–239, 252,
    262, 269, 282–283, 290, 293
Damasio, A., 83–84, 97
Decety, J., 28, 41, 85, 97
Deleuze, G., 324, 336
De Maré, P., xxxvi, xlvi, liv, 72, 119–120
de Mendelssohn, F., xx, 180, 185
Derrida, J., xxxiii, liv
Desmond, J. E., 109, 120
Despotović, T., 228, 232
development
    group, 106, 113–114, 118, 193, 282
    psychological, xlix, 128, 145, 247
    social, 12, 179, 199, 253
Devereux, G., 13, 19, xxxvi, liv
Diez, T., 52, 65
Discépolo, E. S., 49, 51–53, 55–56,
    58–59, 65
Donald, M., 272, 283
Donne, J., 60, 65
Dunning, E., 156, 174
Durkheim, E., xxxi, xxxvi, li, 90, 97,
    99, 120, 238, 240–241
Dusek, J. A., 100, 116, 121

Eagle, M. N., 28, 42
ego, xxiv–xxv, xxxii, xxxiv, xliii,
    10–11, 29–30, 35–36, 51, 71–72, 74,
    79–81, 86, 88–89, 91–96, 162,
    171–172, 224, 267, 275, 290, 292,
    300–301, 304–306, 316, 323–324,
    329–330, 332
    super, xxiv–xxv, 11, 71, 79–80,
        86–89, 157, 171–172, 215,
        223–224, 244, 259, 267
Ehrenzweig, A., 326, 328, 336
Eisold, K., 139–140, 144, 151
Ekman, P., 270, 283
Elias, N., xx, xxviii, 7, 11–12, 14, 19,
    127, 129, 155–164, 168–172, 174,
    235, 237, 241, 249, 252–253, 255,
    257–259, 261–262, 273, 283
Ellenberger, H. F., 266, 283
Erikson, E. H., 10–11, 19, 49, 65
Erös, F., 91, 97

Evans, A., 307, 317
Exodus, 206–207
Ezriel, H., xxviii, 142–143, 151

Fadiga, L., 85, 98
Fairbairn, W. R., 81, 97, 128, 210, 215,
    224, 231, 244, 250, 252–253, 262,
    324
fantasy, xxiv–xxv, xxxiv,
    xxxvii–xxxviii, xlix, 32, 35–39, 51,
    53, 63, 210, 213–214, 218, 225, 266,
    271, 280, 303, 310
Fariss, S., xxi, 290–292, 306, 317
Fenichel, O., 10–11, 19
Feo, M., 36–37, 42
Ferenczi, S., 87, 89, 97, 128, 139, 144
Fernandez-Armesto, F., 323, 336
Ferro, A., 37, 215, 231
Fine, B. D., 271, 285
Fischl, B., 100, 116, 121
Flash, R., 85, 98
Fleury, H. J., xx, 28, 34, 40, 42
Fogassi, L., 85, 98
Fosshage, J., 147, 151
Foucault, M., 138, 151, 255–256, 262
Foulkes, S. H., xviii–xx, xxvi–xxix,
    xxxii, xxxv, xl, xlv–xlvii, l–li, liv,
    3–20, 45, 60–61, 63–65, 72, 74–75,
    81, 89–90, 93, 97, 127, 129–131,
    134, 139, 141, 143, 145, 149–151,
    155–158, 160–161, 163–174, 192,
    207, 211, 235–236, 241, 249–252,
    254–255, 260–262, 265–266,
    268–271, 282–283, 289–290, 298,
    314, 317, 328, 336
Fox, J., 35, 42
Freud, S., xviii, xxiii–xxvi, xxxi, xxxiii,
    xxxvii, xlix, li, liii–liv, 3, 5–6, 9–10,
    14–17, 20, 62, 65, 71, 75, 78–82, 84,
    86, 88–90, 92, 94–95, 97, 133–146,
    148, 150–151, 157, 160, 170–171,
    173–174, 235, 241, 244, 247–248,
    252–253, 259, 262, 266–269,
    273–274, 281, 283–284, 291, 296,
    298–299, 303–304, 314, 325, 332
Friedman, M., 128, 131
Friedman, R., xx, xxxvii, liv, 130–131
Friesen, W. V., 270, 283
Fromm, E., xxv–xxvi, xxxvi, lii, 10–11,

17, 20, 72, 237, 241, 254, 256,
    267–268, 284, 290, 293

Gabrieli, J. D. E., 109, 120
Gage, F. H., 100, 123
Gallese, V., 28, 42, 85, 98
Gantt, S. P., xx, 73–75, 106–107, 109,
    113, 120
Garcia, A., 40, 44
Garfinkel, H., 272, 284
Garwood, A., xxxix, liv
Geertz, C., 236, 241
Gelb, A., 6, 20
Gill, M., 146, 151
Glover, G., 109, 120
Goldberg, A., 141, 147, 151–152
Goldstein, K., 6–8, 15–16, 20, 74
Goleman, D., 110, 120
Gray, J. R., 100, 116, 121, 326, 336
Greenberg, J. R., 150, 152, 259, 262
Greenspan, S., 17, 21
Greve, D., 100, 116, 121
Grosskurth, P., 314, 317
Grotstein, J. S., 209, 212, 215, 224, 231,
    322, 336
group see also: development,
    unconscious(ness)
    analysis, xvii, xx–xxi, xxvii–xxviii,
        xxxii–xxxiii, xxxvi, xxxix–xl, li,
        3, 6, 8, 11, 45, 47–48, 64, 72–75,
        85, 95, 127, 129–130, 134, 141,
        148–150, 155–156, 158–160,
        165–166, 168, 170–171, 187,
        192, 223, 235, 239, 251, 254,
        258, 260, 268, 274, 289, 314
    dynamics, xxvii, 4, 73, 75, 115, 156,
        163–164, 182, 243, 298
    mind, xx, xl–xli, xliv–xlvi, 73, 89,
        99, 103–106, 115, 117–119, 193,
        239, 244
    therapy, xxvii, 5, 102, 105, 129, 143
Group Analysis, 133, 141, 152

Hadfield, J. A., xlix, liv
Halbwachs, M., xxxviii, liv, 274–275,
    284
Haney, C., 105, 121
Harland, R., 257–258, 262
Harmatta, J., 95, 97

Harrison, A., 134, 142, 153
Hartman, H., 90, 97
Hartmann, E., 334–336
Hartzell, M., 101, 103, 123
Harwood, I., 146, 152
Hashmi, N., xli, lvi
Hawkins, J., 119, 121
Heard, D., 113, 121
Hearst, L., 134, 137, 150, 152
Hebb, D. O., 100, 121
Hegel, G. W. F., 47, 255, 262
Henderson, J. L., l, liv, 304, 315, 317
Hernandez de Tubert, R., 45, 59, 67
Hinshelwood, R. D., xlv, liv, 167, 174, 261–262
Hoffmann, S. O., 10, 21
Hoggett, P., 215, 231
Hopper, E., xxviii–xxxi, xxxiv–xxxv, xxxviii–xxxix, xli–xliv, xlvi–xlvii, lii, liv–lv, 14, 39, 42, 62, 65, 71, 75, 89, 95, 97, 99, 121, 128, 131, 155–156, 167, 171, 174–175, 180, 185, 187–188, 199–200, 202, 207, 209–210, 212, 216–217, 224, 230–231, 238–239, 241, 254, 256, 261–262, 267, 277–279, 282, 284, 290, 293, 298–299, 311–312, 317
Horkheimer, M., 17
Horney, K., xxvi, xxviii, 72, 254
Horwitz, L., 107, 121
Hug, E., 27–28, 34, 40, 42
Husserl, E., 127, 131, 141
Hutton, E. H., xl, lv

Iacoboni, M., 85, 98, 103, 113–114, 121
id, xxiv–xxvi, xliii, 5, 11, 71, 79–80, 86, 268
instinct, xviii, xxv, xxxii–xxxv, xxxix, xlix, 10, 14, 17, 47, 60, 77–78, 80–81, 85–86, 89–91, 93–94, 128, 136, 138, 145, 170, 189, 193, 244, 247–248, 253, 266–267, 269, 273, 305, 313
introjection, xxvi, xxxii, xxxvi, xxxviii, xlvii, 49, 79, 81, 128, 166–167, 206, 211, 251

Jackson, P., 85, 97
Janis, I. L., 105, 121

Jaques, E., 220, 231–232
Jolly, C., xli, liv
Jung, C. G., xx–xxi, xxv, xlviii–li, lv, 4, 13, 15–16, 63, 271, 289–293, 296, 298–306, 308, 310–311, 313–318
Jurinetz, W., 9, 18

Kaes, R., xxxvi, lv, 45
Kandel, E. R., 100, 121
Kansteiner, W., xxxviii, lv
Kant, I., 8, 83, 248, 253, 255, 262, 299, 314
Kanzer, M., 139, 152
Karterud, S., 180, 185, 193, 198, 207
Kernberg, O., xlviii, lv
Kerr, C., 100, 116, 121
Kimbles, S., l, lvi, 306, 319
Kirsch, T., 299, 311, 314, 318
Klein, M., xviii, xxviii, xlix, 8, 62, 86–87, 128, 145, 167, 210, 212, 243–244, 248, 250, 252, 260–262, 322
Klein, S., 210, 212, 232
Klímová, H., xxi, 179–181, 202, 207
Knauss, W., xxxv, lv, 282
Knobel, A. M., xx, 35, 38, 42
Knoblich, G., 85, 98
Kohut, H., 142, 145, 152, 180, 189, 207
Kossmann, M. R., 109, 121
Krause, R., 270, 284
Kuhn, T., 255–256, 262

Lacan, J., xviii, xxxiii, lv, 255–256, 262
Lachmann, F., 145, 152–153
Lake, B., 113, 121
Laplanche, J., 196, 207
Lasko, N. B., 110, 122
Lattes, A. E., 50, 66
Lavie, J., xx, 127, 129–130, 171, 175
Lawrence, W. G., xxi, 131, 289–293
Lazar, S. W., 100, 116, 121
Le Bon, G., 99, 121
LeDoux, J., 110, 121
Leibniz, G., xxiii, 314
Lenn, R., xlvi, lv
Le Roy, J., xxxvi, lv, 270, 272, 284
Levy, D., 277, 284
Lewis, E., 3–4, 13, 15, 20
Leyton, L., 255–256, 263
Lichtenberg, J. D., 148, 152

Lintott, B., xlv, lv
living human system (LHS), 73,
    103–104, 106, 119
Loewald, H., 62, 65, 169–170, 175
Lorenzer, A., 17, 21
Lyons-Ruth, K., 134, 142, 153

Macklin, M. L., 110, 122
Macmurray, J., 321, 324, 336
Malan, D., 143, 152
Malinowski, B., xxix, 12–14, 16, 21
Malone, T., xli, lvi
Mannheim, K., 11, 21, 268, 285
Marra, M. M., 40, 42
Martin-Skurski, M. E., 105, 120
Martis, B., 110, 122
Marx, K., xxxvii, li, 9, 47–48, 90, 197,
    200, 201, 240, 251, 254–255, 257
matrix see also: social dreaming
    dynamic, xxi, xlvi–xlvii, 192, 211,
        224, 236, 269, 291, 314
    foundation, xxi, xlvi–xlviii, 187,
        189, 192, 197, 211, 236,
        239–240, 265–266, 269–274,
        276, 278, 280, 282, 290, 314
McCluskey, U., 112–113, 121
McDougall, W., 99, 121–122
McGarvey, M., 100, 116, 121
McGilchrist, I., 75
McLaughlin, J., 147, 152
McMullin, K., 110, 122
McNaughton, B. L., 100, 123
Mead, G. H., xxix, 93, 98
Meltzer, D., 210, 212, 232
Menegazzo, C., 35–36, 42
Menning, H., 100, 122
Menzies Lyth, I., 220, 232
Meyer, M., 28, 41
Mies, T., 281, 285
Migone, P., 28, 42
Milgram, S., 105, 122
Miller, P., xli, lv
Mitchell, S. A., xxix, 134, 152, 156, 169,
    175, 252–253, 259, 262
Mojović, M., xxi, 182–183, 223–225,
    228, 232
Money-Kyrle, R. E., 81, 98
Montevechio, B., 61–63, 65
Moore, B. E., 271, 285

Moore, C. I., 100, 116, 121
Moreno, J. L., xviii–xx, xxvi, xxxii, xl,
    xlv, 23–27, 29–31, 33, 35, 37–40,
    42–43
Moreno, Z. T., 37–38, 43
Morgan, A., 134, 142, 153
Morin, E., 25, 43
Mother Party, 181, 204–206
myth(s), xxxvii–xxxviii, xlix, 13, 16,
    26, 29–30, 33, 35, 39, 46, 62, 78, 89,
    91, 134, 137, 139, 146, 150, 171,
    184, 218, 239–240, 255, 278, 291,
    302, 304, 306, 313, 315

Nahum, J., 134, 142, 153
narcissism, xlii, li, 62–63, 84–85, 88,
    140, 145–146, 191, 211–213, 279
Nava, A. S., 85, 98
Neri, C., 37, 43
Nery, M. P., 40–41, 43
Neumann, E., 300, 306, 318
neurobiology, xx, xxxiii, xli, xliv, 3,
    6–7, 25, 27, 73, 99, 101, 119, 183
    interpersonal (IPNB), xliv, 73,
        99–103, 105–106, 115, 119
neuroscience, xviii, liii, 27, 32–33, 40,
    101, 183
Nietzsche, F., xxiii, 62, 141, 314
Nitzgen, D., xx, 7–8, 16, 21
nos, 71–73, 80, 82–85, 87–96

Obama, B., 261, 300, 309–310, 318
object, xliii, 90, 189–190, 217, 236,
    328–329, 333
    external, xxiv, xxxiv, xxxvi, 60–61,
        84, 167
    internal, xxxiv, xxxvi, 61, 214, 224
    relations, xxviii, 49, 60, 63, 71,
        80–81, 85, 88–89, 143, 189, 209,
        213, 230, 243
    self, 134–135, 140, 145–147
objective/objectivity, xxxv, xlvi, 33,
    37–39, 139, 142, 144, 147, 202,
    245–248, 250–252, 258–259, 261,
    274, 290, 311–312, 322–323, 325,
    328
Oedipal ideas, xxviii–xxix, xxxvi, 14,
    17, 62–64, 143, 171, 196–197, 328,
    332

Ogden, T. H., xxxii, 62, 65, 129, 131, 210, 232
Orange, D. M., 129, 131, 141, 145–147, 150, 152–153
Ormay, T., xx, 71–73, 95, 97
Orr, S. P., 110, 122
Orwell, G., 12, 188, 203

Pagnoni, G., 105, 120
Pampliega de Quiroga, A., 48, 66
Pantev, C., 100, 122
Parsons, A., xxviii
Parsons, T., xxviii
Passeron, J.-C., 282–283
Patel, E., 295–296, 300, 310, 318
Pecotic, B., 217, 232
Penso, M. A., 30, 43
Pentland, A., xli, lvi
personality, xvii, xxiii–xxiv, xxvi, xxviii–xxix, xxxiii, xxxv, xlii, 10, 46, 49, 52, 77–78, 80, 85–88, 167–168, 172, 194, 196, 210, 213, 219, 223, 228, 243, 250, 252, 313–314
phantasy, xviii, xlix, 4, 8, 63, 79, 87, 135, 166, 184, 195–196, 239, 248
Pichon-Rivière, E., xviii, xix–xx, xxvii, xxxii, xl, 45–49, 51–53, 58–61, 63–64, 66
Pines, M., xx, xxix–xxx, xxxv, lv, 4, 21, 89, 98, 142, 146, 152, 156, 170–171, 175, 189, 192, 208, 211, 232
Piontelli, A., 183, 185
Piper, R., 119–120
Pitman, R. K., 110, 122
Plato, xlviii, 86, 98, 133
Plaut, F., 302, 318
Pontalis, J. B., 196, 207
Porges, S. W., 108–109, 122
projection, xviii, xxv–xxvii, xxxii, xxxiv, xxxvi, xli, xlvii, 8, 63, 81, 84, 128, 138, 143, 167, 179–180, 197, 204–206, 211, 219, 226, 228, 251, 259–260, 267, 275, 278, 305–306
Puget, J., xxxii, lv
Pujol, S., 56, 66

Quinn, B. T., 100, 116, 121

Racker, H., 80, 98
Rauch, S. L., 100, 110, 116, 121–122
Rechinni de Lattes, Z., 50, 66
Redl, F., xlviii, lv
Reich, W., 9, 18, 212, 232, 267, 285
relationship(s) see also: object
    human, xvii–xviii, xxv, xlvii, 40, 77, 88–89, 94, 127–128, 130, 171, 194, 209, 224
    interpersonal, xliv–xlv, lii, 31, 63, 100, 210, 216
    social, xxxvi, 5, 7, 14, 84, 87, 89–90, 167
repression, xxiv, xxx, xxxv, 5, 14–16, 54–55, 64, 82, 89, 92, 134, 141, 145, 148–149, 237, 240, 244, 257, 267–269, 281, 290, 302
Rey, F. G., 25, 43
Ribeiro, M. A., 30, 43
Richards, J., 105, 120
Richardson, F., 147, 153
Rizzolatti, G., 85, 98
Roberts, J. P., xlv, lv
Roberts, L. E., 100, 122
Robertson, R., 297, 313, 318
Rodrigues, R. A., 33, 43
Rojas Mix, M., 47, 67
Rosenfeld, H., 210–211, 215, 232
Rouchy, J. C., xxxvi, lvi
Rutzel, T., 37–38, 43

Salas, J., 35, 43
Samuels, A., 302, 318
Sander, L., 134, 142, 153
Sapir, I., 9, 18
Schachtel, E., 328–329, 336
Schaffer, M. C., 300, 318
Schain, J., 142, 152
Scharff, D. E., 324–325, 336
Scharff, J. S., 324–325, 336
Scheidlinger, S., xxxii, lvi
Schivelbusch, W., 9, 21
Schlapobersky, J., 280, 285
Schneider, S., 38, 44
Scholz, R., xxi, 236, 238–239, 274, 285
Schopenhauer, A., xxiii, 314
Schore, A. N., 33, 43, 100–101, 113–114, 122
Schöttler, P., 12, 16, 21

Schulte, P., 135, 152
Searle, J. R., xlii, lvi
Šebek, M., 194, 197, 208, 224, 232
self, 25–26, 31, 72, 84–85, 91, 94,
        144–145, 156, 189, 203, 210–211,
        214–217, 224, 236, 290, 324–325
    false, xxi, 180–181, 193–198, 201,
        205–207
Sennett, R., 312–313, 317
Shakespeare, W., xliii, 51
Shanker, S., 17, 21
Shannon, C. E., 117, 122
Shin, L. M., 110, 122
Shorter, B., 302, 318
Siegel, D. J., xliv, lvi, 73, 100–101,
        103–104, 109, 112–113, 116,
        118–119, 122–123
Simon, A., 117, 123
Singer, T., l, lvi, 306–307, 318–319
social dreaming (SD), xxi, 131,
        289–290, 321, 327–328, 330–334
    matrix (SDM), xxi, 290, 292, 328,
        330–333, 335–336
social science(s), xvii–xviii, xxxvi,
        xl–xli, lii, 17, 93, 156, 164, 237,
        312, 332
social system(s), xvii, xx–xxi,
        xxvii–xxxi, xxxvi–xlviii, l–li, 14,
        48, 63, 129, 179, 182, 188, 209,
        211–212, 216–218, 224, 230,
        235–236, 238–240, 291, 296, 299,
        301, 307, 311–312
Solomon, H., xlix, lvi
Song, H., 100, 123
Spector-Person, E., xxxv, lvi
Spencer, H., xliii, 90, 98, 159
Spinoza, B., xxiii, 83
splitting, xxiv, xxx, xxxv, lii, 12, 46, 51,
        53, 60, 96, 115, 118, 163, 170, 181,
        184, 194, 196, 215–216, 218, 314
Stacey, R., 134, 152, 166, 175
Stefano, K., xlvi, lv
Stein, M., 301–302, 305, 313, 315, 319
Steiner, J., 183, 209–210, 213, 232
Stern, D. N., 28, 31, 44, 80–81, 98, 134,
        142, 153, 270, 272, 285
Sternberg, P., 40, 44
Stevens, C. E., 100, 123
Stewart, H., 142, 153

Stoljarov, A., 9, 18
Stolorow, R. D., 129, 131, 134–136, 138,
        141, 144–146, 148, 150, 152–153
Stone, W. N., 180, 185, 193, 198, 207
Strachey, J., 94, 137, 143, 153
Strenger, C., 180, 185
subjectivity, xlvi, 23, 28, 33, 37–38, 61,
        63, 135, 137, 144, 146, 180,
        189–192, 199, 202–207, 325
    inter-, xx, xlvi, 27, 32–33, 127–131,
        134–135, 138, 140, 142–147,
        150, 166, 172, 189, 253–254,
        323–324, 332
symbol(-ism), xxix, xxxiii, 15–16,
        34–35, 63, 78, 89, 180, 182, 188,
        196, 202–203, 206, 211, 224, 239,
        255, 271–272, 280–282, 297, 300,
        316, 323, 325, 327–328, 334
Symington, J., 217, 232
system-centred therapy (SCT), 73, 75,
        99, 103, 109, 111, 113, 115
Sznaider, N., 277, 284

Tacey, D., 305, 316–317
Tavistock Clinic/Institute, xxviii,
        142–143, 289, 327, 333
Taylor, C., 149, 153
Terrazas, A., 100, 123
Thomashoff, H.-O., 183, 185
Thompson, S., 119–120
Tomasini, M., 35–36, 42
totalitarianism, xxi, xxxvii, 179–182,
        187–189, 191, 194, 199–205, 207,
        213, 215, 221–224, 228, 230
transference, liii, 4, 63, 80–81, 87,
        136–138, 143–147, 150, 224, 236,
        260, 304, 333
trauma/traumata/traumatic
    chosen, 230, 238, 276–281
    collective, 182, 238, 266, 274, 276
    experience, xviii, xxi, xxxiv, xxxix,
        xliii–xliv, 187, 199, 206–207,
        216, 306–307
    social, xvii, xxi, xxix, xxxvii–xxxix,
        xlv, 199, 209, 227, 278, 289
Treadway, M. T., 100, 116, 121
Tronick, E., 112, 120, 123, 134, 142, 153
Tubert-Oklander, J., xx, xxxii, 45, 47,
        59, 63, 67

Tustin, F., 210, 215, 217, 232
Tutu, D., 308–310, 319

unconscious *see also*: conscious
    co-, xx, xxvii, xxxii, 23–27, 29–35,
        37–41, 129
    collective, xxv, xlviii–li, 4, 13, 15,
        291–292, 296, 299, 301,
        303–306, 310
    cultural, xxxv–xxxvi, l, 273, 299,
        301, 304, 306
    dynamic, xxx, 3, 134, 148, 280, 282
    group, xli, 63, 239
    individual, 273, 289, 299, 326, 334
    interpersonal, xxvi–xxviii, xxxii, l,
        5, 269, 291
    life, xxv, 148, 216–217, 265
    mind, xvii, xxiii–xxv, xxxiii, xxxv,
        xl–xli, xliii, xlviii, 15, 322, 334
    processes, xxiv, xxx, lii–liii, 25, 28,
        30, 129, 172, 182, 222, 248,
        255–256, 265–266, 268–269,
        273–274, 282, 290, 298
    social, xvii–xx, xxii–xxiii, xxv–xxxi,
        xxxiii–xxxix, xli, xlv, xlviii,
        l–lii, 3, 5–7, 11, 13–18, 39, 47,
        64, 75, 89, 91–92, 127, 130,
        148–149, 156, 163, 170–172, 181,
        187, 189, 209, 211, 222, 226–227,
        230, 237–240, 250, 253–256, 260,
        265, 267–269, 273, 280, 282,
        289–292, 296–299, 311, 325–327,
        330, 332–334

Vargas, L., 12–13, 16
Vietze, P., 128, 131
vignettes
    Carla, 193–194
    Lili, 195–196
    No. 4, 197–199, 201
    No. 5, 200–202
    Otík, 190
Voegelin, E., 13, 16, 21
Volkan, V. D., xxxviii, lvi, 238, 241,
        276–279, 285
Von Franz, M. L., 299, 319

Wasserman, R. H., 100, 116, 121
Weaver, W., 117, 122

Weber, M., 90, 98
websites, 312, 316, 319
Wechsler, M. F., 25, 44
Wedig, M. M., 110, 122
Weegmann, M., xx, 127–128, 130, 136,
        153
Weinberg, H., xviii–xix, xxxvii–xxxviii,
        xli, xliv–xlv, lvi, 38, 44, 129, 132,
        156, 175, 191, 197, 208–209, 232,
        278, 285, 299, 311, 319
Welzer, H., 275, 285
Wertsch, J. W., 171, 175
Western, S., 224, 232
Weyman, A., 311, 317
Wilke, G., xxi, 235, 240–241
Williams, C., 240
Winnicott, D. W., xxviii, xxxi–xxxii,
        xlii, lvi, 78, 80, 86–87, 98, 128, 132,
        181, 191, 193, 208, 210, 214–215,
        232, 244, 250, 252–253, 263, 322,
        336
Wittgenstein, L., 92, 98
Wolberg, L. R., 136, 153, 166
Wolf, F. A., 323, 332, 336
Woolley, A. W., xli, lvi
world
    external, xxx–xxxi, xxxvi, lii, 8, 10,
        79, 82, 84, 166, 203, 211, 269
    internal, xxxi, 84, 87, 127, 184, 195,
        215, 238, 251, 325
    social, xxv–xxvi, xxix–xxxi, xxxv,
        xxxix, lii, 72, 79, 84, 88–89, 245,
        248–249
    wars, xxvi, 6, 74, 168, 197, 199, 222,
        267, 277
Wright, C. I., 110, 122
Wrong, D. H., 250, 263

Yrigoyen, H., 54–55, 57–58

Zeddies, T., 141, 147–148, 150, 153
Zeisel, E., xxxii, lvi
Zhao, Z., 109, 120
Zimbardo, P. G., 105, 121
Zink, C. F., 105, 120
Zinkin, L., l, lvi, 298, 311, 317, 319
Žižek, S., 224, 232
Zuretti, M., 30, 35–36, 42, 44